W9-BVK-144

Around Cairo
See pp162–173

Sinai and the Red Sea Coast
See pp220–237

aid

lia

SINAI AND
THE RED
SEA COAST

Taba

Ras Gharib

Sharm
el-Sheikh

Hurghada

Qena

Al-Quesir

Red Sea

Edfu

ILE
EY

Aswan

Marsa Alam

Berenice

Halaib

Cairo Area by Area

Central Cairo
See pp72–89

Islamic Cairo
See pp90–115

Rhoda Island and Old Cairo
See pp116–129

Giza and Heliopolis
See pp130–141

EYEWITNESS TRAVEL

EGYPT

EYEWITNESS TRAVEL

EGYPT

DK

LONDON, NEW YORK,
MELBOURNE, MUNICH AND DELHI
www.dk.com

Project Editors Hugh Thompson, Claire Folkard
Project Art Editor Jo Doran
Editors Liz Atherton, Irene Lyford,
Ferdie Mcdonald, Marianne Petrou, Martin Redfern
Designers Emma Rose, Rebecca Milner, Ian Midson,
Sue Megginson, Anthony Limerick
Picture Researchers Monica Allende, Cynthia Frazer,
Katherine Mesquita
Map Co-Ordinators David Pugh, Casper Morris
DTP Designer Maite Lantaron

Main Contributors
Jane Dunford, Dr Joann Fletcher, Carole French, Robin Gauldie,
Andrew Humphreys, Kyle Pakka, Richard Williams

Maps
Era-Maptec Ltd

Photographers
Max Alexander, Jon Spaull, Peter Wilson

Illustrators
Gary Cross, Richard Draper, Claire Littlejohn, Maltings Partnership,
Chris Orr & Associates, John Woodcock

Printed in Malaysia

First American Edition, 2001

16 17 18 19 19 10 9 8 7 6 5 4 3 2 1

Published in the United States DK Publishing, 345 Hudson Street,
New York, New York 10014

Reprinted with revisions 2003, 2005, 2009, 2011, 2013, 2015

Copyright 2001, 2015 © Dorling Kindersley Limited, London

A Penguin Random House Company

Published in the UK by Dorling Kindersley Limited.

A catalog record for this book is available from the Library of Congress.

ISSN 1542-1554

ISBN 978-1-46544-102-7

Throughout this book, floors are referred to in accordance
with European usage: the "first floor" is the floor above ground level

MIX
Paper from
responsible sources
FSC
www.fsc.org   FSC™ C018179

Front cover main image: View of the Nile from the garden at the Old Cataract hotel, Aswan

◀ Detail of the vaulted ceiling of the Mosque of Amir Akhur, Cairo

Camel-trekking in the desert

Contents

The gigantic Colossus of Memnon,
West Bank

Painted relief shows Sennedjem and his wife worshipping, Deir al-Medina

Hatshepsut Temple at the foot of a sheer limestone cliff face

The Great Temple of Abu Simbel

HOW TO USE THIS GUIDE

This guide helps you to get the most from your visit to Egypt by providing detailed practical information and expert recommendations. *Introducing Egypt* maps the country and sets it in its historical and cultural context. The Cairo section and the five area chapters describe important sights using maps, photographs and illustrations.

Features cover topics from food and wildlife to hieroglyphics and mythology. Restaurants and hotel recommendations can be found in *Travellers' Needs*, while the *Survival Guide* has tips on everything from making a telephone call to using local transport, as well as information on money and other practical matters.

Cairo Area by Area

The city is divided into three areas, each with its own chapter. A fourth chapter covers the peripheral areas of Giza and Heliopolis. All sights are numbered and plotted on each chapter's area map. Information on each sight is easy to locate as the entries follow the numbering used on the map.

A locator map shows where you are in relation to other areas in the city centre.

All pages relating to Cairo have the same colour thumb tabs.

Sights at a Glance lists the chapter's sights by category: Streets and Squares, Holy Places, Museums, Historic Buildings and Mosques.

1 Area Map For easy reference, sights are numbered and located on a map. The central sights are also marked on the Street Finder maps on pages 148–57.

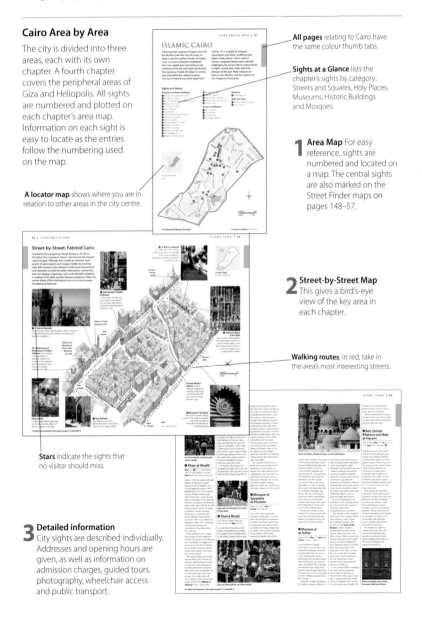

2 Street-by-Street Map This gives a bird's-eye view of the key area in each chapter.

Walking routes, in red, take in the area's most interesting streets.

Stars indicate the sights that no visitor should miss.

3 Detailed information City sights are described individually. Addresses and opening hours are given, as well as information on admission charges, guided tours, photography, wheelchair access and public transport.

1 Introduction The landscape, history and character of each area is described here, along with an account of how the area has developed over the centuries and what it has to offer the visitor today.

Egypt Area by Area

Apart from Cairo, the country has been divided into five areas, each of which has a separate chapter. The most interesting cities, towns, ancient and religious sites, and other places of interest are located on a *Regional Map*.

2 Regional Map This shows the road network and gives an illustrated overview of each area. Interesting places to visit are numbered, and there are useful tips on getting to and around the region by car and public transport.

Each area of Egypt can be quickly identified by its colour-coded thumb tabs (*see inside front cover*).

3 Detailed information All the important towns and other places to visit are described individually. They are listed in order and follow the numbering on the Regional Map. Within each town or city there is detailed information on important buildings and other sights.

For all major sights, a *Visitors' Checklist* provides the practical information you will need to plan your visit.

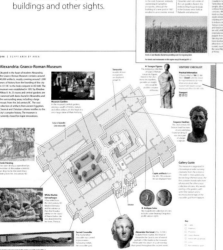

4 Egypt's Top Sights These are given two or more pages. Historic buildings are reconstructed, or dissected to reveal their interiors. Other interesting sights are shown in bird's-eye view, with important features highlighted.

INTRODUCING EGYPT

DISCOVERING EGYPT

The following tours have been designed to take in as many of the country's highlights as possible, while keeping long-distance travel to a minimum. Our first tour covers two days in Cairo, followed by three days spent in Alexandria and along the North Coast. Next comes four days in Sinai and six days on the Red Sea Coast; these itineraries can be followed individually or combined to form a 10-day tour. Finally, we suggest two seven-day tours, covering Luxor and the Nile Valley and the Western Desert. Extra suggestions are provided for those who want to extend their stay. Pick, combine and follow your favourite tours, or simply dip in and out and be inspired.

A Week in the Western Desert

- Be in awe of nature at **Siwa Oasis** where freshwater springs feed thousands of date palms and olive trees.
- Make the lonely jeep journey across the great sand sea between Siwa and Bahariyya oases.
- Unwind in the hot springs of **Bahariyya Oasis** before dining on traditional cuisine.
- Visit **Farafra Oasis**, one of the most isolated places in Egypt, and camp under the stars in the otherworldly White Desert.
- Enjoy the desert landscape and be astonished as **Dakhla Oasis** rises from the sands like a mirage.

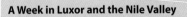

Exact replica of the tomb of Tutankhamun in the West Bank, Luxor

◄ Hieroglyphics on tomb in the Valley of the Kings

A Week in Luxor and the Nile Valley

- Marvel at the **Luxor Temple**, illuminated at night to create a magical ambiance.
- Take a horse-drawn carriage from the centre of Luxor to **Karnak** and its fabulous Temple of Amun.
- Admire the spectacular tombs in the **Valley of the Kings**, and visit the exact replica of the Tomb of Tutankhamun.
- Cruise the Nile from Luxor to **Aswan**, passing mighty temples and villages where little has changed in centuries.
- Learn about Aswan's Nubian community in the excellent **Nubian Museum**.
- Gaze in awe at the **Great Temple of Abu Simbel** and the **Temple of Hathor**, hewn out of solid rock.

4 Days in Sinai

- Unwind in the diving and snorkelling resort of **Sharm el-Sheikh**.

- Head to **Ras Mohammed National Park** to snorkel or dive among 1,000 species of fish.

- Experienced divers may be tempted by **Dahab**'s famous Blue Hole that plunges to depths of 80 m (260 ft).

- Marvel at isolated **St Catherine's Monastery** and ascend **Mount Sinai** where Moses received the Ten Commandments.

- See the spectacular backdrop of the Sinai Mountains and unspoiled beaches between Dahab and **Nuweiba**.

0 kilometres   200
0 miles   100

Mediterranean Sea

Cairo

Monastery of St Anthony
Monastery of St Paul

St Catherine's Monastery
Mount Sinai

Gulf of Suez

Coloured Canyon
Nuweiba
Ras Abu Galum
Dahab

Sharm el-Sheikh
Ras Mohammed National Park

El-Gouna
Hurghada

River Nile

Red Sea

Dendara
Valley of the Kings
Luxor
Esna
Edfu
River Nile

Al-Quseir

Marsa Alam

Temple of Kom Ombo
Aswan
Temple of Philae

Lake Nasser

Abu Simbel

Key

=== The Red Sea Coast tour
=== The Western Desert tour
=== The Luxor and the Nile Valley tour
=== The Sinai tour

The pretty band of pinkish rock provides a wonderful backdrop to the fertile fields of Dakhla Oasis

6 Days on the Red Sea Coast

- Take a boat to **Giftun Island** or a submarine-style trip to see the underwater world off **Hurghada**.

- Wonder at the size and tranquillity of the **Monastery of St Anthony** and see its vivid frescoes.

- Wander around peaceful little **Al-Quseir**, whose long history and active past is revealed in the fort, mosques and shrines of saints.

- Kick back and relax on the expanse of **Marsa Alam**'s endless white beaches, or dive off one of the Red Sea's isolated islands.

2 Days in Cairo

Cairo is crammed with extraordinary monuments including pyramids, palaces, mosques and citadels, and the lively cultural scene is complemented by all-night coffee shops and bars.

- **Arriving** Cairo International Airport lies 20 km (12 miles) northeast of the city centre. Taxis operate from outside the terminal – bargaining on the price is necessary.

- **Transport** Central Cairo is best explored on foot and by taxi. The Metro, buses, mini-buses and taxis are available for travel further afield.

Day 1
Morning Make an early start at the **Giza Plateau** (open from 8am) (pp132–39). The 4,500-year-old Great Pyramid built for King Khufu, the Pyramid of Khafre and the Pyramid of Menkaure are the iconic images of Egypt. Inside, descending narrow shafts and climbing staircases to burial chambers, you begin to understand the scale of the craftsmanship and engineering skills required to build such staggering structures. Take time to visit the Solar Boat Museum, displaying a full-size boat used by the ancient Egyptians that has been painstakingly rebuilt. Stop to admire the enigmatic Sphinx, before seeking out an authentic Egyptian lunch.

Afternoon Head back to the city to explore the relatively compact area of **Coptic Cairo** (pp118–27). Dip into the excellent Coptic Museum before exploring the tiny alleyways dotted with secretive churches. The most famous is the ornate **Hanging Church** (pp124–5), which has an exquisitely inlaid Sanctuary Screen considered the finest in Egypt. Spend the evening in bustling Downtown, admiring the architecture and life along Sharia Talaat Harb and Qasr el-Nil, and choosing between swanky restaurants and local bars.

Day 2
Morning Midan Tahrir (p76) is the heart of modern-day Cairo, and here you'll find the fabulous **Egyptian Museum** (pp78–81). No visit to Cairo is complete without spending a few hours among some of the greatest Pharaonic treasures ever discovered. The Tutankhamun Galleries are a highlight, exhibiting thousands of items from the tomb of the boy king, including his life-size golden mask. Next, take a taxi to **Islamic Cairo** (pp90–115) and get dropped by the **Khan al-Khalili** (p94) – one of the largest bazaars in the Middle East. It will leave you spellbound by the aroma of spices and a seemingly endless array of souvenirs. Explore the adjacent **Bein al-Qasreen** (pp100–1) where soaring mosques and elaborate mausoleums capture the soul of Mamluk Cairo. There are some good spots around the Khan for lunch and people watching.

Afternoon You could take a taxi to the walled **Citadel** (pp108–11), which dominates the skyline of Islamic Cairo, enclosing several mosques and museums, and affording incredible views. Alternatively, strike out on foot from the **Al-Ghouri Complex** (p96), passing through the **Bab Zuweila** (p107) and the **Tentmakers' Market** (p107), along narrow streets crowded by markets and locals, to finish at the **Mosque of Ibn Tulun** (pp114–15). Climb its spiralling minaret and visit the adjoining Gayer-Anderson House, lavishly

The majestic Sphinx on the Giza Plateau, in the suburbs of Cairo

furnished with Middle Eastern treasures. At dusk, soak up the atmosphere at the awe-inspiring **Mosque of Sultan Hassan** (p112), before a relaxing evening in the elegant **Zamalek** (p88–9) district. Start with a drink on the Marriott Hotel's terrace, and maybe catch a performance at Cairo's famous **Opera House** (p88).

> **To extend your trip…**
> Journey south out of the city to see the step pyramid and tombs at **Saqqara** (pp166–8), and the lonely majesty of the **Dahshur** pyramid plateau (p169).

3 Days in Alexandria and the North Coast

- **Arriving** There are direct buses from Cairo International Airport to Alexandria. Trains, buses and shared taxis leave day and night for the 2.5-hour journey from the centre of Cairo.

- **Transport** Alexandria is best explored by foot, tram or minibus. Minibuses and taxis are the most convenient for travel along the coast.

Day 1: Alexandria
Alexandria (pp244–51) was the Graeco-Roman capital of Egypt and, today, is its second largest city. Central **Midan Saad Zaghloul** (p244) is the ideal place to get your bearings. The grand façade of the **Cecil Hotel** (p244) dominates; it opened in 1929 and has, famously, hosted politicians, actors and writers. It's a short walk to the **Bibliotheca Alexandrina** (p244), a modern wonder that echoes the greatest library of the ancient world. Today, it houses an expanding collection of books, along with a Planetarium, museums and exhibition halls. In the afternoon, head to the **National Museum of Alexandria** (p248) to see pieces found in and around the city, encompassing ancient Egyptian, Classical, Coptic and Islamic cultures. The site of **Kom al-Dikka**

For practical information on travelling around Egypt, see pp334–9

Extraordinary colours of marine life in the Red Sea

(p245) contains a small Roman amphitheatre and an exquisite mosaic in the Villa of the Birds. Refresh in nearby Pastroudis, an elegant café that has retained much of its early 20th-century grandeur, or seek out the gorgeous Cap d'Or bar for a beer.

Day 2: Alexandria and Rosetta
Take a tram east to visit the **Royal Jewellery Museum** *(p251)* with priceless glittering displays housed in a restored villa. Continue along the coast to historic **Abu Qir** *(p254)* where you'll find excellent fish restaurants for lunch. Then, spend the afternoon exploring **Rosetta** *(p243)*, a town with many extraordinary Ottoman mansions and mosques. It was here that the famous Rosetta stone was discovered in 1799, enabling scholars to decipher ancient Egyptian hieroglyphics. Return to Alexandria via the eye-catching **Montazah Palace** *(p251)*, which has lush gardens and several restaurants by the seafront.

Day 3: El-Alamein and Alexandria
Hire a taxi to **El-Alamein** *(p255)*, around an hour's drive west of Alexandria. El-Alamein was the site of the World War II battle that pitched British General Montgomery's Eighth Army against Field Marshal Rommel's German-Italian troops and changed the course of the North Africa campaign. Pay your respects at the poignant cemeteries and visit the War Museum. Returning to Alex, pass by iconic **Pompey's Pillar** *(p250)* and explore spooky underground burial chambers in the

Catacombs of Kom ash-Shuqqafa *(p250)*. Finish off the day at the 15th-century **Fort Qaitbey** *(p249)*, dominating the Eastern Harbour. There is a delightful restaurant in the adjacent Greek Club, which offers panoramic views of the cityscape and colourful boats on the water.

To extend your trip…
Take a bus from Alexandria to **Siwa** *(p264)*, via Marsa Matruh, to spend a couple of days in a culturally unique and utterly beautiful oasis.

4 Days in Sinai

- **Arriving** Flights arrive at Sharm el-Sheikh International Airport, 18 km (11 miles) northeast of the city. Taxis operate from outside the terminal.

- **Transport** Sinai is best explored by bus, minibus and taxi, or with an organized tour.

- **Tip** Check the latest travel advice before heading to north Sinai.

Day 1: Sharm el-Sheikh
Spend the day immersed in the warm waters off **Sharm el-Sheikh** *(p230)*, where diving, snorkelling, glass-bottomed boat trips and other watersports are available. The beaches and resorts stretch for some 20 km (12 miles) along the coast, encompassing the popular hub of Naama Bay and quieter Shark's Bay with its offshore reefs. **Ras Mohammed**

National Park *(p230)*, on Sinai's southernmost tip, is a popular day trip for snorkelling and diving – the waters contain over 1,000 species of fish and world-class dive sites. Later, Naama Bay's busy pubs and coffee shops make for a good night out.

Day 2: Dahab
Hit the coast road north to **Dahab** *(p234)*, a mellow yet fun beach town with a range of accommodation. Experienced divers could check out the famed Blue Hole that plunges to depths of 80 m (260 ft), or first-timers can learn to scuba directly off the shore. Dahab is also a great place to try kitesurfing.

Day 3: St Catherine's
Take a sunrise tour to climb mystical **Mount Sinai** *(p228)* where Moses is said to have received the Ten Commandments. At the foot of the mountain is **St Catherine's Monastery** (closed Sundays) *(p226–9)* which contains priceless icons and the lavish early Byzantine Mosaic of the Transfiguration. Return to Dahab to spend the rest of the day relaxing at one of the laidback cafés, bars and restaurants lining the shore.

Day 4: Ras Abu Galum and Nuweiba
Continue on the road north, making a detour to **Ras Abu Galum** *(p234)*, where there is snorkelling off the white-sand beach and a breathtakingly beautiful turquoise lagoon. Alternatively, head inland to the Coloured Canyon for a short excursion along its vivid gorge. Finish up at **Nuweiba** *(p234–5)* where the spectacular Sinai Mountains provide a backdrop to unspoiled beaches and the lights of Saudi Arabia twinkle across the Red Sea at night.

To extend your trip…
Go on a diving safari, south on the Red Sea, spending a few nights on a comfortable "live-aboard" and visiting up to four dive sites a day.

6 Days on the Red Sea Coast

- **Arriving** Flights arrive at Hurghada International Airport located 6 km (4 miles) southwest of the city. Marsa Alam International Airport, 60 km (37 miles) north of town, has daily flights to Cairo. A ferry crosses between Sharm el-Sheikh and Hurghada (see p236).

- **Transport** The Red Sea Coast is best explored by taxi, although infrequent buses and minibuses do travel along the coast.

Hatshepsut Temple, Luxor, at the foot of a sheer limestone cliff face

Day 1: Hurghada
Spend a day in **Hurghada** (pp236–7). Take a boat trip to Giftun Island, a submarine-style excursion to see the underwater world, or enjoy the beaches that stretch 25 km (15 miles) along the coast. There is a range of nightlife, from slap-up meals to discos by the beach.

> **To extend your trip…**
> From Hurghada, it is easy to join a one- or two-day tour to **Luxor** (pp186–207) to dip into Pharaonic history.

Day 2: Monasteries of St Anthony and St Paul
Join a tour, or hire a taxi, to the **Monastery of St Anthony** (p236) and the **Monastery of St Paul** (p236), the country's oldest Coptic monasteries. Be prepared for a full day out, but the reward will be breathtaking scenery and two of Egypt's hidden gems. Don't miss the stunning restored 13th-century frescoes on the walls of the Church of St Anthony.

Day 3: El-Gouna
Make the short hop north to **El-Gouna** (p237) for an indulgent overnight stop. The low-rise resorts are attractively designed in Nubian or Arabesque styles, linked by walkways and interspersed by lagoons. Take a trip to the Mons Porphyrites quarries, go out on a dive boat, or relax by the pool before dinner in one of many high-class restaurants.

Day 4: Al-Quseir
Set off south for the small town of **Al-Quseir** (p237), from where Queen Hatshepsut set off on her expedition to the Land of Punt. It is a sleepy, sultry place, where colourful old-fashioned houses are overlooked by numerous mosques. The 16th-century fort and traditional souq make for a pleasant wander, plus there is snorkelling from nearby resorts.

Day 5 and 6: Marsa Alam
Make the 132-km (82-mile) trip south from Al-Quseir to **Marsa Alam** (p237). This large stretch of coast is scattered with glamorous resorts and occasional rustic beach-camps. The endless expanse of sand glistens white and the diving is superlative.

A Week in Luxor and the Nile Valley

- **Arriving** Flights from Europe arrive at Luxor International Airport, just east of the city, plus there are domestic flights from Cairo. Aswan can be reached by air from Cairo, and Abu Simbel is served by flights from Aswan. Trains run between Cairo, Luxor and Aswan.

- **Transport** Luxor and the Nile Valley are best explored by boat, train, minibus or taxi.

Day 1: Luxor
Take a carriage ride to magnificent **Karnak Temple** (pp192–4) to be dwarfed by the Great Hypostyle Hall and the Colossus of Ramses II. Have lunch and a browse in the souq before visiting **Luxor Museum** (p191), where incredible finds from Thebes are on display. See nearby **Luxor Temple** (p190–91) at dusk, when its avenue of sphinxes and enormous statues and pylons are atmospherically lit. Top off the day with a cool drink on the terrace of the **Winter Palace** (p189), probably the most famous hotel in Egypt.

Day 2: Luxor
Spend the day exploring the West Bank and the **Valley of the Kings** (pp196–8). The most decorated is the Tomb of Ramses VI, but don't miss the exact replica of Tutankhamun's Tomb. The vast **Hatshepsut Temple** (pp200–1) is an absolute must, as are the intimate **Valley of the Queens** (p203) and enchanting **Medinet Habu** (pp202) nearby. On the return route, stop to see the **Colossi of Memnon** (p206), two giant statues of Amenhotep III that stood guard at his mortuary temple. After dinner, sit back and enjoy the **Sound and Light Show** (p194) at Karnak.

> **To extend your trip…**
> Head north from Luxor to **Dendara** (pp182–3) to see the Temple of Hathor.

Day 3 to 5: Nile cruising
Have a relaxing morning in Luxor before stepping aboard a cruise boat to sail up the Nile, first to the farming town of **Esna** (p208) and its Temple of Khnum. You will moor overnight near the mighty

Temple of Horus in **Edfu** (*p208*), which lay buried under sand for almost 2,000 years. Another delightful stop is the Graeco-Roman **Temple of Kom Ombo** (*p209*), although equal pleasure is to be had simply gazing at the timeless scenery and village life along the river. Cruises finish in charming **Aswan** (*pp212–15*), which nestles on the banks of the Nile surrounded by the orange sands of the desert.

Day 6: Aswan
Start the day at the **Temple of Philae** (*p216*), romantically situated on a lake, then return to town via the gigantic **Unfinished Obelisk** (*p212*). Spend a leisurely afternoon strolling around Aswan, purchasing souvenirs from the **souq** (*p212*) and dipping into the excellent **Nubian Museum** (*p212*). Sip a sundowner at the gorgeously renovated **Old Cataract Hotel** (*p212*), made famous by the English crime-writer Agatha Christie's novel *Death on the Nile*.

Day 7: Abu Simbel
Take an early morning flight to see the superb temples of **Abu Simbel** (*pp218–19*), hewn out of solid rock and located on the edge of Lake Nasser. Return to Aswan for lunch, before visiting the Nubian villages and ancient ruins on **Elephantine Island** (*pp212–13*) or strolling magical **Kitchener's Island** (*p214*). Sunset is the perfect time for a felucca ride on this most beautiful part of Egypt's Nile.

Hot-air balloons over Valley of the Kings, near Luxor

A Week in the Western Desert

- **Arriving** Flights arrive at Cairo International Airport. Buses connect Cairo with all the oasis towns, or tour operators provide comfortable minibuses.

- **Transport** The Western Desert is best explored by 4x4 jeep, or there are infrequent buses. Only jeeps can cross the track between Siwa and Bahariyya.

Day 1: Siwa
The 9-hour journey to the isolated oasis of **Siwa** (*p264*) gives a sense of what's ahead in this challenging safari itinerary. The tiny town blends into the desertscape, while palm trees and saltwater lakes appear like mirages. Join locals in the tiny souq, explore the remains of the old mudbrick fortress of Shali, and dine in one of the lovely garden-restaurants.

Day 2: Siwa
Take a bicycle to see the sights encircling the town, including the Mountain of the Dead and the Temple of the Oracle, which Alexander the Great visited in 332 BC. Immense sweeping dunes stretch west of Siwa, and you can make a short jeep excursion to swim in natural pools set among the sands, or simply wander around the dusty atmospheric little streets.

Day 3: Siwa to Bahariyya
Rise early to embark on a full day's journey along the rough desert road to **Bahariyya Oasis** (*p261*), an expanse of desert that is especially wild and inspiring. On arrival unwind in one of Bahariyya's sulphurous hot springs. Lodges and camps are dotted around the edges of town, where you can dine on local cuisine and taste the dates and olives for which the oasis is renowned.

Day 4: The Black and White Deserts
Bahariyya has an ancient history, so be sure to see the famed

Golden Mummies (*p261*) before setting off in a 4x4 for an exhilarating safari through the rolling dunes of the **Black Desert** (*p261*). It won't be hard to find a tranquil picnic spot for lunch, before entering the unearthly **White Desert** (*p261*) – the highlight of this trip – where the wind has sculpted the pale landscape into incredible forms and shapes. Following dinner around a campfire, sleep under a million stars.

Day 5: Farafra to Dakhla
See sunrise on the White Desert's eerie rock formations before hopping into your jeep to **Farafra Oasis** (*p261*), one of the most remote places in all Egypt, for a traditional breakfast. It is a spectacular 310-km (192-mile) drive to **Dakhla Oasis** (*p260*), where palm trees, olive groves and agricultural plains make a remarkable sight rising from the sands. Overnight in one of the charming hotels between Al-Qasr and Mut.

Day 6: Dakhla
In the morning explore Mut, where the delightful Ethnographic Museum is designed to resemble a traditional home; it provides an interesting insight into how oasis dwellers have lived for centuries. Spend the afternoon wandering maze-like **Al-Qasr** (*p260*), a medieval town that is the best preserved of all the oases' mudbrick fortifications.

Day 7: Dakhla to Kharga
The last stop on this tour is **Kharga Oasis** (*p260*), a 190-km (118-mile) journey from Dakhla. Explore the remarkable Necropolis of al-Bagawat, an early Christian cemetery with a myriad domes, and the Persian Temple of Hibis. Archaeological finds are displayed in the quaint antiquities museum. From Kharga, it's around a 7-hour drive back to Cairo.

> **To extend your trip...**
> Travel south from Kharga to **Luxor** (*pp186–207*), on a little-used road, making stops at sites such as the Temple of al-Ghueita along the way.

Putting Egypt on the Map

Sitting on the northeast corner of Africa, with coastlines along the Mediterranean and Red seas, Egypt borders Libya to the west, Israel to the east and Sudan to the south. Over 90 per cent of the country is desert and most of the 85 million population live along the Nile Valley and in the Nile Delta, with a small percentage living in the oases that dot the barren interior.

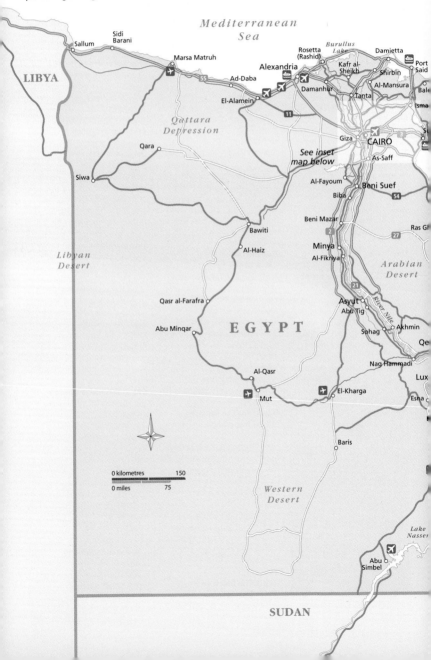

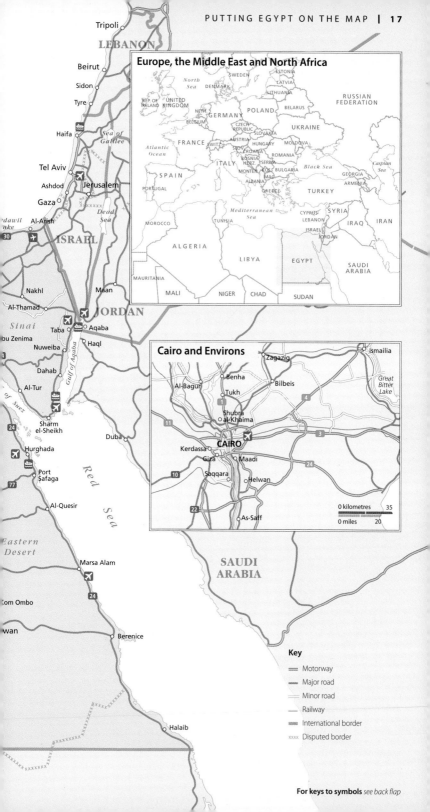

Tripoli

LEBANON

Beirut

Sidon

Tyre

Haifa

Sea of Galilee

Tel Aviv

Ashdod

Jerusalem

Gaza

ISRAEL

Dead Sea

rdawil ake

Al-Arish

Nakhl

Maan

Al-Thamad

JORDAN

Sinai

Taba

Aqaba

ou Zenima

Nuweiba

Haql

Dahab

Al-Tur

Duba

Gulf of Aqaba

Sharm el-Sheikh

Hurghada

Port Safaga

Al-Quesir

Red Sea

Eastern Desert

Marsa Alam

Kom Ombo

wan

Berenice

Halaib

SAUDI ARABIA

Europe, the Middle East and North Africa

North Sea

SWEDEN

DENMARK

ESTONIA

LATVIA

LITHUANIA

RUSSIAN FEDERATION

REP. OF IRELAND

UNITED KINGDOM

NETH

BELGIUM

GERMANY

POLAND

BELARUS

Atlantic Ocean

FRANCE

CZECH REPUBLIC

AUSTRIA

SWITZ

SLOVAKIA

HUNGARY

UKRAINE

MOLDOVA

ROMANIA

SPAIN

ITALY

SLOV CROATIA

BOSNIA HERZ

MONTEN

SERBIA

BULGARIA

Black Sea

Caspian Sea

GEORGIA

ARMENIA

PORTUGAL

ALBANIA

MAC

GREECE

TURKEY

CYPRUS

SYRIA

IRAQ

IRAN

Mediterranean Sea

LEBANON

ISRAEL

JORDAN

MOROCCO

TUNISIA

ALGERIA

LIBYA

EGYPT

SAUDI ARABIA

MAURITANIA

MALI

NIGER

CHAD

SUDAN

Cairo and Environs

Zagazig

Ismailia

Benha

Al-Bagur

Tukh

Bilbeis

Great Bitter Lake

Shubra al-Khaima

Kerdassa

CAIRO

Giza

Maadi

Saqqara

Helwan

As-Saff

0 kilometres   35

0 miles   20

Key

Motorway

Major road

Minor road

Railway

International border

xxxx Disputed border

For keys to symbols see back flap

A PORTRAIT OF EGYPT

Settling along the fertile banks of the Nile, the ancient Egyptians established a magnificent and enduring civilization whose achievements have captured the imagination of the world ever since. Although looking to the future, modern Egypt cannot ignore its glorious past, and the resulting contrasts make it a uniquely fascinating place to visit.

The world's fascination with this country centres on the civilization of ancient Egypt that flourished from around 3000 BC to 30 BC, ruled by approximately 30 dynasties. The river Nile was the powerful force that enabled the ancient Egyptian kingdom to develop. The river's annual cycle of inundation watered the land and replenished the fertile topsoil. This resulted in an agricultural abundance that allowed them to concentrate on developing the knowledge and culture that formed their unique and sophisticated civilization. Over the succeeding millennia, waves of foreign conquerors passed through the country – Persians, Greeks, Romans, crusaders, Arabs and Turks – leaving traces behind in their descendants. Today most Egyptians are classified as being of Eastern Hamitic descent. The once nomadic Bedouin and Berber tribes of the desert are of Arab descent and

the third major racial grouping (less than 200,000) is the Nubian community in the south.

Daily Life

Even today, the river Nile remains the lifeblood of Egypt, with around 96 per cent of the population forced by the harsh environment to live in the Nile Delta or Nile Valley.

The ancient cycle of flooding ended with the completion of the High Dam at Aswan in 1971, forcing the Egyptian *fellaheen* (farmers) to resort to artificial fertilizers. However, it is easy to imagine that life today along the river's edge remains just as it has for thousands of years.

The typical Egyptian rural settlement is a village of between 500 and 10,000 people set amid intensely cultivated fields. Houses are often no more than one or two storeys high and each village also

The fertile Nile Delta, one of the most intensely cultivated areas of the world

◀ Men dressed in local attire at Luxor Temple

Solitary felucca sailing serenely down the tranquil waters of the Nile

has a mosque or church, and perhaps a colourful pigeoncote, a few shops and an official government building. Most of the inhabitants of smaller villages work in agriculture and the landscape is usually dotted with farmers, wearing the traditional *galabiyya* (long smock), working the green fields or tending their precious animals – buffalo, sheep and goats.

The urban population has been expanding rapidly since the 1980s. Increasing pressure on agricultural land and the growth of city-based service industries have led to large numbers of Egyptians moving from the country to urban areas. Dwellings in towns and cities are mainly two-storey houses or higher apartment blocks with flat roofs and balconies, often built close together. The high population density in cities also leads to problems of traffic congestion. Nowhere is this more evident than in Cairo, where there is a constant cacophony of car engines and horns.

Men chatting in a Cairo coffee house, a popular male Egyptian pastime

Throughout Egypt the family has remained the most significant unit of a patriarchal society. Traditionally, an individual's social identity was closely linked to his or her status in the network of relations. Today families are far more likely to disperse and the ideal of an extended family that lives together is less frequent. However, strong ties with in-laws, grandparents, nieces and nephews and the rest of the family still create a strong social fabric that binds the whole community together.

Religion and Culture

Underpinning all levels of Egyptian society is a powerful religious faith. Islam is constitutionally established as the official religion and around 90 per cent of the population are Sunni Muslim *(see p95)*, the rest being Christian, mainly of the Coptic church *(see pp126–7)*. However, say to an Egyptian of either faith "I'll see you tomorrow" and the answer will be the same – "Inshallah", meaning "if God is willing". For the casual tourist, the many casinos, bars, nightclubs and beach resorts can disguise the fact that Egyptians uphold a fairly conservative mix of traditional and religious values, particularly outside the main cities. Gambling or drinking alcohol in public is frowned upon and Egyptian men rarely wear shorts, except maybe at the beach.

Women, too, are almost always well-covered. In the 1970s, as women gained greater independence and access to education, they swelled the numbers of the nonagricultural workforce and many Muslim women discarded their *hijab* (headscarf). With the wide appeal of Islamist conservatives in the 1990s, women started dressing more modestly and, even in Cairo, increasing numbers are once again covering their heads, with some adopting the *niqab*, the full-face covering. However, the number of women in employment has remained at a high level.

Egyptians, governed by outsiders for thousands of years, have only been truly independent since 1952 when Gamal Abdel Nasser removed the last foreign royal and forged a truly Egyptian identity for his people. Despite a climate of political turmoil, this period of Egypt's history was a time of cultural vitality, when Umm Kolthum, the diva of the Arab world,

The *hijab* or headscarf, increasingly worn by Egyptian women

gave concerts for the masses and Naguib Mahfouz penned his most famous novels. Awarded a Nobel Prize in 1988, Mahfouz single-handedly rejuvenated the Egyptian literary scene. However, few other Egyptian writers have managed to emulate his success. Today, as a result of Egypt's population boom and greater exposure to Western music, there is a ready market for home-grown modern pop music. Nevertheless Umm Kolthum's soulful music is as all-pervasive as ever, constantly played in shops and taxis throughout Egypt. Egypt's cinema had its heyday in the 1940s and 50s when its studios made films for the whole Arab world. Apart from a few independent films which gain a wider exposure during international film festivals, little of merit emerges these days.

Modern Cairo with the Pyramids of Giza just visible through the evening haze

Negotiating the streets around Midan Ataba in Cairo on a daily bread round

Politics and Economics

After the abolition of the monarchy in 1952, Nasser went on to dissolve all political parties and introduce a new constitution in 1956, declaring the Republic of Egypt. Led by Nasser, the National Union, later the Arab Socialist Union (ASU), became the sole party. In 1971 a new constitution declared Egypt to be "a democratic, socialist state". But it was not until 1977 that the formation of other political parties was allowed. Three years later the ASU was abolished. The next ruling party, the National Democratic Party (NDP) led by Hosni Mubarak, was a direct descendant of Nasser's ASU. Egypt's "dominant party system" allowed a large ruling party to straddle the centre of the ideological spectrum, surrounded by small pressure parties. This limited the possibility for radical reform, but allowed the government to proceed slowly. In 2011, following widespread public protests, Mubarak's government was dissolved. The military took over interim rule until June 2012, when Mohamed Morsi, a moderate Islamist from the Muslim Brotherhood, was elected president. However, the political situation remains unstable.

Nasser, President of Egypt 1956–70

Egyptian growth has decelerated with the global economic woes. Agriculture is the most important industry. Employing a large amount of the workforce, it feeds much of the country and provides valuable exports, especially the cotton crop. The High Dam project increased arable land and provided a much needed boost to the power supply.

The modern Nile City Towers complex in Cairo, overlooking the Nile

Ancient tombs lying in the path of a motorway

However, in the same period, just as much land was swallowed up by industrial and urban development, constantly building over Egypt's celebrated past. Although slowing down, population growth undermines all efforts to foster the economy. Other important sources of income are oil, gas, mining and, of course, tourism. The brutal murder of 58 tourists in 1997 *(see p180)* and the kidnapping of tourists in a remote southern region in 2007 rocked the country, causing visitor numbers to plummet. Tourism quickly recovered, however, 30 years of Mubarak's rule resulted in stagnation, corruption and the decreasing quality of life among average Egyptians. This led to increasing pent-up frustration and the situation reached a boiling point, exploding into a revolution in 2011 – a part of the Arab Spring.

Egypt Today

Social media played a critical part in the 2011 revolution, sometimes called the Facebook revolution, due to the ability of Egyptians to connect with each other. With increasing Internet accessibility and usage, Egyptians are now able to reach the world beyond the tightly controlled state media. Even more so has been the spread of smartphone use, available to even the poorest of Egyptians thanks to affordable Chinese devices. A level of unprecedented exposure to global culture and politics has led to rapid change among the youth of Egypt, which makes up one third of the population. This has created an increasing strain on traditional Egyptian culture and customs. The current military-backed regime has tried to put the lid back on with harsher repressive laws against dissent and opposition; however, as far as the Egyptian youth is concerned, there is no turning back. An ancient land is rapidly joining the modern world.

A visitor at a Red Sea resort, enjoying Egypt's beautiful beaches and all-year-round sun

Discovering Ancient Egypt

The magnificence and longevity of the ancient Egyptian civilization has always held a timeless fascination. As early as 1400 BC, King Tuthmosis IV undertook excavations at Giza, and the Greek historian Herodotus left a detailed account of his tour of Egypt in 450 BC. However, modern Egyptology really started with the study of the country commissioned in 1798 by Napoleon. Since then the subject has developed rapidly. In the 1980s, computers and electron microscopes begun to replace the pickaxe and shovel.

Napoleon's scholars amassed the material for the authoritative work *Description de l'Egypte* during the French occupation (1798–1802).

Jean-François Champollion (1790–1832) was a French linguist whose brilliant work in deciphering the hieroglyphic script was the single most important event in the development of Egyptology.

Hieroglyphs were used as early as 3200 BC and are the oldest known writing system. Used primarily in religious contexts, their last datable use was in AD 394 at Hadrian's Gate at Philae when the script numbered over 6,000 characters.

Howard Carter (1873–1939)

Carter trained as an artist and joined the Archaeological Survey of Egypt in 1891. In 1922, he achieved fame when he found King Tutankhamun's tomb, virtually untouched, in the Valley of the Kings.

Howard Carter had to carefully remove many layers of solidified perfumes and resins covering Tutankhamun's innermost coffin. The body was protected by several layers of coffins, the last one of solid gold.

The treasures Carter found on opening the tomb were abundant. Most items are on display in the Egyptian Museum *(see pp78–81).*

Relocation of Ancient Temples

Trajan's Kiosk (also known as the Pharaoh's Bedstead) before relocation at Philae

The construction of the Aswan High Dam and Lake Nasser (1960–71) threatened many temples and rock tombs along the Nile with total submersion. Concern over the loss of such archaeological treasures led UNESCO to promote an international relief campaign. Three stages of operations were necessary: a survey of the area, the excavation of sites, and the final movement of as many endangered monuments as was possible. Twenty monuments from Egyptian Nubia and four from the Sudan were carefully dismantled, then reassembled at safe distances from their original sites. The two largest operations involved the Great Temple at Abu Simbel *(see pp218–19)* and the temple complex at Philae *(see p216)*.

Underwater Discoveries

In 1996, a team led by the French marine archaeologist, Franck Goddio, began to explore the submerged Royal City of Alexandria, where Cleopatra held court. The finds so far include statues, sphinxes, ceramics and the remains of Cleopatra's palace.

Tutankhamun's death mask, shown here at the British Museum with Queen Elizabeth II in 1972, was the top exhibit in a display of Carter's finds that toured the major museums of the world, rekindling interest in Egypt's rich history.

Archaeology and Technology

Egyptology is a relatively young science, but huge advances have been made since Champollion's work opened the door on ancient Egyptian history. Today, Egyptologists are greatly assisted by new technologies, both in the laboratory and in the field – and even under water.

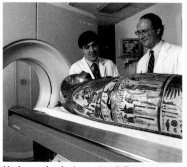

Restoration and preservation work on ancient artifacts involves skilled and painstaking processes, which have to be conducted in a strictly controlled environment.

Modern technologies, such as CAT scanning, radio-carbon dating, DNA and trace element analysis, endoscopy and electron microscopy have all contributed to more accurate dating and a deeper understanding of archaeological finds.

Hieroglyphics

Dating from around 3200 BC, ancient Egyptian hieroglyphics are the world's oldest known writing system. The word "hieroglyph" means "sacred carved letter" and refers to the beautiful pictorial script used by ancient Egyptians to express their religious beliefs and engraved onto nearly every available surface of their monuments. Although pictorial, hieroglyphs convey extremely complex semantic information; they could be read from left to right, right to left or top to bottom. However, when writing on papyrus, the hieroglyphic system was too slow and impractical for everyday use and over the centuries more easily written scripts were developed with the last datable hieroglyphic inscription being at Hadrian's Gate at Philae in AD 394.

Thoth, the ibis-headed god of wisdom and patron deity of scribes, is here portrayed holding his sceptre of power or *was*.

Egyptian scribes, in a virtually illiterate population, were part of society's elite. It took many years to learn the art of hieroglyphics but the rewards could be high – King Horemheb started his career as a scribe.

The Rosetta Stone – Cracking the Code

Until 1822, the ability to read hieroglyphic inscriptions had been lost. It was a black granite stele, discovered in 1799 in Rosetta by Napoleon's army, that held the key. It contained a text in three scripts: hieroglyphic, demotic and Greek. The two main contestants in the race to decipher the symbols were Thomas Young, a British physician, and Jean-François Champollion, a gifted French linguist. By 1819, Young was ahead of the Frenchman, translating the demotic text as well as identifying the cartouches of Ptolemy and Cleopatra. However, Champollion was also able to decipher these names and others, compiling an extensive list of symbols. Using this list, he realized that there were separate types of hieroglyphs with different functions and therefore discovered the basis of the writing system used in hieroglyphic texts.

The Rosetta stone, inscribed by the priests of Ptolemy V (196 BC)

Ptolemaic scribes raised the number of hieroglyphic symbols from 700 to 6,000, in an attempt to keep their knowledge exclusive.

The Importance of Names

Ancient Egyptians believed that names were as vital to one's existence as the soul. Names held great power and speaking the name of the dead could bring them to life. Therefore, funerary texts often included spells to cause the name of the deceased to be remembered in the afterlife and so ensure eternal life.

The oval cartouche forms a protective wall or enclosure.

Hieroglyphs give the name, "Ramses, beloved of Amun".

Egyptian kings protected their names within cartouches and increased their chances of eternal life by the sheer number of epithets they possessed.

This detail of the King List found at Abydos gives some of Ramses II's names, including "the king of Upper and Lower Egypt, Usermaatre Setepenre, son of Ra, and Ramses, beloved of Amun".

Hieroglyphic Text

Hieroglyphs were a decorative art and ritual pictures, combined with texts, played a vital part in religious ceremonies. Funerary texts were designed to protect the dead and help guide their passage to the underworld. This detail from the funeral texts of the scribe Nebked (c.1400 BC), shows the deceased (his writing kit tucked into his belt) worshipping the god Osiris with his wife and mother.

Hieratic script was a faster way of writing. Dating from c.2600 BC, it was used for everyday communications until c.600 BC when it was superseded by the even faster demotic or "popular" script.

Translating Hieroglyphs

Put simply, there are three main types of hieroglyphs. "Phonograms" convey the sounds of the syllables; for example the ancient Egyptian for "son" was spoken *sa* and this is denoted by the duck. "Ideograms" portray the actual object or action, such as a sun on the horizon to indicate "appearance". The final type is "determinatives" which indicate, confirm or modify the meaning of the word to which they are attached, for example, three bars denote a plural. To further complicate matters, many symbols can be either ideograms, phonograms or determinatives. The basket symbol, *neb*, can be a phonogram for "Lord" or simply represent a "basket". Symbols of humans and animals always face the start of the text, indicating the direction the text runs.

Ra *ra*

Son *sa*

Lord *neb*

Appearance *kha*

Determinative plural symbol

Hieroglyphs for "Son of Ra, Lord of Appearances"

Temples and Religious Life

For the ancient Egyptians, the universe was composed of dualities – fertile and barren, life and death, order and chaos – held in a state of equilibrium by the goddess Maat. To maintain this balance, they built enormous temples dedicated to the gods. At the centre of every settlement and devoted to a particular god or set of gods, the "cult" temple served as a storehouse of divine power, maintained by the priesthood for the benefit of all. The temple was also an economic and political centre employing large numbers of the local community and serving as a town hall, medical centre and college.

Goddess Maat, the person-ification of cosmic order and harmony, set the rules by which all kings must govern. Her power regulated the stars, the seasons and humans' relationship with the gods.

Funerary priest in a leopard skin, performing sacred rituals

A Day in the Life of a Temple Priest

Egyptian priests were literally "servants of the god or goddess", responsible for performing the daily rituals that regulated the workings of the universe. The king, although the intermediary between the mortal and the divine, delegated his duties to the high priest of the temple. This priest was then responsible for the most important of the temple rituals – the honouring of the god within its shrine. Twice daily the "cult" statue was bathed and clothed before receiving offerings of food and drink. Incense was burned and holy water from the sacred lake scattered to show the purity of the offerings. After the essence of the food had been consumed by the gods, the priests were able to eat the actual offerings.

Cult Temple Reconstruction

As well as housing the deity, the temple complex symbolized the universe. Its architecture represented the fundamental elements of water, sunlight, stars, forests and, inside the depths of the temple, darkness.

Covered colonnade

Flagstaffs

Entrance to enclosure

Processional route

Pylons, or monumental gateways, had vast towers decorated with giant reliefs of the king warding off his enemies.

The central court, as depicted in this 19th-century reconstruction of the court at Philae *(see p216)*, was a colonnaded courtyard brightly decorated with reliefs showing the king making offerings to the temple's deities.

Tomb decorations, such as this detail from Luxor *(see pp190–91)* illustrating the offering of ducks, depicted typical ritual ceremonies. Reliefs and paintings of rituals ensured that these important ceremonies were continually enacted.

The shrine, like this one from Edfu temple *(see pp208–9)*, was the most essential part of the Egyptian temple. Located in the innermost sanctuary, it housed the statue of the temple god. Daily offerings were made to persuade the divinity's beneficial essence to reside in the statue.

Small hypostyle hall

Outer temple wall

Inner chambers were dimly lit and marked the approach to the sacred inner sanctuary. They were used for storing valuables or worshipping subsidiary deities.

Priests' houses

The hypostyle hall's ceiling was usually painted with constellations of stars, while its great columns were decorated with plant reliefs. It was meant to resemble a primeval forest with the stars and sky overhead.

Sacred lakes, like this one at Karnak *(see pp192–3)*, were an important feature of "cult" temples and were used by religious personnel, who bathed in the lake to ensure ritual purity.

Mortuary Temples

In addition to the local "cult" temples, each king built a mortuary temple to serve as a place where, following his death, offerings could be made for his soul. The temples were originally attached to the royal tombs of the Old and Middle Kingdoms but by around 1500 BC they had developed into vast, elaborate complexes built at separate locations to the tombs which were now hidden away in secluded desert valleys. The great temples on the West Bank at Luxor are fine examples of New Kingdom mortuary temples. The magnificent Temple of Queen Hatshepsut *(see pp200–1)* at Deir al-Bahri has one of the most original mortuary temple designs.

The Ramesseum in Thebes *(see pp204–5)*, the mortuary temple of Ramses II

Mythology

Ancient Egyptian religion was a highly complex belief system involving a great number of deities originally based on aspects of the natural world. As these evolved into more cohesive "personalities", each locality developed myths relating to their own particular deities. These myths were many and varied, with even the story of creation having at least three different versions, based on the belief that life first emerged from the waters of chaos as a mound of earth. A number of places claimed to be the original site of this primeval mound and that the first life was created by the gods associated with that particular place, be they the nine gods of Heliopolis, the eight gods of Hermopolis or the one god of Memphis.

Amun, whose name means "the hidden one", became a national deity when Thebes ruled Egypt, in an attempt to unify the country.

Creation Myth

This detail from a popular creation myth shows the Egyptian gods in relation to the world. In the beginning there was nothing but the sea of chaos, Nun. Then Atum thought himself into being, sneezing to create Shu and then Tefnut. He caused the seas to recede and called forth all the plants and animals. Shu and Tefnut gave birth to two children: Geb, the earth, and Nut, the sky, who in turn gave birth to the stars.

Nephthys pours the waters of fruitfulness over the earth, where men hoe the land.

Nut, mother of all, swallows the sun each night, giving birth to it again in the morning.

Geb, god of the earth; his bent leg represents the mountains.

Statuette of Osiris (centre) with his son Horus and loyal wife Isis

Osiris, Isis and Horus

One of the most universal Egyptian myths is that of Osiris and Isis. The story has it that Osiris was a king who taught the Egyptians how to live, worship and grow corn. He was murdered by his jealous brother Seth, who cut up the body, scattering it over Egypt. Osiris's beloved wife Isis and her sister Nephthys collected up all the pieces and, with the help of the gods Anubis and Thoth, they put him back together as the first mummy. Isis used her magic to revive him and at the same time conceived a son, Horus, who would avenge his father. Osiris, brought back to life, went down to the underworld to be the lord and judge of the dead.

Osiris in a typical pose

The Sun

Fundamental to the Egyptians, the sun was regarded as the source of all life, conquering the forces of darkness each night before emerging victorious at dawn to repeat the eternal cycle. Worshipped under a variety of names and guises, the sun was most often represented by the falcon-headed god Ra, as well as Atum, Khepri, Harakhty and the Aten sun-disk. The sun-god's representative on earth, the king was hailed as the "Son of Ra". When Amun was elevated to supreme deity, for political reasons, his status was validated by linking him with Ra's supremacy to create Amun-Ra, the "King of the Gods".

Khepri was represented as a dung beetle or scarab. Identified with the sun-god Ra, he was said to roll the sun across the sky like a ball of dung.

Ra-Harakhty was the combination of two gods: the sky-god Horus, whose right eye was the sun and left eye the moon, and the all-powerful sun-god Ra.

Ra, creator of the universe, wears the sun on his brow.

Maat keeps the world in balance.

Shu, jealous of Geb and Nut, stands keeping them apart.

Major gods

- **Amun**: powerful local Theban deity.
- **Anubis**: jackal-headed god of embalmers.
- **Atum**: creator aspect of the sun-god.
- **Bes**: household god of women in childbirth.
- **Geb**: god of the earth.
- **Hathor**: goddess of love, pleasure and beauty.
- **Horus**: falcon-headed god closely identified with each pharaoh.
- **Isis**: goddess of magic.
- **Khepri**: a sun-god as a scarab beetle.
- **Maat**: goddess of truth and universal balance.
- **Nekhbet**: vulture-goddess of Upper Egypt.
- **Nephthys**: with Isis, protector of the dead.
- **Nut**: goddess of the sky.
- **Osiris**: god of the underworld.
- **Ptah**: creator god and patron of craftsmen.
- **Ra**: pre-eminent form of the sun-god.
- **Sekhmet**: lioness-goddess of destruction.
- **Seth**: god of chaos.
- **Shu**: god of the air.
- **Tefnut**: goddess of moisture.
- **Thoth**: the ibis-headed god of wisdom.
- **Wadjet**: cobra-goddess of Lower Egypt.

The Benu Bird

The Benu bird flew across the waters of Nun at the dawn of creation and saw land first break the water's surface. The Benu bird was identified with the sun and the primeval mound was symbolized by the Benben stone at Heliopolis, thought to be where the sun's first rays touched land. It was the prototype for obelisks whose tips were gold plated – to catch the first rays of the sun.

Tomb painting showing the worship of the Benu bird

Obelisk, symbol of first land

Burial Traditions

The ancient Egyptians believed in an eternal afterlife and they developed a complex funerary cult aimed at maintaining their life after death. This involved preserving the body of the dead person through a process of mummification so that their soul would live on in their embalmed corpse. The deceased were then supplied with everything they might need in the afterlife before being launched into eternity via a set of elaborate funeral rituals.

Anubis, the jackal-headed god of embalming, is shown putting the finishing touches to a mummy in this 19th-Dynasty tomb relief.

Mummification Techniques

The earliest mummies from prehistoric times were probably accidental. True mummification began in the 4th Dynasty with the development of artificial embalming techniques. Special priests first removed the internal organs of the deceased, leaving only the heart, to be weighed in the afterlife. Then the corpse was dried out with natron and finally wrapped in linen.

Natural mummification occurred when dead bodies were placed in simple sand graves. The sand absorbed the body's moisture, drying out the corpse and preserving soft tissue.

Canopic jars stored the embalmed internal organs of the deceased. The intestines, stomach, liver and lungs had separate jars, which were buried alongside the coffin in the tomb.

Natron, a naturally occurring mixture of sodium salts, was packed in and around the body to dry it out artificially. This took 40 days.

Ramses III, one of the best preserved of the royal mummies, was discovered in 1881 at Deir al-Bahri. The mummy is now on display in the Egyptian Museum *(see pp78–81).*

The mummified body was stuffed with linen and sawdust before being wrapped in tight linen bandages. Finally the wrapped mummy was placed in its painted wooden coffin.

Animal Mummies

The ancient Egyptians believed that all living things contained the divine essence and were, therefore, worthy of respect. In sharing the attributes of the gods they symbolized, animals were venerated as the gods' representatives on earth and mummified after their death. By the Late Period (664–332 BC), animals of all kinds were being mummified and buried in catacombs, from literally millions of ibises and cats to bulls and lions, shrews, snakes and crocodiles.

Ibis mummy

Cat mummy

Mummy Masks

A mask was fitted over the head of the mummy to help the dead person's spirit to recognize its body. From the glittering gold masks of pharaohs such as Tutankhamun to the more common painted masks made of cartonnage (a sort of papier-mâché), mummy masks were idealized portraits of the deceased.

A mummy mask showed the face framed by a stylized wig and wide collar.

Roman portrait masks, painted on flat wooden panels, were laid over the face of the mummy. The portraits were often painted during the lifetime of the deceased and were more realistic than earlier masks *(see p173).*

Accessories

In addition to significant worldly possessions, the mummy was usually buried with funerary items, including amulets, a set of shabti *figures and a model boat to transport the mummy to Abydos.*

***Shabti* figures** were models of workers placed in the tomb to carry out manual work on behalf of the deceased in the afterlife.

Amulets were worn by Egyptians in life and in death to protect the body from evil and to bring good luck.

A model funerary boat symbolized the mummy's journey to Abydos, home of Osiris, god of the dead *(see p30).*

Funerary Rites and Ceremonies

At the funeral, relatives left offerings of food and priests performed special funerary rites. These ceremonies and rituals were meant to protect the deceased, ensure a successful journey into the afterlife and sustain them on their way. As further protection, ritual images and texts were placed with the body or used to decorate the tomb.

The Book of the Dead was a guide through the underworld. The deceased is portrayed here crossing the Lake of Offerings with his gifts.

The Opening of the Mouth ritual was performed on the body prior to burial in the belief that this would reactivate the senses, so the deceased would function in the afterlife.

The Weighing of the Heart was the final stage in the journey to the afterlife. A jury of gods presided over the ceremony to decide whether the deceased deserved eternal life. The jackal-god Anubis weighed the heart against the feather of truth. If the heart was too heavy, it was given to the monster Ammut, who devoured it; only if it balanced would the dead live forever.

Daily Life in Ancient Egypt

In the hierarchical society of ancient Egypt, the importance of the family was fundamental. Early marriages were encouraged, with the hope of producing children to continue the family line and, importantly, to organize a proper burial. Marriage seems to have required no religious or civil ceremony, but simply involved one partner moving into the home of the other. Youngsters enjoyed a brief period of childhood before taking on adult responsibilities. Education was mainly vocational, with boys often being apprenticed to their fathers.

This family group comprises husband and wife *(centre)*, their son *(right)* and older male *(left)*.

Egyptian Housing

Egyptian houses were built of sun-baked mudbricks and so have not survived well. From the evidence that has been preserved it seems that houses were typically square with a central living room, bedrooms and storerooms and sometimes stairs leading to the roof or to an upper floor. Some even had primitive bathroom suites.

Egyptian houses had basic air-conditioning, provided by small windows and roof vents as shown in this painting from the tomb of 18th-Dynasty scribe Nakht.

The roof vent is designed to catch the cool north breezes.

Small, high windows let in light and breezes, but not the sun.

Soul houses, such as this terracotta example, were included in tombs to house the soul of the deceased. The models demonstrate many features of ancient Egyptian housing and even mirror houses in rural Egypt today.

Cooking would take place outside or in outbuildings.

More complex housing, such as this model town house, reflected the higher status of the owner.

The village at Deir al-Medina, founded in the 16th century BC for those working in the Valley of the Kings

Workers' Village at Deir al-Medina

In a secluded valley on the west bank of the Nile opposite Luxor are the excavated foundations of a village that was inhabited by the craftsmen and labourers who constructed the tombs in the Valley of the Kings. In this early example of urban planning, the houses, arranged in rows, all opened off one central street and were enclosed within an outer wall. A typical house in Deir al-Medina had between four and six rooms plus a cellar or two for storage. Around the village are the chapels and tombs of the government-employed workers.

Women often worked and looked after the children. In this 26th-Dynasty tomb relief, a mother with her child sorts fruit in an orchard.

Women In Society

Although their status generally derived from that of their fathers or husbands, women in ancient Egypt enjoyed a relatively high profile. Equal to men before the law, they could own or rent property, engage in business, receive an equal share of inheritances and, in some cases, even rule as pharaoh. Divorce and remarriage were available to them, and if a man divorced his wife, she was entitled to maintenance. Women were expected to manage the household and family, and the poorer ones had to work alongside the men too.

Two women are depicted in this 30th-Dynasty relief using a tourniquet press to extract the essential oils of lilies for perfume.

Three noblewomen are seen in this 18th-Dynasty detail, sharing their pleasure in the perfume of lotus blossoms and mandrake fruit.

Working Life in Ancient Egypt

Most of the farmland was owned by the king, the temples and rich individuals. This was farmed by the bulk of the population, who worked either directly for the owner or as a tenant farmer paying large amounts of rent and tax. Slightly better off were the skilled craftsmen, many of whom worked for the pharaoh, the temples or rich nobles. Their crafts included carpentry, jewellery and stone-working. Near the top of the hierarchy was an elite of professionals who ran the country – the scribes (see p26), the priests (see p28) and top-ranking officials.

Nile-style farming is depicted in this painting from the 19th-Dynasty tomb of Sennedjem and Iyneferti. Although portraying the idealized afterlife, it shows the methods used to reap grain, plough and harvest flax.

The Nile may have provided fish and fertile soil, but it had its share of risks as well as its rewards. As depicted in this Old Kingdom tomb relief scene, herdsmen had to be mindful of the danger posed to livestock from crocodiles.

Dairy produce, as depicted in this tomb relief, played an important part in the diet. Other livestock reared by ancient Egyptian farmers included sheep, goats and even pigs.

Skilled craftsmen were usually employed in large workshops or in special communities such as Deir al-Medina.

Peasant farmers also supplied most of the labour for large building projects. This was a requirement for everybody except officials. In this tomb painting a team of unskilled workers are making mudbricks.

Islamic Egypt

Islam was founded by Mohammed, a merchant who was born in around AD 570 in Mecca. At the age of 40 he began to receive revelations of the word of Allah (God) and these were transcribed as the Quran. Mohammed's preachings were not well received in Mecca and, in AD 622, he and his followers fled to Medina. This flight (hejira) constitutes year zero in the Islamic calendar. Before he died in AD 632, Mohammed returned to conquer Mecca. The armies of Islam swept through the Byzantine provinces of the eastern Mediterranean, arriving in Egypt in AD 640.

The crescent moon, a familiar symbol of Islam, has resonances with the lunar calendar, which orders Muslim religious life.

The Quran, the holy book of Islam, is regarded as the direct word of Allah. Muslims believe that it can only be fully understood if read in Arabic. It is divided into 114 chapters, or suras, which cover many topics, including matters relating to the family, marriage, and legal and ethical concerns.

This house is decorated with pilgrimage scenes, which include a depiction of the great mosque in Mecca. The picture indicates that the house-owner has made the pilgrimage to Mecca.

Muslims praying outside the Mosque of Sayyidna al-Hussein

The Five Pillars of Faith

Islam rests on the "five pillars of faith". The first of these, the *Shahada*, is a simple declaration that "there is no God but Allah and Mohammed is his Prophet". The second is the set of daily prayers that are supposed to be performed five times a day, facing in the direction of Mecca. The third is fasting during the daylight hours of the holy month of Ramadan. The fourth is the giving of alms. The fifth is *Haj*: at least once in their lifetime all Muslims must, if they are able, make the pilgrimage to Mecca, the birthplace of Mohammed.

Visiting a Mosque

Apart from at prayer times and during the Friday congregation, most mosques in Egypt are open to visitors. Very few require an entrance ticket, but it is customary to give a tip to the guardian and to the person who looks after your shoes or provides a scarf to cover your head during your visit. Mosques are open 24 hours, but only open to visitors from 9am–7pm. They close earlier in winter and during the month of Ramadan *(see also p322)*.

Arcaded courtyard of the Mosque of al-Azhar, Cairo

Muslim festivals are relatively infrequent, with just four major dates in the calendar *(see p43)*. The most important of these are Eid al-Adha, marking the time of the pilgrimage *(Haj)*, and Eid al-Fitr, which is held at the end of Ramadan. Islamic celebrations tend to be communal affairs and usually take the form of great feasts, often held outdoors.

The Call to Prayer

A muezzin traditionally makes the call to prayer five times each day from the balcony of a mosque's minaret. Today, microphones and loudspeakers are used to allow the muezzin to be heard from afar.

Mosques have been built in a variety of styles but they all share some common features. Chief of these is the *mihrab*, the niche that indicates the direction of Mecca. Most mosques also have a *minbar*, from which the *imam* delivers his Friday sermon.

Balcony, from where the call to prayer is traditionally made

Minaret

Crescent-shaped finial

Prayer hall entrance, where footwear must be removed

Islamic Architecture

The term Islamic architecture refers not only to mosques but also to a wide range of interesting buildings. The styles used were developed primarily under the early Islamic dynasties (the Tulunids, Fatimids and Ayyubids) and reached the height of creativity during the Mamluk era *(see p61)*. Craftsmen from all over the Near East were brought to Egypt to build palaces and mausoleums for rich and vainglorious sultans. They also created public institutions such as hospitals, schools and street fountains, many of which are still in use. The last great period of Islamic architecture in Egypt was under the Ottoman Turks *(see p62)*. Although reserving their best work for the imperial city of Istanbul, the Ottoman legacy includes some impressive structures.

Typical mosque-style building with domes and minarets *(see p97)*

Domestic Architecture

Private houses (called *beit* in Arabic) owed their design to both climatic and social conditions. Certain features, such as small windows covered with wooden screens, large airy rooms, shady arcades and fountains, kept the rooms cool. Typically these houses would be partitioned into separate male and female zones, known as the *salamlek* and *haramlek* respectively.

Mashrabiyya screens allowed the women of the house to look out without being seen.

Rooftop wind catchers channelled cool breezes into the rooms below.

The grandest private houses could rise as high as three or four storeys. They used recurring features such as *ablaq* (striped layers of stone), arcades and fountains.

Indoor fountains were built into the homes of the wealthy to keep the room temperature down.

The House of Amasyali is one of numerous examples of the exquisite Ottoman merchants' houses that have survived in the town of Rosetta *(see p243)*.

Wooden ceilings were often carved with beautifully intricate geometric patterns and then painted in rich colours.

A *qaa* or reception room typically formed the sumptuous centrepiece of the wealthy merchants' houses.

Sabil-Kuttab (Fountain and School)

Sabils (public fountains) are a typical element of Islamic architecture – some no more than a tap and a trough, some grand like the Sabil-Kuttab of Abdel Katkhuda. The *kuttab* was an open loggia or gallery where teachings of the Quran took place.

Tiles painted with scenes from Mecca were used to decorate some *sabil-kuttabs* in keeping with the religious nature of these buildings.

Sabil-Kuttab of Abdel Katkhuda *(see p102)*

Madrassa (Law School)

A *madrassa* is a Quranic school, where law and theology are taught. Usually a mosque and *madrassa* are one and the same building. Sunni Islam, the variant of Islam followed in Egypt, has four schools of law (Hanafi, Malaki, Shafii and Hanbali), and so typically a *madrassa* will have four separate teaching areas, one for each. These often take the form of *iwans*, which are large arched spaces arranged around a central courtyard.

Fountains existed for the ablutions that had to be carried out before prayer.

Madrassa of Sultan Barquq *(see p101)*

Wikala (Hotel)

Also known as a caravanserai, the *wikala* is the precursor of the modern inn. It provided hospitality to the travelling merchant caravans that brought such great wealth to medieval Egypt. Animals were kept on the ground floor, along with goods placed in storage, while upstairs were the lodgings. At night, the whole building was sealed behind a sole gate for security purposes.

The rooms for the travellers overlooked the tiled central courtyard of the *wikala*.

Fountains provided water for the animals.

The Wikala of al-Ghouri *(see p96)*

Mausoleum (Tomb)

Some of the most splendid pieces of architecture in Egypt are mausoleums. Just like the pharaohs before them with their pyramids and immense mortuary temples, medieval sultans sought to glorify themselves in death. This they did by spending lavish amounts on enormous funerary complexes that often incorporated mosques and *madrassas* beside a domed tomb chamber. Inside, the bodies of the dead were laid above ground in a cenotaph marked by a pillar-like headstone. During Ottoman times, soldiers' headstones were frequently decorated with a carved turban.

Elaborate wrought-iron decoration was used to adorn the tomb.

The crescent moon symbol of Islam was an essential component of any Islamic mortuary structure.

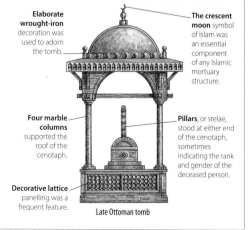

Four marble columns supported the roof of the cenotaph.

Pillars, or stelae, stood at either end of the cenotaph, sometimes indicating the rank and gender of the deceased person.

Decorative lattice panelling was a frequent feature.

Late Ottoman tomb

The Landscape and Wildlife of Egypt

Although Egypt comprises over 90 per cent desert, it is not a totally barren landscape. A number of plants and animals have developed strategies to cope with extreme temperatures and long periods of drought. Humans, however, are less adaptable and while a tiny percentage lives in desert oases *(see p265)*, 96 per cent live close to water in the green Delta or along the Nile Valley. However, despite plentiful water and rich soil, this land struggles to provide enough food for the rapidly growing population. Around Egypt's coastline the seas teem with marine life and the colourful coral reefs of the Red Sea *(see p231)* are probably the one of the richest natural environments on the planet.

Desert travel, reliant on camels and date palms

Deserts

The popular image of deserts is of endless seas of sand. However, the rocky interior of Sinai also counts as a desert – strictly defined as an area with less than 25 cm (10 inches) of rainfall a year. Strong winds are also characteristic of the desert, eroding the rocks into bizarre shapes and creating sand which accumulates as slowly moving sand dunes.

Agriculture in the desert oases is vital to the economy of the country, providing large quantities of sugar cane, dates, figs and other fruit and vegetables.

Scorpions are perfectly adapted to the desert environment: they rarely need to drink, as they obtain their fluids from a diet of insects.

Fennec foxes sleep during the day, only leaving their burrows in the cool dusk. Exceptional hearing enables them to catch insects and small mammals in the dark.

Date palms thrive in the rocky desert environment. Growing "with their head in fire and feet in water", they are a sure sign of a hidden water source.

Sinai's red massif rises in places to over 2,000 m (6,700 ft). Crisscrossed with *wadis* (dry river beds), the area is brought to life by sporadic flooding.

Nile Valley and Delta

The Nile creates a habitable tract of land never more than 20 km (13 miles) wide from Lake Nasser to the Delta. In the past, floods replenished the soil with rich silt deposits which enabled the land to support a wide range of flora and fauna. The Aswan Dam (see p215) ended the floods, making farmers reliant on chemical fertilizers. Today, the Delta is one of the most intensely farmed areas in Egypt.

Farmland is irrigated by a complicated system of canals and dykes. The resulting wet croplands provide the ideal environment for cattle egrets, which hunt for frogs, insects and small rodents.

Acacia is easily identified along the banks of the Nile by its eye-catching balls of yellow flowers.

Papyrus, widely used in ancient times, was all but extinct by the 19th century. It is only grown in a few select areas.

The Purple Gallinule is a colourful duck-sized water bird found the length of the Nile. Its long, slender toes enable it to walk on lily pads.

The Spitting Cobra, a symbol of Lower Egypt in Pharaonic times, hunts its prey at night in crop fields. It is not usually a danger to humans, but it might attack if threatened, spitting venom accurately at its attacker's eyes.

Coastal Regions

Egypt's northern coastline is on the Mediterranean Sea where fishing is a key industry. While Egypt's Red Sea and Sinai coastlines also maintain fishing communities, they are far more important as a resource for the tourist industry. These coastlines support several large strips of coral reef (see p231) which attract divers from all over the world. A fragile environment, the reefs are under serious threat from overdevelopment of the coastline.

Mangrove Swamps

The mangrove swamps of the Sinai peninsula perform an important function protecting the shoreline against erosion and filtering pollutants from the water. The mudflats they create provide a vital environment for crabs and wading birds. Mangroves are able to live in salt water by excreting excess salt via their leaves.

Mangrove swamps fringing the Sinai coastline

Coral reefs provide a colourful environment for an equally spectacular array of marine life.

EGYPT THROUGH THE YEAR

The Egyptian calendar is crowded with Muslim, Christian, national and local festivals. The dates of these events can be difficult to predict as they are often calculated in different ways. The Islamic calendar is based on twelve 29- or 30-day lunar months, while Egypt's Christian Coptic Church uses the Julian calendar and the solar Coptic calendar. Extra confusion is caused by the frequently changing dates of nonreligious events or festivals. Visitors should confirm the date of the event locally. Whatever the calendar, these are mostly joyous events and a great way to experience Egyptian culture at close hand as both Muslims and Copts often enjoy celebrating *moulids* or festivals together. A wide range of esoteric sports events is staged throughout the year which range from the interesting to the bizarre, from camel-racing to long-distance swimming in the Nile at Cairo.

Spring

Springtime is a pleasant time to visit Egypt. The main visitor attractions such as the Pyramids at Giza, Luxor and Aswan are not too crowded and the temperature has yet to reach the scorching highs of summer. One weather phenomenon that can cause problems is the *khamseen*, a hot, dry wind that blows up from the Sahara Desert in the south. This can turn the air orange with dust and drive everyone indoors.

The main spring festivals are the beginning of the Egyptian New Year in March and the Christian festival of Easter. On the Monday after Easter Sunday, all Egyptians celebrate Sham an-Nessim or the "sniffing the breeze". They go on picnics or hold events outdoors to take in the fresh spring air.

March
Feast of the Annunciation *(Mar 25)*. This Coptic feast celebrates the announcement to the Holy Virgin that she was to give birth to Jesus.
Easter is the most important date on the Coptic calendar. The Coptic Pope celebrates Easter Mass at St Mark's Cathedral in Cairo.

April
Flower Show takes place at the Orman Gardens, Sharia Giza, Giza. Originally a one-day event, it now lasts for over a month.
Sham an-Nessim, celebrated by both Copts and Muslims, is a day when families enjoy outdoor pursuits and reputed to date from Pharaonic times.
Sinai Liberation Day *(Apr 25)*, celebrates Israel's withdrawal from the Sinai peninsula in 1982.

Coptic Christians celebrating Palm Sunday, a week before Easter

Ragabiyya is a local festival in Tanta. The festival lasts for three days in celebration of the Sufi saint, Sayyid Ahmad al-Badawi, and is held when the Nile rises in late spring.

May
Labour Day *(May 1)* is a public holiday when most businesses will be closed.
Moulid of St Damyanah *(May 15–20)*, a Coptic festival celebrating one of their important saints.
National Fishing Competition, Sharm el-Sheikh. Top fishermen compete to see who can catch the biggest specimen.
South Sinai Camel Festival, in the vast desert around Sharm el-Sheikh, raises clouds of dust with the running of the world's bumpiest race, the International Camel Race Competition.

Families celebrating the arrival of spring, known as Sham an-Nessim

Muslim Festivals

Celebrated with great feasts, family gatherings, music and street processions, Muslim festivals are joyous occasions. The largest of the festivals are Eid al-Fitr, which takes place at the end of Ramadan, the month of ritual fasting, and Eid al-Adha, which marks the time of the pilgrimage to Mecca. Other Muslim festivals include the Moulid an-Nabi which celebrates the birth of the Prophet Mohammed, Ras as-Sana, the Islamic New Year, and various saints' name days known as *moulids*.

Zikrs are a feature at *moulids*, where Sufi sheikhs and their followers chant and sway for hours in an effort to achieve unity with God. A *munshi* leads with hypnotic singing, and often women both sway and sing.

Cookies for Eid al-Fitr are traditionally baked in preparation for the three-day feast that marks the end of Ramadan. Food plays an important part of Muslim festivals and preparing it is often a social affair.

Islamic Calendar

The Islamic calendar has twelve months, each with 29 or 30 days. Purely lunar based, the Islamic year is around 11 days shorter than that of the Western calendar. Because Islam relies on actual sightings of the crescent moon at a given place, it is difficult to give dates in advance. Local Islamic centres will be able to provide the dates for the current year.

Eid al-Adha This four-day festival marks the time of the *Haj*, or pilgrimage to Mecca.

Ras as-Sana The Islamic equivalent of New Year's Day and quite a low-key affair.

Moulid an-Nabi Birth of the Prophet and one of the major holidays of the year. The streets burst into colour and noise with the celebrations.

Ramadan The ninth month of the Muslim calendar when most Muslims observe a degree of fasting and abstinence. The *iftar*, or breaking of the fast, occurs every evening when the sun sets.

Eid al-Fitr The end of Ramadan and the signal for a joyous, three-day feast.

Eid al-Fitr is a happy celebration marking the end of Ramadan. During the festivities, which usually last for three days, new clothes are worn and gifts are exchanged.

Religious holidays provide the perfect opportunity for family gatherings. Muslim celebrations often centre around the enjoyment and sharing of food and picnics are therefore a popular choice.

Donkey-trekking in the heat of summer, Valley of the Kings, Luxor

Summer

From June to August the temperature in Egypt climbs to unbearable levels in Upper Egypt, although the sights are often less crowded and hotel accommodation is plentiful. Many Egyptians choose to holiday on the North Coast where the temperature is slightly cooler. The Red Sea coastal resorts, although also very hot, have beautiful, clear water in which visitors can keep themselves cool. In the summer heat and smog, Cairo can get very uncomfortable and there are fewer interesting festivals.

June

Ahlan Wa Sahlan Belly-Dance Festival *(end Jun)*, Cairo. Performances and classes by some of the world's best belly dancers accompany a competition.

Evacuation Day *(Jun 18)* celebrates the departure of the British Forces from the Canal Zone in 1956 and the start of the Egyptian Republic.

July

International Shopping and Tourism Festival, Sharm el-Sheikh *(Jul)*. In an effort to boost tourism during the scorching summer months,

discounts are offered in shops, hotels and restaurants.

Revolution Day *(Jul 23)* commemorates the 1952 coup which toppled the puppet monarchy *(see p66)*.

Shopping and Tourism Festival, Cairo *(Jul–Aug)*.

August

Nile Festival Day or Wafaa an-Nil, Cairo. This is a series of processions, parades and sporting competitions which take place on the Nile.

Autumn

Autumn brings cooler weather to Egypt and a proliferation of events and festivals. While some of these are obvious attempts to boost tourist revenues, the best can be truly magical events that are well worth making the effort to go to. However, it is worth noting that the time of year some of these events take place is liable to change at the whim of the Egyptian authorities so check nearer the time.

September

Alexandria Film Festival, Alexandria. This festival

Coptic Festivals

Christmas, Epiphany, Easter and the Annunciation are the main Christian festivals of the year and all are celebrated by Copts, with Easter being the most important. Saints' days also feature strongly and, as with Islamic feasts, they are usually celebrated with a lively *moulid*. The main saints' days include the Moulid of St Damyanah, the Feast of the Apostles Peter and Paul and various *moulids* of

the Virgin and St George which take place throughout August. The spring festival of Sham an-Nessim is celebrated by both Muslims and Christians with family picnics of painted eggs and salted fish.

The Coptic pope presides over important religious ceremonies and events. Pope Shenouda III (above) died in March 2012.

Coptic Calendar

While some Coptic festivals correspond to the Julian calendar, others rely on the solar Coptic one. This calendar has 13 months, 12 of 30 days each and an intercalary month at the end of the year of five or six days, depending whether it is a leap year or not.

Easter This is the most important date in the Coptic calendar. However, it can differ by up to a month from the date of the Orthodox Church's festival.

Coptic festivals are primarily religious affairs with celebrations centred around church services for the young and old.

A colourful pageant at the Arabian Horse Festival, Az-Zahraa

features more home-produced films than the very popular Cairo festival.

Arabian Horse Festival, Az-Zahraa. Egypt holds two horse festivals. The other is held at Sharkeya in the Delta during September.

International Folkloric Festival, Ismailia, attracts energetic tribal performances from all over the world.

October

Aida Opera, Giza. This spectacular Egyptian-themed extravaganza was written by Verdi for the opening of the Suez Canal. Performed in front of the pyramids, this is a very popular production.

National Day (Armed Forces Day) *(Oct 6)* is a day of parades, fly-bys and nonstop patriotic songs and films.

The Battle of El-Alamein Commemoration *(Oct 24)*, with services conducted by former Allied and Axis countries, remembers those that died in the campaigns in North Africa during World War II.

Sun Festival of Ramses II, Abu Simbel *(Oct 22)*. On this day, and again in February, the sun reaches 55 m (185 ft) into the inner chamber of the Temple of Ramses and illuminates the statues inside.

Moulid of Sayyid Ahmed al-Badawi, Tanta. Egypt's largest festival – up to two million revellers attend this week-long celebration at the end of the cotton harvest.

National Liberation Day *(Oct 23)* and **Suez Victory Day** *(Oct 24)* are popular celebrations of Egypt's martial past.

Pharaoh's Rally (International Egypt Rally) is a gruelling 3,100-km (1,900-mile) motor vehicle race through the Egyptian deserts. Major car manufacturers and competitors come from all over the world to participate.

November

International Fishing Competition, Sharm el-Sheikh. These competitions are staged at several of the Red Sea resorts.

Luxor National Day *(Nov 4)* is combined with a commemoration of the discovery of the Tomb of Tutankhamun in 1922.

Cairo International Film Festival, Cairo, is an often chaotic festival which shows the best of world cinema. However, its popularity is partly due to the fact that it is the only time that Egyptians get to see uncensored films.

Pharaonic Race, Cairo. This 100-km (62-mile) run started in 1977, inspired by a similar race by royal soldiers in the 7th century BC.

Arab Music Festival, Cairo. The Opera House hosts the best in Arab music.

One of the cultural highlights of the Egyptian calendar, Verdi's spectacular opera, *Aida*

Winter

Winter brings some slight relief from the heat and, in Cairo and Alexandria and along the North Coast, even the odd shower of rain. The days are still sunny and warm but the nights can be quite cold, especially in desert areas. It also brings the start of the tourist season and a large influx of foreign visitors seeking winter sun and a glimpse into the fascinating, civilization of ancient Egypt. Cruise tours and hotels in Upper Egypt tend to get busy during this period and prices increase accordingly.

December

Alexandria Mediterranean Biennale (for artists) brings Mediterranean artists together for an exchange of cultural and artistic ideas, featuring exhibitions and activities.

The organized chaos of the International Book Fair, Cairo

Competitors in the International Egyptian Marathon, Luxor

January

New Year's Day (1 Jan) is a widely celebrated public holiday.
Coptic Christmas (7 Jan). On this day, Copts throughout Egypt dress up in their Sunday best, visit their relatives and feast together. It is not an official public holiday, but many Egyptian Copts take this day off.

Epiphany (19 Jan), a Coptic celebration of the revelation of Jesus's divinity after his baptism by John.
International Egyptian Marathon, Luxor. As many as 2,000 competitors brave the heat to take part in this run around Luxor.
International Nile Regatta, Alexandria. Organized by the Egyptian Rowing Federation, this event attracts teams of young and more experienced rowers from all over the world.
Belly-Dancing World Cup takes place each year in the Taba Heights resort in Sinai. There are competitions for advanced dancers, as well as workshops for beginners, lectures and classes.
International Cairo Biennale, (Dec–Feb). This major cultural event in the Middle East features contemporary art shows, concerts, films and installations.
Cairo International Book Fair, Nasr City. Ostensibly for the book trade, this event also attracts regular book lovers and Cairenes simply looking for a day out among the fast food stalls. During the event a bus service departs for Nasr City from Midan Tahrir.

February

Abu Simbel Sun Festival (22 Feb). This festival celebrates one of the two days in the year (the other is in October) when the sun's rays penetrate the sanctuary of Ramses's Great Temple at Abu Simbel.

The Climate of Egypt

Egypt's weather is predominantly hot, sunny and very dry. The only rain that falls regularly is on the North Coast during winter, but this is under 100 mm (4 inches) a year. There are two seasons – May to October, the hot season, and November to April, the cool season. In general, it is warm all the year round, although the deserts can get cold during winter nights. The most striking meteorological phenomenon is the *khamseen*, a dry wind during April and May that causes sandstorms.

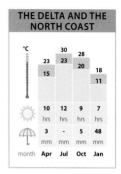

THE DELTA AND THE NORTH COAST

°C	Apr	Jul	Oct	Jan
high	23	30	28	18
low	15	23	20	11
☀	10 hrs	12 hrs	9 hrs	7 hrs
☂	3 mm	- mm	5 mm	48 mm
month	Apr	Jul	Oct	Jan

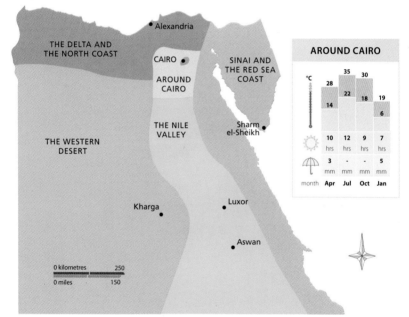

THE DELTA AND THE NORTH COAST

Alexandria

CAIRO

AROUND CAIRO

SINAI AND THE RED SEA COAST

THE NILE VALLEY

Sharm el-Sheikh

THE WESTERN DESERT

Kharga

Luxor

Aswan

0 kilometres 250
0 miles 150

AROUND CAIRO

°C	Apr	Jul	Oct	Jan
high	28	35	30	19
low	14	22	18	6
☀	10 hrs	12 hrs	9 hrs	7 hrs
☂	3 mm	- mm	- mm	5 mm
month	Apr	Jul	Oct	Jan

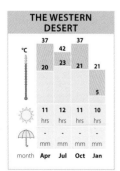

THE WESTERN DESERT

°C	Apr	Jul	Oct	Jan
high	37	42	37	21
low	20	23	21	5
☀	11 hrs	12 hrs	11 hrs	10 hrs
☂	- mm	- mm	- mm	- mm
month	Apr	Jul	Oct	Jan

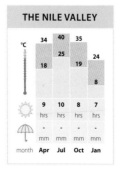

THE NILE VALLEY

°C	Apr	Jul	Oct	Jan
high	34	40	35	24
low	18	25	19	8
☀	9 hrs	10 hrs	8 hrs	7 hrs
☂	- mm	- mm	- mm	- mm
month	Apr	Jul	Oct	Jan

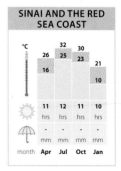

SINAI AND THE RED SEA COAST

°C	Apr	Jul	Oct	Jan
high	26	32	30	21
low	16	25	23	10
☀	11 hrs	12 hrs	11 hrs	10 hrs
☂	- mm	- mm	- mm	- mm
month	Apr	Jul	Oct	Jan

ΚΡΟΚΟΔΙΛΟΠΑΡΔΑΛΙϹ

THE HISTORY OF EGYPT

Egypt's history has been crucially influenced by its environment. When lack of rain forced the early nomadic inhabitants to migrate towards the Nile Valley, the fertile floodplain gave birth to a nation that produced some of the most important achievements in human history and established a culture that would remain largely unchanged for over 3,000 years.

Although the beginning of Egyptian history is generally given as 3100 BC, human activity in the Predynastic Period can be traced back many thousands of years before this date. The Sahara Desert used to be a green and fertile savannah, home to a nomadic population who hunted the wildlife they portrayed in rock drawings (petroglyphs). Archaeologists have also discovered that cattle-herders in Nabta Playa in the Western Desert built stone-circle calendars dating from 8000 BC.

The way of life of these early peoples remained much the same for around 4,000 years, but as the climate became increasingly arid, the population left the growing areas of desert (*deshret* or red land) for the banks of the river Nile where the annual flooding sustained a region of great fertility (*kemet* or black land). The excavation of their settlements has revealed the rapid development of a sophisticated culture of mudbrick houses and workshops, together with primitive temple structures.

The need to organize these settlements led to the invention of the world's first form of writing – hieroglyphs. Excavations at Abydos have shown that this script was in use from around 3250 BC, several centuries before the earliest writing in Mesopotamia. Further expansion meant settlements inevitably came into conflict with each other. The country polarized into two opposing kingdoms of north (Lower Egypt) and south (Upper Egypt). Around 3100 BC, the two were unified for the first time into a single state. However, each kept their own emblems of royalty; for Lower Egypt the *deshret* or Red Crown and for Upper Egypt the *hedjet* or White Crown. From then the pharoahs were officially referred to as the rulers of the Two Lands, wearing a double crown called *pschent*, with each half symbolizing one of the two kingdoms. The unification of Egypt was commemorated on the cosmetic slate palette of King Narmer (sometimes known as Menes), found at Hierakonpolis. The palette is possibly the most important historical document from the whole of Egyptian history, recording the creation of the world's first nation state. The dramatic pose as he is about to smash the skull of his defeated foe became the standard way to portray Egypt's kings throughout the next 3,000 years.

8000 BC Early human settlement of Nabta Playa in Western Desert builds huge sculptures and a stone-circle calendar

Pots from 4000–3000 BC

3400 BC Egypt's oldest temple built at Hierakonpolis

3250 BC Invention of hieroglyphs – world's first script

| 10,000 BC | 5000 BC | 4500 BC | 4000 BC | 3500 BC | 3000 BC |

10,000 BC Nomadic population of Sahara draw petroglyphs of the animals they hunt

Earliest known human sculpture

c.4000 BC Earliest known human figure sculpted in Africa, at Neolithic settlement in western Delta

3100 BC Political unification of Egypt by King Narmer. Memphis becomes the capital city

◀ Graeco-Roman mosaic showing the flooding of the Nile, Egypt's temples and its fabled wildlife

The Old Kingdom (3100–2180 BC)

The power base of the Old Kingdom was established at Memphis, the first capital of a united Egypt. This was strategically located where Upper Egypt meets Lower Egypt at the apex of the Delta close to modern Cairo. Whereas the earliest kings chose Abydos as their funeral site to reflect their southern origins, later rulers preferred to be buried close to their new capital in its necropolis, Saqqara. The site of Egypt's earliest pyramid (c.2650 BC), Saqqara is also home to many stone *mastaba* (bench-shaped) tombs built for members of the royal court and beautifully decorated. The king was seen as the living incarnation of the god Horus and his court sought to be buried close to his divine power.

King Narmer's successors managed to suppress any outside threat to Egypt's stability while organizing the country into 42 provinces or *nomes*. These were administered by means of a highly efficient bureaucracy of officials. The great wealth created through a carefully organized system of taxation – based on the collection and redistribution of Egypt's abundant grain supplies – was also used to fund ambitious building schemes. This culminated in the massive pyramid complexes of the Old Kingdom god-kings such as Djoser, Sneferu, Khufu and Khafre. The organization required for such huge projects helped to unify the nation, while the vast numbers of skilled craftsmen involved meant that art and technology developed at a rapid pace.

Of all the pyramid-building pharaohs, Sneferu was the greatest, building three such structures, including the first true pyramid at Dashur. It was only with techniques perfected by Sneferu that his son Khufu was able to construct the largest of all Egypt's pyramids at Giza around 2589 BC.

Eventually centuries of pyramid-building, together with a series of poor harvests, severely depleted the economy. This led to a decline in royal power, which was reflected in the small size of the later pyramids built at Abusir and Saqqara.

Statue of King Khafre protected by the falcon god Horus

The Pyramids at Giza, magnificent symbols of the divine power of the early Egyptian kings

2665 BC The world's oldest stone monument, the Step Pyramid of King Djoser, built at Saqqara

2613–2589 BC Reign of King Sneferu, builder of three pyramids at Dashur and Meidum

2900 BC	2800 BC	2700 BC	2600 BC	2500 BC

Figurine from a unified Egypt fashioned in c.2900 BC

2686 BC Oldest surviving mudbrick building built by King Khasekhemwy at Hierakonpolis

c.2589 BC The Great Pyramid of Khufu (Cheops) built at Giza

c.2558 BC Pyramid of Khafre (Chephren) built at Giza. Its complex includes the oldest surviving temple in Egypt

The incredibly long reign of Pepi II (2278–2184 BC), only added to the problem and with the pharaoh seen as a feeble old man, royal authority was further undermined. After an incredible 94 years on the throne Pepi II was succeeded by Egypt's first female pharaoh Nitocris, but despite being remembered as "the bravest and most beautiful" of her time, it was too late to reverse the decline in royal fortunes.

First Intermediate Period, Middle Kingdom and Second Intermediate Period (2180–1550 BC)

Statue of Montuhotep II, Theban founder of the 11th Dynasty

As royal power declined, officials began to relocate to their home provinces. No longer reliant on the king, they created their own small kingdoms maintained with private armies. As the country gradually fragmented, central authority finally broke down into anarchy and the First Intermediate Period began c.2180 BC.

The lack of overall authority is clearly expressed in provincial and rather "idiosyncratic" art styles typical of local trends. The breakdown of social order is also reflected in the literature – "All is ruin…men kill their brothers…blood is everywhere".

The remnants of royal power relocated to Herakleopolis, at the entrance to the Fayoum Oasis, and attempted to rule through the forging of alliances with the southern regions. However, any temporary unity was shattered when Thebes formed

an independent monarchy. Civil war and fierce fighting between neighbouring tribes tore the whole country apart. After a long and bitter struggle the powerful Theban warlord Montuhotep II conquered the north to reunite the country under the 11th Dynasty. His reign took Egypt from the chaos of the First Intermediate Period into the stability of the Middle Kingdom (c.2055 BC). Thebes now grew into a major metropolis, home to skilled craftsmen who created new art styles at a rate not seen since the Age of the Pyramids. The old trade routes and mines were reopened and expansionist policies prevailed. Although the office of pharaoh would never again reach the absolute divinity of earlier times, the Theban monarchy restored royal power as growth in revenue led to a resumption of building projects. The greatest new structure was Montuhotep's imposing funerary complex built at Deir al-Bahri which, 500 years later, would serve as the prototype for Hatshepsut's temple.

Model of the private army of the Governor of Asyut (c.2000 BC)

| 2400 BC | 2300 BC | 2200 BC | 2100 BC | 2000 BC |

2278 BC Pepi II ascends throne and rules for 94 years

2184 BC Reign of Nitocris begins, Egypt's first female ruler

2180 BC First Intermediate Period – decentralization of authority and civil war

2004 BC Montuhotep II buried at Deir al-Bahri

Life-size copper statue of King Pepi I 2321–2287 BC

2160 BC Kings of the 9–10th dynasties based at Herakleopolis

2125 BC Warlords of Thebes form independent 11th ruling dynasty

2055 BC Montuhotep II of Thebes defeats Herakleopolis and reunites Egypt ruling from Thebes. The local god Amun becomes important

Teams of workers dragging a huge stone statue, from the Middle Kingdom tomb of Djehutyhotep (c.1850 BC)

The kings of the 12th Dynasty, which lasted from c.1985–1795 BC, moved the royal residence back to the traditional capital, Memphis, in order to be closer to the centre of the country. They continued with ambitious building projects, and the art and literature of this time is regarded as the "classic" period of Egyptian culture. Pharaohs such as Senusret III and Amenemhat III constructed impressive pyramids at Saqqara, Dahshur, Lahun and Hawara, where they were buried alongside their relatives with beautiful jewellery made of gold, amethyst, carnelian and lapis lazuli.

Successful military campaigns expanded Egypt's borders, while at home the crown centralized its authority by removing power from provincial governors and replacing these governors with a vast bureaucracy of loyal officials. Many of these officials were migrants from nearby Palestine who had

Sphinx bearing the face of Amenemhat III

settled peacefully in northern Egypt and had been gradually absorbed into Egyptian society over a period of about 150 years. By infiltrating the government they took advantage of the instability caused by a series of short-lived rulers during the 13th and 14th Dynasties. In 1650 BC, these settlers, referred to as the Hyksos (Rulers of Foreign Lands), finally assumed control.

This marks the beginning of the Second Intermediate Period, when Egypt was once again divided geographically. Based in their northern capital Avaris, the Hyksos formed an alliance with Nubia to help them to control southern Egypt, where the native Egyptian opposition to foreign rule had organized itself in Thebes. The country was once again subject to intermittent civil war until the Theban warlord Seqenenre Taa II and his sons Kamose and Ahmose finally drove the Hyksos out of Egypt to reunite the Two Lands.

1965 BC Assassination of Amenemhat I and accession of his son Senusret I

Statue of Senusret III

1795–1725 BC Unstable 13th Dynasty of 70 kings

1750–1650 BC Minor rulers of the 14th Dynasty

1900 BC

1800 BC

1700 BC

1874–1855 BC Reign of Senusret III

1799–1795 BC Reign of Egypt's second female ruler, Sobekneferu

1855 BC Senusret III and his family buried at Dahshur

Middle Kingdom Horus head pendant

The New Kingdom (1550–1069 BC)

With the reunification of north and south, the New Kingdom began. This is Egypt's "Golden Age", when a series of unrelenting warrior pharaohs turned the country into the most powerful empire in the ancient world. The expulsion of the Hyksos was followed by vigorous military campaigns as far north as the river Euphrates and as far south as Nubia. The enormous wealth amassed from foreign tribute was channelled into massive building projects in and around Thebes, with successive monarchs trying to outdo their predecessors. The magnificent temple of Karnak – the cult centre of the local Theban deity Amun – was embellished by successive pharaohs, built as Amun was linked with the sun-god Ra to create Amun-Ra, "King of the Gods". Meanwhile, pharaohs built huge funerary temples for themselves on the west bank of the Nile, and were buried in spectacular rock-cut tombs in the Valley of the Kings, designed to ensure their eternal afterlife.

As the first king of the New Kingdom, Ahmose continued his family's military successes and established a pattern for his successors. His son Amenhotep I followed in his father's footsteps by pacifying Nubia. He also founded a village for royal tomb builders at Deir al-Medina, where both he and his mother and co-ruler Ahmose-Nofretari were worshipped long after their deaths.

Then began the succession of the Tuthmosis pharaohs: men born to minor wives of the king who strengthened their claims to the throne by marrying into the female royal line. Tuthmosis II was succeeded by his wife and half-sister Hatshepsut, the most familiar of Egypt's female pharaohs, who is often portrayed in statues as a bearded pharaoh. Her successor, Tuthmosis III, the so-called "Napoleon of Ancient Egypt", expanded the Egyptian Empire into Asia Minor and as far as the Euphrates. His son Amenhotep II, a great warrior like his father and an accomplished athlete, consolidated Egypt's control over the vassal states of Asia Minor. Their foreign conquests created the wealth used so wisely by the greatest of all the pharaohs, Amenhotep III, known as "the Magnificent". His peaceful 38-year reign marks the height of Egypt's cultural and artistic achievement.

Statue of Hatshepsut as a bearded pharaoh

Tuthmosis III making offerings to Amun-Ra, the national deity during the New Kingdom

1650 BC Palestinian Hyksos take power

c.1560 BC Theban warlord Seqenenre Taa II killed fighting the Hyksos

c.1500 BC Valley of the Kings becomes royal burial ground

Head of Tuthmosis III

1458–1425 BC Tuthmosis III campaigns as far as the Euphrates

1600 BC

1500 BC

1400 BC

1550 BC Seqenenre Taa II's younger son Ahmose drives the Hyksos out of Egypt and becomes the first ruler of the 18th Dynasty

1525 BC Amenhotep I founds royal tomb builders' village of Deir al-Medina

1473–1458 BC Reign of Hatshepsut

1390–1352 BC Peaceful reign of Amenhotep III, "the Magnificent"

The Egyptian Pharaohs

The ancient Egyptians dated events to the particular year in the reign of a king or pharaoh (regnal dating). It was a Ptolemaic scholar, Manetho, who later sorted the kings into dynasties, a system still used today along with ancient king lists, astronomical dating records and modern archaeological dating methods. The resulting chronology is, however, neither fixed nor complete and liable to change.

Early Dynastic Period

3100–2890 BC		2890–2686 BC	
Ist Dynasty		**2nd Dynasty**	
Narmer	3100	Hetepsekhemwy	2890
Aha	3100	Raneb	2865
Djer	3000	Nynetjer	
Djet	2980	Weneg	
Den	2950	Sened	
Anedjib	2925	Peribsen	2700
Semerkhet	2900	Khasekhemwy	2686
Qaa	2890		

# aka Amenhotep IV *(see p179)*	† aka Amenophis
* denotes female pharaoh	‡ aka Sesostris

First Intermediate Period

2181–2125 BC	2160–2055 BC	
7th & 8th Dynasties	**9th & 10th Dynasties Herakleopolitan**	
During this unstable period of ancient Egyptian history there were numerous ephemeral kings. The weakening of centralized power led to the establishment of local dynasties.	Kheti	
	Merykare	
	Ity	
	11th Dynasty (Thebes Only)	
	Intef I	2125–2112
	Intef II	2112–2063
	Intef III	2063–2055

Middle Kingdom

2055–1985 BC		1985–1795 BC	
11th Dynasty all Egypt		**12th Dynasty**	
Montuhotep II	2055–2004	Amenemhat I	1985–1955
Montuhotep III	2004–1992	Senusret I ‡	1965–1920
Montuhotep IV	1992–1985	Amenemhat II	1922–1878
		Senusret II ‡	1880–1874
		Senusret III ‡	1874–1855
		Amenemhat III	1855–1808
		Amenemhat IV	1808–1799
		Sobekneferu*	1799–1795

"Block" statue from the 12th Dynasty

Overlaps in dates indicate periods of co-regency

New Kingdom

Bracelet of Queen Ahotep, mother of Ahmose, first king of the 18th Dynasty

1550–1295 BC		1295–1186 BC		1186–1069 BC	
18th Dynasty		**19th Dynasty**		**20th Dynasty**	
Ahmose	1550–1525	Ramses I	1295–1294	Sethnakhte	1186–1184
Amenhotep I †	1525–1504	Seti I	1294–1279	Ramses III	1184–1153
Tuthmosis I	1504–1492	Ramses II	1279–1213	Ramses IV	1153–1147
Tuthmosis II	1492–1479	Merneptah	1213–1203	Ramses V	1147–1143
Tuthmosis III	1479–1425	Amenmessu	1203–1200	Ramses VI	1143–1136
Hatshepsut*	1473–1458	Seti II	1200–1194	Ramses VII	1136–1129
Amenhotep II †	1427–1400	Siptah	1194–1188	Ramses VIII	1129–1126
Tuthmosis IV	1400–1390	Tawosret*	1188–1186	Ramses IX	1126–1108
Amenhotep III †	1390–1352			Ramses X	1108–1099
Akhenaten #	1352–1336			Ramses XI	1099–1069
Nefertiti					
Smenkhkare*	1338–1336				
Tutankhamun	1336–1327				
Ay	1327–1323				
Horemheb	1323–1295				

Head of Ramses III, who built the great mortuary Temple at Medinet Habu

Late Period

672–525 BC		525–359 BC		404–c.380 BC		380–343 BC	
26th Dynasty		**27th Dynasty**		**28th Dynasty**		**30th Dynasty**	
(Saite)		**(Persian Period 1)**		Amyrtaios	404–399	Nectanebo I	380–362
						Teos	362–360
Necho I	672–664	Cambyses	525–522	**29th Dynasty**		Nectanebo II	360–343
Psamtek I	664–610	Darius I	522–486				
Necho II	610–595	Xerxes I	486–465	Nepherites I	399–393		
Psamtek II	595–589	Artaxerxes I	465–424	Hakor	393–380		
Apries	589–570	Darius II	424–405	Nepherites II	c.380		
Ahmose II	570–526	Artaxerxes II	405–359				
Psamtek III	526–525						

One of the stone sphinxes from Luxor Temple, carved with the face of Nectanebo I

Old Kingdom

2686–2613	2613–2498 BC	2494–2345 BC	2345–2181 BC
3rd Dynasty	**4th Dynasty**	**5th Dynasty**	**6th Dynasty**

3rd Dynasty		4th Dynasty		5th Dynasty		6th Dynasty	
Sanakht	2686–2667	Sneferu	2613–2589	Userkaf	2494–2487	Teti	2345–2323
Djoser	2667–2648	Khufu	2589–2566	Sahure	2487–2475	Userkare	2323–2321
Sekhemkhet	2648–2640	Djedefre	2566–2558	Neferirkare	2475–2455	Pepi I	2321–2287
Khaba	2640–2637	Khafre	2558–2532	Shepseskare	2455–2448	Merenre	2287–2278
Huni	2637–2613	Menkaure	2532–2503	Raneferef	2448–2445	Pepi II	2278–2184
		Shepseskaf	2503–2498	Nyuserre	2445–2421	Nitocris*	2184–2181
				Menkauhor	2421–2414		
				Djedkare	2414–2375		
				Unas	2375–2345		

The Pyramids at Giza, built in the 4th Dynasty

Second Intermediate Period

1795–1650 BC	1650–1550 BC	1650–1550 BC
13th Dynasty	**15th Dynasty**	**17th Dynasty**
1795 – c.1725	**(Hyksos)**	In addition, several kings ruled from Thebes including the following:
14th Dynasty	Salitis	
1750–1650	Khyan c.1600	Intef
Minor rulers probably contemporaneous with the previous dynasty.	Apepi c.1555	Ta I
	Khamudi	Seqenenre Taa II c.1560
	16th Dynasty	Kamose 1555–1550
	1650–1550	
	Minor Hyksos rulers contemporary with the 15th Dynasty.	

Limestone relief of Senusret I from the Temple at Karnak

Third Intermediate Period

1069–945 BC	945–715 BC	818–715 BC	Late Period
21st Dynasty	**22nd Dynasty**	**23rd Dynasty**	747–656 BC

21st Dynasty		22nd Dynasty		23rd Dynasty		25th Dynasty	
Smendes	1069–1043	Sheshonq I	945–924	Several continuous lines of rulers at Herakleopolis Magna, Hermopolis Magna, Leontopolis and Tanis including the following:		Piy	747–716
Amenemnisu	1043–1039	Osorkon I	924–889			Shabaqo	716–702
Psusennes I	1039–991	Sheshonq II	c.890			Shabitqo	702–690
Amenemope	993–984	Takelot I	889–874			Taharqo	690–664
Osorkon the Elder	984–978	Osorkon II	874–850			Tanutamani	664–656
Siamun	978–959	Takelot II	850–825	Pedubastis I	818–793		
Psusennes II	959–945	Sheshonq III	825–773	Sheshonq IV	c.780		
		Pimay	773–767	Osorkon III	777–749		
		Sheshonq V	767–730	**24th Dynasty**			
		Osorkon IV	730–715	Bakenrenef	727–715		

Silver coffin of Psusennes I from Tanis

Ptolemaic Period

343–332 BC	332–305 BC	305–80 BC	80–30 BC
Persian Period 2	**Macedonian Dynasty**	**Ptolemaic Dynasty**	**Ptolemaic Dynasty (Cont.)**

Persian Period 2		Macedonian Dynasty		Ptolemaic Dynasty		Ptolemaic Dynasty (Cont.)	
Artaxerxes III		Alexander		Ptolemy I	305–285		
Ochus	343–333	the Great	332–323	Ptolemy II	285–246	Ptolemy XI	80
Arses	338–336	Philip Arrhidaeus	323–317	Ptolemy III	246–221	Ptolemy XII	80–51
Darius III		Alexander IV	317–305	Ptolemy IV	221–205	Cleopatra VII*	51–30
Codoman	336–332			Ptolemy V	205–180	Ptolemy XIII	51–47
				Ptolemy VI	180–145	Ptolemy XIV	47–44
				Ptolemy VII	145	Ptolemy XV	44–30
				Ptolemy VIII	170–116		
				Ptolemy IX	116–107		
				& (second reign)	88–80		
				Ptolemy X	107–88		

Alexander the Great in Egyptian headgear

Egypt becomes part of the Roman Empire in 30 BC (see pp60–61)

With the death of Amenhotep III in 1352 BC, the succession passed to his son Akhenaten *(see p179)*. His mismanagement of the political situation, relocation of the capital to Akhetaten (modern Tell al-Amarna) and attempts to overturn the traditional religious hierarchy destabilized Egypt and brought the country close to ruin. Akhenaten's successor, probably his wife Nefertiti, restored order by returning the seat of power to Thebes and re-establishing the traditional religion. The reign of Akhenaten's son Tutankhamun was largely devoted to restoring internal stability before trying to reverse Egypt's fortunes abroad. But it took the military prowess of Horemheb, who had worked his way up from scribe to general and finally king, to restore the country to its former greatness. The last king of the 18th Dynasty, he soon began recovering Egypt's empire. This military policy was continued by the rulers of the 19th Dynasty, which began in 1295 BC. Under Seti I, Egypt regained much of her prestige abroad, while at home the monarchy's reputation was consolidated and

Philistines, one of the "Peoples of the Sea", being taken prisoner by Egyptians, from Ramses III's mortuary temple at Medinet Habu

Bust of Queen Nefertiti, 18th Dynasty

enhanced by great new building projects such as Karnak's hypostyle hall *(see pp192–3)* and Seti's temple at Abydos. Seti was succeeded by his son Ramses II – also known as Ramses the Great – whose 66-year reign saw royal construction on a massive scale. Huge monuments, including the awesome Great Temple of Abu Simbel *(see pp218–19)*, were erected in a deliberate effort by Ramses to impress his subjects and preserve his reputation for posterity.

Ramses was succeeded by his son Merneptah, and four more pharaohs in less than 20 years. In c.1186 BC, Sethnakhte inaugurated the 20th Dynasty; nine kings followed, all named Ramses. The greatest of these was Ramses III, who successfully defended Egypt's northern borders against repeated invasions by Libyans and settlers from the Mediterranean region – the so-called "Peoples of the Sea". But his weak successors could not sustain his victories, and foreign infiltration grew rapidly. With internal disorder and social unrest, even the royal tombs were ransacked. The New Kingdom finally collapsed in 1070 BC.

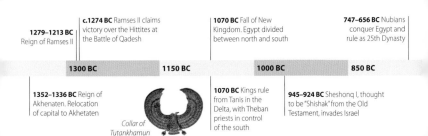

1279–1213 BC Reign of Ramses II

c.1274 BC Ramses II claims victory over the Hittites at the Battle of Qadesh

1070 BC Fall of New Kingdom. Egypt divided between north and south

747–656 BC Nubians conquer Egypt and rule as 25th Dynasty

1300 BC **1150 BC** **1000 BC** **850 BC**

1352–1336 BC Reign of Akhenaten. Relocation of capital to Akhetaten

Collar of Tutankhamun

1070 BC Kings rule from Tanis in the Delta, with Theban priests in control of the south

945–924 BC Sheshonq I, thought to be "Shishak" from the Old Testament, invades Israel

Third Intermediate Period, Late Period and Ptolemaic Period (1070–30 BC)

The New Kingdom gave way to four centuries of disunity and foreign infiltration, known as the Third Intermediate Period. Egypt was again divided between north and south: the south remained under the control of the semi-royal high priests of Thebes, while the monarchy was located in the north and ruled from Tanis in the eastern Delta.

Alexander the Great

Egypt was further fragmented by the Libyan invasion of the western Delta, but in 747 BC the country was united by the Nubians, who managed to hold onto power for over a century, ruling as the 25th Dynasty.

The Late Period began with the Assyrian invasion of Egypt in 669 BC. The Assyrians meant to rule the country through their vassal king Nekau then Psamtek of the western Delta city Sais, but Psamtek outmanoeuvred his former masters and the 26th "Saite" Dynasty saw a brief flowering of native Egyptian culture.

Hopes of a permanent revival were, however, cut short by the Persian's invasion in 525 BC. Two hundred years of Persian domination was only interrupted by the short-lived 30th Dynasty – the last native Egyptian rulers. Finally the Macedonian king Alexander the Great "liberated" Egypt from the Persians and founded his new capital Alexandria on the Mediterranean coast, followed by the Ptolemaic Period.

On Alexander's death in 323 BC, his most trusted general assumed power, and over the next three centuries (305–30 BC) 14 of Ptolemy's successors and namesakes ruled from their capital Alexandria. The Ptolemies were accepted by the native Egyptians because they ruled as traditional pharaohs and built temples, such as Edfu, Dendara and Philae, in deliberate imitation of ancient Egyptian design. They also embellished Alexandria, which became the most important city of the ancient world. The last of the Ptolemies, Cleopatra VII, inherited the throne in 51 BC. Her 21-year reign briefly restored Egyptian greatness in the face of the expansionist ambitions of Rome. Her suicide marks the notional end of ancient Egypt, as the country finally became a Roman province.

Ptolemy V, wearing traditional Pharaonic clothing, making offerings to the sacred Buchis bull

669 BC Ashurbanipal of Assyria invades Egypt

Female mummy head from Late Period

332 BC Alexander the Great conquers Egypt and founds Alexandria

323 BC Death of Alexander in Babylon and burial of his body in Egypt

30 BC Egypt becomes Roman province

51–30 BC Reign of Cleopatra VII

700 BC   550 BC   400 BC   250 BC   100 BC

672–525 BC Native Egyptian renaissance under 26th "Saite" Dynasty

525 BC Invasion by Persian King Cambyses

380–343 BC 30th Dynasty, the last native Egyptian rulers

305 BC Ptolemy I establishes Ptolemaic dynasty, ruling from Alexandria

Coin of Cleopatra

Cleopatra VII (69 BC–30 BC)

Perhaps the most familiar of ancient Egyptian figures, the real Cleopatra is hidden beneath centuries of misinformation. Most of the detail about her is supplied by Roman sources who waged a propaganda war against her. To them she was the ruler of a decadent eastern culture who seduced two of Rome's generals in order to seize the Roman Empire. In fact, Cleopatra was an educated Macedonian Greek, who had one child with Julius Caesar and three during her 11 years with Mark Antony. These two men used Egypt's wealth for their imperial ambitions as much as she used their military might to assure her position.

Ptolemy I (305–285 BC) ruled Egypt after his close friend Alexander the Great died, founding a dynasty that lasted nearly 300 years.

Orientalist Painting of Cleopatra

Part inspired by reliefs on temple walls, part by a confusion of the exotic and the erotic, this painting by Alexandre Cabanel (1823–89) misrepresents Cleopatra in seductive Pharaonic attire.

This Classical bust is probably a more realistic representation of Cleopatra. She was portrayed in Pharaonic dress on the walls of temples such as Dendara *(see pp182–3)* to reinforce her position in the eyes of her subjects as the rightful heir to the great pharaohs.

This Ptolemaic papyrus bears Cleopatra's signature. Although fluent in seven languages, including Egyptian, she used Greek for official documents.

Egypt and Roman Expansion

Rome's expansion from the 4th to the 1st century BC was fuelled in part by the need for ever-increasing quantities of grain. Grain's importance to the ancient economies is somewhat analogous to the value of oil to modern economies. Thanks to its efficient Greek administration, Egypt's vast grain harvests made it incredibly wealthy and a threat to Rome if the country fell into the wrong hands. Therefore the Romans knew they had either to ensure Egypt's ruler was sympathetic towards them, or annex the country. At first, Egypt avoided being absorbed by Rome through a skilful combination of bribery and diplomacy – on different occasions, Julius Caesar and Mark Antony were paid large sums of money to restore the throne of Egypt to Cleopatra's father, Ptolemy XII. When Cleopatra and her brother were installed on the throne in 51 BC, Rome expected simply to add Egypt to their empire.

Key

- Rome 300 BC
- Rome 51 BC
- Ptolemaic Kingdom 51 BC

Cleopatra and Rome

In 51 BC, Cleopatra and Ptolemy XIII, her brother, were named co-rulers of Egypt. When they fought for sole control, Rome sent Julius Caesar to settle the dispute. He put Cleopatra on the throne and formed a close relationship with her. Three years after Caesar's murder, Mark Antony paid a visit to Cleopatra seeking funding for his expeditions. They became lovers and when Antony handed Roman territories over to Egypt in 34 BC, Rome, at Octavian's urging, declared war on Cleopatra.

Julius Caesar, after moving Cleopatra to Rome, was killed by Republicans who feared that, under her evil influence, he wanted to return Rome to monarchy.

Octavian, with the prize of the Roman Empire at stake, decided to fight Antony at sea near Actium, off the coast of Greece.

Mark Antony was derided by Rome for his lack of self control towards Cleopatra. Forced to marry the sister of Octavian, he later returned to his Egyptian lover.

At the Battle of Actium (31 BC) the two fleets quickly clashed, opening up a gap in Octavian's formation. Seeing her chance, Cleopatra headed for Egypt closely followed by Antony. His men, thinking him a deserter, defected to Octavian. A year later Octavian's army routed Antony's troops and marched on Alexandria.

The African asp is a cobra, which, as the uraeus snake, protected the pharaoh in this world and the next. It is possible, therefore, that Cleopatra did in fact choose to die by snake bite.

The Enduring Appeal of Cleopatra

The appeal of Cleopatra's story is magnified by her tragic death: defeated by Octavian and believing reports that Cleopatra was dead, Antony committed suicide; Cleopatra realizing all was lost then took her own life. As told by Roman writers, this tale of sex, power, greed and ultimately tragedy proved irresistible for artists from the Renaissance, Shakespeare and Hollywood.

Shakespeare's play was based on Plutarch's *Lives* (c.AD 75), the Roman account most sympathetic to Cleopatra.

Hollywood films such as *Cleopatra*, starring Liz Taylor and Richard Burton, used grand sets and outrageous outfits and did not let historical accuracy ruin a good story.

Eye make-up was one detail Hollywood did not get wrong, except that it was worn by both sexes. Ancient Egyptians used ground minerals mixed with water and stored in tubes.

From Christic to Mohammed

Egypt was now a province of mighty Rome, whose emperors established themselves as the successors of the pharaohs. As Christianity spread throughout the Roman Empire, its Egyptian adherents, known as Copts, came into conflict with the Roman authorities. Even when Christianity was

Salah ad-Din al-Ayyubi (1138–93), the scourge of the European Crusaders

adopted as the official religion of the eastern half of the now divided Roman Empire in 323 AD, there were differences in theology, and the Copts were mercilessly persecuted.

The Eastern Romans, later known as Byzantines, remained largely unchallenged in power until in the 7th century they were confronted by a new force sweeping up from Arabia. Following the teachings of the Prophet Mohammed, the army of Islam defeated the Byzantines in battle and entered Egypt. Ignoring Alexandria, the Arab army, led by the general Amr ibn al-Aas, marched on the fortress of Babylon-in-Egypt near to the old capital of Memphis. After a brief siege it surrendered and Amr settled his men just to the north, where he founded a new city known as Fustat.

Egypt became a province of an already vast Islamic empire ruled first from Damascus (the Umayyad dynasty), then from Baghdad (the Abbasids). Ahmed Ibn Tulun, an administrator sent from Baghdad, decided to declare the territory independent. His mosque still stands but his dynasty did not outlive him long; his son was assassinated and rule from Baghdad reimposed.

In AD 969 Egypt was seized by the Fatimids from Tunisia. They built a new city north of Fustat, encircled by fortified walls and containing palaces, great mosques and plazas. They called their new city Al-Qahira, "The Conqueror", a name later corrupted by European tongues to "Cairo". Their reign in Egypt lasted for barely more than 200 years until it was brought to an end in 1171 by the arrival of a Syrian warrior-general, Salah ad-Din al-Ayyubi, known in English as Saladin. In Cairo, Salah ad-Din expanded the city walls and added a fortress that survives as today's Citadel (see pp108–11). A hero of the Arab world, who recaptured Jerusalem from the European Crusaders, Salah ad-Din's role in Egyptian history is, however, overshadowed by the dynasty that succeeded him, a warrior caste called the Mamluks.

Detail of a manuscript showing Mamluk cavalry in training (1348)

30 BC–395 AD
Roman Period

Roman mummy portrait from 4th century AD

451 Egypt's Coptic Church splits from Eastern Christianity at the Council of Chalcedon

527 St Catherine's Monastery founded in Sinai

AD 1	**150**	**300**	**450**	**600**

394 End of ancient Egypt as Roman Empire accepts Christianity as official religion and closes all temples

640 Islamic army under Amr ibn al-Aas invades and conquers Egypt

19th-century lithograph of Sultan Baybars I (c.1265) executing Christians who refuse to convert to Islam

Slaves and Soldiers

The word "Mamluk" means "one who is owned", and reflects their origins as slaves brought to Egypt to be palace guards. Their service was rewarded by land and eventual freedom. By the middle of the 13th century the Mamluks were the most powerful force in the land, and were able to claim Egypt for themselves.

The Mamluks retained the slave system, and whoever had the largest slave army installed himself as sultan at the top. There was no hereditary lineage, instead it was succession by the strongest. Once in power, there remained constant challenges, and only the exceptionally able and ruthless survived.

The Mamluks prided themselves on their martial skills and were known particularly for their masterful horsemanship. From their base in Cairo they fought victorious campaigns throughout Palestine and Syria, completing the job begun by Salah ad-Din by finally evicting the Crusaders from the Holy Land in 1291. They governed Jerusalem and Damascus, and carved out an empire that extended north as far as eastern Turkey. With these territories came control of East–West trade. The taxes raised on spices, perfumes, silks and dyes made Cairo one of the richest cities in the world. This wealth remains evident in the legacy of superb architecture left behind from this time, built with fine marble panelling, intricate ivory-inlaid woodwork and carved stone ornamentation.

Mamluk monopolies forced Europe to seek alternative routes to the East, and when, in 1498, Vasco da Gama rounded the Cape of Good Hope, the fortunes of Egypt were dealt a crippling blow. Worse still, the Ottoman Turks from their capital of Constantinople were eroding the Mamluks' empire from the north. Sultan Qansuh al-Ghouri (1501–16) rode out to meet this new threat. His Mamluk army was defeated, and the following year the Ottoman Turks entered Cairo to take control of Egypt.

Magnificent interior of the Mosque of Qaitbey (1475), built with money raised by taxes

969 Fatimids found the city of Al-Qahira, forerunner of modern Cairo

1250 Mamluks accede to power

1468–96 Reign of Qaitbey, enthusiastic patron of architecture

Mamluk tile from the 15th century

900 — 1050 — 1200 — 1350 — 1500

876–9 Construction of the Mosque of Ibn Tulun

1171 Salah ad-Din becomes ruler of Egypt

Mamluk jacket (c.13th century)

1516 Al-Ghouri's Mamluk army defeated by Ottomans, who take control of Egypt

The defeat of the Mamluks by Napoleon's army during the 1798 Battle of the Pyramids

Ottoman Rule

Under Ottoman rule, Egypt ceased to be the centre of the Mediterranean world and Cairo became just one of numerous provincial capitals ruled from Constantinople. The Turkish sultan Selim "the Grim", so called for his habit of executing his advisers, ruled Egypt and the Mamluks lived on as lords or *beys* still wielding considerable power.

The Ottoman empire reached its peak during the reign of Suleiman the Magnificent, but his death in 1566 heralded a long era of decline for the empire. A succession of weak Ottoman sultans enabled the Mamluks to re-emerge in the mid-17th century as the most powerful force in Egyptian politics. However, internal rivalry and bloody feuding prevented them from exploiting

Sultan Selim I (1467–1520),
also known as Selim "the Grim"

power to the full. At the same time, economic decline and recurrent outbreaks of plague further weakened the country.

Europe "Discovers" Egypt

In 1798 Egypt was invaded by a French army under the command of Napoleon Bonaparte. With France and Britain at war, Napoleon saw the occupation of Egypt as a way of threatening British rule in India. The French defeated the Mamluks at the Battle of the Pyramids but this success was short-lived. Napoleon's fleet was destroyed at Abu Qir *(see p254)* by the British Navy, led by Admiral Nelson. A declaration of war by the Ottoman sultan followed, and by 1801 the French expedition had come to an end. Their legacy is the *Description de l'Egypte*, an

1520–66 Reign of Suleiman the Magnificent		1566 Death of Suleiman the Magnificent		1650 Mamluks re-emerge as a powerful force
	1550		**1600**	**1650**
1528 Egypt's first Ottoman mosque (Suleiman Pasha) built at the Citadel		*Suleiman the Magnificent*	1623 First overt rebellions in Egypt against rule from Constantinople	

exhaustive scientific study of the country which encouraged many other writers and artists to visit Egypt.

Mohammed Ali and his Heirs

In the resulting power vacuum, the Mamluks, Ottoman troops and a contingent of Albanian mercenaries locked horns in a struggle for power which was won, in 1805, by Mohammed Ali, commander of the Albanians. To consolidate his position he eliminated the threat of the Mamluks by inviting the leading *amirs* to a banquet and having them massacred on the way home. He then began to transform Egypt into an industrialized nation. Bringing agriculture under state control, he built textile plants, shipyards and munitions factories to supply his new Western-style army. After a series of military victories in Greece, Arabia and the Sudan, Mohammed Ali threatened the Ottoman sultan, but was forced to back down after the British intervened and he died in 1849.

Two successors followed before Khedive Ismail acceded to power. Determined to

Mohammed Ali in negotiations with the British, following his threat to overthrow the Ottoman sultan

transform Egypt into a modern nation, he introduced the first national postal service and extended railroad networks throughout the country.

His greatest achievement was to preside over the opening of the Suez Canal in 1869 *(see pp64–5)*. Such projects were funded by loans from European banking houses at exorbitant rates of interest. As the national debt rose, Ismail was forced to sell the majority of Suez Canal shares to the British and the French.

19th-century advertisement showing Europeans at Giza

In 1882, Egyptian army officers led by Colonel Ahmed Orabi staged popular uprisings in an attempt to establish a more independent regime. The breakdown in local order led the British to send in the warships, shelling Alexandria and landing an army of occupation which routed Orabi's forces at Tell al-Kebir.

The 1811 massacre of the leading Mamluk *amirs* ordered by Viceroy Mohammed Ali

1719 Plague decimates the population of Egypt

1798 Egypt invaded by Napoleon

1805 Mohammed Ali wins control of Egypt

1882 British troops occupy Egypt

00   1750   1800   1850

1707 Mamluk power struggle reaches new heights in Cairo

Napoleon Bonaparte

1822 Translation of hieroglyphs by French scholar Champollion

1869 Khedive Ismail opens the Suez Canal

Khedive Ismail

The Construction of the Suez Canal

As early as the 7th century BC, the ancient Egyptians had connected the Nile and Red Sea with an east–west canal. A north–south canal, slicing through the Isthmus of Suez to connect the Mediterranean with the Red Sea was first considered in the Middle Ages by Venetian merchants. At the end of the 18th century, Napoleon's engineers took up the idea but dropped it when they mistakenly calculated that one sea was 10 m (33 ft) higher than the other. The canal project was taken up by Ferdinand de Lesseps, the French consul to Egypt, who received the go-ahead during the reign of Khedive Said. Construction began on 25 April 1859.

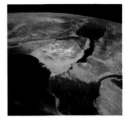

This impressive satellite picture shows how the Suez Canal separates Africa (Egypt) from Asia (Sinai).

The Canal Route

This 19th-century painting by Albert Rieger shows how the Suez Canal utilizes lakes as passing places for shipping – Lake Manzila at its northern end, Lake Timsah, and the Bitter Lakes at the midpoint of the canal. This route is 163 km (101 miles) in length.

Rosetta branch of the Nile

Cairo

The Bitter Lakes provided a natural passing point for shipping.

Suez remains the most important of Egypt's ports.

Ferdinand de Lesseps (1805–94) was a French diplomat descended from a long line of civil servants. It took him 20 years to receive approval for his canal plans.

Digging the Suez Canal

At the outset, the building of the canal was largely carried out by hand, but acquiring the 20,000 workers needed each month proved extremely difficult. In addition, fatalities were high, running at about 200 per year, and work was periodically halted by waves of infectious diseases, such as cholera.

After five years of construction, the Egyptian government discontinued its supply of unhappily drafted peasant labour and work continued with the use of mechanical diggers and a smaller number of labourers. It took 10 years to plough through the 96 km (60 miles) of lake and 64 km (40 miles) of land, but finally, in March 1869, the waters of the Mediterranean flowed into the basins of the Bitter Lakes at long last bringing into existence a new sea route between Europe and Asia.

Construction of the canal began in a manner that recalled the great building projects of ancient Egypt. Hampered by a lack of drinking water, huge numbers of labourers worked in awful conditions, aided only by camels with baskets.

The Cairo Marriott Hotel, built along the lines of Spain's Alhambra as a palace for Empress Eugénie of France, was one of the extravagant projects designed for the opening of the canal.

Building Boom

The construction of the Suez Canal inspired a building boom in Cairo where grand new buildings, such as the Khedival Apartments on Sharia Emad al-Din, were constructed to house the various dignitaries invited for the opening celebrations. An opera house was erected for their entertainment and a palace (now the Marriott Hotel) built for the guest of honour Empress Eugénie, wife of Napoleon III of France. A tree-lined road, still in use today, was also laid for the Empress's visit to the Pyramids. The canal also resulted in the founding of three new towns – Port Said, Ismailia and Suez.

Ismailia was the headquarters of the Suez Canal Company.

Lake Timsah

Lake Manzila

Port Said is the Mediterranean gateway to the canal.

Inaugural celebrations for the canal began on 17 November 1869. Khedive Ismail, escorting the French Empress Eugénie and Austro-Hungarian Emperor Franz Josef in this painting by Mahmoud Said, offered weeks of lavish hospitality to visiting dignitaries.

The opera *Aida* was written by Giuseppe Verdi for the canal opening. However, it was not completed in time and another Verdi opera, *Rigoletto*, was performed in its place.

The Suez Crisis

President Gamal Abdel Nasser (1918–70)

The cost of building the canal and financing the accompanying lavish celebrations bankrupted Egypt. Ismail was forced to sell his shares and full ownership passed to the French and British who kept control over the canal for the next 80 years. When, in the wake of Egyptian independence, President Nasser nationalized the canal in 1956, Britain and France, in collusion with Israel, invaded the canal zone in an attempt to take it back by force. In the face of widespread international condemnation they were forced to retreat, leaving the canal in Egyptian hands.

British troops at Port Said during the 1956 invasion

Early 20th-century photograph of members of the British elite at Shepheard's Hotel in Cairo

British Occupation

When Egypt's soaring national debt rendered the country unable to repay British loans, Britain invaded. The occupation, motivated by the need to protect British interests in the Suez Canal, was intended as a temporary policing measure. Although the *khedives*, the heirs of Mohammed Ali, remained on the throne, all real power was held by the British.

With the outbreak of World War I in 1914, Britain took an even firmer hold on Egyptian affairs. The demands of the British war effort fell hard on the country's peasants and popular discontent spread. At the end of the war, Egyptian demands for autonomy, led by nationalist leader Saad Zaghloul, were curtly dismissed, causing the 1919 rebellion. The violence of the rebellion forced Britain to proclaim the end of its protectorate and recognize Egypt as an independent state with a hereditary monarch, King Fuad I, sixth son of Khedive

Nasser receives a hero's welcome after the successful coup of 1952

Ismail. Despite the king, Britain still controlled Egypt's legal system, communications, foreign policy and the Suez Canal. During World War II, Egypt was vital to British war aims. At El-Alamein the Eighth Army under Montgomery repulsed Rommel's Afrika Korps, changing the course of the war in North Africa.

1952 Revolution

At the conclusion of the war, the British withdrew most of their soldiers from the country, but new forces in Egyptian politics were demanding nothing less than full independence. The disaster of the 1948 War, in which the Egyptian army was defeated by the newly formed state of Israel, contributed to the mood for independence. Fuad's son, King Farouk, who was rumoured to have made a fortune by selling faulty equipment to Egyptian troops, was blamed for the disaster. In 1952 Egyptian anger resulted in "Black Saturday", when European businesses in central Cairo were torched by rampaging mobs. Six months of rioting and political instability followed until, on 23 July, a group calling itself the Free Officers, led by Gamal Abdel Nasser, seized power in a bloodless coup. The monarchy was deposed, King Farouk went into exile and Mohammed Neguib, an army general, became prime minister, commander-in-chief and, later, president. He was deposed in 1954 by Nasser, who succeeded him first as prime

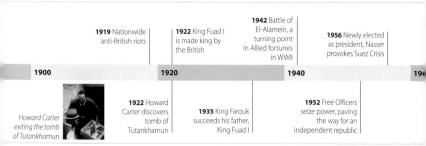

1919 Nationwide anti-British riots

1922 King Fuad I is made king by the British

1942 Battle of El-Alamein, a turning point in Allied fortunes in WWII

1956 Newly elected as president, Nasser provokes Suez Crisis

1900   1920   1940   19◄

Howard Carter exiting the tomb of Tutankhamun

1922 Howard Carter discovers tomb of Tutankhamun

1935 King Farouk succeeds his father, King Fuad I

1952 Free Officers seize power, paving the way for an independent republic

minister, then in 1956 as president. Nasser's ideology of socialism, allied with Arab nationalism, made him a hero to the masses. During the Suez Crisis of 1956 he took on the combined forces of Britain, France and Israel, who invaded following Nasser's announcement of his intention to nationalize the Suez Canal. The invaders were forced to withdraw after intervention by the United Nations and USA.

President Mohamed Morsi holding a press conference at the EU headquarters in Brussels in 2012

This golden era for Nasser was brought to an abrupt end in 1967, with the shattering defeat of Egypt by Israel in the Six-Day War. Nasser died a broken man three years later.

Sadat, Mubarak and Morsi

Nasser's successor, Anwar Sadat, rejected his socialist policies and sought private and foreign investment. On 6 October 1973, he launched a surprise attack on Israeli lines along the Suez. This early success, though quickly reversed, paved the way for peace talks that culminated in the signing of the Camp David peace treaty in 1979. Sadat was assassinated in 1981 by Islamic extremists. His successor, Hosni Mubarak, inherited an ailing economy and recovery was slow. For much of his reign Egypt was ostracized by

Thousands of Egyptian protestors gather in Cairo's Midan Tahrir in 2011

the other Arab nations because of its peace with Israel. In the 1990s and 2004 and 2005, Egypt was hit by Islamist-inspired violence, including fatal attacks on tourists. Visitor numbers fell, damaging the economy, though the situation was stabilized. The country maintains a cool peace with Israel and plays a key role as a peace broker in the Middle East crisis.

On 25 January 2011, spurred on by the Arab Spring sweeping across the region, Egypt exploded into a revolution. Within 18 days Mubarak had been swept from power, and Egypt entered a turbulent period. Elections held in 2011 gave Egypt its first democratically elected president, Mohamed Morsi, from the conservative Muslim Brotherhood. He took office in 2012, but after a year of mismanagement and a rapidly collapsing economy, mass protests again filled Midan Tahrir on 30 June 2013. This led to a military takeover by General Sisi on 3 July. In the 2014 presidential elections, Abdel Fattah el-Sisi ran as a civilian and won. A clampdown followed, with protests being banned, the Muslim Brotherhood outlawed and opposition silenced. Sisi's main focus has been to restore security and the battered economy.

1967 Defeat by Israel in the Six-Day War

1970 Nasser dies and is succeeded by Anwar Sadat

Anwar Sadat (1918–81)

1980

1981 Sadat is assassinated and succeeded by Hosni Mubarak

1988 Egyptian novelist Naguib Mahfouz wins Nobel Prize for Literature

Naguib Mahfouz

1999 Egyptian scientist Ahmed Zewail wins Nobel Prize in Chemistry

2000 International coverage of Millennium celebrations at the Pyramids

2000

2005 President Hosni Mubarak re-elected following landslide victory in multi-candidate election

2011 President Mubarak resigns after anti-government protests

2014 General Sisi steps down and is elected a civilian President

2020

2013 President Morsi ousted after mass protests

2012 Mohamed Morsi is elected president

CAIRO
AREA BY AREA

Cairo at a Glance

Cairo is one of the most densely populated cities in the world. Though its suburbs have spilled over onto the Nile's west bank, its top attractions lie on the eastern bank. Central Cairo is the heart of the modern city and boasts some fine 19th-century architecture. Gezira and Rhoda islands, cooled by the Nile, seem quieter than the centre, while Old Cairo's Roman and early Christian history predates the capital itself. Islamic Cairo is the highlight of the city; its minarets and domes, bazaars and alleyways recall scenes from *1001 Nights*. Further afield, the suburb of Heliopolis spreads northeast, while Giza and the Pyramids lie to the west.

Cairo Tower *(see p88)* offers the best vantage point from which to see the city, as shown above. Amid this modern cityscape, feluccas slide slowly down the Nile, as they have done for thousands of years.

The Egyptian Museum *(see pp78–81)* houses the world's largest collection of ancient Egyptian artifacts. Exhibits include ceramics like this hippopotamus and the riches of the boy king Tutankhamun.

The Hanging Church *(see pp124–5)* is one of a cluster of churches built in the ancient fortress of Babylon in Old Cairo. This beautiful church's name derives from its position, suspended above two Roman gate towers.

CENTRAL CAIRO
(See pp72–89)

**RHODA ISLA
AND OLD CA**
(See pp116–12·)

◄ Domes and minarets dominate the skyline of Cairo

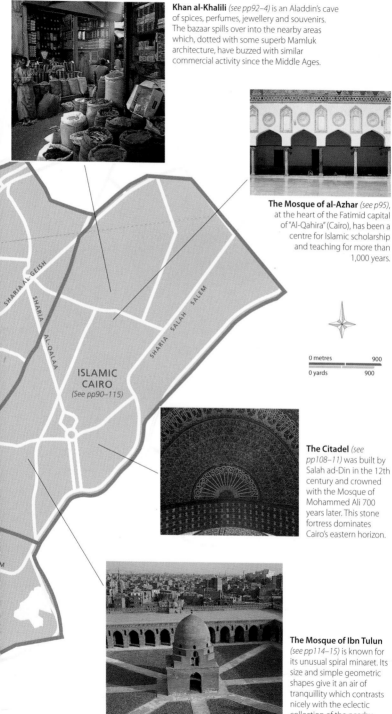

Khan al-Khalili *(see pp92–4)* is an Aladdin's cave of spices, perfumes, jewellery and souvenirs. The bazaar spills over into the nearby areas which, dotted with some superb Mamluk architecture, have buzzed with similar commercial activity since the Middle Ages.

The Mosque of al-Azhar *(see p95)*, at the heart of the Fatimid capital of "Al-Qahira" (Cairo), has been a centre for Islamic scholarship and teaching for more than 1,000 years.

ISLAMIC CAIRO
(See pp90–115)

0 metres 900
0 yards 900

The Citadel *(see pp108–11)* was built by Salah ad-Din in the 12th century and crowned with the Mosque of Mohammed Ali 700 years later. This stone fortress dominates Cairo's eastern horizon.

The Mosque of Ibn Tulun *(see pp114–15)* is known for its unusual spiral minaret. Its size and simple geometric shapes give it an air of tranquillity which contrasts nicely with the eclectic collection of the nearby Gayer-Anderson House.

CENTRAL CAIRO

When Ismail (see p63) came to power in 1863, Cairo was an almost medieval city with a street plan little changed in 500 years. But the khedive, educated in France, set about transforming his capital into a modern, fashionable city that could compare with Paris. Rather than try to impose order on the existing city, he chose to drain the marshy flood plains between it and the Nile and start again. His creation is the heart of Central Cairo. Fine 19th-century European architecture – albeit battered and worn – is the backdrop to thoroughly Middle Eastern streetlife, with the placid Nile offering a refuge from the noise and crush of people and cars.

Sights at a Glance

Areas, Streets & Squares
❷ Midan Tahrir
❹ Sharia Talaat Harb
❺ Sharia Qasr el-Nil
❻ Midan Ramses
❼ Midan Opera and Midan Ataba
⓬ Garden City
⓭ Corniche el-Nil
⓳ Zamalek

Museums & Historic Buildings
❶ Egyptian Museum pp78–81
❸ American University in Cairo
❾ Museum of Islamic Art
❾ Abdeen Palace Museum
❿ Beit as-Sennari
⓫ Mausoleum of Saad Zaghloul
⓮ Manial Palace
⓯ Mahmoud Khalil Museum

⓰ Opera House Complex
⓱ Cairo Tower

Walks
⓲ River Promenade

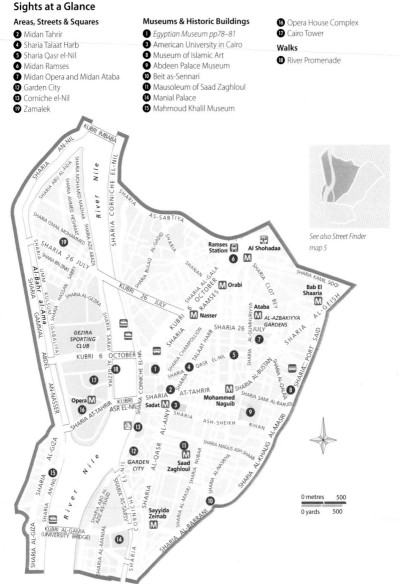

See also Street Finder map 5

◀ Cairo Tower, the capital city's landmark building   For keys to symbols see back flap

Street-by-Street: Around Midan Tahrir

Overrun by traffic and far from pretty, Midan Tahrir is the hub
of Central Cairo and was the site of extensive public protests
against the government in 2011. All routes lead here and most
visitors become very familiar with its Brutalist landmarks: for
example the Mogamma, home to 18,000 bureaucrats. Brighter
spots include the dusky pink Egyptian Museum, the
Arab League Building and the elegant curve of
façades between Sharia Qasr el-Nil and Sharia
Talaat Harb – the location of airline offices,
travel agents, souvenir shops
and cafés.

Ramses Station

Bus Station

SHARIA RAMSES

SHARIA CHAMPO

KUBRI 6 OCTOBER

CORNICHE EL-NIL

Central Cairo
Cairo's bustling modern centre
is flanked to the west by the
tranquil waters of the Nile.

Zamalek

❶ ★ Egyptian Museum
The museum has the
greatest collection of
Pharaonic treasures
in the world and is
one of Cairo's most
popular sights.

**The Nile Ritz-
Carlton Hotel** *(see
p77),* built in 1959,
was Egypt's first
modern hotel. It was
orginally named
the Nile Hotel.

Gezira

0 metres   130

0 yards   130

❸ Corniche el-Nil
This boat-lined
boulevard is wide
and shady and the
city's favourite
place for an
evening stroll.

Key

— Suggested route

For hotels and restaurants in this region see pp272–3 and pp284–6

Groppi's café
(see p76)

Locator Map
See Street Finder map 5

❺ Sharia Qasr el-Nil
The shops along Qasr el-Nil are filled with glitzy paraphernalia. The street is situated in the heart of the financial district where some fine architecture can still be seen.

Felfela restaurant
(see p284)

❹ Sharia Talaat Harb
Central Cairo's main street is a bustling thoroughfare filled with colourful hoardings, shops and cafés.

❷ Midan Tahrir
The cafés located on the south and east sides of Midan Tahrir are ideal spots to break during sightseeing or to simply sit and people-watch.

Mogamma
Building

Omar Makram
Mosque

Semiramis
InterContinental
Hotel *(see p272)*

The Arab League Building, meeting place for Arab world leaders.

❸ American University in Cairo
The Neo-Islamic-style building still houses some of the American University, although most of its faculties have now been relocated. A café, bookshop and art gallery are housed here.

Two Cairenes, dressed in traditional garments called *galabiyyas*, in Midan Tahrir

❶ Egyptian Museum

See pp78–81.

❷ Midan Tahrir

Map 5 B4. Ⓜ Sadat.

Midan Tahrir was not always the dauntingly urban square that it is today. Until the 19th century, the area was a swampy plain, flooded each summer by the Nile. When Khedive Ismail (1863–79) came to power, however, he had the land drained as part of his grand scheme to transform Cairo into a European-style city of tree-lined boulevards and grand public squares.

The Qasr el-Nil (Palace of the Nile) was built beside the river, fronted by an extensive plaza named Midan Ismailia (Ismail's Square). However, Ismail's glory was short-lived: his ambitious scheme drained not only the swamps, but also the state coffers, as Egyptian debt to European lenders spiralled out of control.

In 1882, the British stepped in to take control *(see p63)*, requisitioning Qasr el-Nil as their headquarters, and later as the barracks for their army of occupation. Overcrowded with Allied soldiers during World War II, the barracks were evacuated at the end of the war and the palace was demolished. In 1959, the Nile Hotel was built on the site – the first modern international hotel to be built in Egypt. The 1952 revolution saw all traces of the old regime wiped away, including the

name of Ismail, and the largest square in the city was reincarnated as Midan Tahrir (Liberation Square).

Midan Tahrir is the closest Cairo gets to having a centre, and several major airlines have their offices here, along with tourist agencies, the Omar Makram Mosque, which serves as a venue for state funerals, and the massive monolithic structure of the Mogamma Building, housing around 18,000 civil servants. In January 2011, Midan Tahrir was the main location – and the symbol – of the anti-government protests *(see p67)*.

❸ American University in Cairo

Qasr al-Ainy, Midan Tahrir.
Map 5 B4. Ⓜ Sadat. **Tel** (02) 2794 2964. **Open** 8:30am–5pm Sun–Thur, 10:30am–5pm Sat.

The American University in Cairo (AUC) has its roots in this attractive Neo-Islamic building, although most faculties are now in a state-of-the-art campus in the outlying area of New Cairo. Attending the private AUC is Egypt's equivalent of an Ivy League education and beyond the means of most Egyptians.

The historic downtown building houses a branch of the AUC bookstore, a café and the Margo Veillon Gallery for

Flags fly above the Neo-Islamic façade of the American University

Contemporary Egyptian Art. Regular lectures and discussions are held on the campus, and non-students are welcome to attend. Visitors are admitted upon proof of identity.

Shar Hashamaim Synagogue, near Sharia Talaat Harb

❹ Sharia Talaat Harb

Map 5 C3. Ⓜ Sadat.

Running from Midan Tahrir to Midan Orabi, Sharia Talaat Harb is quintessential modern Cairo. Its pavements are permanently crowded and the road is jammed with horn-honking traffic. As you walk along, music blares from cars on one side and shops on the other, while the air is heavy with car fumes mingled with the smells of cooking and incense. Rising above this pandemonium is some grand architecture, especially around Midan Talaat Harb, where Parisian-style buildings dwarf the statue of Talaat Harb, founder of the National Bank.

On the square is **Groppi's**, a tearoom that once supplied confectionery to the royalty of Great Britain; the only clues to its more glamorous past are the delightful, spangly mosaics around the entrance. More memories of a golden era now passed are evoked by the Art

Paris by the Nile

Inspired by Baron Haussmann's plans for the modernization of Paris in the mid-19th century, Khedive Ismail turned to foreign architects to realize his dream of a modern Cairo. Drawing on Renaissance, Baroque and even Gothic styles, their buildings were adorned with wrought-iron grilles, plaster mouldings, carved foliage, cherubs and angels, plus some local flavouring in the form of scarabs and sphinxes. Later buildings began to take more account of Egypt's heritage, incorporating Islamic motifs such as striped stonework and crenellations. Downtown streets, including Qasr el-Nil and the intersecting Mohammed Farid and Emad ad-Din, still contain a wealth of these beautiful buildings.

Kubri Qasr el-Nil (Qasr el-Nil Bridge), part of the European-style Cairo planned by Khedive Ismail

Deco lines of the Metro Cinema, which opened in 1939 with *Gone With the Wind*. It now screens low-budget action movies – fun to attend for the experience of Egyptian cinema-going, where the bad guys are dispatched to a round of applause.

Little mention is made, in the current climate of Arab-Israeli tension, of Egypt's own Jewish community. However, in Sharia Adly (which joins Sharia Talaat Harb beside the Metro Cinema) the Babylonian-style Shar Hashamaim Synagogue is evidence of their historical presence. You must show your passport in order to enter.

Talaat Harb terminates in another elegant square, named after the nationalist politician Ahmed Orabi who sought political reform in 1881. Off to the east is pedestrianized Sharia Alfy, full of small bars and restaurants, including the excellent Alfy Bey.

❺ Sharia Qasr el-Nil

Map 5 C3. Ⓜ Sadat.

A frenetically busy shopping street, running in front of the Nile Ritz-Carlton Hotel in Midan Tahrir to Midan Opera, Qasr el-Nil is taken up almost exclusively with shop windows that display the brightest and gaudiest of goods. The streets on either side of Sharia Qasr el-Nil traditionally constituted Cairo's financial district. At the junction with Sharia Sherif is the National Bank of Egypt building. Here, too, is the Bourse, or stock exchange, which is enjoying a new lease of life since the government undertook a programme of privatization in the late 1990s. The boom in trading was reflected in a renovation

Statue of Mustafa Kamel overlooking his square

programme that covered a 60,000-sq m (645,000-sq ft) section of downtown Cairo. The area around the Bourse has been pedestrianized and many of the roads are now paved. These walkways are also furnished with 19th-century-style lampposts, along with flowerbeds, greenery and palm trees. Some of the buildings in this area have also been renovated, including the lovely Trieste Insurance Building on the corner with Sharia Sherif. This was designed by the Italian architect Antonio Lascaic (1856–1921), who was responsible for many of central Cairo's most beautiful belle époque buildings.

Sharia Qasr el-Nil crosses over Midan Mustafa Kamel, named after the founder of the Egyptian Nationalist Party, formed in 1907. Kamel was an early opponent of British occupation and his statue looks out over the square.

Sharia Qasr el-Nil continues past jewellers' shops and a few outlets selling street signs (you can have your name put on one) to emerge on Sharia al-Gumhuriyya. This leads into Midan Opera (*see p82*), which was once one of Cairo's grandest squares, but is now occupied by a vast car park and the derelict Continental-Savoy hotel.

Small fruit stall set up in an alleyway off Sharia Talaat Harb

● Egyptian Museum

Founded by a Frenchman, Auguste Mariette (1821–81), Egypt's first national museum of Pharaonic antiquities opened in 1863. It outgrew two homes before settling in these premises in 1902. More than 120,000 items are on display here, with another 150,000 stored in the basement. Pride of the collection are the Tutankhamun Galleries containing artifacts from Tutankhamun's tomb, but there are great pieces from every period of ancient Egyptian history, from the Narmer Palette, dating from around 3100 BC, through to the Graeco-Roman Fayoum Portraits of the 2nd century AD. Some of these items may be transferred to the new Grand Egyptian Museum, currently under construction at Giza and due to open in 2018.

Gallery Guide

The museum has two floors and confusingly the rooms on each floor are numbered the same. Artifacts on the ground floor are organized in a roughly chronological order, running clockwise from the entrance and atrium, while the first-floor collection is arranged by themes. The central hall houses large monumental statuary and the annexe in the basement houses the Children's Museum.

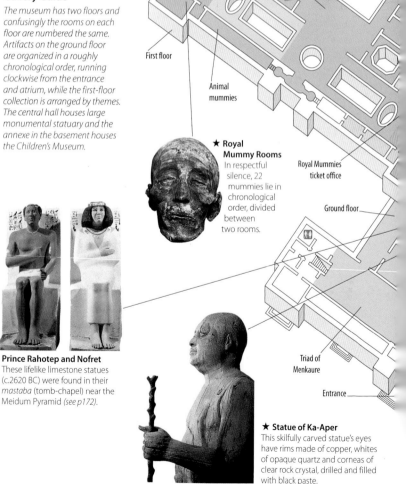

Royal Tombs of Tanis

Middle Kingdom Models

Yuya and Thuyu collection

First floor

Animal mummies

★ **Royal Mummy Rooms**
In respectful silence, 22 mummies lie in chronological order, divided between two rooms.

Royal Mummies ticket office

Ground floor

Prince Rahotep and Nofret
These lifelike limestone statues (c.2620 BC) were found in their *mastaba* (tomb-chapel) near the Meidum Pyramid *(see p172)*.

Triad of Menkaure

Entrance

★ **Statue of Ka-Aper**
This skilfully carved statue's eyes have rims made of copper, whites of opaque quartz and corneas of clear rock crystal, drilled and filled with black paste.

★ **Tutankhamun Galleries**
This life-size gold mask is just one in a collection of 1,700 items from the tomb of the boy king.

VISITORS' CHECKLIST

Practical Information
Midan Tahrir, Cairo. **Map** 5 B3.
Tel (02) 2578 2448, (02) 2578 2452. **Open** 9am–5pm daily (last admission 4pm). 🏛 🅿 ♿ 📷 💻 ✏ 🎒 🔒 Left luggage facilities available. 🎨

Transport
Ⓜ Sadat. Ⓣ 🚌 to Midan Tahrir.

Ancient Egyptian Jewellery
Made with beads of gold and lapis lazuli, this c.11th-century BC necklace is one of several examples of the royal jewellers' exquisite skill.

The Fayoum Portaits are remarkably lifelike studies of Egyptians from the Graeco-Roman period.

Tutankhamun's Throne
On the back of the lavishly decorated throne is this portrayal of Tutankhamun and his wife under the rays of Aten, the sun.

★ **Amarna Room**
During Akhenaten's 15-year rule, not only was the old religion abandoned (see p179) but also its art. A new style developed which depicted figures with elongated heads (as in this bust of the king) and protruding bellies.

Colossus of Amenhotep III and Queen Tiye

Key

- ☐ Old Kingdom
- ☐ Middle Kingdom
- ☐ New Kingdom
- ☐ Late Period/Graeco-Roman
- ☐ Coffins and Sarcophagi
- ☐ Tutankhamun Galleries
- ☐ Royal Mummy Rooms
- ☐ Middle Kingdom Models
- ☐ Miscellaneous exhibits
- ☐ Non-exhibition space

Exploring the Egyptian Museum

While not particularly large, the museum is densely packed with artifacts and anybody with more than a passing interest in ancient Egypt will need more than one visit to take everything in. When the museum is busy, long queues can form outside the room holding Tutankhamun's funeral mask. To view the mask at some leisure, it is best to visit the museum just as it opens or late in the afternoon and make straight for the Tutankhamun Galleries, visiting the rest of the museum afterwards. Independent guides tout for business at the entrance to the museum and, as the labelling inside is sparse, it may be worthwhile hiring one.

Wall frieze, known as the Meidum Geese, painted on plaster (c.2620 BC)

Old Kingdom

All the museum's great pieces of monumental statuary are on the ground floor. These start in the museum's atrium with King Djoser's empty-eyed statue carved in limestone nearly 5,000 years ago. It was discovered at Saqqara (see pp166–8) in his *serdab*, a small sealed room beside his Step Pyramid. Other Old Kingdom highlights on the ground floor include a statue of Khafre, builder of the middle pyramid at Giza, in Room 42. He is seated on his throne with the wings of the falcon-god Horus wrapped protectively around his head, symbolizing the divine sanction of the king's rule (the term *pharaoh* was rarely used before 1500 BC). Also in Room 42, the wooden figure of Ka-Aper, a 5th-Dynasty official, puts his left foot forward in a stylized pose that suggests movement and, along with his gleaming eyes, brings the statue to life. Further examples of the vitality of the ancient artists are exhibited in Room 32 in the lifelike, seated statues of Prince Rahotep and Princess

Nofret, whose real hairline can be seen poking out from under her wig, and in the Meidum Geese panels, which were discovered at Fayoum (see p172). Room 37 contains a touchingly personal collection of alabaster ornaments and bedroom furniture, including a golden four-poster bed, an armchair and a jewellery box all of which belonged to Hetepheres, the mother of Khufu, builder of the Great

Pyramid. Her jewellery is on display on the second floor. The room also contains an alabaster canopic chest that was used to store the internal organs of the deceased. The chest was found in Hetepheres's tomb at Giza, with the remains of its contents still visible.

Middle Kingdom Models

The daily life of the less-exalted ancient Egyptian is well illustrated in rooms in the west wing, which hold finely detailed 11th-Dynasty models of domestic scenes. The models provide a wealth of detailed information about Egyptian life, as well as reflecting an interest in factual artistic representation. Room 22 holds an exquisite rendering in cedarwood of Senwosret I. Its companion statuette (wearing the red crown of Lower Egypt) is housed in the Metropolitan Museum of Art in New York.

Model servant girl (c.2010 BC)

New Kingdom

Ancient Egypt's New Kingdom represented an artistic golden age, but many of the best pieces are housed at the Luxor

18th-Dynasty relief of Amenhotep III riding over bound Nubian captives

Museum *(see p191)*. However, Room 11 holds the painted limestone face of Hatshepsut from her mortuary temple in Thebes, and Room 3 contains fine artifacts from Amarna, the short-lived capital of the "heretic king" Akhenaten *(see p179)*. Here, the sleek muscular forms of traditional Pharaonic art are replaced by swollen bellies and almost cartoon-like elongated faces. This is particularly evident on a set of reliefs showing the sun-god, Aten, whose solar rays end in hook-like hands. One of the notable exceptions to this style is an unfinished, sculpted head of Nefertiti, Akhenaten's wife, which is stunning in its human beauty.

Head of Queen Nefertiti (c.1340 BC)

Tutankhamun Galleries

The Tutankhamun Galleries fill the upper floor's east and north wings. Entering via the southeast stairs, visitors pass the two life-size statues of the young king that stood guard at the entrance to his tomb. Out of the 5,000 items discovered, some 1,700 are on display, ranging from board games and hunting implements to couches and beds and, of course, the fabulous death mask. A glass cabinet is filled with some of Tutankhamun's

One of Tutankhamun's gilded fans

Tutankhamun's carved throne inlaid with gold and ebony

shabtis. These were small effigies of the deceased that were buried with the body to carry out any tasks that the deceased might be asked to do in the afterlife. In all, 413 *shabtis* were found in the tomb; one for each day of the year, plus foremen. Nearby is the dazzling royal "lion" throne, named after the golden lion heads and legs on each side. Aside from the craftsmanship, this throne is of great interest in that it reveals influences of the "Amarna period" when the Aten cult still thrived *(see p179)*. The Aten sun-disk and rays resemble reliefs from Amarna, and the pharaoh's name from this period, Tutankhaten, is inscribed on the back of the throne. In the north wing is the alabaster canopic chest holding four jars with Tutankhamun-head stoppers. Room 3 holds Tutankhamun's solid gold death mask and the two inner coffins, one of gilded wood set with semiprecious gems, the other solid gold. The king's body lies in its tomb in the Valley of the Kings on the west bank of the Nile.

Royal Mummy Rooms

There is a separate fee to see the mummies, which is payable at the ticket desk at the top of the southeast stairs. This allows the experience of coming face to face with some legendary kings such as Tuthmosis II, Seti I and the mighty Ramses II. The good condition of the bodies belies the fact that they all died more than 3,000 years ago. The beak-nosed face of Ramses II barely resembles his sleek bust downstairs in the New Kingdom galleries.

Miscellaneous Exhibits

In addition to the human mummies, the museum holds a fascinating collection of animal mummies in Rooms 52 and 53 (upstairs). The ancient Egyptians revered certain animals; for example, the ibis and baboon were sacred to the god Thoth and cats sacred to Bastet. In the regions where these cults thrived, great numbers of these mummified creatures have been unearthed.

Across the hall, in Room 43, are 18th-Dynasty funerary artifacts from the tomb of Yuya and Tuya, the great-grandparents of Tutankhamun. Discovered in 1905, the beautiful sarcophagi and other lustrous items here are undeservedly ignored by most visitors. Better known are the Graeco-Roman funerary paintings known as Fayoum Portraits, after the oasis where many of them were found *(see p172)*; Room 14 (upstairs) contains a collection of these haunting faces, along with some of the mummies to which they were attached.

Two galleries devoted to the Royal Tombs of Tanis and Ancient Egyptian Jewellery contain some of the museum's finest small pieces. Tanis was a major city in the Delta during the 21st and 22nd Dynasties *(see p243)*. In 1939 archaeologists found a series of intact royal tombs that held a marvellous haul of death masks, coffins and jewellery. One of the items, the coffin of Shashanq II, is interesting not just for its striking hawk's head but also because it is made of solid silver. Rare in Egypt, silver had to be imported, making it a highly prized commodity. The Children's Museum is in an annexe beneath the main building and displays statues, miniatures and some impressive creations made of Lego.

❻ Midan Ramses

Map 2 D3. Ⓜ Al Shohadaa.

Marking the northernmost extent of central Cairo, Midan Ramses is the gateway to the city. In ancient times, when the river followed a different course, a port here served the Pharaonic city of Heliopolis. When Salah ad-Din (Saladin), ruler of Egypt, refortified Cairo in the 12th century, he built a great gate here, the Bab al-Hadid, or Iron Gate, which remained standing until 1847, when it was demolished to make way for the new railway station.

Mahattat Ramses (Ramses Station) is still Cairo's main rail terminus and the place to catch trains for most destinations, although Giza Railway Station is also in use *(see pp334–5)*. The **Egyptian National Railway Museum**, housed at the eastern end of the station, has a fascinating collection of engines, carriages and models.

The 11-m- (36-ft-) high colossus of Ramses II, found at Mit Rahina near Memphis *(see p169)* in 1882, stood in the square for more than 50 years. The red granite statue was restored in 1955 and erected here, becoming one of the city's most imposing landmarks. In 2006 the 3,200-year-old statue was moved in a carefully orchestrated 10-hour journey to its new home on the Giza

Former Tiring department store designed by Oscar Horowitz in 1911, Midan Ataba

plateau, where Cairo's Grand Egyptian Museum is currently under construction.

🏛 **Egyptian National Railway Museum**
Midan Ramses. **Map** 2 D3. Ⓜ Al Shohadaa. **Tel** (02) 2576 3793. **Closed** until further notice. ♿

❼ Midan Opera and Midan Ataba

Map 6 D2 & E2. Ⓜ Ataba.

In just five months in 1868, labour gangs constructed a completely new opera house for the inaugural celebrations marking the opening of the Suez Canal. To mark the occasion, the Italian composer Giuseppe Verdi had been commissioned to write a new opera, *Aida*, but he was unable to finish it in time, so the new Cairo Opera House opened instead with a performance of Verdi's *Rigoletto*.

Modelled on Milan's La Scala and built entirely of wood, the Opera House was the loveliest landmark in central Cairo – until it was burned to the ground in 1971. A less lovely multistorey car park was built on the site, but the square is still known as Midan Opera. In the middle of the paved plaza is a statue of Ibrahim Pasha (1789–1848), general and viceroy of Egypt, who successfully campaigned in Syria in 1832–3.

Just beyond Midan Opera is Midan Ataba, which forms a dividing point between so-called "European" Cairo to the west and the old medieval city, known as Islamic Cairo, to the east. From this point, the streets get narrower, the buildings smaller and more decrepit. The square itself can be a knot of snarled traffic, but in the surrounding streets are various markets. To the northwest is a small area of secondhand bookstalls; there is a clothing market to the northeast,

Clothes stall in front of mosque in Midan Ataba

electronics to the southeast and, in the southwest, a few stalls sell cards and stationery. The latter run, appropriately enough, in front of the central post office, an old building with an attractive courtyard and an annexe where the **National Postal Museum** is housed. Egypt was one of the first countries in the world to issue stamps (1866). The museum is small, but there is a lot crammed into the space, including models of carriages and delivery bikes, old mail boxes and a vast collection of stamps.

Also on Midan Ataba is the **Cairo Puppet Theatre**, which puts on regular colourful puppet shows for children and adults.

🏛 **National Postal Museum**
Midan Ataba. Ⓜ Ataba. **Tel** (02) 2391 0011. **Open** 8am–2:30pm Sun–Thu. ♿

🎭 **Cairo Puppet Theatre**
Midan Ataba. Ⓜ Ataba. **Tel** (02) 2591 0954. **Open** Oct–May: show at 6:30pm Thu & Fri. ♿

❽ Museum of Islamic Art

Sharia Port Said. **Map** 6 E3. Ⓜ Mohammed Naguib. **Tel** (02) 2390 1520. **Open** 9am–5pm daily (9am–3pm Ramadan). **Closed** for renovation until 2016. ♿

Often overlooked by the crowds that throng the Egyptian Museum, this museum contains

Ibrahim Pasha's statue, Midan Opera

some beautiful pieces of medieval decorative art salvaged from the houses, mosques and palaces of Islamic Cairo at the instigation of Khedive Tawfiq. Most striking of all are the large *mashrabiyya* screens, which are constructed of thousands of individual pieces of wood. Still seen today in many old buildings, such screens shaded rooms from the sun while admitting cooling breezes. They were also important as they allowed the women of the house to look out without being seen.

The museum houses other examples of creative woodworking taken from mosques around the city, including huge ivory-inlaid doors, carved friezes and a fine 14th-century *minbar* (pulpit).

Three ornamental fountains provide the best examples of another speciality of Egyptian craftsmen – inlaid stone and marble-work. These pieces, dating from the Mamluk and Ottoman periods, would have decorated the reception halls of rich merchants' houses. Look out, also, for enamelled glass lamps; these beautiful objects, many of them decorated with stylized Arabic

A manuscript in the Museum of Islamic Art

lettering, would have been suspended by chains from the ceilings of mosques. Other exhibits include Persian and Turkish ceramics, illuminated manuscripts and books, and carpets and rugs. The museum has been renovated and is a true highlight among Cairo's many attractions.

❾ Abdeen Palace Museum

Sharia Abd ar-Raziq, Midan Abdeen. **Map** 6 D4. Ⓜ Mohammed Naguib. **Tel** (02) 2391 0130. **Open** 9am–3pm Sat–Thu (10am–1pm Ramadan).

Abdeen is a former royal palace, part of which is now open to the public as a museum that embraces several collections. These include displays of weaponry, presidential gifts, royal acquisitions and silver plates.

From the time of Salah ad-Din in the 12th century, Egypt was ruled from the safety of the Citadel *(see pp108–11)*, but tradition was broken 700 years later by Khedive Ismail, who ordered a European-style residence to be built on the edge of his new city. Designed by the French architect

Cannon yard of the Abdeen Palace Museum

Rousseau, the 500-room palace was begun in 1863 and took over 10 years to complete. Over the years, it was constantly remodelled and expanded, with the addition, in the 1930s, of a Byzantine throne room.

Following the overthrow of King Farouk in 1952, the Abdeen Palace was vacated, but later put to its present use as a venue for receiving visiting heads of state.

In the late 1980s, President Mubarak ordered that the palace be restored. The work took longer than anticipated because the palace was hit by the 1992 earthquake. The museum was inaugurated by the president in 1998.

Entered via neat gardens at the rear of the palace, the museum occupies a complex of unadorned halls; the more extravagantly decorated state rooms remain off-limits to the public. A lot of space is given over to the collection of guns, swords and daggers, many of which were gifts to Egypt's various *khedives*, kings and presidents. There are also displays of medals and other decorations, as well as a room of awards and gifts presented to President Mubarak. A silverware section contains a display of silver, crystal and *objets d'art* belonging to the family of Pasha Mohammed Ali.

Centrally located in the museum is the fountain courtyard, where the fountain is surrounded by the busts of Mohammed Ali, Khedive Ismail and King Fuad I.

Entrance to Abdeen Palace, museum and gardens

⑩ Beit as-Sennari

Harat Monge, off Sharia Khayrat, Saida Zeinab. **Map** 4 D2. Ⓜ Saad Zaghloul. **Tel** (02) 2390 9471. 🖼

Napoleon invaded Egypt in 1798, bringing with him an army of scientists, scholars and artists to establish a French cultural base in the country. Over the next few years, they carried out the first European study of Egypt and published their findings in the *Description de l'Egypte (see p24)*.

This *beit* (house), which was built in 1794 for Ibrahim Katkhuda as-Sennari, an occultist from Sudan, was requisitioned by Napoleon and housed many of his artists during the occupation. It has some fine wooden *mashrabiyya* screens, an attractive courtyard and well-preserved rooms. Extensive renovation works have been completed, and it is hoped that the building will open in the future as the Institute for Applied Arts, with displays of glassware, textiles, pottery and other work by local artists.

⑪ Mausoleum of Saad Zaghloul

Sharia Mansour. **Map** 5 B5. Ⓜ Saad Zaghloul.

Saad Zaghloul (1853–1927) spent most of his life trying to get the British out of Egypt. He became a national spokesman for self-rule and held the post of prime minister for a time. Zaghloul was highly respected, even by the foreign governors he opposed, and shortly after his death this vast mausoleum was erected in his honour. Built of granite, the mausoleum was designed to echo that of a Pharaonic temple, with an outward-curving cornice and entrance flanked by two great lotus pillars.

It is also possible to visit Zaghloul's house, **Beit al-Umma** (House of the Nation), which is just a short distance west. Most of the rooms have been pre-served with Zaghloul's original furnishings and belongings still in place. The study is worth

visiting, as it shows Zaghloul's concern for his safety, which led him to put mirrors in the room and arrange the furniture to allow him to keep an eye out for potential assassins.

🏠 Beit al-Umma

2 Sharia Saad Zaghloul. Ⓜ Saad Zaghloul. **Tel** (02) 2794 5399. **Open** 10am–5pm Tue–Thu, Sat & Sun. 🖼

⑫ Garden City

Map 5 A5. Ⓜ Sadat.

Garden City, one of the most attractive and tranquil of Cairo's quarters, was created by the British in the early years of the 20th century as a leafy green suburb, where officers and administrators could pretend they were still living in rural England, far from the dusty, dry streets of Cairo. The roads were designed to curve and wind like country lanes but, instead of England's oaks and beeches, leafy coverage was provided by native palms, rubber and mango trees.

As well as housing the British, the villas of this exclusive suburb were home to Egypt's most prominent doctors, lawyers, bankers and politicians.

Today, Garden City suffers from an onslaught of concrete high-rise buildings, but it remains a very desirable address: the British, American and several other embassies

Elegant, curving façade of a building in Garden City flanked by tree-lined pavements

are located here. Garden City still offers a welcome respite from the hustle of Cairo, and a walk through the area reveals a wonderfully eclectic array of architecture, including the building known as **Grey Pillars** – the British Army's headquarters in Egypt during World War II. This can still be seen on Sharia as-Suraya.

⑬ Corniche el-Nil

Map 5 A4. Ⓜ Sadat.

Although it is one of the city's busiest highways, the Corniche el-Nil is also where Cairo comes to relax. In a city chronically short of public green spaces, this is as close as it gets to a

View across the Nile from the Corniche north of Rhoda Island

◀ Interior of the Egyptian Museum in Central Cairo

park. Each evening, the wide pavements of the Corniche are packed with promenading families, roaming college kids and young lovers, all enjoying the pleasant waterborne breezes and the sense of open space that the river provides.

An even better way to enjoy the river is on a felucca, one of the small triangular-sailed boats used on the Nile since antiquity. The boats (which can be hired by the hour) and their captains gather at various landing stages, including one opposite the Semiramis Hotel and another at Dokdok, opposite the northern tip of Rhoda Island. Lazily scudding about the river while the sun drops towards the skyline makes for a calming end to a hectic day of sightseeing.

Regnault's painting of a fleeing Mamluk, in the Manial Palace

🟤 Manial Palace

Sharia al-Saray, Rhoda. **Map** 3 B2. Ⓜ Sayyida Zeinab. **Tel** (02) 2368 7495. **Open** 9am–4pm daily. 🖼

Located on the northern tip of the island of Rhoda is the Manial Palace, a former royal residence. It it open to the public, although parts of it may be closed for renovation, so check ahead. The palace was built for Prince Mohammed Ali Tawfiq, a descendant of Egypt's famed ruler Mohammed Ali, and the uncle of King Farouk. It was constructed between 1899 and 1929 and is a curious ensemble of five separate buildings in a

Façade of Cairo's Mahmoud Khalil Museum

variety of Islamic styles. Beside the mock-Medieval gateway is a Moorish tower attached to the Turkish-tiled Mosque of Mohammed Ali. Nearby, the Hunting Museum has a somewhat grim display of over 300 mounted gazelle heads strung along its narrow gallery.

The eccentrically contrived design extends to the interiors. The Main Residence is a series of rooms decorated in a mixture of styles. The Syrian room has an elaborately painted wooden ceiling, an Ottoman room is furnished with turquoise ceramics from Anatolia, while the Egyptian corner has windows featuring *mashrabiyya* screens. Also included among the valuable displays is a painting of a Mamluk and his mount leaping over the Citadel walls. The painting, by Henri Regnault (1843–71), hangs in the Blue Salon, and depicts an alleged incident that took place during Mohammed Ali's suppression of the Mamluks' 1826 revolt.

Behind the residence, through the banyans, palms and Indian rubber trees, is the Throne Hall, complete with red carpet, sunburst ceiling and portraits of the prince's illustrious forebears. While Prince Mohammed Ali Tawfiq never attained the throne, he was able to hold his own court here.

Detail of Mohammed Ali Mosque, Manial Palace

🟤 Mahmoud Khalil Museum

1 Sharia Kafour, off Sharia Giza. **Map** 3 A2. Ⓜ Dokki. **Tel** (02) 3748 2142. **Closed** for renovations until 2017. 🖼

It may come as a surprise to learn that Cairo has a fine collection of Impressionist paintings. They were amassed by Mohammed Mahmoud Khalil (1876–1953), a devout Francophile and patron of the arts, and an important figure on the political scene during the 1930s and 40s. Khalil bequeathed his art collection to the state, along with the house – a beautiful late 19th-century Parisian-style mansion overlooking the Nile.

Khalil's paintings were removed when the house was taken over as the official residence during Sadat's term as Egyptian president (1970–81). In the early 1990s, after the assassination of Sadat, however, the house was refurbished and returned to the public domain.

The paintings on show include works by Degas, Ingres, Monet, Pissarro, Renoir, Sisley and Toulouse-Lautrec. Pride of place goes to van Gogh's *Genêts et Coquelicots* and Gauguin's *La Vie et la Mort*. No longer on display is van Gogh's *Poppy Flowers*, which was stolen in 2010.

For hotels and restaurants in this region see pp272–3 and pp284–6

Sculpture in the grounds of the Opera House Complex

⑯ Opera House Complex

El Borg Gezira, Gezira. **Map** 1 A5. Ⓜ Opera. **Tel** (02) 2737 0602.

A gift to Egypt from Japan, the Opera House Complex was opened in 1988, replacing the original Opera House, which burned down in 1971 *(see p82)*. At the heart of the complex is the **Cairo Opera House**, where a busy programme of classical music and dance, including visits from international performers such as the Bolshoi Ballet, is staged *(see p302)*.

Situated across the lawn, the **Museum of Egyptian Modern Art** displays the work of Egyptian artists since 1908. One who deserves far greater recognition than he is currently given is Mahmoud Said (1897–1964), whose use of warm, glowing colours and subject matter of dignified, proud *fellaheen* (peasants) is reminiscent of the Mexican artist Diego Rivera (1886–1957). Several of Said's paintings are displayed in the museum. There

are two more art galleries within the grounds: the Nile Gallery and the Hanager Gallery, which both host changing exhibitions of contemporary work.

🏛 **Museum of Egyptian Modern Art**
Opera House Complex, Gezira. Ⓜ Opera. **Tel** (02) 2736 6667. **Open** 10am–2pm, 4–8pm Tue–Thu, Sat & Sun. 🖼

⑰ Cairo Tower

Sharia Hadayek el Zuhreya. **Map** 1 A5. Ⓜ Opera. **Tel** (02) 2736 5112. **Open** 9am–midnight daily. 🖼

The southern half of Gezira (the Arabic word for "island") is almost completely flat, making it the ideal site for the 185-m (610-ft) Cairo Tower, which affords excellent views of the city and is beautifully lit at night. Built in the late 1950s, the tower takes the form of a lattice-work tube that fans out slightly at the top, supposedly in imitation of the lotus blossom. From the top, it is possible to make out the easternmost extent of Cairo, where the dark grey buildings run up against the cliff face of the Muqattam Hills. To the west, the Pyramids mark the limits of the city and the start of the desert, while below the Nile flows north to the Mediterranean, slicing Cairo in two.

The best time to go up the tower is at sunset, when millions of lights twinkle into life, accompanied by the haunting evening call to prayer.

⑱ River Promenade

Gezira. **Map** 1 B5. Ⓜ Opera.

Created in the late 1990s, Gezira's river promenade is a wide paved avenue down by the Nile, with fine views of the central city skyline opposite. The promenade starts at the foot of the elegant Qasr el-Nil Bridge, which was designed and built by Dorman Long & Co., the British architects responsible for Australia's Sydney Harbour Bridge.

Between the promenade and the main road is the small, neat **Andalusian Garden**, with lawns, benches and an obelisk from Heliopolis. A small admission charge keeps out the crowds, and it makes for a restful break. On the street beside the garden, *hantours* (also called *caleches*) wait for hire. A quick spin in one of these horse-drawn black carriages is a fine way to see the island – but expect to pay inflated prices for the pleasure.

Horse-drawn carriage (*hantour*) for hire on the River Promenade

Moored off the promenade is a string of former Nile cruisers, most of which have now been converted into upmarket floating restaurants and bars.

⑲ Zamalek

Gezira. **Map** 1 A3. 🚇

Occupying the northern half of Gezira, Zamalek is a well-to-do residential district. The main thoroughfare, Sharia 26 July, which runs diagonally through the area, is the best place to come for European-style comforts. Simonds makes a classic venue for a coffee or an orange juice, and Maison Thomas does great pizza and desserts. European newspapers and magazines are sold at local newsstands and there are a couple of well-stocked supermarkets, plus several bars which attract a mixed Egyptian and

View from Rhoda Island of Cairo Opera House and Cairo Tower

Entrance to Cairo Marriott Hotel, formerly the Gezira Palace

expat crowd. Zamalek's most prominent landmark is the twin orange towers of the Cairo Marriott. This atmospheric and luxurious hotel *(see p272)* was built around the palace created for Empress Eugénie of France when she attended the opening of the Suez Canal in 1869. It has an attractive garden terrace, open to nonresidents, which is an excellent spot for lunch or a beer.

Tucked away behind the Cairo Marriott is a small 19th-century, Islamic-style villa, now home to the **Islamic Ceramics Museum and Gezira Arts Centre**. This little-visited museum displays exquisite ceramics from Egypt, Iran, Morocco and Andalusia, while the Arts Centre, located in the basement of the same building, hosts changing exhibitions by contemporary artists. To the north of the island, the quiet, orderly streets are a treasure-trove of splendid villas and mansion blocks in a variety of styles, from Gothic to Baroque to Arts and Crafts. Many of the finest properties here are embassies, but the **Greater Cairo Library** is open to visitors. This is now Egypt's main resource for information about its capital and contains many interesting books, maps, documents and surveys relating to the history of the city.

🏛 Islamic Ceramics Museum and Gezira Arts Centre
1 Sharia Sheikh al-Marsafi. **Tel** (02) 2737 3298. Arts Centre: **Open** 10am–2pm, 5–9pm Sat–Thu.

🏛 Greater Cairo Library
15 Sharia Mohammed Mazhar. **Tel** (02) 2736 2278. **Open** 10am–2pm, 4–9pm Sat–Thu.

Houseboats

On the narrow stretch of water separating Zamalek from the Nile's western bank sits a small flotilla of tatty, two-storey wooden houseboats. They are all that remains of the floating neighbourhood that once lined the river from the city's southern edge to the north. The community flourished in the early 20th century when, supplied with gas, electricity, fresh water and telephones, the boats provided homes or served as cafés, casinos and nightclubs. In 1943, on a houseboat owned by belly dancer Hekmat Fahmy, a German spy, John Eppler, was arrested. The episode formed the basis of Ken Follett's thriller *The Key to Rebecca*. Most boats are now private residences, although a couple are garish cafés.

One of the houseboats moored near 15th May Bridge

Looking south from 15th May Bridge towards high-rise buildings lining the waterfront in west Zamalek

ISLAMIC CAIRO

Following their conquest of Egypt in 641 AD, the Muslims built their city, Al-Fustat, on what is now the southern border of modern Cairo. Successive dynasties established their own capital, each one further to the northeast of the old, until Salah ad-Din built the impressive Citadel (Al-Qalaa) on a rocky spur and settled the capital's location. During the Mamluk era, which lasted from 1250 to 1517, a wealth of mosques, mausoleums and Islamic buildings were added. Today, Islamic Cairo's maze of narrow, congested streets teems with life, challenging the senses with its unique blend of sights, sounds and smells, and vivid glimpses of the past. Most mosques are open to non-Muslims, and the majority do not charge an entrance fee.

Sights at a Glance

Mosques and Historic Buildings
- ❸ Mosque of Sayyidna al-Hussein
- ❹ Mosque of al-Azhar
- ❺ Beit Zeinab Khatoun and Beit al-Harawi
- ❻ Wikala of al-Ghouri
- ❼ Al-Ghouri Complex
- ❽ Bein al-Qasreen
- ❾ Qasr Beshtak
- ⓫ Sabil-Kuttab of Abdel Katkhuda
- ⓬ Mosque of al-Aqmar
- ⓭ Beit as-Suhaymi
- ⓮ Sharia al-Muizz li-Din Allah
- ⓯ Mosque of al-Hakim
- ⓱ Northern Cemetery
- ⓴ Mosque of as-Salih Talai
- ㉒ The Citadel pp108–11
- ㉓ Mosque of Sultan Hassan
- ㉔ Mosque of ar-Rifai
- ㉕ Dervish Theatre
- ㉖ Sabil-Kuttab of Qaitbey
- ㉗ Mosque of Ibn Tulun pp114–15
- ㉘ Al-Azhar Park

Bazaars and Markets
- ❶ Khan al-Khalili
- ❷ Sharia Muski
- ⓲ Carpet Bazaar
- ㉑ Tentmakers' Market

Museums
- ❿ Textile Museum

Walls and Gates
- ⓰ Northern Walls and Gates
- ⓳ Bab Zuweila

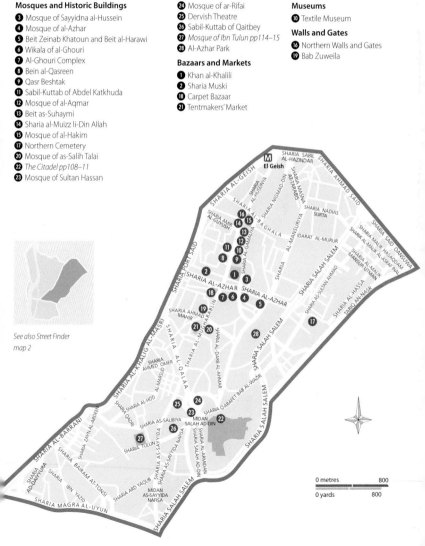

See also Street Finder map 2

◀ Mohammed Ali Mosque in the Citadel

For keys to symbols *see back flap*

Street-by-Street: Around Khan al-Khalili

Any exploration of Islamic Cairo begins at the medieval bazaar of Khan al-Khalili, the commercial heart of the quarter. The original Khan area lay between Al-Muizz li-Din Allah and Midan Hussein but today it encompasses a wider area made up of several markets selling everything from souvenirs to spices. Traders line the streets all the way to the old city gates, but the bazaar's narrow alleyways are at their densest and most beguiling in the original Khan area. The quarter's mosques, houses and palaces offer an escape from the incessant sales pitches.

Mosque of al-Ashraf Barsbey
Built in 1423, this mosque boasts a beautifully carved wooden pulpit, inlaid with ivory.

Al-Muizz li-Din Allah
This narrow thoroughfare was for centuries the main route through the medieval city of Cairo.

SHARIA AL-MUIZZ LI-DIN ALLAH

SHARIA AL-MUSKI

Pedestrian overpass

SHARIA AL-AZHAR

❼ ★ Al-Ghouri Complex
The mosque-*madrassa* and mausoleum complex of Al-Ghouri is housed in twin striped buildings and boasts a unique, red-chequered minaret.

Egyptian Pancake House

Mosque of Abu Dahab

❻ Wikala of al-Ghouri
This *wikala* or caravanserai is Cairo's best-preserved example of a medieval merchants' hostel. It is now a cultural centre that hosts whirling-dervish performances.

0 metres   50
0 yards   50

❶ ★ Khan al-Khalili
Filled with glittering paraphernalia, this bazaar is Cairo at its most magical. The lanes of the original Khan area are lined with shops selling everything from waterpipes and handicrafts to silks and spices.

Locator Map
See Street Finder map 2

Medieval gates

❸ Mosque of Sayyidna al-Hussein
The holiest site in Cairo, this mosque is said to contain the head of Hussein, grandson of the Prophet Mohammed. Built in 1870 on the site of a 12th-century mosque, it is off-limits to non-Muslims.

SIKKET AL-BADESTAN

MIDAN AL-HUSSEIN

Fishawi's coffee house *(see p94)*

❷ Sharia Muski
This busy market street is where Cairenes come for serious bargains on everything from wedding dresses to plastic furniture and children's toys.

SHARIA AL-AZHAR

Pedestrian underpass

❹ ★ Mosque of al-Azhar
Founded in AD 970, this mosque and centre for Islamic study is one of the oldest in the city. It displays a mix of architectural styles including this 18th-century Gate of the Barbers.

Key
— Suggested route

One of two medieval, carved stone gates in Khan al-Khalili

❶ Khan al-Khalili

Map 2 F5. 🚌 77, 102 (from Midan Tahrir) or taxi to Midan al-Hussein.
Open daily (most shops closed Sun).

Built in 1382 by Garkas al-Khalili, Master of Horses to Sultan Barquq, Khan al-Khalili is one of the biggest bazaars in the Middle East. This is the oriental bazaar of fable, where gold, silver, brass and copper goods glitter enticingly in the cave-like interiors, and sacks overflowing with exotic spices fill the air with their pungent scents. Its maze of narrow, canvas-covered alleyways is crammed with shops selling a huge variety of goods. Here, too, traditional Egyptian crafts, such as dyeing, carving and sewing, are practised as they have been for centuries.

Khan al-Khalili is, of course, also a major tourist attraction. Hordes of tourists arrive here, by the coachload, to haggle and stock up on the kitsch trinkets and souvenirs that are sold in nearly every shop in the main part of the bazaar.

The bazaar grew up around several *khans* (also known as *wikalas*), which served as both warehouses and lodgings for travelling merchant caravans. Most have been swallowed up by later structures, but a few remain. On a side street off Sharia Muski, stairs lead to the upper level of the **Wikala of Silahdar** (1837), where the former living quarters can be made out, ranged around the central courtyard. Two carved stone gates in the Badestan area, added during the reign of Sultan al-Ghouri (1501–16), are the oldest surviving part of Khan al-Khalili.

Apart from exploring and haggling, the bazaar's other great attraction is **Fishawi's**, located in an alley one block in from Midan al-Hussein. Open day and night for the past 200 years, it is possibly Cairo's oldest coffee house and is crammed with small copper-topped tables, while huge antique mirrors line the walls. Here, patrons puff on *shishas* (waterpipes) and sip mint tea round the clock.

For further information on shopping in Egypt and Cairo, see Shopping in Cairo (*pp144–5*) and What to Buy in Egypt (*pp298–9*).

Apple vendor in the bustling street market of Sharia Muski

❷ Sharia Muski

Runs between Midan Ataba and Midan al-Hussein. **Map** 6 F3, 2 F5.

In a city that is bursting at the seams, Sharia Muski is possibly the single most crowded street of all. Before Sharia al-Azhar was bulldozed through the area in the mid-20th century, Muski was the main route between Khan al-Khalili and downtown Cairo. The street is crammed with budget-end clothing emporia and bargain-basement market stalls that are piled high with synthetic goods: clothing that is guaranteed to bobble and fade, wedding outfits, plastic toys and garden furniture. At the Khan al-Khalili end of the street, clothing gives way to perfume and "antiques" but, just before Midan al-Hussein, there is one last glorious burst of glitzy glamour in the form of outfitters selling lavishly decorated belly-dancing outfits.

The sounds that fill Sharia Muski are as much part of the experience as the goods on display. The sales patter of the stall-keepers, the warning cries and hisses of barrow-men as they push through the crowds, the drink vendors selling liquorice water, all contribute to the lively character of the street.

❸ Mosque of Sayyidna al-Hussein

Midan al-Hussein. **Map** 2 F5.
Closed to non-Muslims.

This is the most important mosque in all Egypt, so sacred that only Muslims are allowed to enter. Hundreds come here to pray each day, and as many as 10,000 on Fridays. Replacing an earlier 12th-century mosque, it was built in 1870 and is reputed to shelter one of the

Brass and leather goods for sale in Khan al-Khalili

Domes and minarets of Mosque of al-Azhar seen from Zeinab Khatoun

holiest relics of Islam – the head of Al-Hussein, grandson of the Prophet Mohammed. After the Prophet's death in AD 632, control of the caliphate was assumed by the Umayyad clan. The Prophet's son-in-law Ali, claiming to be the natural successor, took up arms and was killed. His son, Al-Hussein, led a revolt but died in AD 680 at the battle of Kerbala, Iraq, where the rest of his body is said to lie. Islam is still divided into followers of Al-Hussein (Shiites) and Sunnis, who hold the Umayyads to be the true successors to Mohammed.

During the annual 10-day Moulid of Al-Hussein and other feast days, thousands throng Midan al-Hussein to enjoy the fair and join in the festivities.

❹ Mosque of al-Azhar

Sharia al-Azhar. **Map** 2 F5. **Open** daily. **Closed** 11:30am–1:30pm Fri.

Just southwest of Midan al-Hussein is one of Cairo's most venerable institutions. Al-Azhar was founded in AD 970 as the main mosque and centre of learning for the city that had just been built by the new Fatimid rulers from North Africa. Though the Fatimids were swept from power some 200 years later, their mosque and university remained central to religious and political life in Egypt.

Today, the Sheikh of al-Azhar is the highest religious authority in

the land and the university the most revered centre of learning in the Sunni Islamic world. Although now housed in several modern campuses around the country, including a separate faculty for women, the university continues to provide free education and board for Muslim students from all over the world. They come to study the Quran and Islamic law along with other traditional subjects such as grammar, logic and rhetoric.

Since a reorganization of Al-Azhar in 1961, faculties have been formed for the study of medicine, agriculture, engineering and commerce.

Little remains of the original structure of the mosque, which now exhibits a mix of styles from different periods. The double-arched **Gate of the Barbers**, where students traditionally had their heads shaved, dates from the mid-18th century. Visitors now enter through this gate, which leads into an enclosure flanked by two *madrassas* (places of study). Both *madrassas* date to the early part of the 14th century; the one on the left is usually open and is worth visiting to see the beautifully ornate *mihrab* (niche indicating the direction of Mecca).

In the centre of the mosque is the main *sahn* (courtyard), which dates as far back as Fatimid times. Although classes are no longer held here, small circles of students still come to sit in the peace and shade of its

arcades to memorize their Quranic texts, much as they have done for centuries.

Before entering the mosque, women must cover their heads; no admission will be granted to anyone with bare legs.

❺ Beit Zeinab Khatoun and Beit al-Harawi

Harat al-Azhar. **Map** 2 F5. **Tel** (02) 2510 4174. **Open** 9am–5pm daily.

Running between the south wall of Al-Azhar Mosque and a long, low, medieval *wikala*, a narrow alley leads to a small garden square. Projecting into the square on its northern side is Beit Zeinab Khatoun, an Ottoman-era house (*beit*) originally built in 1486 and restored in the 1990s. On the southern side of the square is the restored Beit al-Harawi, built in 1731 as the home of a rich Cairo merchant.

Both houses are beautiful examples of the sophisticated domestic architecture that once filled the city. Beit al-Harawi, in particular, contains some fine *mashrabiyya* (carved wooden screens) and elegant painted ceilings. Built around central courtyards, both houses are designed to stay as cool as possible with their airy rooms, shaded stone floors and interior fountains.

The houses are open to visitors during the day and, since being restored, also operate as cultural centres, where regular performances of music and theatre are staged (*see pp300–3*).

Wooden *mashrabiyya* screen covering the window of Beit Zeinab Khatoun

Tapestry of women, an example of the craft items on sale in the Wikala of al-Ghouri

❻ Wikala of al-Ghouri

Off Sharia al-Azhar. **Map** 2 F5.
Open 8am–5pm daily.

Also known as *khans* or caravanserais, *wikalas* were hostels used by merchants arriving in caravans from North Africa, Arabia and the East. As well as rooms, they provided stables, storage space and a place where merchants could trade. *Wikalas* were typically rectangular in shape with a central courtyard and a main gate that could be locked at night. During the Mamluk era, Cairo's golden age, some of the city's *wikalas* were up to four or five storeys high. Unfortunately, none of these have survived. The finest remaining example is the Wikala of al-Ghouri, which dates from the early

Fine architectural detail at the three-storey Wikala of al-Ghouri

17th century and is three storeys high. It boasts a fine courtyard and beautiful *mashrabiyya* (carved wooden screens) on the upper floors. Parts of the building serve as an arts and crafts centre, with rooms converted into artists' studios and shops. The courtyard is used as a concert hall, theatre and venue for the free whirling-dervish performances that take place on Monday, Wednesday and Saturday nights *(see below).*

❼ Al-Ghouri Complex

Sharia al-Muizz li-Din Allah.
Map 2 F5. **Tel** (012)
2590 3737. Mosque:
Open 9am–midnight
daily. Mausoleum:
Open 9am–5pm daily.
Closed 11:30am–
1:30pm Fri.

Carpenter at work in the Wikala of al-Ghouri

One of the finest buildings in Cairo, the Al-Ghouri Complex is made up of twin, boldly striped black-and-white buildings situated opposite each other across a narrow market street. Dating from 1505, the structure was

constructed by Qansuh al-Ghouri, the last of the powerful Mamluk sultans, who ruled between 1501–16 and died at the hands of the Ottoman Turks. The sultan's body was never recovered from the battlefield and his mausoleum, the building on the east side of the complex, was used for his short-lived successor, Tumanbey. The Al-Ghouri's four beautifully renovated floors and courtyards deserve exploration. The interiors are stunning, although the stairs up to the roof are not for the faint of heart. Opposite the mausoleum, on the west side of the complex, is the Al-Ghouri Mosque and Madrassa offering fine views from its rooftop. Of particular note is the mosque's unique square minaret which is topped by five bulbs. A replica of the 18th-century wooden roof that linked the two buildings re-creates the covered area that once housed the city's silk market.

Whirling Dervishes

Cairo's whirling dervishes are members of the Mawlaiyya sect of Sufis, followers of a semimystical branch of Islam. Sufis were originally associated with poverty and self-denial and wore rough woollen clothes next to their skin – the name Sufi originates from *suf*, the Arabic for wool. Sufis aspire, through meditation, recitation, dance and music, to attain union with God. The whirling dervishes, so called because of their ritual spinning dance, offer a rare glimpse of this otherwise underground phenomenon. The group performs thrice weekly at the Wikala of al-Ghouri. Questions of authenticity aside, the show is a marvellous spectacle. Dancers turn like spinning tops while a line of musicians create a hypnotic pulse, tossing their heads jerkily from side to side. Performances are popular, so it is recommended that you pick up a free ticket at 6:30pm and return for the start at 8:30pm. See p300 for more details.

Whirling dervishes performing their mesmerizing dance ritual

Minarets and Domes

One of the greatest achievements of Cairo's medieval artisans was the decorative carving of stone surfaces, seen at its best on the city's myriad minarets and domes. The craft flourished under the Mamluk dynasty (1250–1517) during which time minarets evolved from short, stubby towers, with little decorative detail, to slender, elegant spires boasting carved balustrades and stalactites. The stone domes of the city's mausoleums are also characteristic of Mamluk architecture, beginning their development in the early 14th century and reaching their zenith in the latter part of the 15th century. Originally small and plain, domes rapidly progressed to vast structures adorned, in the first instance, with a simple rib pattern followed by zigzags and finally explosions of star patterns and floral arabesques. The flourishing of this art form was brought to an abrupt end by the Ottoman invasion.

Minarets

These elegant towers, attached to Cairo's mosques, fall broadly into three categories: the square-based towers of the Fatimid period, the lavish three-tiered spires of the late Mamluk era and the pencil minarets of the Ottoman Turks.

Pepperpot caps adorn these early, square-based minarets.

This external staircase is a unique feature of the Mosque of Ibn Tulun.

Brass crescent

Pear-shaped bulb

A pavilion of eight columns supports a crown of stalactites.

Stalactites or *muqarnas* decorate the transitional area between sections.

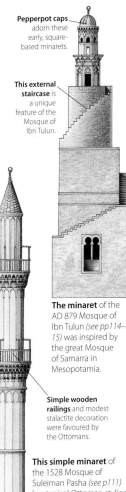

The minaret of the AD 879 Mosque of Ibn Tulun *(see pp114–15)* was inspired by the great Mosque of Samarra in Mesopotamia.

Simple wooden railings and modest stalactite decoration were favoured by the Ottomans.

This three-tiered spire, adorning the Mosque of Qaitbey *(see p106)*, displays the elaborate decorative stonework typical of late Mamluk minarets.

This simple minaret of the 1528 Mosque of Suleiman Pasha *(see p111)* has typical Ottoman styling such as a pointed cap and little decorative detail.

Stone Domes

Developed by the Mamluks, decorating domes became an increasingly sophisticated art form.

The dome of Madrassa Sultaniya (c.1370) in the City of the Dead *(see p107)* has a rib design.

This cupola, in the City of the Dead, illustrates the progression to a more elaborate zigzag pattern.

The dome of the Mosque of Qaitbey (1474) combines geometric and floral designs in its decoration.

Street-by-Street: Fatimid Cairo

Founded by the conquering Fatimid dynasty in AD 969 as
"Al-Qahira" (the Conqueror), Islamic Cairo became the imperial
capital of Egypt. Although they created an extensive royal
quarter of grand palaces and mosques hidden by towering
walls, little remains of the Fatimids' architectural achievements.
Later dynasties recycled the earlier monuments, constructing
their own displays of grandeur, such as the Mamluk complexes
on al-Muizz li-Din Allah and fine Ottoman residences. Today, the
narrow streets of this small quarter serve as a living museum
of medieval architecture.

⓫ Sabil-Kuttab of Abdel Katkhuda
In the centre of what was once Cairo's main street is one of many *sabil-kuttabs* (structures with fountains) in Islamic Cairo.

❽ ★ Bein al-Qasreen
Once the site of two Fatimid palaces, Bein al-Qasreen is now dominated by the minarets of three grand Mamluk complexes.

Madrassa of Sultan Barquq *(see p101)*

Textile Museum

Madrassa and Mausoleum of Sultan an-Nasr Mohammed *(see p100)*

The Madrassa and Mausoleum of Sultan Qalawun is an example of the ambition of Mamluk architecture. As well as the *madrassa* and mausoleum it also houses an ancient hospital *(see p100)*.

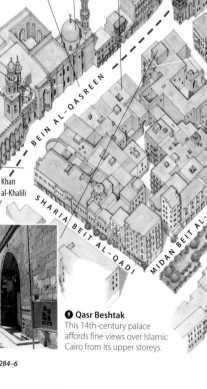

Khan al-Khalili

BEIN AL-QASREEN

SHARIA BEIT AL-QADI

MIDAN BEIT AL-Q

Glass Goods
Locally made "Muski" glassware can be found in the alleys off Sharia al-Muizz li-Din Allah.

❾ Qasr Beshtak
This 14th-century palace affords fine views over Islamic Cairo from its upper storeys.

For hotels and restaurants in this region see pp272–3 and pp284–6

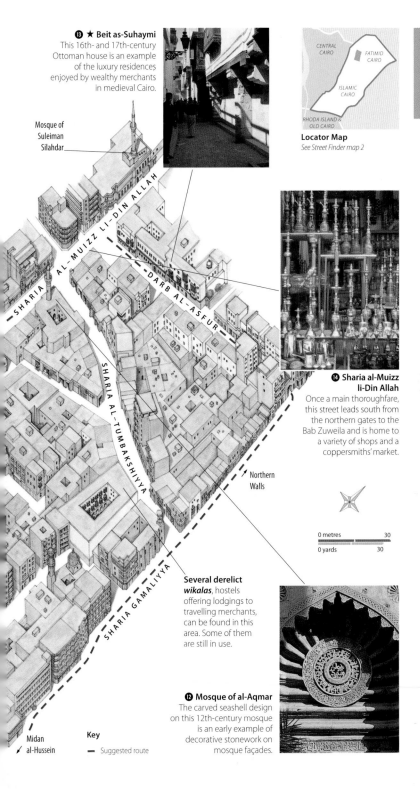

⓭ ★ Beit as-Suhaymi
This 16th- and 17th-century
Ottoman house is an example
of the luxury residences
enjoyed by wealthy merchants
in medieval Cairo.

Mosque of
Suleiman
Silahdar

Locator Map
See Street Finder map 2

CENTRAL
CAIRO

FATIMID
CAIRO

ISLAMIC
CAIRO

RHODA ISLAND &
OLD CAIRO

AL–MUIZZ LI–DIN ALLAH

DARB AL–ASFUR

SHARIA

SHARIA AL–TUMBAKSHIYYA

SHARIA GAMALIYYA

Midan
al-Hussein

Key

— Suggested route

Northern
Walls

**⓮ Sharia al-Muizz
li-Din Allah**
Once a main thoroughfare,
this street leads south from
the northern gates to the
Bab Zuweila and is home to
a variety of shops and a
coppersmiths' market.

0 metres   30
0 yards   30

**Several derelict
wikalas,** hostels
offering lodgings to
travelling merchants,
can be found in this
area. Some of them
are still in use.

⓬ Mosque of al-Aqmar
The carved seashell design
on this 12th-century mosque
is an early example of
decorative stonework on
mosque façades.

Detail of inscription and motifs in the Mausoleum of Sultan Qalawun

❽ Bein al-Qasreen

Sharia al-Muizz li-Din Allah. **Map** 2 F4.

Bein al-Qasreen, which translates as "between the two palaces", is the local name for the stretch of Sharia al-Muizz li-Din Allah that runs immediately to the north of Khan al-Khalili. The name is a testament to the tenacity of history in Cairo, because the two palaces to which it refers ceased to exist more than 600 years ago. Facing each other across a busy public square, the two palaces formed the splendid centrepiece of Al-Qahira (the Victorious), the original Fatimid city, which was founded in AD 969.

Subsequent dynasties replaced them with buildings of their own, but the area was always reserved for only the grandest of building projects.

Today, Bein al-Qasreen is lined on the western side by a sequence of spectacular façades, belonging primarily to three early Mamluk religious complexes. The most southerly is the **Madrassa and Mausoleum of Sultan Qalawun**, which also happens to be the oldest of the three, having been completed in 1279. Three hundred Crusader prisoners took part in its construction, which was completed in only 13 months. The Christian involvement may account for its almost Gothic façade. Inside, a long, dark corridor separates the *madrassa*, on the left, from the mausoleum, on the right. The latter is one of the most spectacular and stunning interiors in Cairo. Inspired by Jerusalem's Dome of the Rock, it has an octagonal arrangement of columns, two pairs of which are massive granite pillars that originated in some Pharaonic structure. The walls are covered in vivid geometric mosaics tracing the name "Mohammed" in florid strokes. Lavish amounts of gold gleam as they are picked out by the coloured rays of sunlight filtering through countless stained-glass windows. Despite the sumptuous restored interior, the complex as a whole receives few visitors, which adds to its charm. Built as part of the complex, set back from the street, is a *maristan* or hospital which treated the sick for free

View across the rooftops to the balconies on the minaret of the Madrassa of Sultan Barquq

and amazingly, over 700 years later, still operates as a clinic.

As you head north, adjoining the Qalawun complex is the lower, less expansive façade of the **Madrassa and Mausoleum of Sultan an-Nasr Mohammed**. It was erected between 1299 and 1304 by a sultan who, despite being deposed twice, fought back to regain the throne on both occasions and reigned for a total of 42 years. During this time, he endowed Cairo with over 200 buildings, the best known of which is his mosque at the Citadel *(see pp108–11)*. Sultan an-Nasr's monument in Bein al-Qasreen has also been restored and now houses a mosque, *madrassa* and tomb. The exterior boasts detailed North African-style stuccowork covering the minaret and the Gothic black-and-white

Naguib Mahfouz

Naguib Mahfouz

The West was introduced to the work of writer Naguib Mahfouz (1911–2006) in 1988, when he won the Nobel Prize for Literature. Mahfouz grew up in the backstreets of Islamic Cairo, and his work was greatly influenced by the neighbourhoods and people of his youth. His best-known work is *The Cairo Trilogy*, a vast work spanning the generations of one family. Each title in the trilogy takes its name from a particular locale: the first, *Bein al-Qasreen*, was translated as *Palace Walk*. The award of the Nobel Prize rekindled opposition to Mahfouz's earlier novel *Children of the Alley*, which caused uproar when serialized in *Al-Ahram* in 1959. In 1994 the author was attacked near his home, receiving injuries that affected his physical ability to write.

Dome and minaret in Bein al-Qasreen

doorway. The latter was removed from a church in Acre (now Akko, Israel) and re-erected in Cairo to mark the final defeat of the Crusaders by the Mamluks in the Holy Land in 1291.

The northernmost building in Bein al-Qasreen is the **Madrassa of Sultan Barquq**, built around 1384–6. While a *madrassa* does not appear to be noticeably different to a mosque on the outside, it is actually a school for teaching Islamic law. Barquq's complex has four doors, each intricately decorated with bronze, leading off the main courtyard to four separate sets of classrooms and student cells – one for each of the schools of Islamic law. The mausoleum, just off the prayer hall, resembles an ornate jewellery box, with marbled walls under a lovely gilded dome. It is not Barquq but rather his daughter who lies here: the sultan is buried in the Northern Cemetery *(see p106)*.

The three complexes that make up Bein al-Qasreen make an excellent break from the hustle and bustle of the market streets all around. They are especially magical after dark, when the lighting is dim and atmospheric.

C **Madrassa and Mausoleum of Sultan Qalawun**
Map 2 F4. **Open** 9am–9pm daily.

C **Madrassa and Mausoleum of Sultan an-Nasr Mohammed**
Map 2 F4. **Open** 9am–9pm daily.

C **Madrassa of Sultan Barquq**
Map 2 F4. **Open** 9am–9pm daily.

9 Qasr Beshtak

Sharia al-Muizz li-Din Allah.
Map 2 F4. **Open** 9am–5pm daily.
Closed 11:30am–1:30pm Fri. 🗺
(includes admission to the Sabil-Kuttab of Abdel Katkhuda, *see p102*).

Qasr Beshtak, or Beshtak Palace, is easy to miss: from the outside it presents just a plain, two-storey façade, decorated with a few small *mashrabiyya* windows. However, a narrow alleyway on the left leads to a courtyard with steps leading up to an impressive reception hall, complete with a marble floor and inlaid panelling.

Beshtak was a powerful emir in the 14th century, a notorious rake who married the sultan's daughter and accrued great wealth and influence. His palace, which was built in 1334, was the sumptuous venue for fabulous balls.

During the Mamluk era, however, great wealth and influence was a dangerously double-edged sword, and so it was almost inevitable that a jealous rival succeeded in having Emir Beshtak arrested and executed, at the same time seizing all his possessions.

From what is now the roof of the palace (but which used to be just the second storey of five), there is an excellent

Mashrabiyya screens on the façade of Qasr Beshtak

panoramic view of Islamic Cairo, looking down Sharia al-Muizz li-Din Allah and over the rooftops to the impressive collection of minarets and domes around the Citadel.

The second-floor chamber (*qaa*), with its *mashrabiyya*-screened galleries, arches, stained-glass windows and gilt-and-painted wood panelling is a fine example of a private chamber of the period.

Recycling History

Since Pharaonic times, the rocky Muqattam Hills to the east of Cairo have been quarried for stone. However, it was often found to be more convenient to use materials from closer to hand – in particular, from other buildings. Throughout history, Cairo has been shaken by earthquakes that have reduced great swathes of the city to rubble. Just as frequently, succeeding dynasties have not been above dismantling the existing monuments and reusing the materials for new ones. The Mausoleum of Qalawun, for example, is supported on red granite pillars of Pharaonic origin, while the Mosque of an-Nasr Mohammed at the Citadel *(see pp108–11)* has a

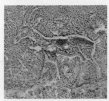

Pharaonic carving on Cairo's Northern Walls

courtyard arcade that is made up of oddments of Roman and Coptic columns and capitals. Most striking of all, though, are the blocks embedded in the interior corridors and rooms of the Northern Walls, which are carved with ancient Egyptian gazelles, hippos and figures – clear evidence of the fact that the stone for these fortifications was scavenged from the ruins of the ancient city of Memphis.

❿ Textile Museum

Sharia al-Muizz li-Din Allah.
Map 2 F4. **Tel** (02) 2786 5227.
Open 9am–4:30pm daily.

Housed within a restored *sabil-kuttab* (a school built around a fountain), this museum presents the 7,000-year-old history of weaving in Egypt. On display are pieces of linen from the time of the pharaohs, including shrouds and the decorated bandages used to wrap mummies. The vibrant designs of the Coptic weaving tradition, whose geometric patterns and floral motifs were incorporated by Islamic artists, are showcased. Immense black and golden woven coverings made for the *kaba'a* in Mecca (the structure at the centre of the mosque), which were produced in Egypt up until the 20th century, are impressive. The museum is, as yet, a relatively undiscovered place and a quiet respite from the hustle of nearby Khan al-Khalili.

⓫ Sabil-Kuttab of Abdel Katkhuda

Sharia al-Muizz li-Din Allah. **Map** 2 F4.
Open 9am–5pm daily. **Closed**
11:30am–1:30pm Fri. (includes
admission to Qasr Beshtak, *see p101*).

Islamic Cairo is dotted with odd-shaped buildings with large windows covered by lacy grilles and what looks like a water trough where the windowsill should be. The *sabil*, or fountain, was kept full of fresh water and copper cups were attached to the grille so that passers-by

Carved stone stalactites between ribbed arches on Mosque of al-Aqmar

could help themselves to a drink. Wealthy warlords and nobles would build a *sabil* to curry favour with both the city populace and their god above.

On an upper floor was often a terrace open to the breezes on three sides, which was set aside for the teaching of the Quran and known as a *kuttab*. Thus a *sabil-kuttab* provided two things commended by the Prophet Mohammed – water for the thirsty and spiritual enlightenment for the ignorant.

Built in 1744, this structure has been carefully renovated. Faïence tiles depicting Mecca adorn the lower floor, while the upper floor is decorated with carved wooden pillars and beams. The exterior of the building has some fine "joggling" – panels of different coloured blocks of marble fitted together like a jigsaw.

⓬ Mosque of al-Aqmar

Sharia al-Muizz li-Din Allah.
Map 2 F4. **Open** daily.
Closed 11:30am–1:30pm Fri.

The name of the Mosque of al-Aqmar (the Moonlit Mosque) was supposedly inspired by the luminous quality of its grey stone. These days, coated in centuries of Cairo grime, the mosque does anything but shine. Nevertheless it is an architectural gem.

The mosque was built in 1125 by one of the last Fatimid caliphs, and is the oldest stone-built mosque in Egypt (earlier buildings were made of brick faced with plaster). The layout of the mosque is interesting as it uses an outer wall of varying thickness to realign the interior, reconciling the conflicting geometry imposed by the street plan and the direction of Mecca. The façade also displays the earliest use of decorative features that were later to become popular under the Mamluks, such as the sculpted stone "stalactites" (*muqarnas*) and carved ribbing in the hooded arch.

⓭ Beit as-Suhaymi

19 Darb al-Asfar, off Sharia al-Muizz
li-Din Allah. **Map** 2 F4.
Open 9am–5pm daily.
Closed 11:30am–1:30pm Fri.

Beit as-Suhaymi is really two houses, one built in 1648 and the other in 1796, joined to create a structure of almost palatial proportions. Its traditional design means entry is gained through a right-angled passage (which ensured complete privacy) into a central courtyard. Originally this would have had been filled with copious greenery ranged around a fountain.

The rooms on the ground floor comprise the *salamlek*, an area reserved for men; those on the upper floor form part of the *haramlek*, for women and the family. Here, the effect of the stained glass and painted ceilings combined with the dappled light from the *mashrabiyya*-covered windows is entrancing. These large wooden screens overlook the courtyard, filtering sunlight and cool breezes inside as well as allowing the women to observe the goings-on below without themselves being seen.

"Joggling" on southern facing arch of Sabil-Kuttab of Abdel Katkhuda

For hotels and restaurants in this region see pp272–3 and pp284–6

Stalls setting up along Sharia al-Muizz li-Din Allah

Some of the restored decoration is sumptuous, particularly in the ground floor *qaa* or reception room, which features intricate paintwork and a polychrome marble fountain set into the floor. The Beit hosts free concerts every Sunday at 8pm.

Shisha pipe manufacturer on Sharia al-Muizz li-Din Allah

⓮ Sharia al-Muizz li-Din Allah

Map 2 F5.

Al-Muizz li-Din Allah was the Fatimid caliph who conquered Cairo in AD 969. This street was the former main thoroughfare of medieval times, entering the city through the southern gate of Bab Zuweila and exiting out of Bab al-Futuh to the north. Over the centuries, buildings have encroached on its width and it is no longer very grand, but it is still vital and busy. Lined with stalls, at Khan al-Khalili it is home to the coppersmiths' market and an assortment of workshops. Further along are shops selling a miscellany of coffee-house equipment such as tin-topped tables and *shishas*.

⓯ Mosque of al-Hakim

Sharia al-Muizz li-Din Allah.
Map 2 F4. **Open** daily.
Closed 11:30am–1:30pm Fri.

Al-Hakim, the third Fatimid caliph (997–1021), was one of the most notorious rulers in Egyptian history. He ruled from the age of 11 and had his tutor murdered when he was 15. Infamous for his bizarre laws and arbitrary acts of violence, he proceeded to burn areas of Cairo when people objected to the substitution of his name for Allah at Friday prayers. He was also a virulent misogynist and banned the manufacture of women's shoes in order to keep them indoors.

The mosque that bears his name was actually started by his father, but completed by Hakim in 1013. Since that time it has been variously used as a prison for captured Crusaders, a stable by Salah ad-Din, a warehouse by Napoleon and a boys' school. After a somewhat heavy-handed restoration during the 1980s, it gleams with polished marble and glitzy golden chandeliers. The minarets are the only original features of the mosque.

⓰ Northern Walls and Gates

Sharia al-Galal. **Map** 2 F4. **Open** daily.
Closed 11:30am–1:30pm Fri.

The medieval city of Cairo was completely walled with at least 10 huge gateways, but only a short northern section of the ramparts and two gates now remain, as well as one other gate to the south, Bab Zuweila (*see p107*). The two northern gates, the square-towered Bab an-Nasr (Gate of Victory) and the rounded Bab al-Futuh (Gate of Conquests), were built in 1087 and later strengthened by Salah ad-Din.

Steps in the gate towers lead into a vaulted corridor running the whole length of the wall, through which mounted guards could ride. The passage is lit by daylight filtering through arrow slits. These were widened to accommodate cannons in 1789 when Napoleon garrisoned troops within the walls. Evidence of their stay remains in the names the French gave to the towers, which they painted over the doorways.

Unique style of minaret at the Mosque of al-Hakim

Intricate Mamluk designs on the Mosque of Qaitbey's minaret, Northern Cemetery

⑰ Northern Cemetery

East of Sharia Salah Salem.
🚇 🚌 102, 103 from Midan Tahrir.

On the edge of the city, across the six-lane Salah Salem highway, the Northern Cemetery (al-Qarafah) is not only a place of burial, but also home to the living. While several magnificent funerary complexes dominate the area, a lot of the more modest, low-rise tombs double as family homes.

By the end of the 14th century, Cairo's population may have numbered 500,000, making it the largest urban centre in the world. Land was at a premium, so the Mamluk sultans looked beyond the city walls for the building space to match their egos. The great mausoleums they built here rank as some of their finest achievements. Best of these is the **Mosque of Qaitbey**, completed in 1474. A beautifully proportioned structure, with a simple but dazzling sunlight-infused interior, it is topped by the most elegant of minarets and intricate carved stone domes. The Qaitbey mosque features on the Egyptian one pound note.

Further south, down the sandy main street, a stone wall encloses the **Complex of Sultan Ashraf Barsbey**. Much of this has been lost over the centuries but the central mosque remains, topped by a beautiful dome carved with interlocking stars. If the door is unlocked,

it is worth looking at the fine marble floor and the ivory-inlaid *minbar*.

Further north lies the fortress-like bulk of the **Mausoleum of Ibn Barquq**. This was built by the son of the Barquq whose complex sits on Bein al-Qasreen *(see p100)*. The building is quite unique in being perfectly symmetrical with two domes and two minarets. It served as a *khanqah*, a monastery for Islamic mystics called Sufis *(see p96)*, and has rows of small cells ranged around the courtyard. Beneath the twin domes are tomb chambers, one for the women, one for the men, with bright, painted ceilings. It is possible to get up onto the roof and climb the minarets.

The best route to the cemetery is to walk east for 10 minutes along Sharia al-Azhar from the Khan al-Khalili area.

C Mosque of Qaitbey
Sharia Sultan Qaitbey. **Map** 4 D2. **Open** daily. **Closed** 11:30am–1:30pm Fri.

C Complex of Sultan Ashraf Barsbey
Sharia Sultan Qaitbey. **Map** 4 D2. **Open** daily. **Closed** 11:30am–1:30pm Fri.

C Mausoleum of Ibn Barquq
Sharia Sultan Qaitbey. **Map** 4 D2. **Open** daily. **Closed** 11:30am–1:30pm Fri. 🖼

⑱ Carpet Bazaar

Sharia al-Muizz li-Din Allah. **Map** 6 F3.

Khan al-Khalili's markets continue south of Sharia al-Azhar, where tourist trinkets give way to items that the locals might want to buy. The alleyways east of the Al-Ghouri Complex *(see p96)* are home to the Carpet Bazaar. Here, rugs of coarse wool or camel hair are sold, either striped in varying shades of beige and brown, or featuring colourful, stylized images of birds, camels and country scenes.

Back on Sharia al-Muizz li-Din Allah, just south of the Al-Ghouri Complex, are two *tarboush*

Northern Cemetery, including dome of Sultan Ashraf Barsbey Mosque

◀ Interior of the Mohammed Ali Mosque in the Citadel

workshops, making the hat better known in the West as a fez. Once common streetwear, they are now a parody of their former elegant self, sported only by a few waiters and restaurant staff.

Courtyard of Mosque of Sultan al-Muayyad, by Bab Zuweila

⑲ Bab Zuweila

Sharia Ahmed Mahir. **Map** 6 F4. **Open** 8:30am–5pm daily.

Bab Zuweila is the sole remaining southern gate of the city walls of Fatimid Cairo. It was built in the late 11th century. In Mamluk times, it was from the platform of Bab Zuweila that the sultan would watch the start of the annual pilgrimage to Mecca. This was also the site of executions, and the heads of criminals were displayed on top of the walls. This bloody habit persisted until the 1800s: after the 1811 Citadel massacre (*see p63*), the heads of the slain Mamluks were mounted on spikes here.

The towering minarets that soar over the gate were added when the adjacent **Mosque of Sultan al-Muayyad** was built in 1415. It is possible to climb the minarets for one of the best views of the city.

Across the entrance to Bab Zuweila is the Sabil-Kuttab Nafisa al-Bayda, a splendid building that combines a water dispensary with a school for orphans.

C Mosque of Sultan al-Muayyad
Sharia Ahmed Mahir. **Map** 6 F4. **Open** daily. **Closed** 11:30am–1:30pm Fri.

⑳ Mosque of as-Salih Talai

Sharia Ahmed Mahir. **Map** 6 F4. **Open** daily. **Closed** 11:30am–1:30pm Fri.

The last of the Fatimid mosques of Cairo, the Mosque of as-Salih Talai was built in 1160. It was the first mosque to be built on an upper storey, resting on top of a layer of shop units. However, over the centuries, through the gradual accumulation of rubbish and dirt, the street level has risen by some 3 m (10 ft), so the mosque is now at ground level and the shops are in the basement.

The façade has five pointed arches, while the interior reveals columns with florid capitals taken from pre-Islamic sites. The prayer hall walls are decorated with superb stained-glass windows. The mosque also features a splendid *minbar* (pulpit), which was donated in 1300 by Amir Baktimur al-Jugandar.

㉑ Tentmakers' Market

Sharia al-Khaimiyya. **Map** 6 F4.

Leaving the Fatimid city via Bab Zuweila, the old main street runs south, passing through a venerable covered market known in Arabic as Sharia al-Khaimiyya, or the Street of the Tentmakers. This covered market was built in 1650 by Radwan Bey, who was in charge of the annual pilgrimage to Mecca. It is here that at one time a huddle of small workshops produced the brightly coloured printed fabrics that adorned the caravans bound for Mecca. Similar decorative material is now used in the large pavilions frequently seen around Cairo. These are erected for events such as weddings and funerals and the opening of new businesses. Huge rolls of the mainly blue or orange cloth are sold at the small, open-fronted kiosks that line the dimly lit street. These places also stitch detailed appliqué work, usually in workshops nearby.

Appliqué motif from the Tentmakers' Market

Living with the Dead

Death has always been a significant part of Egyptian life. Even when the country abandoned Pharaonic beliefs, becoming first Coptic and then Islamic, practices such as visiting the dead were maintained. Most family tombs included a room where visitors could eat and rest and even stay overnight. Inevitably, the city's homeless took to occupying these tombs, some as early as the 14th century. Today, the Northern (and Southern) Cemeteries contain a mixure of tombs and homes, as well as tombs that are homes, where the living and the dead coexist side by side.

Children playing among the tombs in the Northern Cemetery, sometimes known as the "City of the Dead"

㉒ The Citadel

Home to Egypt's rulers for almost 700 years, the Citadel (Al-Qalaa) is today one of the most popular tourist sites in Cairo. Originally founded in 1176 by the famed Muslim commander Salah ad-Din (also known as Saladin), its mosques, museums and battlements reflect a diverse heritage. The Citadel's main tourist area is in the Southern Enclosure, where the Mosque of an-Nasr Mohammed (the Citadel's only surviving Mamluk structure) is dwarfed by the 19th-century Mosque of Mohammed Ali. The upper terraces of the Citadel offer spectacular views over the city.

Police Museum
Entered via a mock-Gothic gateway, the museum traces the gory history of Egyptian crime and punishment.

Mosque of an-Nasr Mohammed
The Persian-style tiling on the minarets is unique in Egypt.

★ Mohammed Ali Mosque
Built in a wholly Turkish style between 1830 and 1848, this mosque has nevertheless become a symbol of Cairo.

KEY

① **Southern Enclosure**

② **Qasr al-Gawhara**, also called the Jewelled Palace, is a museum depicting the court life of Mohammed Ali. It is currently closed for renovation.

③ **Lower Enclosure**

④ **Bab al-Azab** (1754) was built in the Ottoman period as the new main gate.

⑤ **Bab al-Gadid**

⑥ **The statue of Ibrahim Pasha** is a replica of the one in Midan Opera (see p82).

⑦ **Northern Enclosure**

⑧ **The upper ramparts**, entered at ground level, can be explored, offering views across the Citadel.

⑨ **Sand Tower**

⑩ **The Garden Museum** contains monuments and statues.

★ Views over Cairo
Superb views of the city's minarets and domes are afforded from the Citadel's fortifications. In the foreground here is the Mosque of Sultan Hassan.

For hotels and restaurants in this region see pp272–3 and pp284–6

The Hippodrome

Now a large roundabout known as Midan Salah ad-Din, the area to the west of the Citadel walls was once the Hippodrome, an important site in medieval Cairo. Created by An-Nasr Mohammed as a cavalry training ground, this was where the Mamluks – renowned for their feats of horsemanship – practised complex military manoeuvres. Equestrian games were also frequently held here, including horse racing and polo.

19th-century engraving of Bab al-Azab and the Hippodrome area

VISITORS' CHECKLIST

Practical Information
Sharia Salah Salem.
Map 4 F2. **Tel** (02) 2512 1735.
Open summer: 8am–4:30pm daily (Military Museum closes at 4pm).

Transport
🚌 🚇

★ **Mosque of Suleiman Pasha**
Dating from 1528, this beautiful mosque has a cluster of domes and brightly painted interior woodwork, which has been restored.

Bab al-Gebel
(entrance)

Military Museum
Once the Harem Palace of Mohammed Ali, the museum has displays of weapons, uniforms and decorations, and a scale model of the Citadel.

Exploring the Citadel

Although its main attraction is the Mohammed Ali Mosque, the Citadel has a great many other features worthy of attention. This fortified complex serves as a museum of Islamic architecture, with numerous fine examples of Mamluk and Ottoman-era mosques and fortifications from the time of Salah ad-Din (1171–91). With four separate museums also enclosed within its walls, a visit to the Citadel can occupy the best part of a day. Visitors should be aware that certain parts of the complex are out of bounds, notably the lower enclosure leading down to the Bab al-Azab gate.

Detail of a water fountain in the Mosque of Mohammed Ali

◖ Mosque of Mohammed Ali

Dominating the eastern Cairo skyline, the Mohammed Ali Mosque is a relative newcomer, having been constructed as recently as the mid-19th century. It was erected on the orders of the reformist ruler Mohammed Ali, who is regarded as the founder of modern Egypt. When he came to power in 1805, Egypt was a backwater province of the Ottoman empire. By the time of his death in 1849, however, the country was once again a regional superpower.

Mohammed Ali's imposing mosque was a grand gesture that was meant to echo the great imperial mosques of the Ottoman capital. It is modelled along classic Turkish lines, with a great central dome and two towering, yet slender, minarets. The ornate clock in the courtyard near the entrance to the mosque was a gift from King Louis-Philippe of France, in exchange for the obelisk in the Place de la Concorde in Paris.

The clock was damaged on delivery and has yet to be repaired. Mohammed Ali's body lies in a marble tomb to the right on entering the vast space of the prayer hall.

◖ Mosque of an-Nasr Mohammed

When Mohammed Ali came to power, the greatest threat to his authority came from the Mamluks, former overlords of Egypt who were still a force to be reckoned with. In addition to his infamous massacre of 500 Mamluks at the Citadel in 1811 (see p63), Mohammed Ali ordered all the Mamluk structures in the Citadel to be destroyed. This one mosque survived because it had been put to use as a stable.

Situated just behind the Mosque of Mohammed Ali, this simple structure is all that remains of a massive building programme undertaken by Sultan an-Nasr Mohammed (1294–1340), whose madrassa and mausoleum stand on Bein

Arcaded courtyard of the Mosque of an-Nasr Mohammed

al-Qasreen (see p100). Built between 1318 and 1335 as a congregational mosque, where everyone gathered to pray, the building has two unique, corkscrew minarets with bulbous finials, covered with faïence tiles in a fashion more Persian than Egyptian.

There are two entrances to the mosque: one is in the form of a three-lobed arch and was used by soldiers, while the other arch was used exclusively by the sultan.

Although many of the columns within the arcaded courtyard were salvaged from Pharaonic, Roman and Byzantine buildings, they nevertheless blend together surprisingly well.

The marble panelling that once graced the mosque's courtyard was removed by Sultan Selim I in 1517 and sent to Constantinople.

A view of the Mosque of Mohammed Ali, within the Citadel walls

Mihrab (prayer niche) and *minbar* (pulpit) in Mosque of an-Nasr Mohammed

Police Museum
Built on top of the former Mamluk-era Lion's Tower – so-called because of the statues of big cats at the base of the building – this small museum illustrates the history of Egyptian policing through the ages. Exhibits include uniforms and weapons, a small display on political assassinations and accounts of infamous Egyptian criminals, including Raya and Sakina *(see box, below)*. Included in the museum is the small row of cells that were in use as recently as 1983. Among their last inhabitants were President Sadat's assassins, held here while awaiting trial in 1981. The museum terrace offers some of the best views over the city.

Statue of a lion at the entrance of the Police Museum

Military Museum
Built by Mohammed Ali in 1827, this was the residence of the Egyptian royal family until 1874, when Khedive Ismail moved into the newly built Abdeen Palace *(see p83)*.

The building served as a military hospital during British occupation in World War II but it became a military museum when control of the Citadel reverted to Egypt in 1946.

Displays include uniforms, weaponry and dioramas of battles. Some of the palatial interiors are impressive, especially the superb *trompe l'oeil* in the main salon.

Mosque of Suleiman Pasha
This mosque was built in 1528 by Suleiman Pasha, who ruled Cairo after the Turks defeated the Mamluks in 1517. It was the first of many Ottoman mosques to be built in Egypt and, though modest in scale, it is one of the most charming. On the underside of the domes is some exquisitely painted decoration inspired by Turkish tiling. There are also some fine examples of traditional inlaid marblework. In the mosque is a small mausoleum with tombs marked by turban-like headstones. These mark the burial places of Ottoman military officers, who were known as Janissaries.

Towers, Gates and Walls
Punctuated by towers and gates, the Citadel walls extend for over 3 km (2 miles). The former main gate, the Bab al-Azab, has been closed for decades and entrance is now through the Bab al-Gebel (Mountain Gate), created in 1786. The enormous vaulted portal of the Bab Al-Gadid (New Gate) was built in 1826 by Mohammed Ali.

The oldest parts of the walls are those around the northern enclosure. Fortifications here date back to the Ayyubid era. Salah ad-Din built the original walls and all the small half-round towers (1171–93). These were strengthened in the early 13th century by his successors, who also added most of the larger towers. It is possible to visit the interiors of Salah ad-Din's two easternmost towers, Burg al-Haddad and Burg al-Ramla.

Other Museums
Al-Gawhara Palace was built by Mohammed Ali in 1814 to house his administration and as a place to receive guests. The former Audience Hall now serves as a museum and is crammed with furniture, portraits and life-size models of Mohammed Ali and other monarchs and their courtiers. The **Seized Museum**, which is currently closed, contains stolen Pharaonic, Coptic and Islamic works of art which were retrieved from dealers on the black market.

Raya and Sakina – Sisters in Notoriety
Egypt's most infamous criminals, sisters Raya and Sakina, were tried and hanged in 1921 for the murders of 17 young women. The sisters lived in the poorest quarter of Alexandria where, with the connivance of their husbands, they ran a string of brothels. Their victims were picked up in the marketplace, lured back to one of their houses and strangled. The motive was money: only girls wearing expensive-looking jewellery were selected. The eventual arrest of Raya and Sakina occurred after a policeman became suspicious of the strong smell of incense emanating from Raya's home. He ordered a search that led to the discovery of the corpses. Since then, the grisly murders have provided lasting inspiration for writers, dramatists and film-makers, and Raya and Sakina have become part of popular Egyptian mythology.

Raya   Sakina

Mosque of Sultan Hassan (*left*) and Mosque of ar-Rifai (*right*) seen from the Citadel

❷❸ Mosque of Sultan Hassan

Midan Salah ad-Din. **Map** 4 E2.
Open 8am–4:30pm daily.
Closed 11:30am–1:30pm Fri.

One of the most interesting of the capital's mosques, this is also Cairo's finest example of early Mamluk architecture. The mosque overlooks what were the fields of the Hippodrome (now Midan Salah ad-Din), across from the precipitous walls of the Citadel. The dimensions of this massive structure are truly staggering: 150 m (492 ft) long, with walls 36 m (118 ft) high, the tallest minaret rising to 68 m (223 ft).

The construction of the mosque was funded with money from the estates of people who had died in the Black Death (which struck Cairo in 1348). This policy increased the unpopularity of the sultan, An-Nasr Hassan, who was already renowned for his greed. Building work began in 1356 and five years later, in 1361, one of the minarets collapsed, killing hundreds of people. By the end of 1361, two years before his mosque was completed, Hassan had been murdered. Despite the unhappy history of Hassan's grand monument, the interior of the mosque is overwhelming. Through a magnificent portal, a

dimly lit corridor leads to a high-walled central courtyard. On the four sides of the courtyard are great, recessed arches, known as *iwans*, which were formerly used for teaching. Each *iwan* was devoted to one of the main schools of Sunni Islam.

At the rear of the eastern *iwan*, situated to the right of a particularly beautiful *mihrab* or niche, a bronze door leads to the mausoleum. The largest in Cairo, it was never occupied by the sultan, whose body was not recovered. However, the mausoleum was used for the burial of two of his sons. Tickets for the mosque are sold at a kiosk outside. The exterior gates are locked outside of visiting hours.

Detail of wall and steps from the Mosque of Sultan Hassan

❷❹ Mosque of ar-Rifai

Midan Salah ad-Din. **Map** 4 E2.
Open 8am–4:30pm daily.
Closed 11:30am–1:30pm Fri.

Separated from the Mosque of Sultan Hassan by a pedestrian street, the Mosque of ar-Rifai has a similar scale and symmetry but 450 years separate them.

Founded in 1819, this mosque was not completed until 1912. Its patron was Princess Khushyar, mother of the Europhile Khedive Ismail, who intended the mosque as a tomb for her family. Built in a pseudo-Mamluk style, with decoration copied from existing period mosques, the result is rather clumsy compared with the Mosque of Sultan Hassan. The overwrought interior is filled with glitzy tombs of members of the royal family, including Farouk, the last king of Egypt. Also buried here is the last shah of Iran, who found refuge in Egypt after fleeing Khomeini's Islamic revolution in 1979.

Directly in front of the mosque is the **Mosque of Amir Akhur**, a building distinguished by its *ablaq* banding of red and white stone, its imposing dome and double minaret finial.

❻ Mosque of Amir Akhur
Midan Salah ad-Din. **Map** 4 F2. **Open** daily. **Closed** 11:30am–1:30pm Fri.

㉕ Dervish Theatre

Sharia as-Suyufiya. **Map** 4 E2.
Open daily.

In the gardens behind the Mosque of Hassan Sadaqa (also known as Sunqur Sadi) is a restored 19th-century theatre. It is accessed from a small courtyard garden, which is reached via a door on the right of the façade of the mosque, in Sharia as-Suyufiya. Its circular, polished-wood stage is surrounded by a two-storey gallery. The theatre was built by an order of Mevlevi dervishes, who extended the complex to include a hostel (*khanqah*). The dervishes (*see p96*) are Sufis, who follow a spiritual offshoot of Islam, and who believe that their whirling dance leads to oneness with Allah. From the theatre, you can go down into the beautiful mausoleum containing the tomb of Hassan Sadaqa, for whom the mosque was built.

Part of a complex dating from 1321, the Mosque of Hassan Sadaqa is distiguished by fine stuccowork on its minaret and dome, visible from the street. The complex originally included a monastery (*ribat*), which was replaced by the theatre.

⌂ Mosque of Hassan Sadaqa
Sharia as-Suyufiya. **Map** 4 E2. **Open** daily. **Closed** 11:30am–1:30pm Fri.

Al-Azhar Park with the mosque of Muhammad Ali Pasha in the background

㉖ Sabil-Kuttab of Qaitbey

Sharia as-Saliba. **Map** 4 E2.

Just 200 m (650 ft) west of Midan Salah ad-Din, at the western end of Sharia as-Saliba, is the huge, block-like structure of the 15th-century Sabil-Kuttab of Qaitbey. Now restored and in use as a library, this old Quranic school is notable for the fine marble inlay on its western façade.

Qaitbey was a ruthless sultan who started life as a slave-boy to the previous sultan. He built some of Cairo's most beautiful monuments, including his spectacular mosque in the Northern Cemetery (*see p106*).

Further west, Sharia as-Saliba passes between the **Mosque of Sheikhu** on the right and the **Khanqah of Sheikhu** on the left. These 14th-century buildings are still in use. A *khanqah* is a Sufi hostel, where the sheikh resides, teaching his disciples.

Also on Sharia as-Saliba, a short walk straight ahead takes you to Midan Sayyida Zeinab – a good place to get a taxi back to the centre.

⌂ Mosque and Khanqah of Sheikhu
Sharia as-Saliba. **Map** 4 E2. **Open** daily. **Closed** 11:30am–1:30pm Fri.

㉗ Mosque of Ibn Tulun

See pp114–15.

㉘ Al-Azhar Park

Sharia Salah Salem. **Map** 2 F5. **Tel** (02) 2510 3868. **Open** 9am–10pm daily.

Providing panoramic views of Islamic Cairo from its lush, landscaped gardens, this park was created by the Aga Khan Trust for Culture. Once a derelict mound of rubble between the eastern edge of the 12th-century Ayyubid city and the 15th-century Mamluk "City of the Dead", Al-Azhar Park now has orchards, cultural venues and restaurants. An Ayyubid city wall, built by Salah ad-Din in the 12th century and discovered as work on the park began, is undergoing excavations.

Decorative Mamluk Motifs

The buildings created between 1250 and 1517, in the time of the Mamluk sultans, represent the pinnacle of Islamic art in Egypt. A fusion of the building traditions of the Near East, they blend Armenian stonework with North African stucco, Byzantine golden mosaics and Syrian polychrome marble inlays. It is the last that provide the most striking element. Created by painstakingly cutting small pieces of different coloured stone and fitting them together like a jigsaw puzzle, the intricate ornamentation forms incredibly complex geometric patterns that are completely abstract in character. Repetitive and hypnotic, it has been suggested that the complex decoration aided prayer by heightening the viewers' sensory experience.

Detail of the marble inlay on the Sabil-Kuttab of Qaitbey

㉗ Mosque of Ibn Tulun

One of the largest and oldest mosques in the country, Ibn Tulun was built between AD 876 and AD 879 by an Abbasid governor sent from Baghdad to rule Egypt. It is called a "Friday Mosque", becasue its open-air courtyard is large enough to hold the whole male congregation of the district for prayers on the holiest day of the week. Built entirely of mudbrick, the mosque is surrounded by an outer courtyard, which was meant to act like a moat and keep the secular city at bay. This, and its curious spiral minaret, make it unique in Egypt. Contrasting with the geometric simplicity of the mosque, the maze of rooms in the adjacent Gayer-Anderson House is filled with a diverting collection of artifacts.

★ Mihrab
A niche indicating the direction of Mecca, this *mihrab* dates back to the 13th century. Next to it is the *minbar*, or pulpit, one of the finest in Egypt.

Lectern
Called a *dikka* in Arabic, the wooden platform, in line with the *mihrab*, is used for Quranic recitations and calls to prayer inside the mosque.

Entrance

KEY

① **Outer courtyard**

② **Gayer-Anderson House**

③ **Inner courtyard or *sahn***

④ **Pointed arches** are inscribed with geometric designs.

⑤ **The windows** have ornately decorated stucco grilles, no two of which are the same.

⑥ **Outside staircase**

Arcades
Running around the courtyard, the arcades (*riwaq*) provide shade for worshippers. The largest, on the southeast side, is five columns deep and serves as the mosque's prayer hall. Quranic verses are inscribed along the whole length of the ceiling in the arcade.

Gayer-Anderson House

This charming museum is the legacy of John Gayer-Anderson, a British officer serving in Cairo. In the 1930s, he lovingly restored two adjacent 16th- or 17th-century houses. Lavishly decorated with *mashrabiyya* screens and marble inlays, they were further ornamented by a vast amount of interesting and often intriguing orientalia. He also added a room, decorated in lacquer and gold, taken from a 17th-century house in Damascus. The cumulative effect of all these items makes the museum one of the most magical places to visit in Cairo.

Reproduction bust of Nefertiti

★ **Fountain**
The original had a beautiful gilded dome but this collapsed in AD 968. The current dome is a 13th-century replacement.

★ **Ziggurat Minaret**
Inspired by the tower at the Great Mosque of Samarra in Iraq, Ibn Tulun's minaret is an easy climb, rewarded by excellent views of the city.

Crenellations
The design of these brick-built crenellations is supposed to have been inspired by ranks of standing soldiers.

RHODA ISLAND AND OLD CAIRO

For several centuries following the decline of the old Pharaonic religions and before the arrival of Islam, Egypt was a predominantly Christian country. Alexandria was then the country's capital, while Cairo had yet to be founded. Around the 6th century AD the site of the city consisted of little more than a Roman fortress beside the Nile, guarding a crossing point on the route between the ancient Egyptian cities of Heliopolis and Memphis. When Arab general Amr ibn al-Aas set up camp in its shadow and built a capital nearby, he was placing the marker for the future foundation of Cairo. Known today as Old Cairo (Misr al-Qadima), this ancient part of the city contains a bastion of Egyptian Christianity, known as Coptic Cairo, and many historic churches. The area also takes in the southern tip of the island of Rhoda, site of the Nilometer which has been used to measure the height of the river Nile since Pharaonic times.

Sights at a Glance

Holy Places
1 Greek Orthodox Church of St George
3 Ben Ezra Synagogue
4 Church of St Barbara
5 Church of St Sergius and St Bacchus
6 Coptic Convent of St George
7 Hanging Church

9 Mosque of Amr ibn al-Aas
10 Monastery of St Mercurius
11 Tomb of Suleiman al-Faransawi

Archaeological Sites
8 Fustat

Museums & Historic Buildings
2 Coptic Museum
12 Nilometer

0 metres 500
0 yards 500

See also Street Finder map 3

Street by Street: Coptic Cairo

Coptic Cairo is the modern name for the oldest part of the city. The compound lies within the walls of the 3rd-century AD Roman fortress of Babylon and is a haven of quiet, narrow lanes and ancient holy places. Separate entrances, leading to the Coptic Museum and the Hanging Church, are located between two round Roman towers, against which the Nile once lapped before it shifted course. A third, stepped entrance to the north leads along a sunken alley to the rest of the churches, the synagogue and the cemeteries. Conservation work is ongoing in various locations across Coptic Cairo.

❻ Coptic Convent of St George
While not allowed inside, visitors can re-enact the persecution of Palestinian St George, famed for his dragon slaying, and be wrapped in chains.

❶ Greek Orthodox Church of St George
Coptic Cairo is also home to some other significant Christian sights. The Greek Orthodox Church of St George is built upon the Northern Roman Tower and is flanked by a cemetery.

Subterranean entrance to compound

Entrance to Coptic Museum

SHARIA MAR GIRGIS

Mari Girgis Station Ⓜ

Old Roman Tower

Entrance to Hanging Church

❷ ★ Coptic Museum
Artifacts here trace the origins of Christian art in the Near East. The building itself is beautiful, especially the older, southern wing. There is also a lovely garden and a small café.

❼ ★ Hanging Church
This most beautiful of Cairo's churches has an ornately decorated interior consisting of three barrel-vaulted, wooden-roofed aisles, ivory inlaid screens and a finely carved marble pulpit.

Key
▨ Built-up area
▨ Roman wall
— Railway line
— Suggested route

For hotels and restaurants in this region see pp272–3 and pp284–6

❹ Church of St Barbara
Dedicated to the saint who was beaten to death by her father for trying to convert him to Christianity, St Barbara's is one of Egypt's largest and finest churches. There is a domed apse behind the altar with seven steps decorated in bands of black, white and red marble.

Locator Map
See Street Finder map 3

0 metres 50
0 yards 50

Coptic Cemetery

The Nuptial Hall was part of a church first founded in AD 681.

ır Ibn
-Aas
osque

❸ Ben Ezra Synagogue
This is Egypt's oldest synagogue and it has been heavily restored. Ben Ezra is a testament to the ancient and significant presence of Jews in this region.

❺ Church of St Sergius and St Bacchus
Since this, the oldest church in Coptic Cairo, was built, ground levels have risen. It is now entered down a flight of steps. Legend says that the Holy Family sheltered in a cave below the altar.

Cemeteries
The cemeteries around the compound belong to the Coptic, Greek Orthodox and Catholic communities. They are filled with impressive statues and elaborate mausoleums, such as this one.

Catholic Cemetery

For keys to symbols *see back flap*

A 7th-century painting in the Coptic Museum depicting the Virgin Mary and the infant Jesus flanked by apostles

❶ Greek Orthodox Church of St George

Coptic Cairo compound. **Map** 3 B5.
Ⓜ Mar Girgis. **Open** 9am–4pm daily.

Long before the Crusaders carried tales of his legendary exploits back to Europe, St George was venerated throughout the Christian Middle East as Mar Girgis. He is said to have been a Roman legionary who defied a decree by the Emperor Diocletian outlawing the worship of Christ and was martyred for his beliefs in the 3rd century.

There has been a church dedicated to St George on or near the site since at least the 10th century, but today's striking round structure dates only to the beginning of the

Worshippers attending church in Coptic Cairo

20th century. The circular form of the church echoes the shape of the 1st century AD Roman gate tower on top of which it was built. Follow the sign to the small Church of the Sleeping Mary; below is a crypt dedicated to the Holy Family who reputedly sheltered there.

❷ Coptic Museum

Coptic Cairo compound. **Map** 3 B5.
Ⓜ Mar Girgis. **Tel** (02) 2362 8766.
Open 9am–4pm daily.

Largely built in 1947, this charming museum houses the finest collection of Coptic art in the world. The building itself has undergone extensive renovation since suffering earthquake damage in 1992, and boasts elaborately painted wooden ceilings, elegant *mashrabiyya* windows and a garden courtyard.

The exhibits date back to Egypt's Christian era and both Pharaonic and Islamic influences are evident in the artifacts on display. Early exhibits carry motifs and symbols, such as *ankhs* and Horus-like falcons, that are recognizably ancient Egyptian. Elsewhere, carved capitals from an early Coptic cathedral in Alexandria display a mastery of stone carving that would later come to fruition during the era of the Mamluks. A 6th-century Coptic stone pulpit resembles the stairs and shrine

of the pyramid complex at Saqqara (see pp166–8), and also prefigures the *minbars* found in all Cairo mosques. Still more fascinating are the crudely painted depictions of Mary suckling Jesus, which directly echo images found all over Egypt of Isis nursing Horus. Many of the pieces are also Classical in inspiration, a legacy of Alexander's Ptolemaic dynasty and Roman rule.

On the upper floor are the finely woven textiles for which the Copts were once famous. There are also lavishly embroidered silk garments, icons, and what is claimed by some to be the oldest book in the world, the Coptic book of the Psalms of David, with its original wooden cover.

Carved stone capital, Coptic Museum

❸ Ben Ezra Synagogue

Coptic Cairo compound. **Map** 3 B5.
Ⓜ Mar Girgis. **Open** 9am–4pm daily.

Jewish history in Egypt dates back to the era of the Old Testament and the stories of Moses and the persecution by the pharaohs. After the Roman expulsion of Jews from Jerusalem in the 1st century AD, Alexandria became the world's most important centre of

Judaism. As recently as the early 20th century the Jewish community in Egypt remained significant and prominent. This changed dramatically with the creation of Israel in 1948. Those Jews that had not already left by choice were forced out of Egypt when the country went to war against the newly formed Jewish state. Monuments to the long history of the Jews in Egypt are few and, of these, Ben Ezra is the oldest. Legends link it with Moses but in fact the synagogue was formerly a church, built in the 8th century. Around 300 years later the church was destroyed and the site and its ruins given to Abraham ben Ezra, a 12th-century rabbi of Jerusalem.

Repairs in the 19th century unearthed hundreds of Hebrew manuscripts from the synagogue's intact *geniza*, or treasury. In Egypt any paper bearing the name of God had to be preserved and this has resulted in a legacy of thousands of documents dating largely from the 11th and 12th centuries. Together, they amount to a minutely detailed chronicle of life in medieval Cairo.

The synagogue underwent extensive renovation in the 1980s and although it is no longer used for worship it is in a pristine state.

❹ Church of St Barbara

Coptic Cairo compound. **Map** 3 B5. Ⓜ Mar Girgis. **Open** 9am–4pm daily.

This church was named after an early Christian martyr who lived in the 3rd century AD. Daughter of a merchant, she was killed by her father for trying to convert him to Christianity. Occupying the site of an earlier church dedicated to St Cyrus and St John, the church of St Barbara was built in the 11th century and is one of the largest and finest in Egypt. It boasts a beautiful 13th-century iconostasis, or sanctuary screen, of wood inlaid with finely carved ivory. There is also a series of striking icons, dating

Carved 13th-century iconostasis in the Church of St Barbara

to around 1750, depicting Jesus, Mary, two archangels and various saints and apostles.

❺ Church of St Sergius and St Bacchus

Coptic Cairo compound. **Map** 3 B5. Ⓜ Mar Girgis. **Open** 9am–4pm daily.

This is perhaps Egypt's most famous church, owing its reputation to the widely held belief that the Holy Family sheltered in a cave here during their "Flight into Egypt"

(see p127). The cave is preserved as a crypt, but it often floods with underground water.

Whatever the truth of the Holy stopover, the church is likely to be the oldest existing structure within the fortress, with foundations dating back to the 5th century AD. Rebuilt and reconstructed many times, most of the fabric of the building dates to between the 10th and 12th centuries.

❻ Coptic Convent of St George

Coptic Cairo compound. **Map** 3 B5. Ⓜ Mar Girgis. **Open** 9am–4pm daily.

This convent dates back at least as far as the 15th century when it was written about by the Arab chronicler Al-Maqrizi. Nuns still live at the convent but visitors are permitted to enter the Great Hall where there is a shrine with a famed icon of St George. The hall is currently being renovated.

The convent is also known for its unusual chain-wrapping ritual still practised by the nuns. The chains symbolize the persecution of St George.

The shrine dedicated to St George in the Coptic Convent of St George

❼ Hanging Church

Dedicated to the Virgin Mary, this church is popularly called the "Hanging" or "Suspended" Church (Al-Muallaqa in Arabic) because it was built on top of the Water Gate of the old Roman fortress of Babylon. The original structure was built possibly as early as the 4th century AD, but it was destroyed and rebuilt in the 11th century. Expansion and reconstruction have gone on ever since, making it difficult to date precisely any specific part of the church. A marble pulpit and the inlaid ivory screens that hide the three altar areas date from between the 10th and 13th centuries. Despite its venerable nature, the church is still used for regular public services, which are held every Wednesday, Friday and Sunday morning.

Outer Porch
Decorated with geometrical and floral designs, the porch dates from the 11th century.

Carved Frieze
The church incorporates some fine old decoration, but this frieze of Christ flanked by angels and many of the earliest pieces are now housed in the nearby Coptic Museum (see p120).

KEY

① **Priests' quarters**

② **The inner courtyard** has souvenirs for sale, such as crosses, CDs and painted papyri.

③ **Icons** of St George, the Virgin and John the Baptist also adorn the walls.

④ **Barrel-vaulted roof supported on columns**

⑤ **Top of the screen adorned with icons**

⑥ **The Chapel of Takla Haymanot** was part of the original 4th-century church. Built in one of the bastions of the Water Gate, it honours the patron saint of Ethiopia.

★ **Façade**
Surmounted by its distinctive twin bell towers, the whole front section is a relatively recent addition, dating only from the 19th century.

 Mosaic on the wall of the Hanging Church, Old Cairo

★ Sanctuary Screen
Carved from cedarwood and delicately inlaid with ivory, the central screen that shields the main altar is the finest of its kind in Egypt.

VISITORS' CHECKLIST

Practical Information
Coptic Cairo compound, Sharia Mar Girgis. **Map** 3 B5. **Open** 8:30am–5pm daily. 7–10am Wed, 8–11am Fri, 7–11am Sun.
W coptic-cairo.com

Transport
M Mar Girgis. from Midan Tahrir. from Maspero terminal.
T Tel (02) 2363 6305.

Pulpit
Made of marble and dating from the 11th century, the exquisite pulpit rests on 13 columns representing Christ and his disciples.

Roman Towers
The towers belonged to the southwestern bastion of the original Roman fortress of Babylon and date from the 1st century AD.

Interior of Church
Three barrel-vaulted roofs are supported on columns with Corinthian capitals, indicating that they were recycled from earlier buildings.

Coptic Christianity

The word "Copt" is a corruption of the Arabic *Qibti*, which is derived from the Greek word *Aegyptios*, meaning "Egyptian". According to tradition, St Mark, one of the 12 apostles, introduced Christianity into Egypt in the first century AD. Alexandria was one of the first five patriarchates – branches of the Christian Church headed by patriarchs claiming descent from the apostles – and by the 4th century, Christianity was the official religion of Egypt. Egyptian Christians split from the orthodox Church after the Council of Chalcedon proclaimed, in AD 451, the dual human and divine nature of Christ. Dioscurus, patriarch of Alexandria, refused to accept this definition, believing only in Christ's divinity.

The ankh, symbol of eternal life in ancient Egypt, is transformed into a Christian cross.

This sculpture of Isis with the infant Horus, dating from c.1400 BC, is an image akin to later depictions of the Virgin Mary and the infant Christ. This, along with the *ankh* and the belief in the afterlife, are some of the more obvious parallels between the ancient Egyptian religion and Christianity, and may explain the ease of Egypt's conversion to the new religion.

Pope Shenouda III

The 117th patriarch of the Coptic Church, Pope Shenouda III (shown above at midnight mass in St Mark's Cathedral in Cairo) was once a monk at Wadi Natrun (see p173). He died in March 2012 and was succeeded by Pope Tawadros II.

The Coptic language, shown here on an early engraving, has its origins in ancient Greek and Egyptian hieroglyphics. Copts claim to be direct descendants of ancient Egyptians. The Coptic language is still used today in religious ceremonies.

Boutros Boutros-Ghali, the former UN Secretary-General, is an internationally renowned Copt. Always an economically powerful minority, Copts have long provided an educated elite in Egypt, filling many of the country's important posts.

The Holy Family in Egypt

According to biblical tradition, the Holy Family fled to Egypt to escape Herod's "massacre of the innocents". Coptic tradition links their visit to several sites. At Matariyya, a northeastern suburb of Cairo, the Virgin's Tree is a gnarled sycamore under which Mary is said to have rested. In Coptic Cairo *(see pp118–21)*, part of the Church of St Sergius and St Bacchus is a cave in which the family supposedly dwelled, while the town of Asyut *(see p180)* is the southernmost point associated with their route.

The Flight into Egypt by Jean-Léon Gérôme (1824–1904)

Monks, like this one from the Monastery of St Anthony in the Eastern Desert, wear traditional black robes and a hood with gold embroidery. During the time of Pope Shenouda III, monasticism experienced a renaissance and attracted many new recruits. It continues to thrive today.

St Anthony's Monastery *(see p236)* represents the beginning of the Christian monastic tradition. It was later followed by Coptic monasteries like Wadi Natrun *(see p173)* and St Catherine's in Sinai *(see pp226–9)*.

This is a typical Egyptian town in Middle Egypt, dominated by a Coptic church and surrounded by fertile fields. There are approximately eight million Copts – 10 per cent of Egypt's population – and most live in Middle Egypt. Despite the odd claim and counterclaim, Copts and Muslims live harmoniously side by side.

❽ Fustat

Sharia Ain as-Sirah. **Map** 3 C5.
Ⓜ Mar Girgis. 🖼

Fustat represents almost 1,400 years of Egyptian history. When the armies of Islam, led by their general Amr ibn al-Aas, conquered Egypt in AD 640 they chose not to occupy any of the existing cities of Alexandria, Memphis or Karnak. Instead they set up camp immediately north of the Roman fortress of Babylon beside the Nile.

In time the canvas city was replaced by one of mudbrick and stone but was still known as Fustat, meaning "tent". It flourished and became Egypt's first Islamic capital. Under the Fatimid dynasty (969–1171), however, the new rulers built their own city further to the north (see pp98–9) and in 1168 put Fustat to the flame rather than risk its capture by the Crusaders. From the 13th to the 16th century, the Mamluks used the area as a rubbish dump and today it is a vast wasteland. It was once inhabited by thousands of people who earned a living as potters and rubbish-collectors, but now only a few remain on the outskirts. To archaeologists Fustat is a treasure chest waiting to be opened – an ancient city preserved under the garbage of centuries.

Fustat is the location of the National Museum of Egyptian Civilization, which is dedicated to exploring the evolution of Egypt's society. The museum overlooks Ain el Seera Lake.

A pottery on the edge of Fustat, Egypt's first Islamic city

❾ Mosque of Amr ibn al-Aas

Midan Amr ibn al-Aas. **Map** 3 B4.
Ⓜ Mar Girgis. **Open** daily. **Closed** to non-Muslims at prayer times. 🖼

Named after the general who conquered Egypt for Islam in AD 640, the original Mosque of Amr ibn al-Aas was the first place of Islamic worship in Egypt and therefore the first mosque on the continent of Africa.

According to contemporary accounts, the mosque was a basic building of mudbrick walls, unpaved floor and a palm-thatch roof supported on palm columns. It had no mihrab, courtyard or minaret, but it was large enough to hold Amr's army at prayer. Apart from the site, however, nothing of the original remains in the present mosque, which is a patchwork of countless rebuildings and restorations. It is said that no two of its 200 or so columns are the same. The earliest existing parts date to the 9th century, when the original mosque was rebuilt, almost doubling in size. However, other areas, such as the entrance, were reconstructed in the 1980s.

The mosque has retained an air of simplicity in keeping with its humble origins and it still fills each day for prayers with a devout congregation. Visitors to the mosque are welcome at other times.

❿ Monastery of St Mercurius

Sharia Abu Seifan. **Map** 3 B4. Ⓜ Mar Girgis. **Open** 9am–5pm daily. 🖼

To the northwest of the Mosque of Amr ibn al-Aas is a complex consisting of three churches and a convent. Surrounded by a high wall, the compound is entered via a small doorway off the main street. This leads to a narrow, sunken alleyway that connects the various buildings. The monastery complex was reputedly named after a martyred Roman legionary and dates from the early 6th century, but it has been destroyed and rebuilt on at least four occasions.

Relief painting, Church of St Mercurius

The main building in the complex is the **Church of St Mercurius**, which in its current form dates back to 1176. It was destroyed in the blaze when the Fatimid overlord Vizier Shawar ordered Fustat to be razed to the ground.

The church is now a repository of fine early Coptic art with unique wall paintings, an extraordinary collection of icons and a fine wooden altar canopy. A flight of stairs in the north aisle of the church leads down to a small crypt where, in the 4th century, the ascetic St Barsum the Naked is said

Façade and entrance to the Mosque of Amr ibn al-Aas

Ornate ironwork exterior of the Tomb of Suleiman al-Faransawi

to have spent the last 20 years of his life with only a snake for company.

The **Church of the Holy Virgin** and the **Church of St Shenouda** are both open to visitors but the **Convent of St Mercurius**, also part of the complex, is still inhabited by nuns and is off-limits.

⓫ Tomb of Suleiman al-Faransawi

Sharia Mohammed Fouad Galal. **Map** 3 B5. M Mar Girgis.

A small cast-iron tomb in a residential square, this is one of the most unusual monuments in Cairo, built in the 19th century in honour of an extremely unusual man.

Suleiman "the Frenchman" (originally a soldier named Joseph Sèves) was a veteran of Napoleon's campaigns who came to Egypt to train the armies of the viceroy Mohammed Ali *(see p63)*. It is said that the Frenchman, who died in 1860, was so despised by his conscripts that they would shoot at him during target practice. Sèves later converted to Islam, taking the name Suleiman, and was rewarded with the honorary title "Pasha" following Egypt's successful campaigns against Greece and Syria. A statue of Suleiman mounted on his horse used to stand in Downtown Cairo on what was Sharia Suleiman Pasha. During the 1952 revolution the statue was

consigned to the Citadel and the street renamed in honour of the Egyptian nationalist and banker, Talaat Harb.

⓬ Nilometer

Sharia al-Malik Salih. **Map** 3 B5. M Mar Girgis. **Open** 10am–5pm daily.

Until the construction of the dams at Aswan, Egyptian life was governed by the annual flooding of the Nile. Most years, its waters rose to swamp the river valley, then retreated, leaving behind richly fertile deposits of alluvial soil. Occasionally, however, the floods failed to cover the whole agricultural area and this resulted in low crop yields and sometimes famine. In order to forecast what kind of harvest a

Nilometer on Rhoda Island showing the simple calibration used to predict the floods

particular year might bring, the ancient Egyptians constructed a series of Nilometers, one of which is cut into the bedrock of the island of Rhoda. It takes the form of a deep, square pit containing an octagonal column, marked off with graduations. Water was let in through three channels – these are now blocked up but are still visible. At the annual meter-reading ceremony, a sufficiently high level of water would be greeted with festivities, while a shortfall would trigger anxious prayers.

Although there is evidence that a Nilometer has been here since Pharaonic times, in its existing form it dates from the 9th century – hence the elaborate Islamic inscriptions adorning the walls. Set over the Nilometer is a small Ottoman kiosk with a distinctive conical cap, dating from the 19th century. Decorating its wooden ceiling are some impressive painted arabesques.

Adjacent to the Nilometer is the **Umm Kolthum Museum**, dedicated to the revered Egyptian singer and worth a visit. The nearby **Rococo Manasterly Palace**, built in the 1850s, holds occasional classical concerts during the winter.

Umm Kolthum: the Voice of Egypt

For much of the 20th century Umm Kolthum was the greatest living cultural icon not just in Egypt, but in the whole of the Arab world. She began singing with her father at weddings in the villages of the eastern Delta around 1910. Astonished by the strength of her voice, friends and family encouraged her to move to Cairo and establish her career. From the 1930s onwards for almost the next 40 years the whole of the country came to a standstill on one Thursday night each month when her concert would be broadcast live on national radio to audiences of millions. During this time she also recorded over 300 songs and appeared in countless films. When she died in 1975 her funeral was the biggest ever witnessed in Cairo. She remains inescapable today; her music is played constantly in coffee houses and taxis, her voice providing a powerful soundtrack to any visit to Egypt.

Umm Kolthum, Egypt's favourite singer

GIZA AND HELIOPOLIS

Giza and Heliopolis are two Cairo suburbs that are not only geographically opposed, they also epitomize two extremes of Egypt's history. Giza, in the southwest, is famed for its ancient monuments. The Sphinx, usually dated to around 2500 BC and the earliest known monumental sculpture, stands guard over the Pyramids at Giza, and their attendant queens' pyramids, temples and tombs. The Pyramids are the only one of the Seven Wonders of the Ancient World to survive. Even the accompanying circus of camel and horse rides, souvenir and soft drinks vendors, persistent beggars and the nightly Sound and Light Show do not diminish their splendour. In the diagonally opposite suburb of Heliopolis, history moves on to the late 19th century and Baron Edouard Empain, the entrepreneur whose vision inspired this garden city in the desert. Built in a mixture of European and Moorish styles, Heliopolis attracted wealthy Egyptians to its leafy grandeur. Although it is no longer separate from Cairo, visitors still come to enjoy its stylish architecture, restaurants and nightlife.

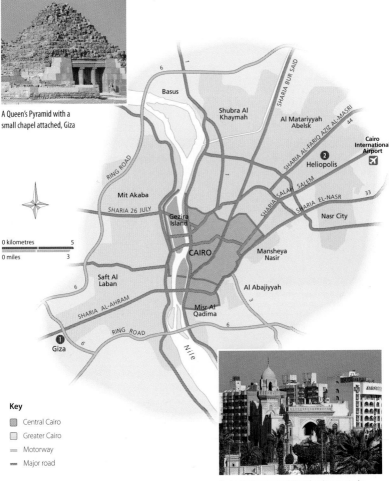

A Queen's Pyramid with a small chapel attached, Giza

0 kilometres 5
0 miles 3

CAIRO

Basus
Shubra Al Khaymah
Al Matariyyah Abelsk
SHARIA BUR SAID
Cairo International Airport
RING ROAD
Mit Akaba
SHARIA 26 JULY
Gezira Island
SHARIA AL-FARIQ AZIZ AL-MASRI
44
2 Heliopolis
SHARIA SALAH SALEM
SHARIA EL-NASR
33
Nasr City
Mansheya Nasir
Saft Al Laban
Al Abajiyyah
SHARIA AL-AHRAM
Misr Al Qadima
RING ROAD
Nile
1 Giza

Key
■ Central Cairo
□ Greater Cairo
— Motorway
— Major road

Contrasting European and Moorish architecture in the suburb of Heliopolis

◀ The Sphinx in front of the Pyramid of Khafre, Giza

For keys to symbols *see back flap*

❶ The Giza Plateau

Nearly 5,000 years ago, Giza became the royal burial ground (necropolis) for Memphis, capital of Egypt. In less than 100 years, the ancient Egyptians built the three pyramid complexes to serve as the tombs for their dead kings. After the king's death, his body was brought by boat to the valley temple for preparation before being taken up the causeway and buried under, and in some cases within, the pyramid. The mortuary temples were maintained for many years afterwards with priests making daily offerings to the dead god-king. The king's close family and the royal court were buried in satellite pyramids and stone tombs called *mastaba* nearby, seeking to share in the king's power in death, as they had in life.

Pyramids of Giza
Three successive generations built these monumental structures during the 4th Dynasty of the Old Kingdom (2613–2498 BC).

Giza Plateau Reconstruction

The funerary complex included the main pyramid, covered in white limestone, various satellite pyramids and a mortuary temple joined by a causeway to a valley temple.

Pyramids of Menkaure and Khafre
While Khafre's Pyramid is nearly as grand as that of his father, Khufu, the Pyramid of Menkaure, Khafre's successor, is much smaller, hinting perhaps at a decline in power and commitment or simply a change in priorities.

Tomb of Khentkawes
This was the last major tomb built at Giza. Queen Khentkawes, daughter of Menkaure, probably gave birth to a new dynasty that moved its necropolis to Abu Sir.

KEY

① **Causeway**

② **Queens' Pyramids** were constructed for the wives and important relatives of the kings. These pyramids were built in two locations.

③ **Pyramid of Menkaure**

④ **Pyramid of Khafre**

⑤ **Khafre's Mortuary Temple**

⑥ **Mastaba tombs** were built in the 4th and 5th Dynasties.

⑦ **Boat pit**

⑧ **Mastaba tombs**

⑨ **Khafre's Valley Temple** held the king's body prior to burial.

★ **The Sphinx**
Guardian of the Giza Plateau, the leonine Sphinx is known to the Arabs as *Abu al-Hol*, the "father of terror".

VISITORS' CHECKLIST

Practical Information
Sharia al-Ahram (Pyramids Road), Giza, 12 km (8 miles) SW of Cairo. (02) 3383 8823. Giza Plateau: **Open** 8am–4pm daily. The Giza Pyramids: **Open** 8am–4pm daily (5pm in summer). for each pyramid (one or more may be closed for restoration). Solar Boat Museum: **Open** 9am–4pm daily (5pm in summer). Sound & Light Show: 7pm, 8pm, 9pm by reservation in winter (2.5 hours later in summer).

Transport
355, 357 from Midan Tahrir.

★ **The Great Pyramid**
The oldest and largest of the Pyramids was built by the 4th-Dynasty king, Khufu (2589–2566 BC).

Meaning of the Giza Pyramids

Archaeologists agree that pyramids served as monumental structures for the burial of kings. They were topped with gold-covered pyramidions (pyramid-shaped capstones) which caught the first rays of the sun, and their shape perhaps symbolized the mythical, primeval mound of creation *(see p30)*. However, because the exact purpose of some of the rooms and shafts of the Giza Pyramids is unknown, the fact that some air shafts point towards important constellations, that the southeast corners lie on a near perfect diagonal and that their sides align with true north inspires many to look hard for fanciful explanations. However, such alignments are simply consistent with ancient Egyptian funerary beliefs that the king's soul would rise up to join the "eternal stars".

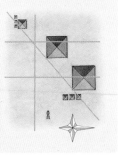

The Giza Plateau: The Great Pyramid

The facts of Khufu's Pyramid, commonly referred to as the Great Pyramid, are staggering. It is estimated to contain over two million blocks of stone weighing on average around 2.5 tonnes, with some stones at the base weighing as much as 15 tonnes. Until the 19th century it was the tallest building in the world. Yet for such a vast structure the precision is amazing – the greatest difference in length between the four 230-m (756-ft) sides is only 4 cm (2 inches). The construction methods and exact purpose of some of the chambers and shafts are unknown, but the fantastic architectural achievement is clear.

Statue of Khufu
(Cheops)
Khufu's only surviving statue is this 7.5-cm- (3-inch-) high ivory figure from Abydos, now kept in the Egyptian Museum.

Queens' Pyramids
These three small pyramids were built for members of the king's family, although the actual identity of the occupants is unknown.

★ King's Chamber
Probably emptied 600 years after being built, the chamber, despite holding only a lidless sarcophagus, was often broken into by treasure seekers.

KEY

① **The "air shafts"** may have been symbolic paths for the king's soul to ascend to the stars.

② **The Queen's Chamber** probably held a statue representing the *ka* or life force of the king.

③ **This vertical shaft** probably served as an escape route for the workers.

④ **Unfinished underground chamber**

⑤ **Underlying bedrock**

★ Great Gallery
Soaring nearly 9 m (30 ft) high, this is thought to have been used as a slipway for the huge blocks that sealed the passageway.

◀ The Pyramids at Giza set in a stunning desert landscape

Reconstruction of the King's Chamber

Built to protect the chamber, the stress-relieving rooms also hold the only reference to Khufu in the pyramid – graffiti, from the time of construction, stating the names of the gangs who built the pyramid - one such name being "How powerful is the great White Crown of Khufu".

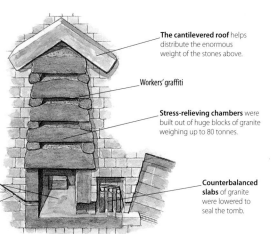

The cantilevered roof helps distribute the enormous weight of the stones above.

Workers' graffiti

Stress-relieving chambers were built out of huge blocks of granite weighing up to 80 tonnes.

King's Chamber

Counterbalanced slabs of granite were lowered to seal the tomb.

The "air shaft" would have been closed off by the outer casing.

The Development of Pyramids

It took the ancient Egyptians around 400 years to progress from mudbrick *mastaba* to smooth-sided pyramid. The last stage, from stepped to "true" or smooth-sided pyramid, took only 65 years. In this time each pyramid was a brave venture into the unknown. Rarely in the history of mankind has technology developed at such a rate.

The Red or North Pyramid, at Dahshur (c.2600 BC)

Mastaba
Around 3000 BC the sandy mounds of the graves of the upper echelons of society were formalized into low, box-like *mastabas*.

Stepped pyramid (c.2665 BC)
A more impressive memorial was made by putting six stone *mastabas* on top of each other (*see King Djoser's Pyramid pp166–7*).

Prototype pyramid (c.2605 BC) The first smooth-sided pyramid was achieved by filling in the steps of a stepped pyramid (*see Meidum Pyramid p172*). This was followed by purpose-built, smooth-sided pyramids.

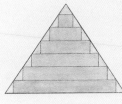

Entrance
The original entrance is now blocked and visitors use a lower opening made by the Caliph Maamun in AD 820.

Exploring the Giza Plateau

For preservation purposes, each of the Pyramids is closed for a spell on a rotating basis and the number of visitors allowed inside is limited. Early morning is the best time to visit, before the heat and crowds become unbearable; it is also worth a trip in the evening for the kitsch but spectacular Sound and Light Show. It can get hot and airless inside the pyramids so clambering inside is not recommended for claustrophobics or the unfit. Camel owners tout expensive rides between the monuments but the area is compact enough to get around on foot.

Egyptian offering camel rides or simply a photo opportunity

The space-age shape of the Solar Boat Museum

🏛 Solar Boat Museum

On the south side of the Great Pyramid sits the pod-shaped Solar Boat Museum. This holds a full-size ancient Egyptian boat discovered in pieces in 1954, lying in a pit beside the pyramid. Experts spent 14 years putting its 1,200 pieces together again using only ancient Egyptian materials of wooden pegs and grass rope.

It is called a solar boat by archaeologists because it resembles the vessels seen in tomb paintings in which the sun-god makes his daily trip across the heavens. It is not clear whether the boat was buried for the sun-god or for the pharaoh's own journey across the heavens. Marks on the wood suggest that the boat had been sailed before being buried. It might have served as a funerary barque, carrying the body of Khufu from Memphis to his tomb at Giza. A similar boat was also found in 1954 in a nearby pit. Excavation work is ongoing.

🏛 Pyramid of Khafre

The base of the Pyramid of Khafre (also called Khephren), is just 15 m (50 ft) shorter than the Great Pyramid, while in height there is a difference of only 3 m (10 ft). Today, however, Khafre's pyramid appears the larger by virtue of being built on higher ground, and because its summit remains intact. This summit is the only area that retains the limestone casing that originally covered all three pyramids. The rest was taken by the medieval rulers of Cairo who used it for their own monuments.

The interior is simpler than that of the Great Pyramid. It has two descending passageways converging and leading to a single tomb chamber. Whereas Khufu's tomb chamber sits high up inside the structure,

Khafre's is dug deep into the bedrock beneath his pyramid. There is little to see except the king's granite sarcophagus. Khafre's mortuary temple still has parts of a small sanctuary and a courtyard, and sections of the 500-m (550-yard) granite-lined causeway are still visible.

🏛 Pyramid of Menkaure

The last pyramid built on the Giza Plateau, the pyramid of Menkaure (also known as Mycerinus) has a base area less than a quarter of that of its two neighbours. Some attribute this to a reduction in the power of the king. However, others point to a change in priorities; the size of the pyramid has been reduced but its valley and mortuary temples are larger and more elaborate. This can perhaps be viewed as the start of a process that eventually saw pyramids abandoned, in favour of secret, rock-cut tombs with separate large funerary temples.

In the 12th century one of Cairo's sultans attempted to dismantle this pyramid. After eight months the project was abandoned, merely having achieved the vertical scar visible on the north face.

Inside, a passageway descends from the entrance to an antechamber decorated with a stylized false-door motif. Beyond that is another antechamber, from where a

Idu, guardian of the burial complexes

The Sphinx and Pyramid of Khafre viewed from the edge of the plateau

passage leads down to the tomb chamber carved from the bedrock. Its barrel-ceiling is carved from a giant granite roof slab. A beautifully decorated sarcophagus was discovered here in the early 19th century but it was lost at sea while being shipped to the British Museum in London.

The Sphinx

Standing guard at the approach to the Pyramid of Khafre, the Sphinx is the earliest known monumental sculpture of ancient Egypt. Archaeologists date it to around 2500 BC, crediting Khafre as the inspiration. It stands 20 m (66 ft) high with an elongated body, outstretched paws and a royal headdress framing a fleshy face, possibly that of the king himself. It is carved from an outcrop of natural rock, augmented by shaped blocks around the base, added during repeated renovations from the 18th Dynasty onwards.

Although it is often written that the Sphinx's nose was shot off by the Mamluks, Ottomans or Napoleon's French army, it was in fact lost some time before the 15th century. Originally the Sphinx also had a stylized false beard, symbol of royalty, but that too fell off. A piece taken from where it lay on the sand is now held by the British Museum in London.

Directly in front of the statue are the remains of the Sphinx Temple, closed to the public. Access to the area around the Sphinx is gained via the adjacent Valley Temple of Khafre, one of the oldest surviving temples in Egypt. At the time the Pyramids were built, during the annual Nile flood, the waters came up to the edge of the Giza Plateau. Khafre's Valley Temple stood on a quay and served as a gateway to the pyramid, connected by a long, mostly covered, causeway. Buried in the sand, this was discovered by Auguste Mariette in 1852 and traces of it can still be seen today. The other two pyramids had similar complexes but their temples are not so well preserved.

The historic Mena House hotel, at the edge of the Giza Plateau

Around the Giza Plateau

There are also several tombs worth a visit. The *mastaba* tombs near Khufu's Queens' Pyramids include the 6th-Dynasty **Tombs of Qar and Idu**. Qar was a high-ranking official in charge of maintaining the Pyramids and their associated ceremonies and his son, Idu, was the royal scribe. These have reliefs and statues of the deceased. The nearby tomb of Khufu's son **Khufukhaf** has some perfectly preserved reliefs, while the tomb of Khafre's wife **Meresankh III** is intriguing. Its painted reliefs show Meresankh, a priestess dressed in the leopardskin usually associated with male priests, while her mother, the blonde-haired Hetepheres III, wears a dress with pointed shoulder pads.

After the dusty heat of the plateau, it makes a nice end to the day to have a drink at the luxurious **Mena House** hotel *(see p273)* and to contemplate the Pyramids as they take on the colour of the setting sun.

Climbing the Great Pyramid

At one time, a complete visit to the Great Pyramid entailed not only an exploration of the passages within, but a clamber to the top as well. A 1902 guidebook to Egypt describes how it was done: "Assisted by two Bedouins, one holding each hand, and, if desired, by a third (no extra payment) who pushes behind, the traveller begins the ascent of the steps." Once up there, many commemorated their climb by carving their names in stone. An archaeological project has catalogued each block of the pyramid. The graffiti noted includes the will of someone who climbed to the top and committed suicide and the names of two lovers carved together for all eternity. As early as 1840 writers complained about the excessive amount of graffiti. This is no longer an issue as since the 1980s climbing the pyramids has been forbidden, although some people still try. The ban is as much to protect the monuments as to prevent injury and even death to climbers.

19th-century photograph of tourists climbing the Great Pyramid

❷ A Walk Through Heliopolis

A product of the visionary ambitions of a wealthy Belgian entrepreneur, Baron Edouard Empain (1852–1929), Heliopolis was built in the first decade of the 20th century. It was designed by a team of European and Egyptian architects as a self-contained garden city in the desert to the northeast of Cairo, linked to the centre by a tram system. Known in Egypt as Masr al-Gedida (New Egypt), Heliopolis has since been swallowed up by the expanding capital, but still retains some of its extraordinary original architecture. A magnet for wealth, this elegant, leafy suburb has good shops, restaurants and nightlife.

On the terrace of the L'Amphitrion cafeteria, Heliopolis

Around Uruba Palace

The walk begins where the bus or tram from Cairo swings left beside the high walls of the Uruba Palace ①. Formerly the Heliopolis Palace Hotel, one of the grandest hotels in the African continent, this was the official residence of former President Hosni Mubarak, and entry is strictly forbidden. Do not wave your camera around, either, as it is not permitted to photograph the buildings. The palace's distinctive, drum-shaped wing once housed a magnificent ballroom.

Diagonally opposite the palace, at the junction of Sharia al-Ahram and Sharia Ibrahim Laqqany, is the venerable L'Amphitrion ②, a bar/restaurant that is as old as Heliopolis itself.

Sights on Walk

① Uruba Palace
② L'Amphitrion
③ Sharia Ibrahim Laqqany
④ Normandy Cinema
⑤ Basilica
⑥ Baron's Palace
⑦ Sharia Baghdad
⑧ Le Chantilly

(map of Heliopolis walk, showing Sharia Ibrahim Laqqany, Sharia Sayyid Abdel Wahid, Sharia al-Ahram, Sharia al-Sumal, Sharia Baghdad, Sharia Sizustris, with numbered sights ①–⑧)

Colonnaded façades and teardrop turrets in Sharia Ibrahim Laqqany

The food is basic, but the back courtyard is one of the few places in Cairo where you can enjoy a beer in the open air.

Turn left from Sharia al-Ahram into Sharia Ibrahim Laqqany ③, which is the most complete remaining example of the original city planning. Baron Empain's architects designed elaborate façades that owe more to Western fantasies inspired by *The 1001 Nights* than to any authentic Islamic architectural traditions. This particular street has a wonderful sweep of arcades with Moorish arches and balconies, punctuated by

Tips for Walkers

Starting point: Sharia al-Ahram.
Length: 4 km (2.5 miles).
Duration: 1.5 hours.
Getting there: Airport bus No. 356 from the bus station behind the Egyptian Museum, trams from Midan Ramses, or taxi.

For hotels and restaurants in this region see pp272–3 and pp284–6

pretty little towers and turrets. The baron, a train enthusiast, was also responsible for what was then a state-of-the-art electric tramway connecting his satellite city to central Cairo. Trams still rattle up the middle of Sharia al-Ahram, but now they are Eastern European models rather than the quaint double-deckers of old.

Turning right from Sharia Ibrahim Laqqany into Sharia Sayyid Abdel Wahid and right again, return to Sharia al-Ahram where, a little further along, on the left, is the Normandy cinema ④. Operating as an

Baron Empain's Byzantine-style basilica, modelled on Istanbul's Aya Sofya

open-air auditorium during the summer months, the cinema screens Egyptian movies and the very occasional English-language film.

Basilica to Sharia Baghdad

As you continue up Sharia al-Ahram, the distinctive central arch of Empain's basilica ⑤ can be seen straight ahead, serving as a reminder that Heliopolis was built by and for (Christian) Europeans. Empain and his family are buried in a crypt within the basilica, which is designed in a highly stylized Byzantine manner, in order to resemble the Hagia Sofia church in Istanbul.

Turning right at Shahid Tayyar Nazih Khalila, a 10-minute walk leads to the most magnificent of follies, known as the Baron's Palace (Qasr al-Baron) ⑥. Built in 1910, this was Baron Empain's Cairo residence and, for reasons unknown, he had it designed to resemble a Hindu temple. The French architect, Alexander Marcel, based his design on a temple at Angkor Wat in Cambodia. Its sandstone exterior is covered with carved animals, Hindu symbols and gods. Legend has it that the building originally had a revolving tower, which allowed the owner to follow the sun throughout the day. The palace has been empty for decades and despite the fact that the building has been renovated, sadly, the palace and its grounds are closed to visitors.

Return to central Heliopolis along Sharia Abd al-Salaam Zaky, turning left onto Sharia Baghdad ⑦, which, like Sharia Ibrahim Laqqany earlier, contains a wealth of fantastical Oriental architecture. About halfway along, on the left, is Le Chantilly (see p286) ⑧, a Swiss-style restaurant and an excellent place to stop for a meal or a beer on the shady back terrace.

Key

••• Walk route

= Tram route

0 metres 250
0 yards 250

Carved sandstone façade of the Baron's Palace

For keys to symbols *see back flap*

SHOPPING IN CAIRO

The hardest thing about shopping in Cairo is knowing when to stop. Souqs, or markets, sell all manner of goods. Khan al-Khalili is the best known: here you will be able to buy jewellery, statues, papyrus and many other items. Artisans such as coppersmiths and glass-makers tend to be gathered together, which helps keep prices low. Alternatively, shop in a modern mall. Here you will find many Western-style shops with recognizable brand names, but prices will be higher. Haggling, usually acceptable in the big shops, is vital in the souqs. Start at below half the asking price and go up in small amounts.

One of the many stalls in the Khan al-Khalili market

Souqs and Markets

Khan al-Khalili (see p94) is a large area of souqs and workshops. Bordering it on its west side is **Sharia al-Muizz li-Din Allah** (see p103), where you will find coppersmiths, goldsmiths, perfumes, spices and carpets. Sections of this wide alley are unofficially named according to the goods on offer: Souq al-Nahhasin (Coppersmiths' Market), Souq al-Sagha (Goldsmiths' and Jewellers' Market) or Souq al-Attarin (Spices Market). Al-Muizz li-Din Allah becomes Sharia al-Khaimiyya, site of **Souq al-Khaimiyya** (Tentmakers' Market) (see p107). The **New Khan al-Khalili** is a market within a market, in the form of a miniature shopping mall in the heart of the souq.

Wikalit al-Balah (Dates Market) is close to the Nile, between Kubri 26 July and the Conrad International Hotel. Everything is sold here – from fruit to car parts – and prices for textiles, curtains and lace are the lowest in Cairo.

Malls

The **Four Seasons** has designer brands. **Dandy Mall**, **Mall of Arabia** and **Citystars** are vast and glitzy malls with many outlets. Others include the **Ramses Hilton Annexe**, **Four Seasons First Mall** and **Nile City Towers**.

Souvenirs

Shisha pipe

Most "papyrus" souvenirs are actually machine-printed banana stalk. For the genuine article, head to a store in a high-end hotel or to **Al-Ghouri Papyrus Art**. **Dr Ragab's Papyrus Institute** gives you a fascinating insight into papyrus's history and manufacture. Admission to the institute is free and its shop sells high-quality papytus products.

You can purchase *shisha* pipes from **Al Tarbiaa** or, much cheaper, from workshops in Khan al-Khalili. The **Old Shop Gallery** in Khan al-Khalili sells antiques.

Handicrafts

You will always get a good deal at hard-to-find workshop **El-Eraki**. Workshops are also the best places to buy mother-of-pearl boxes, since the artisans will be keen to show you their best work. Muski glass can be found at most malls; for the rarer red Muski glass, head to **Saed Abd El-Raouf**. Good-quality *mashrabiyya* ornamental woodwork can be found at the workshop of **El Osta Hussein**. For quality leather goods, head downtown to **Vero Chic** and **Silver Eagle**. **Oum El Dounia** sells a variety of locally made crafts, from ceramics and glassware to jewellery and postcards. Hand-woven shawls from the small village of Naqda can be bought at **Turath**.

Musical Instruments

Most music shops are on and around Sharia Mohammed Ali (al-Qalaa), south of Midan Ataba. Instruments for sale include the *rababa*, a sort of fiddle, and

A dazzling array of silver jewellery on display in a market

◀ The solar boat on display at the Solar Boat Museum, Giza

the *oud*, a round-bodied stringed instrument. A good shop to visit is **Gawharet El Fan**.

Jewellery

The Souq al-Sagha in Khan al-Khalili is thick with jewellers. Try **Mohamed Amin**, **Atlas Jewellery**, **Bedouin Shop** or **Azza Fahmy**. Gold and silver are sold by weight: the shopkeeper will weigh the item and quote a price. This is only a starting price to haggle around.

Textiles

For belly-dancing costumes, try **Saad Hassan Bazaar**, in Khan al-Khalili. Traditional Bedouin jewellery, crafts and costumes can be found at **Nomad**. If you are in search of appliqué, head

to the Souq al-Khaimiyya (Tentmakers' Market), and to the **Fattoh Sons** and **El Khiamiah Star** stores in particular.

One of the oldest and largest conventional places to purchase carpets and rugs in Khan al-Khalili is **El Kahhal Carpets**. Here you can spend hours taking tea with the owner while every carpet in the shop is displayed for you.

Spices and Perfumes

Spices and herbs make excellent gifts to bring back home from Egypt. Head to Khan al-Khalili for the widest selection at the best prices.

Perfume shops such as **Al-Haroun Bazaar** sell quality perfumes and aromatic oils and you will get a good deal if you haggle hard.

Spices for sale at a market in Cairo

DIRECTORY

Malls

Citystars Mall
Stars Centre, Heliopolis.

Dandy Mall
Cairo–Alexandria Desert Road, Cairo.

Four Seasons First Mall
Sharia al-Giza, Giza.

Four Seasons Nile Plaza
Corniche el-Nil, Garden City.
Map 3 B1.

Mall of Arabia
Midan Juhaynah, 6th October City, Cairo.

Nile City Towers
Corniche el-Nil, Boulaq.
Map 1 B2.

Ramses Hilton Annexe
1115 Corniche el-Nil, Downtown.
Map 5 B2.

Souvenirs

Al-Ghouri Papyrus Art
(upstairs, beside Wikala al-Ghouri),
Sharia al-Azhar.
Map 2 F5.

Al Tarbiaa
51 Ramses Hilton Annexe.
Map 5 B2.
Tel (02) 2575 2399.

Dr Ragab's Papyrus Institute
Houseboat on Corniche el-Nil, Giza.
Tel (02) 3571 8675.

Old Shop Gallery
7 Khan al-Khalili.
Map 2 F5.
Tel (02) 2787 0378.

Handicrafts

El-Eraki
55 Sharia Mossadak, Dokki.
Tel (02) 3337 0646.

El Osta Hussein
22 Tabozada (off Sharia Mohammed Ali/Al-Qalaa).
Map 6 E4.

Oum El Dounia
1st floor, 3 Sharia Talaat Harb, Downtown.
Map 5 B3.
Tel (02) 2393 8273.

Saed Abd El-Raouf
8 Khan al-Khalili.
Map 2 F5.

Silver Eagle
18 Sharia Adly, Downtown. **Map** 5 D2.
Tel (02) 2393 6704.

Turath
114 Sharia 26th (entrance on Sharia Hassan Sabry), Zamalek.
Tel (012) 0222 1185.

Vero Chic
19 Sharia Talaat Harb, Downtown.
Map 5 C3.

Musical Instruments

Gawharet El Fan
160–168 Sharia Mohammed Ali (Al-Qalaa), Al-Ataba.
Map 6 E4.
Tel (02) 2391 5243.

Jewellery

Atlas Jewellery
10 Khan al-Khalili.
Map 2 F5.
Tel (02) 2591 8833.

Azza Fahmy
15C Sharia Taha Hussein, Zamalek.
Map 1 A2.
Tel (02) 2735 8354.
w azzafahmy.com

Bedouin Shop
7 Khan al-Khalili.
Map 2 F5.
Tel (012) 2365 6818.

Mohamed Amin
5 Sharia Taha Hussein, Zamalek. **Map** 1 A3.
Tel (02) 2736 4375.

Textiles

El Kahhal Carpets
Khan al-Khalili. **Map** 2 F5.
Tel (02) 2590 9128.

El Khiamiah Star
Bab Zuweila.
Map 6 F4.

Fattoh Sons
Bab Zuweila.
Map 6 F4.
Tel (02) 2512 8853.

Nomad
14 Sharia Saray al-Gezira, Zamalek.
Map 1 B4.
Tel (02) 2736 1917.

Saad Hassan Bazaar
Sharia Gouhar al-Kaad (off Midan al-Hussein), Khan al-Khalili. **Map** 2 F5.
Tel (02) 2588 0834.

Spices and Perfumes

Al-Haroun Bazaar
Garden City House Hotel, 1101–1103 Corniche el-Nil, Garden City.
Map 5 A4.

ENTERTAINMENT IN CAIRO

Cairo is a big, bustling city, with plenty to keep you occupied. Be aware that Cairenes are night owls, often not dining until 11pm and then partying on until morning. For a predominantly Muslim city, there is a surprising number of bars, particularly in upmarket districts such as Zamalek, catering mainly to the young and the expat community. The Cairo Opera House is the venue for Arabic music, classical opera and ballet. The Al-Ghouri Complex puts on regular shows of whirling-dervish dancing, and you can find displays of belly dancing in many places, though the standard varies.

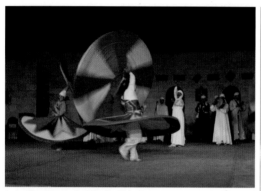
A colourful performance of whirling-dervish dancing

Information and Listings

Your hotel concierge should be able to suggest a range of entertainment options. The listings in local publications will help with any specialized interests, such as classical or jazz music, art exhibitions, theatre or cinema. Get a copy of *Al-Ahram Weekly*, the local newspaper, or the glossy monthly *Egypt Today*. Last-minute changes of programme or venue are possible, so call ahead.

Belly Dancing

Belly-dancing shows are held twice weekly in some of the larger hotels – including the **Haroun al-Rashid** at the Semiramis InterContinental. Alternatively, embark on a dinner-and-belly-dancing cruise. Try the **Nile Maxim**, where you have a choice of two sessions (8–10pm or 10pm–midnight), or **Lessa Faker**, on the Blue Nile Boat. Less touristy are the many clubs along the Pyramids Road in Giza and Sharia al-Alfy, Downtown. **Sheherazade**, in Downtown, has a good local flavour.

Whirling Dervishes

Whirling-dervish dancing developed from a religious rite connected with Sufism. Sufis claim that the centuries-old dizzying dance produces a state of trance that brings protagonists closer to God. Wonderfully intense, colourful displays can be seen at the **Wikala al-Ghouri**, just south of the Al-Azhar mosque, on Monday, Wednesday and Saturday nights at 8pm. There is no charge for entry, but collecting a ticket at 6:30pm is recommended.

Classical and Arabic Music

The huge, domed **Cairo Opera House** complex in Gezira is the home to most classical music, in the form of the Cairo Symphony Orchestra and the Cairo Opera. There are regular performances in the Main Hall, the Small Hall and the Open-Air Theatre. Look also for performances at **Beit al-Harawi**, the **Goethe Institute Gardens** at Midan al-Missaha in Doqqi and the **Gumhuriyya Theatre**, just south of Al-Ataba.

Jazz and Rock Music

The **Cairo Jazz Club** is the main venue for jazz, electronic, funk and Oriental music. It also offers good food and drink, not to mention a hip ambience that makes it popular with young barhoppers. Downtown's **After 8** is a smoky den that features local talent. Jazz events are also held at the various venues within the Cairo Opera House. Most of the big hotels have live music in their bars and cafés too. The **Jazz Bar** at Kempinski Hotel in Garden City is an especially good venue.

A classical quintet performing at the Cairo Opera House

Bars and Nightclubs

There is no real centre to the nightlife in Cairo, so a night out on the town usually involves taxi-hopping from bar to restaurant to nightclub. Wednesdays and Thursdays tend to be the busiest nights.

The upscale **Bistro Bar**, a few blocks from Midan Tahrir, serves food and has a fine playlist of retro 80s music. The **Promenade Café** at the Cairo Marriott Hotel is a good place to enjoy a beer and a *shisha*. Most top-end hotels have roof-top bars with great views of the city, though less well-heeled Cairenes prefer the terrace bar of the **Odeon Palace Hotel**, where the beer is much cheaper. Three restaurants in Zamalek, **La Bodega**, **Amici Bar** and **L'Aubergine**, have trendy bars that stay open late.

Some of the best nightclubs are at the big hotels – for example, **The Bar** at the Four Seasons Nile Plaza, which is open until 3am. For dancing under the stars, try the floating restaurants moored up at Zamalek: **Le Pacha 1901** and the **Moon Deck** on the Blue Nile Boat. The **ACE Club (Association of Cairo Expatriates)** is open only to foreign-passport holders. There is a pool table upstairs and a terrace bar and garden.

The upmarket club **TIU**, in the Nile City Towers, offers an extremely glamorous night out. There's an outdoor terrace, and the bar serves excellent cocktails.

Other Entertainment

There is no denying that the **Sound and Light Show** held against the stunning backdrop of the Giza Pyramids is impressive. Travellers with children may enjoy a visit to **Cairo Zoo**, while **Dr Ragab's Pharaonic Village**, also at Giza, involves a boat trip and a wide choice of museums, historic reconstructions and activities.

DIRECTORY

Belly Dancing

Haroun al-Rashid
Semiramis InterContinental, Corniche el-Nil, Downtown. **Map** 5 A4.
Tel (02) 2797 1818.
W intercontinental. com

Lessa Faker
Blue Nile Boat, 9A Sharia Saray al-Gezira, Zamalek.
Map 1 B4.
Tel (02) 2735 3114.

Nile Maxim
Sharia Saray al-Gezira (opposite Cairo Marriott Hotel), Zamalek.
Map 1 B4.
Tel (02) 2738 8888.

Sheherazade
Sharia Alfy Bey, Downtown.
Map 2 D4.

Whirling Dervishes

Wikala al-Ghouri
off Sharia al-Azhar, Islamic Cairo.
Map 2 F5.

Classical and Arabic Music

Beit al-Harawi
Harat al-Azhar, Islamic Cairo. **Map** 2 F5.
Tel (02) 2510 4174.

Cairo Opera House
Sharia at-Tahrir, Gezira.
Map 1 A5.
Tel (02) 2737 0602.

Goethe Institute
13 Sharia Hussein Wassef, Midan al-Missaha, Doqqi.
Tel (02) 2574 8261.

Gumhuriyya Theatre
12 Sharia al-Gumhuriyya, Downtown.
Map 6 D3.
Tel (02) 2390 7707.

Jazz and Rock Music

After 8
6 Sharia Qasr el-Nil, Downtown.
Map 5 B3.
Tel (0100) 339 8000.

Cairo Jazz Club
197 Sharia 26 July, Mohandiseen.
Tel (02) 3345 9939.

Jazz Bar
Kempinski Hotel, 12 Sharia Ahmed Ragheb, Corniche el-Nil, Garden City.
Map 5 A5.
Tel (02) 2798 0000.
W kempinski.com

Bars and Nightclubs

ACE Club (Association of Cairo Expatriates)
2 Midan Victoria, Degla, Maadi. **Tel** (02) 2519 4594.
W theaceclub-maadi. com

Amici Bar
22 Taha Hussein St, Zamalek. **Map** 1 A2.
Tel (010) 9332 3333.

L'Aubergine
5 Al-Sayyid al-Bakri, Zamalek. **Map** 1 A3.
Tel (02) 2738 0080.

The Bar
Four Seasons Hotel Cairo at Nile Plaza, 1089 Corniche el-Nil, Garden City. **Map** 3 B1.
Tel (02) 2791 7000.
W fourseasons.com/ caironp

Bistro Bar
8 Hoda Shaarawi St, Downtown.
Map 5 C3.
Tel (012) 2489 1943.

La Bodega
157 Sharia 26 July, Zamalek.
Map 1 A3.
Tel (02) 2735 6761.

Moon Deck
Blue Nile Boat, 9A Saray al-Gezira, Zamalek.
Map 5 A3.
Tel (02) 2735 3114.

Odeon Palace Hotel Bar
6 Abdel Hamid Said (off Sharia Talaat Harb), Downtown. **Map** 5 C2.
Tel (02) 2576 7971.

Le Pacha 1901
Saray al-Gezira, Zamalek.
Map 5 A3.
Tel (02) 2735 6730.

Promenade Café
Cairo Marriott Hotel, Sharia Saray al-Gezira, Zamalek.
Map 1 B3.
Tel (02) 2728 3000.

TIU
Nile City Towers, Rhod al-Farag.
Map 1 B2.
Tel (012) 0399 9906.
W tiu-egypt.com

Other Entertainment

Cairo Zoo
Sharia Mourad, Giza.
Tel (02) 3570 8895.

Dr Ragab's Pharaonic Village
3 Sharia al-Bahr al-Aazam, Giza. **Tel** (02) 3571 8675.

Sound and Light Shows
All sites.
Tel (02) 3385 7320.
W soundandlight. com.eg

CAIRO STREET FINDER

The map below shows the areas of the city covered by the *Street Finder*. The maps include the major sightseeing attractions and railway, bus and Metro stations. Map references are given for Cairo's restaurants *(see pp284–6)*, hotels *(see pp272–3)*, entertainment venues *(see pp146–7)* and shopping venues *(see pp 144–5)*. Some of Cairo's small streets and alleyways may not be named on the maps. Some

monuments have two names: one in Arabic and often a commonly used English-language form. What we call the Citadel, taxi drivers sometimes know only as Al-Qalaa. Refer to the Survival Guide for guidance on taxis *(see p336)*. In this guide and on the following maps, where there is a well-recognized English name, we have used it; otherwise we have used the local Arabic names.

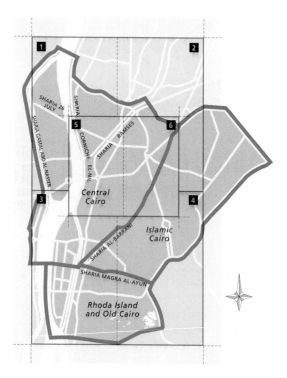

Scale of Map above

0 metres   1000
0 yards   1000

Scale of Maps 1–4

0 metres   200
0 yards   200

Scale of Maps 5–6

0 metres   200
0 yards   200

Key to Cairo Street Finder

- Major sight
- Place of interest
- Other building
- M Metro station
- Bus station
- Railway station
- Tram stop
- River bus boarding point
- Felucca boarding point

- *i* Tourist information
- Hospital
- Police station
- Church
- Synagogue
- C Mosque
- — Railway line
- Pedestrianized street

Street Finder Index

Because of different preferences in the transliteration of Arabic into English, our spellings of street and place names may differ from those on street signs – which, of course, also carry Arabic script.

Note that the word "Sharia" denotes a street. Other Arabic words used here include "Midan" (a square), "Bab" (a gate), "Beit" (a house), "Kubri" (a bridge) and "Qasr" (a palace).

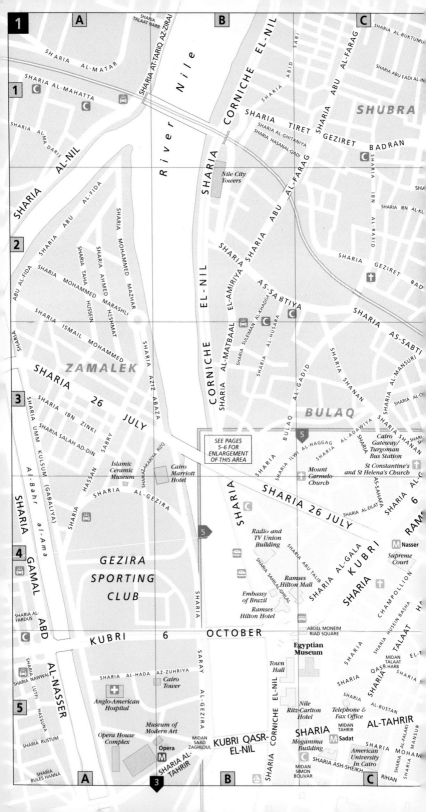

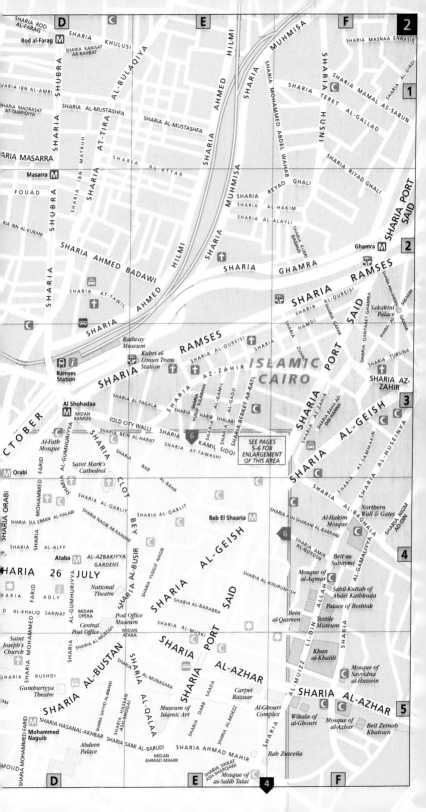

3 SHARIA NABIL AL-WAQAD   **A**   MIDAN AL-GALA   **1**   **B**   Embassy of United States   **C**   Parliament   SHARIA MANSUR

SHARIA AT-TAHRIR

SHARIA MESAHA

1   SHARIA IBN MARWAN

SHARIA AR-RAFI

SHARIA WASIF

Mabmoud Kahil Museum

2

River Nile

KUBRI AL-GAMAA (UNIVERSITY BRIDGE)

SHARIA GAMAL ABD AN-NASSER

3

SHARIA AL-GIZA

SHARIA GAMAL ABD AN-NASSER

SHARIA AL-AZIZ AS-SUUD

SHARIA YUSUF-ADIGAWI

SHARIA MUHMUD ZID ALFAQQAR

KUBRI AL-GIZA   SHARIA AL-RHODA

4

GAMAL ABD AN-NASSER

ABD AL-AZIZ

SHARIA AL-MALIK

SHARIA AL-MUZAFFAR

AL-RHODA

SHARIA AL-MANIAL

SHARIA AL-MALIKSALIH

SHARIA ALI AL-GARIM

C

GIZA

5

SHARIA AL-BAHR AL-AZAM

AL-QORSAIAH ISLAND

A

Embassy of United Kingdom   **5**

SHARIA CORNICHE EL-NIL

SEE PAGES 5–6 FOR ENLARGEMENT OF THIS AREA

SHARIA ABD AL-AZIZ AL-SAUD

Cairo University Hospital

C

AS-SARSY

SHARIA EL-NIL

AL-MANIAL

Manial Palace

SHARIA EL-NIL

Sayyalet AR-RHODA

Sayyalet ar-Rhoda

SHARIA EL-NIL

Suez Canal Office

SHARIA SIFA AL-KAMAL AS-SINAWI

SHARIA DAR AS-SIFA   **5**

SHARIA AL-HADIQA

SHARIA AL-MAWARDI

SHARIA AR-RASHIDI

SHARIA CORNICHE

SHARIA AS-SABA SAKKYAT

SHARIA MASR HELWAN

SHARIA ABU SEIFAN

SHARIA ABUL SUUD

SHARIA MAR GIRGIS

El-Malik el-Salih   **M**

SHARIA GABANA MUSALLAMA

SHARIA SIDI SAD

Monastery of St Mercurius

SHARIA GAM AMR IBN AL-AAS

SHARIA SEIFAN

CORNICHE

SHARIA IBRAHIM AL-GIBALI

Manasterly Palace

Nilometer

SHARIA ABU

Tomb of Suleiman al-Faransawi

Coptic Convent of St George

Greek Orthodox Church of St George

Church of St Sergius & St Bacchus

Church of St Barbara

Coptic Museum

Ben Ezra Synagogue

Mar Girgis   **M**

Hanging Church

SHARIA MOHAMMED ASSUGHAYYAR

B

MAGLIS AS-SHAAB

SHARIA HUSEIN HIGAZI

SHARIA SAAD ZAGHLOUL

SHARIA DARIH SAAD

SHARIA ISMAIL

Saad Zaghloul   **M**

SHARIA AL-QASR AL-AINY

ASSURAYA

SHARIA MOHAMMED IZZAR-ARAB

SHARIA ISMAIL SIRRI

MANSUR

Sayyida Zeinab   **M**

SHARIA AD-DAIYURA

SHARIA

SHARIA HASSAN AL-ANWAR

SHARIA SIDI MALIK

SHARIA ABAZA

SHARIA NUBAR

SHARIA AL-MASRI

SHARIA ALKHALIG

SHARIA IBN ZID

SHARIA YAHYA

SHARIA MUMT

SHARIA EIN AS-SIRA

SHARIA SIDI HASSAN

SHARIA IBN

YAZ

SHARIA MAGI

SHARIA AL-FUSTAT

SHARIA AL-MADABI

SHARIA AL-FUSTAT

SHARIA YAQUBAL-QIBTI

SHARIA AL-BARRANI

SHARIA

SALAH

OLD CAIRO

Amr ibn al-Aas Mosque   **C**

Ruins of Fustat

C

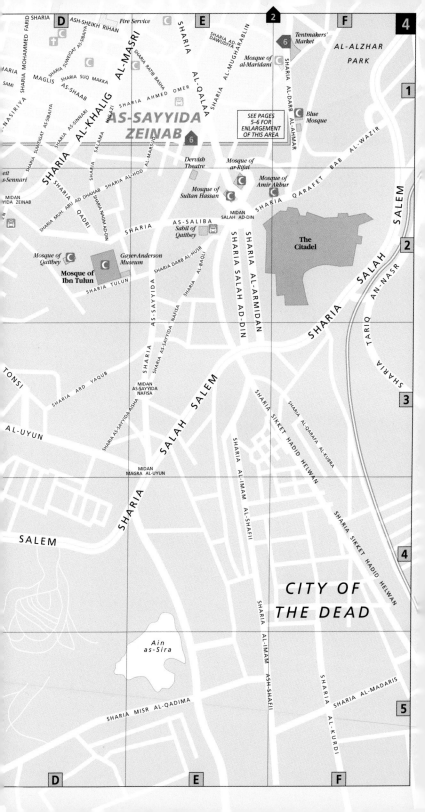

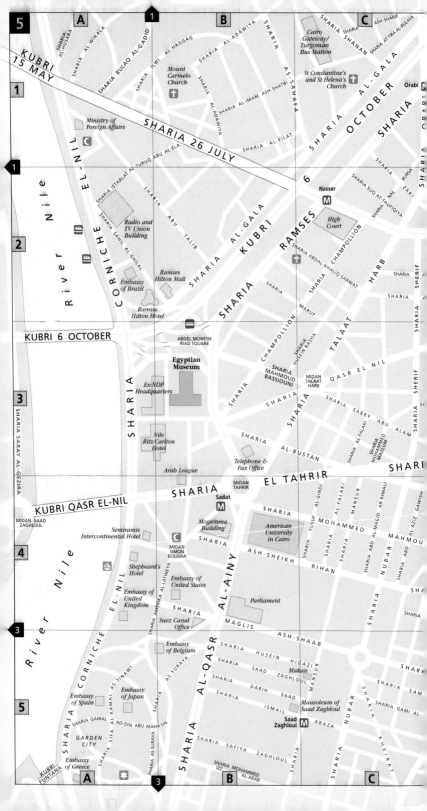

EGYPT
AREA BY AREA

Egypt at a Glance

Most of Egypt's great Pharaonic monuments lie along the Nile Valley, but visitors should not ignore the variety of sights and activities on offer elsewhere. From the vast desert expanses to the biblical scenery of the rocky Sinai interior, Egypt fully engages the senses. For those who need to be near the sea, the North Coast is lined with Mediterranean-influenced cities and beaches, while the resorts and dive centres on the Red Sea Coast allow access to the stunning coral reefs.

The Bent pyramid at Dahshur *(see p169)* in the Pyramid fields around Cairo

Statue in the Graeco-Roman Museum gardens in Alexandria *(see pp246–7)*

Sallum

Alexandria

THE DELTA AND THE NORTH COAST
(See pp238–55)

Siwa

AROUND CAIRO
(See pp162–

Bawiti

Minya

Asyut

Abu Minqar

So

Al-Qasr

THE WESTERN DESERT
(See pp256–65)

El-Kharga

Siwa *(see p264)*, the most isolated of Egypt's oases and a living antiquity in the midst of the Western Desert

Farmer working in the well-watered fields around Dakhla Oasis *(see p260)*

◄ An early morning hot-air balloon ride over Luxor

0 kilometres 150
0 miles 100

Port Said

Ismailia

SINAI AND
THE RED
SEA COAST
(See pp220–37)

ez

Taba

s Gharib

Sharm
el-Sheikh

Hurghada

*Red
Sea*

Qena

Al-Quesir

or

Marsa Alam

Edfu

Aswan

Berenice

THE NILE
VALLEY
(See pp174–219)

el

Halaib

St Catherine's Monastery *(see pp226–9)* nestling at the foot of
Mount Sinai in spectacular surroundings

The majestic Colossi of Memnon *(see p206)* on the way to the
monuments of the Theban necropolis, Luxor

One of the many feluccas that glide among the leafy
islands at Aswan *(see pp212–15)*

AROUND CAIRO

Desert expanses around the modern capital offer escapism in many forms. Cairenes flock to the greenery of Fayoum and Qanater, while visitors can explore millennia of human ingenuity and achievement in the glorious monuments of Egypt's Old Kingdom burial sites and the monastic retreats of early Christians.

The ruins of Memphis, a religious and commercial centre of vast importance nearly 4,000 years before the birth of Egypt's present capital, are situated on the left bank of the Nile about 30 km (19 miles) south of Cairo. One of the main necropolises of Memphis, Saqqara is rich in fascinating sites: prototype pyramids; tombs with the earliest known examples of Pharaonic decorative writing; the mysterious Serapeum, an underground tomb dedicated to the sacred Apis bulls, and some of the deepest burial chambers in Egypt. Other ancient burial sites nearby include Abusir, where a cluster of pyramids built for the principal 5th-Dynasty pharaohs is located on the edge of the desert, and remote Dahshur, home to several stone and mudbrick pyramids including the intriguing Bent Pyramid.

West of the Delta region, between Alexandria and Cairo, are the monasteries of Wadi Natrun. Valued by the ancient Egyptians as a source of natron, the salt used during mummification, Wadi Natrun became, in the Roman era, a bolthole for persecuted Christians, and later a centre of monasticism. Of several monasteries here, Deir as-Suriani, Deir Abu Makar and Deir Anba Bishoi are the most beautiful.

Fayoum is famed for its abundant fruits and vegetables, fragrant flowers and orange blossom. Its vast salt lake hosts a rich population of waterfowl. The area is renowned for its prehistoric remains and has numerous Ptolemaic and Roman archaeological sites. To sail along the Nile from Cairo to the gardens of Qanater is another favourite excursion for city residents.

Boating on the lake at Wadi Rayyan, a popular leisure activity for modern Cairenes

◄ Painted frieze on the west wall of the Step Pyramid of Djoser, Saqqara

Exploring Around Cairo

When the hustle of Cairo gets too much, it is easy to slow down the pace a little by visiting one of the many interesting sights outside the capital. Saqqara attracts far fewer visitors and covers a larger area than the Pyramids at Giza and so rarely feels crowded, while the pyramid fields of Abusir and Dahshur are often practically deserted. Pharaonic remains are also dotted throughout Fayoum Oasis, although most people make the trip for the lush vegetation. The other option for grassy spaces and trees is to sail down the Nile to Qanater, but this is so popular at the weekends that it is often just as congested as the city everyone is looking to escape. For real peace and quiet the best option, as the early Christians discovered, is to head out into the desert. Wadi Natrun is one of the founding sites of monasticism and the monks, although on holy retreat, are gracious when receiving visitors.

The mortuary temple and Pyramid of Sahure at Abusir

Farmers tending their sheep near Memphis, the first capital of ancient Egypt

0 kilometres 25

0 miles 15

Getting Around

Abusir, Saqqara, Memphis and Dahshur all lie on the same road; unfortunately, it is not served by public transport and the only option is to hire your own. Most hotels in Cairo can arrange a taxi or, even better, a car and driver for the day. Birqash camel market is only really accessible by car or taxi, too. Buses for Wadi Natrun and Fayoum depart from the Cairo Gateway bus station (formerly known as Turgoman Station).

For hotels and restaurants in this region see p273 and pp286–7

Alexandria

WADI NATRUN 8 11 Medinet el Sadat

10

Bahariyya Oasis

Gebel Qatrani

Birket Qarun San

Wadi al Hitan Qarun FAYO(

El Shawashna

Tubhar

Wadi Rayyan Abu Gandir

El Gharaq el Sultani

Sights at a Glance

1. Abusir
2. *Saqqara pp166–8*
3. Memphis
4. Dahshur
5. Fayoum
6. Birqash Camel Market
7. Nile Barrages (Qanater)
8. Wadi Natrun

Date palms at Fayoum Oasis, inspiration for Pharaonic columns

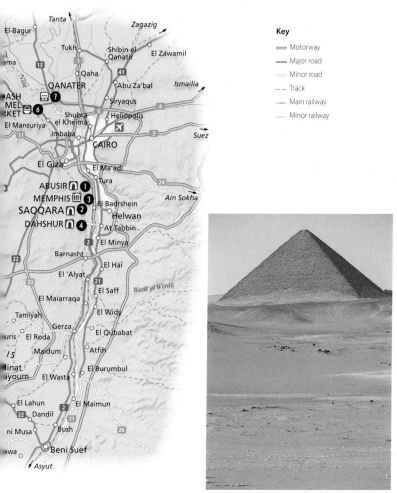

Key

━━ Motorway
━━ Major road
── Minor road
─ ─ Track
━━ Main railway
── Minor railway

The Red Pyramid at Dahshur, so called because of ancient red graffiti found inside

For keys to symbols see back flap

❶ Abusir

Off Hwy 27, 27 km (17 miles) S of Cairo. 🚇 **Closed** to the public. 🅿️

The cluster of four 5th-Dynasty pyramids at Abusir has not aged as well as the Giza complex (see pp132–9). Instead, the site's appeal comes from its location at the edge of the desert and the fact that few tourists ever venture here.

Only the northernmost and best-preserved **Pyramid of Sahure** can be entered, though this is not recommended for claustrophobics. The pyramid is fronted by a mortuary temple, which has partially reconstructed walls with reliefs of sea voyages and scenes of the king hunting. To the left, the **Pyramid of Nyuserre** is badly dilapidated but has the most complete causeway linking its valley and mortuary temples. Further south is the **Pyramid of Neferirkare**. The brother and successor of Sahure, Neferirkare died while his pyramid was still being constructed, so it was hastily completed with a facing of perishable mudbrick. This has since crumbled away to reveal a six-stepped stone inner core, similar to Djoser's pyramid at Saqqara. Finally, to the southwest lies the unfinished **Pyramid of Neferefre**, still being excavated by Czech archaeologists.

Abusir has also been the site of two major archaeological finds. In the 19th century, a famed set of Old Kingdom papyri, describing schedules of ceremonies and festivals, was discovered. Then, in 1998, a team of Czech archaeologists found the undisturbed tomb of a 6th-century BC Egyptian priest, Iufaa, containing Iufaa's mummy and hundreds of artifacts such as amulets and shabtis (see p33).

The pyramids of Abusir on the edge of the desert

❷ Saqqara

Saqqara is one of the richest archaeological sites in Egypt. Its monuments span 3,000 years, from the earliest ancient Egyptian funerary structures to Coptic monasteries. Saqqara developed as the royal necropolis for the Old Kingdom capital of Memphis, just to the west. As Memphis grew, so did this city of the dead until it covered an area of 7 km (4 miles), north to south. While Saqqara continued to be used as a burial site for officials for a time, it was eventually abandoned and, apart from Djoser's pyramid, lay buried under sand for centuries. Then, in 1851, Auguste Mariette discovered the Serapeum, since when regular finds continue to be made at Saqqara.

Step Pyramid of Djoser at Saqqara, built by the architect Imhotep

🔝 Step Pyramid of Djoser

The centrepiece of the Saqqara necropolis is the Step Pyramid of Djoser, the prototype for all other pyramids. This remarkable structure was built for 3rd-Dynasty King Djoser by his architect, the high priest Imhotep, in the 27th century BC, and is currently undergoing extensive exterior conservation work. This pyramid marks an unprecedented leap forward in the history of world architecture. Until then, Egyptian royal tombs had been underground rooms covered with low, flat, mud-brick mastabas (see p137). The great innovator Imhotep chose to use stone rather than mudbrick, and to build not just one mastaba but six, one on top of the other, with each additional layer smaller than the one beneath it. The vast enclosure surrounding the step pyramid marked yet another major achievement. Bounded by a finely cut lime-stone wall originally 10.5 m (34 ft) high, this complex included vast open courts, pavilions, shrines and chapels.

A part of the ancient wall has been restored in the southeast corner, and this provides the entrance to the enclosure. A colonnaded corridor of 40 pillars, ribbed in imitation of palm stems, leads into the Great South Court, where things to look out for include a restored section of wall bearing a frieze of cobras.

Frieze of cobras, Saqqara

Some of the oldest known examples of tourist graffiti, dating from the 12th century BC, can be seen preserved under perspex in buildings east of the pyramid. On the north side of the pyramid, there is a life-size painted statue of Djoser in a serdab, a stone box designed to allow the dead king's ka (spirit) to interact with the living world. The statue is a replica – the original is in Cairo's Egyptian Museum *(see p80)*. The excellent Imhotep Museum has six galleries with pieces found both here and at Abusir. One gallery is dedicated to the French archaeologist Jean-Philippe Lauer who died in 2001 having devoted 75 years to restoring these monuments.

Pyramid of Unas

Unas was the last king of the 5th Dynasty. His tomb is covered with vertical columns of hieroglyphic text designed to protect the king in the afterlife. These so-called Pyramid Texts are the earliest known examples of decorative writing in a Pharaonic tomb chamber. They later formed the basis of the New Kingdom Book of the Dead *(see p33)*. Unfortunately, deterioration

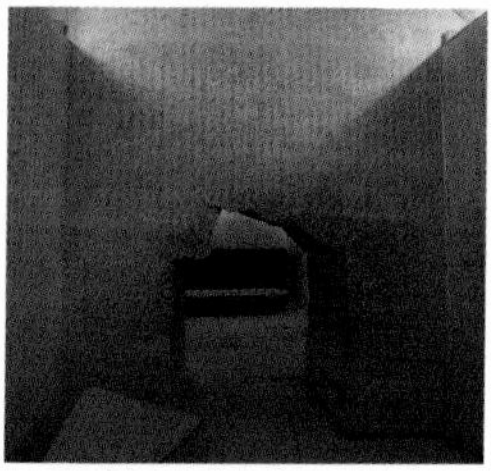

Pyramid Texts in the chambers of the Pyramid of Unas, Saqqara

caused by too many visitors means that the pyramid is now closed to the public.

More than 200 *mastabas* and tombs line the causeway running east of the pyramid. Many of them are beautifully decorated and open to visitors.

Persian Tombs

Some of the deepest underground burial chambers discovered in Egypt, the Persian Tombs, are situated immediately south of the Pyramid of Unas. Found here were the resting places of three Persian noblemen. Psamtik, Djenhebu and Pediese were all officials of the 27th Dynasty. Colourful inscriptions on the walls of the tombs reveal that Psamtik was chief physician of the pharaoh's court and Djenhebu was a famous Persian admiral. Pediese was Psamtik's son and held various official titles. This site is closed to the public.

VISITORS' CHECKLIST

Practical Information
Off Hwy 27, 44 km (27 miles) S of Cairo. **Tel** (02) 3815 1560. **Open** daily.

Transport
Ⓣ or tour from Cairo.

Map of Saqqara

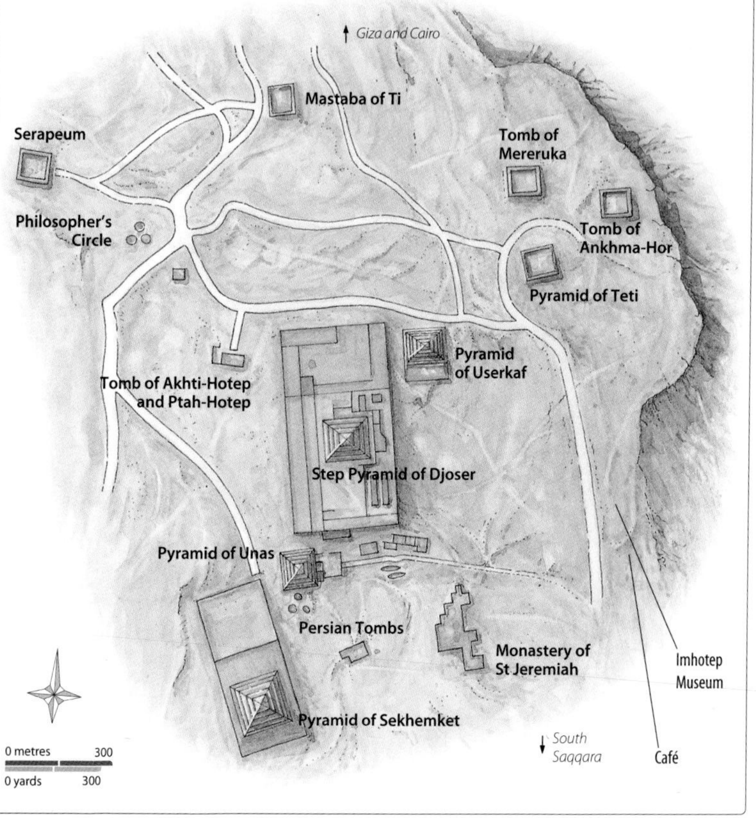
Giza and Cairo
Mastaba of Ti
Serapeum
Tomb of Mereruka
Philosopher's Circle
Tomb of Ankhma-Hor
Pyramid of Teti
Pyramid of Userkaf
Tomb of Akhti-Hotep and Ptah-Hotep
Step Pyramid of Djoser
Pyramid of Unas
Persian Tombs
Monastery of St Jeremiah
Imhotep Museum
Pyramid of Sekhemket
South Saqqara
Café
0 metres 300
0 yards 300

Pyramid of Teti

The pyramid of Teti, who was the first king of the 6th Dynasty, looks like nothing more than a mound of rubble. However, it is worth visiting for its burial chamber, which contains the king's well-preserved giant basalt sarcophagus. The ceiling of the chamber is decorated with carved stars, and the walls are inscribed with sections of Pyramid Texts. Though found in several pyramids on the Saqqara site, this is currently the only place where these ancient funerary writings are accessible to the public.

Statue of Mereruka emerging from a false door in his tomb at Saqqara

Tomb of Mereruka

An extensive complex of 33 chambers, the tomb of Mereruka, Teti's son-in-law, is one of the highlights of Saqqara. The tomb has some magnificent wall paintings, including a marsh scene with Mereruka hunting among birds, fish and hippos, and in another chamber a scene showing tax evaders being punished. The largest hall, which has a stone ring at its centre for tethering sacrificial animals, contains a life-size statue of Mereruka striding forward from a false door.

Tomb of Ankhma-Hor

A short walk from Mereruka's tomb is the tomb of Ankhma-Hor, also referred to as the "Physician's Tomb" because of its fascinating wall reliefs depicting surgical operations. These

include surgery being performed on a man's toe and, apparently, a circumcision, as practised in the 6th Dynasty. The tomb is currently closed to the public.

Serapeum

Saqqara's strangest monument is the eerie underground burial chamber of the sacred Apis bulls. The Serapeum consists of a series of long, dark passageways lined with side chambers, which house 25 giant granite sarcophagi. Weighing up to 70 tons each, the sarcophagi once contained the mummified corpses of the Apis bulls. Seen as an incarnation of Ptah, god of Memphis, these bulls were looked after by priests. When they died they were buried with great ceremony in the Serapeum's rock-cut, subterranean galleries. The catacombs were begun by Amenhotep III (1390–1352 BC) and remained in use until 30 BC.

When Auguste Mariette discovered the site in 1851, he found that all the tombs had been broken into and pillaged except for one. Inside was a sarcophagus containing a mummified bull, now in the Agricultural Museum in Cairo.

Mastaba of Ti

East of the Serapeum, the Mastaba of Ti is the tomb of a court official who served three kings during the 5th Dynasty. Its wall paintings are unrivalled for the wealth of information they provide about everyday life in Old Kingdom Egypt. The far chamber has the best reliefs and also three slits in the wall revealing Ti's statue in its *serdab*. This was a room for the deceased's statue in which his spirit or *ka* resided.

Philosopher's Circle

This grouping of statues, near the Serapeum, was set in place by the Ptolemaic Greeks. The circle of figures includes Plato and Homer, although most are in a very poor condition. The circle was originally designed as an adjunct to a temple built by the last truly Egyptian pharaoh, Nectanebo, in the 4th century BC. The temple has long since disappeared, leaving the philosophers sitting alone.

Statue in the Philosopher's Circle, built by the Ptolemies at Saqqara

Environs

Beginning 2 km (1 mile) south of the main complex, **South Saqqara** is a field of smaller, dilapidated pyramids built by pharaohs Pepi I, Pepi II, Djedkare and Merenre. Pepi II's pyramid contains some fine examples of hieroglyphic text. Nearby, the Mastabat al-Faraun, or "Pharaoh's Bench", is a large monolithic mortuary complex of a 4th-Dynasty king. Hiring a horse, donkey or camel from near the Serapeum is the best way to reach these secluded southern sites.

An agricultural scene from the Mastaba of Ti, Saqqara

Palm groves at Memphis, covering the site of the ancient city

❸ Memphis

Off Hwy 27, 47 km (29 miles) S of Cairo. Ⓣ from Cairo.

The ancient city of Memphis was the capital of Egypt during the Old Kingdom and most of the Pharaonic period. It is thought it was founded in about 3100 BC by King Menes, the ruler responsible for uniting Upper and Lower Egypt. Situated at the head of the Nile Delta, this majestic city controlled important overland and river routes. While Thebes (the site of modern-day Luxor) became the ceremonial centre of Egypt during the New Kingdom, Memphis was still an important administrative and commercial centre until well into the Ptolemaic era. There are many descriptions of the city in texts from Greek writers and historians such as Plutarch and Strabo. In the 5th century AD, the historian Herodotus described Memphis as a "prosperous city and cosmopolitan centre". The extent and grandeur of the city's necropolis, centred on Saqqara, give some indication of how large and prosperous Memphis must once have been. Sadly, there is little remaining

Giant calcite sphinx at Memphis

evidence of this former glory. The city has almost completely vanished. Its magnificent temples and palaces were torn down and pillaged by foreign invaders from the Romans onwards, and the ruins were then buried under the alluvial mud deposited by the annual flooding of the Nile. Palm groves, cultivated fields and villages now cover the site of this once impressive city. What little has been discovered at Memphis is gathered together in a small open-air **museum** in the village of Mit Rahina. The showpiece is a colossal limestone statue of Ramses II, which lies, truncated at the knees, in a viewing pavilion. The statue's more complete twin once stood in Midan Ramses but was moved in 2006 to Giza (see p82). In the garden there are more statues of Ramses II and an 18th-Dynasty sphinx, at 80 tons the largest calcite statue ever found. The garden also contains several calcite slabs, on which the sacred Apis bulls were mummified before being buried in nearby Saqqara.

🏛 Museum
Open 8am–4pm daily (5pm in summer, 3pm during Ramadan). 🎫

❹ Dahshur

Off Hwy 27, 64 km (40 miles) S of Cairo. Ⓣ from Cairo. **Open** 8am–4pm daily (5pm in summer, 3pm during Ramadan). 🎫

Dahshur is a remote desert pyramid field of great significance in the history of pyramid building. The two Old Kingdom pyramids at the site were constructed by 4th-Dynasty king Sneferu (2613–2589 BC), father of Khufu, the builder of the Great Pyramid (see pp136–7). Chronologically they come after Saqqara and Meidum and before Giza and Abusir. The **Bent Pyramid** is considered to be Egypt's first proper pyramid because until this time pyramids were stepped, like Djoser's at Saqqara. The prevailing theory is that the pyramid is bent because once it began to rise the whole structure became unstable and so it had to be completed at a shallower slope. Unusually for pyramids dating from this period, much of its outer limestone casing is still intact, giving a good indication of what a stunning sight it must once have been.

Not happy with his Bent Pyramid, in the 30th year of his reign Sneferu began construction of the northern **Red Pyramid**, so called because of its ancient red graffiti. Second in size only to the Great Pyramid, it can be entered via a passage on the north face. At the foot of a long shaft are three chambers, two of which have corbelled ceilings – where the arch is formed by a series of steps.

The two smaller pyramids at Dahshur date from the Middle Kingdom, when there was a revival in pyramid building, and are badly dilapidated.

Sneferu's Bent Pyramid at Dahshur with much of its outer limestone casing still visible

Fishermen mending their nets on the shores of Lake Qarun, Fayoum

❺ Fayoum

Off Hwy 27, 100 km (62 miles) SW of Cairo. 🚐 2 million. 🚌 from Cairo. ℹ️ Governorate Building, Medinat al-Fayoum (084) 6342 313.

Just an hour-and-a-half's drive from Cairo, Fayoum is Egypt's largest oasis and a popular escape for the smog-choked inhabitants of the big city. They avoid the ugly, modern town of Medinat al-Fayoum (Fayoum City), the oasis's administrative centre, and head instead for the heart of the area, **Lake Qarun**.

This tranquil lake, which existed in antiquity, was linked to the Nile by a series of canals built by the 12th-Dynasty pharaoh Amenemhat III. The area later became a favoured Pharaonic vacation spot.

The Greeks knew the area as Crocodilopolis, named after the reptiles in the lake, which they worshipped. Remains of crocodile temples can be seen at **Kom Aushim**, once the 3rd-century BC city of Karanis, north of Medinat al-Fayoum on the road to Cairo. Some of the objects found on the site are exhibited at the nearby museum. Although the crocodiles are long gone, Lake Qarun is home to an amazing variety of birds. As well as the indigenous species, there are also many migrants and winter visitors.

◀ Beautiful Lake Qarun, Fayoum

The ancient Egyptians were aware of birdlife throughout the country, which they recorded here in friezes on tomb walls – most famously the Meidum Geese, now in Cairo's Egyptian Museum *(see p80)*.

Birding opportunities also exist at **Wadi Rayyan**, a stunning bit of land reclamation, in which excess water from the oasis has been channelled into the desert to create lakes and waterfalls among the dunes. The lakes are well stocked with fish and are a major nesting ground for birds, as well as a big draw for picnicking day trippers.

Of the pyramid sites around the Fayoum oasis, two are worth visits – but only by keen pyramidologists: the **Pyramid of Hawara** and the **Pyramid of Meidum**.

Within Fayoum, **Wadi al-Hitan** is a remote valley where whale skeletons dating back 40 million years were discovered in 1902. The site is so important that it is now a UNESCO World Heritage Site. The area is accessible by 2WD vehicles and can be undertaken as a day trip from Cairo. Alternatively, accommodation is available in nearby Tunis.

The inner core of the Meidum Pyramid at Fayoum

🏛️ Kom Aushim
30 km (18 miles) N of Medinat al-Fayoum. 🚌 **Open** 8am–4pm daily (5pm in summer, 3pm Ramadan). 📷

☒ Wadi Rayyan
45 km (28 miles) SW of Medinat al-Fayoum. Ⓣ **Open** see Kom Aushim. 📷 includes Wadi al-Hitan.

🏛️ Pyramid of Hawara
12 km (7 miles) SE of Medinat al-Fayoum. Ⓣ **Open** see Kom Aushim. 📷

🏛️ Pyramid of Meidum
32 km (20 miles) NE of Medinat al-Fayoum. 🚂 to Al-Wasta, then taxi. **Open** see Kom Aushim. 📷

🏛️ Wadi al-Hitan
60 km (35 miles) SW of Wadi Rayyan. **Open** daily. 📷 includes Wadi Rayyan.

❻ Birqash Camel Market

Off Mansuriyya Canal Road, 30 km (18 miles) NW of Cairo. Ⓣ from Cairo. **Open** mornings. 📷

Contrary to popular belief, the camel is not indigenous to Egypt: it was probably introduced here by the Persians or the Ptolemies in the 6th century BC. Now reputed indispensable, camels are brought up to Egypt in their thousands from western Sudan. Most are taken to Birqash, Egypt's largest camel market. Hundreds of camels are sold every morning, but trade is at its briskest on Fridays. The sound of the animals bawling competes with traders' haggling voices, and the smell is truly awful.

Camels and traders at the daily Birqash camel market

❼ Nile Barrages (Qanater)

16 km (10 miles) N of Cairo. 🚶 56,000. 🚌 Corniche el-Nil, Maspero Terminal. 🚍 from Midan Tahrir, Cairo.

The Nile divides into its eastern Damietta and western Rosetta branches at Qanater, where the main attraction is the Nile Barrages, built to control the flow of water to Lower Egypt. Work on the barrages began in 1834, under Mohammed Ali, and was completed in 1863, when it was discovered that they were ineffectual. The barrages were abandoned until 1883 when a group of British engineers, led by Sir Colin Scott-Moncrieff, finally completed the work. Today the Nile Barrages

View across Deir Anba Bishoi monastery at Wadi Natrun

are surrounded by gardens and are popular with picnickers. Although busy at weekends, Qanater is a pleasant destination for day trips from Cairo, the journey by river bus taking approximately 2 hours.

❽ Wadi Natrun

Off Desert Hwy, 100 km (62 miles) NW of Cairo. 🚍 from Cairo.

Just west of the Delta region, Wadi Natrun was valued by the ancient Egyptians as a source of the salt deposit natron, a vital ingredient in the mummification process (see p32). Later, during the Roman era, the valley's isolation made it an ideal retreat for early Christians escaping Roman persecution. Initially these

Nile Barrages at Qanater, where the two branches of the river fork

monks and hermits lived in caves, but over the years they built many monasteries, of which only four remain today.

The monasteries are easily reached from Cairo by bus, which terminates at the small village of Bir Hooker. All four are surrounded by high, mudbrick walls and resemble desert fortresses. Within the fortified keep of **Deir Anba Bishoi** (the Monastery of St Bishoi), are a well, kitchens, church and storerooms large enough to hold provisions for a year. The church is believed to contain the body of St Bishoi, perfectly preserved in a sealed tube on the altar. He is also commemorated at the Monastery of the Syrians, **Deir as-Suriani**, whose main church (dedicated to St Mary) is built over a cave where St Bishoi is believed to have received a vision of Christ. A bigger draw are the icons and wall paintings, some of which date back to the 8th century.

A little to the north is **Deir al-Baramus**, where the bodies of two sons of the Roman emperor Valentinus are reputed to be buried in a crypt below one of its five churches. Some 20 km (12 miles) to the southeast is **Deir Abu Makar**, the most secluded of the monasteries: permission to visit must be arranged in advance. Each monastery has a full complement of monks, who will show visitors around and may provide a simple meal, for which a small donation should be offered.

The Fayoum Portraits

Although Fayoum is visited by few tourists, many know the name because of the Fayoum Portraits. Several of the portraits, which have been exhibited throughout the world, were discovered here. Some of the earliest ever examples of portraiture, these eerily lifelike faces with their wide staring eyes date back to the Graeco-Roman period. What makes the portraits particularly haunting is that these are funerary artifacts, painted on wooden boards during the subject's lifetime then, at death, laid over the face of the mummified corpse. Many portraits are now on display to the public at the Egyptian Museum (see pp78–81).

Portrait of an Egyptian dating from 3rd century AD, found at Fayoum

THE NILE VALLEY

Egypt has been described as the "gift of the Nile" because without the river the whole country would be a barren desert. Instead, a narrow and verdant strip of cultivated land cuts through the arid country. In ancient times, a great civilization flourished along the river's banks and the incredible wealth of temples and tombs left behind makes the Nile Valley the greatest open-air museum in the world.

For Egypt's *fellaheen* (farmers), the Nile is as central to life today as it was to the farmers and fishermen depicted in the Pharaonic tombs dotted along the valley. For thousands of years the annual flooding of the Nile deposited fresh, fertilizing silt on the surrounding land. Once the flood subsided, the peasants built irrigation channels, planted their crops and waited for the harvest. Though the construction of Aswan's High Dam in the 1960s put an end to the annual inundation, many of Egypt's farmers still live in simple, mudbrick villages and cultivate the precious fertile belt using the same age-old methods.

Since the 19th century, visitors have come to the Nile Valley to gaze in awe at the countless treasures that have been excavated along the banks of the river.

Most of the ancient monuments here were rediscovered after being buried for centuries under sand and debris. As a result, some have been preserved in amazing condition.

In addition to the magnificent monuments, the Nile itself is part of the region's attraction. The traditional feluccas, with their distinctive white sails, are part of the Nile Valley landscape as they dart between cruise ships gliding up and down the river between Luxor and Aswan.

Tourism remains the region's main industry. Despite the setback caused by a series of attacks on foreign tourists in the 1990s, visitors continue to flock to the Nile Valley to experience the sense of living history found along the banks of this majestic river – the lifeblood of Egypt.

Villager in Luxor, setting out his vegetable stall with crops grown in the fertile Nile Valley

◀ Intricately carved columns in the Temple of Hathor, Dendara

Exploring the Nile Valley

Most visitors to the Nile Valley head for the tourist magnet of Luxor, where the magnificent Luxor and Karnak temples and the Theban necropolis are the major attractions. Further south, the beautiful ancient garrison town of Aswan is a relaxing place to stay and a good base for exploring the temples on the banks of Lake Nasser, including the stunning Abu Simbel. The sheer number of ancient monuments in the Nile Valley can be overwhelming and to enjoy the region fully it is a good idea to combine sightseeing with a felucca trip on the Nile or a visit to the colourful souqs of Luxor and Aswan.

Sights at a Glance

1. Minya
2. Beni Hasan
3. Hermopolis
4. Tell al-Amarna
5. Asyut
6. Sohag
7. Abydos
8. *Dendara pp182–3*
9. *Luxor & Thebes pp186–207*
10. Esna
11. Edfu
12. Temple of Kom Ombo
13. Daraw
14. *Aswan pp212–15*
15. Temple of Philae
16. Temple of Kalabsha
17. Temple of Wadi as-Sebua
18. Temple of Amada
19. Qasr Ibrim
20. *Abu Simbel pp218–19*

Donkey and cart, a traditional mode of transport for Nile farmers

Getting Around

Luxor and Aswan have airports served by regular international and domestic flights and Abu Simbel has daily domestic flights. Trains run frequently between Cairo, Luxor and Aswan, stopping at major towns. However, the current political situation means that care should be taken if visiting sites between Cairo and Luxor *(see p180)*. The road from Cairo to Aswan is good, and buses and service taxis operate between the main cities. Dendara and Abydos are best visited on a day trip from Luxor, and Abu Simbel can be reached by air or road from Aswan. Many cruises operate between Luxor and Aswan, and on Lake Nasser. A felucca trip may appeal to the more adventurous, while a *dahabiya* boat is one of the best ways to travel in luxury *(see pp314–17)*.

For hotels and restaurants in this region see p274 and pp287–9

The graceful Kiosk of Trajan on the enchanting island of Philae, near Aswan

A selection of exotic spices on sale in Aswan's famous souq, one of the most colourful markets in Egypt

Key

- Motorway
- Major road
- Minor road
- Scenic route
- – – Track
- Main railway
- International border
- ▪ ▪ Disputed border

0 kilometres   100
0 miles   50

For keys to symbols *see back flap*

❶ Minya

Al-Minya governorate, 245 km
(152 miles) S of Cairo. 200,000.
Governorate Building,
Corniche el-Nil (086) 2362 722.

Situated on the west bank of
the Nile, the regional capital
Minya was a wealthy centre of
the cotton industry in the early
20th century. Today it is a semi-
industrial city, although it still
feels distinctly rural. With its
green squares, pretty, tree-lined
corniche and run-down Italian
villas built by cotton magnates,
Minya is a pleasant place to
simply wander around.
Unfortunately, the surrounding
countryside's association with
Islamic militants and the
relatively high police presence
mean that few tourists now
venture here. However, Minya
makes an excellent base from
which to explore historical sites
such as Beni Hasan. The tourist
office is keen to encourage
people to come to the town
and will help arrange tours to
the sites, although the police
may insist on escorting visitors.

❷ Beni Hasan

Al-Minya governorate, 20 km
(12 miles) S of Minya. to Abu
Qirkis, then ferry. **Open** 6am–4pm
daily (5pm in summer).

Carved into limestone hills on
the east bank of the Nile, the
rock tombs of Beni Hasan date
from the Middle Kingdom
(2055–1650 BC). The necropolis
belonged to military and
regional rulers who, in a clear

Tall granite columns, which once supported a Coptic basilica, amid the ruins of Hermopolis

assertion of their growing independence, chose to be buried in
their own *nome* (province) rather
than close to the king at Saqqara
(see p166). With their deeper
shafts and more elaborate layout
and decoration than earlier
mastabas, these tombs mark a
transition in style between the
Old and New Kingdoms.

Only a handful of the 39
tombs are open to the public
but the vivid murals on some
of the walls reveal much
about life in the Middle
Kingdom. Among the
most beautiful is the
Tomb of Khnumhotep
(No. 3), which shows
Khnumhotep, a
12th-Dynasty regional
governor, hunting
with a throwstick
and fishing with
spears. The **Tomb of
Amenemhat** (No. 2)
is decorated with desert
hunting scenes, while wall
paintings in the **Tomb of Kheti**
(No. 17) depict many aspects
of rural life, including wine-
making. The wrestling scenes in
the **Tomb of Baqet** (No.15) are
precursors of the battle reliefs
found in New Kingdom tombs.

Sandstone baboon from
Amenhotep III's Thoth temple

❸ Hermopolis

Al-Minya governorate, 8 km (5 miles)
N of Mallawi. to Al-Ashmunein.
Open daily.

Believed by ancient Egyptians
to be one of the sites of
creation, the city of Khmun was
the cult centre of Thoth, god
of writing and wisdom. The city
was later renamed Hermopolis
Magna by the Ptolemies, who
associated their own god
Hermes with Thoth. Standing
out among the rather
scant remains are 24 huge
columns from a Christian
basilica and two **sand-
stone baboons** from
Amenhotep III's original
Thoth temple.

Environs
The ancient
city's vast
necropolis, **Tuna
al-Gebel**, lies to the southwest.
Thousands of mummified
baboons and ibises, animals
sacred to Thoth, once filled
the labyrinth of catacombs here.
A short walk further
south is the "City of the Dead",
where streets lined with
chapels and tombs lie

The Tomb of Kheti (No. 17) in Beni Hasan with detailed scenes of daily life during the Middle Kingdom

semi-buried in sand dunes. Most remarkable is the family tomb of Petosiris, high priest of Thoth in the 4th century BC, which resembles a small temple. It is decorated with detailed reliefs featuring an unusual blend of Greek and Egyptian art. The Tuna al-Gebel necropolis bordered on Akhetaten (see below) and a boundary stele showing Akhenaten and his family is visible just to the north of the tombs.

Relief showing wine-pressing in the Tomb of Petosiris, Tuna al-Gebel

❹ Tell al-Amarna

Al-Minya governorate, 12 km (7 miles) SW of Mallawi. 🚉 to Deir al-Mawas, then ferry. **Open** 6am–4pm daily (5pm in summer). 🔲

The remains of the city of Akhetaten, built by the rebel pharaoh Akhenaten and his wife Queen Nefertiti, lie at a site known today as Tell al-Amarna. The site, which once stretched an impressive 15 km (9 miles) north to south and boasted magnificent temples and palaces, is now almost desolate but the sense of history and romance remains.

The widely dispersed ruins are spread around a desert plain bounded by the Nile to the west and surrounded by cliffs. South of the landing stage at At-Till, a cemetery covers part of what was once the **Great Temple of Aten**. In contrast to traditional Egyptian temples which had darkened sanctuaries (see pp28–9), this temple had a roofless sanctuary, designed to allow the rays of the sun-god Aten to flood in. To the south is the **Small Temple of Aten**. Better preserved are the remains of Nefertiti's **Northern Palace**, to

the north of At-Till. Here, the remains of some mosaics can still be seen on the floor of summer residence.

The highlights of Tell al-Amarna are the two sets of cliff tombs at either end of the city. Of the **Northern Tombs**, 3 km (2 miles) north of At-Till, one of the finest is the **Tomb of Huya** (No. 1), Superintendent of the Royal Harem and Steward to Queen Tiye, Akhenaten's mother. This fascinating tomb is carved with royal banquet scenes, including one that shows the queen wining and dining with her son and his family. In the highly decorated **Tomb of Mery-Re I** (No. 4), Akhenaten is shown presenting Mery-Re I with the high priest's golden collar. Reliefs depicting Akhenaten and the Great Temple on the eastern wall of the tomb give an indication of what the city must have looked like during its brief period of glory. Grouped in clusters, 8 km (5 miles) south of At-Till, the **Southern Tombs** are less accessible but equally rewarding. The **Tomb of Ay** (No. 25), Akhenaten's vizier, is

Relief of Nefertiti and her daughter praying to the sun-god Aten, in Cairo's Egyptian Museum

considered the finest tomb in Tell al-Amarna. The wall paintings show Ay and his wife receiving ceremonial golden collars from Akhenaten and Nefertiti, watched by a crowd of cheering onlookers. The well-preserved **Tomb of Mahu** (No. 9) contains reliefs of Mahu carrying out his duties as Akhenaten's chief of police. Malawi has a small museum exhibiting finds from across the Al-Minya area.

Akhenaten the Heretic

In the 14th century BC, Amenhotep IV turned his back on Thebes and the practice of worshipping several gods to establish a religion based on the worship of just one god, Aten, god of the sun-disk. He changed his name from Amenhotep to Akhenaten, meaning servant of Aten, and built a huge city dedicated to Aten at Akhetaten. The city was the capital of Egypt for 14 years but, when Akhenaten died, Thebes was re-established as the capital by Akhenaten's son-in-law and successor Tutankhamun. Akhetaten was destroyed on the order of the priests of Karnak who were determined to eradicate all trace of the heretical pharaoh's new religion.

The rebel pharaoh Akhenaten

❺ Asyut

Asyut governorate, 110 km
(68 miles) S of Minya. ⛰ 280,000.
🚂 🚌 ℹ Sharia ath-Thawra
(088) 2324 000.

In Pharaonic times Asyut was
capital of the 13th *nome*
(province) and centre of the cult
of Wepwawet, the wolf-headed
god and avenger of Osiris. At
the crossroads of caravan routes
to the Western Desert oases and
across the Sahara, the city has a
long history as a centre of trade.
Until the mid-19th century,
slaves who had survived the
torturous "Forty Days Road" from
Darfur in Sudan were sold here
alongside camels in Egypt's
biggest slave market.

Today Asyut is the largest city
in Upper Egypt and has the third
largest university in
the country. Known
for its carpet-
making, Asyut
remains the region's
main agricultural
trading centre.
The area is also
associated with
the Virgin Mary. In
August 2000, the
Virgin was reportedly seen above
St Mark's Church. For a few
months afterwards there were
reports of lights around the
church towers and many
thousands flocked to see them.
The apparitions have now ceased.

Convent of the Holy Virgin, built into the cliffs at Dirunka, near Asyut

Icon showing the Holy Family in the Convent of the Holy Virgin

Environs
Coptic Christians believe that
Mary, Joseph and the baby

Jesus sheltered in caves at
Dirunka, 12 km (7 miles)
southwest of Asyut. They were
escaping from King Herod,
who had ordered the killing
of all baby boys under the
age of two in
Bethlehem.
A large convent,
the **Convent of
the Holy Virgin**,
was built nearby.
During the
annual Moulid of
the Virgin, held
between 7 and
22 August,
around 50,000 pilgrims flock
here to see icons paraded
around the cave-church.

Another place held sacred by
Christian Copts is the **Burned
Monastery** (Deir al-Muharraq).
This is situated on the edge
of the desert, 5 km (3 miles)
outside Al-Qusiya, a small town
42 km (26 miles) north of Asyut.
The Holy Family is said to have

lived in a cave here for a month
and it is thought that the
church built over it was the
first in Egypt. What is now
the church's altar stone once
blocked the entrance to the
cave. The annual *moulid*, which
is held here between 21 and
28 June, attracts many
thousands of visitors.

A further 7 km (4 miles) west
of the monastery are the
Tombs of Mir, a burial ground
dating from the Old and
Middle Kingdoms.

❻ Sohag

Sohag governorate, 115 km (71 miles)
S of Asyut. ⛰ 210,000. 🚂 🚌
ℹ Governorate Bldg (093) 4604 493.

An agricultural town and
commercial centre, Sohag
has a large Coptic Christian
community and, like many
other cities in Middle Egypt,
is a place of sporadic unrest.
A museum housing a wealth
of local archaeological finds,
including those from the
ongoing excavations of the
temple of Ramses II in Akhmim,
opened in 2011 and aims to
increase tourism in the town.
Many visitors usually prefer a
brief visit to Sohag as a day trip
from Luxor. A large animal
market is held in the town
each Monday.

Environs
A short drive west of Sohag,
the **White Monastery** (Deir
al-Abyad) dates from the early
5th century AD. Named for
the colour of its masonry,

Security in the Region

Police at the Temple of Hathor gateway

This area has long been associated with religious
extremists who want to turn the country into an
Islamic state. Asyut University was a hotbed for
Islamic fundamentalists in the late 1970s, and
the early 1990s saw several attacks on tourists
around Qena, Asyut and Dairut. The Egyptian
government has tightened security, especially
since the 1997 massacre at Luxor, but tension
continues and police presence is high. Although
tour groups tend to avoid the region, officially it
is possible to travel freely in this area and visitors
rarely encounter trouble. The most common way
to see sites such as the Temple of Hathor at Dendara *(see pp182–3)*
is on a day trip from Luxor, usually with a police escort. The situation
is always changing, however, and visitors should contact local tourist
authorities and their embassy for the latest advice.

the monastery was built using chunks of white limestone taken from local Pharaonic temples. The monastery, founded by the Coptic saint Pjol, was once home to 2,000 monks. Today very little remains within its high fortress walls apart from a church, dedicated to Saint Shenouda. On 14 July every year thousands of pilgrims attend a *moulid* at the site.

Four kilometres (2.5 miles) north of the White Monastery lies the **Red Monastery** (Deir al-Ahmar). Built in the 6th century AD by Shenouda's disciple Bishoi – a repentant robber who became a saint – the monastery has two churches within its grounds. The main church is decorated with beautiful frescoes dating from the 10th century. These wall paintings are being restored, and the colours and designs that have been revealed are extraordinary.

On the eastern bank of the Nile, just across the river from Sohag, is **Akhmim**, which can be reached by microbus. The town is known for its hand-woven hangings and throws. The town's main attraction is an 11-m (36-ft) high statue of Queen Meret Amun – the fourth daughter of Ramses II.

White Monastery
10 km (6 miles) W of Sohag. 🚌 **Open** daily. 📅14th July.

Red Monastery
14 km (9 miles) NW of Sohag. 🚌 **Open** daily.

The chapel of Osiris in the Cenotaph Temple of Seti I in Abydos

❼ Abydos

Sohag governorate, 46 km (29 miles) SW of Sohag; 10 km (6 miles) W of Al-Balyana. 🚌 or day trip from Luxor, with convoy.

Abydos, the cult centre of Osiris, god of the dead, was regarded as the holiest of Egyptian towns in Pharaonic times. All ancient Egyptians tried to make the pilgrimage to the town during their lifetime or hoped to be buried here. Many tombs were painted with scenes of the deceased making the posthumous journey to Abydos. Tradition had it that Osiris – or at least his head – was laid to rest here after he was murdered by his brother Seth and his mutilated body strewn over the country.

Icon of Christ in the White Monastery

Abydos was once a vast walled town with several ancient cemeteries, lakes and temples, including the important Temple of Osiris. Today, almost all that can be seen is the stunning 19th-Dynasty **Cenotaph Temple of Seti I**. Built during Seti I's reign between 1294–1279 BC, it is one of the most intact temples in Egypt. Constructed using white limestone, this secondary mortuary temple possesses some of the finest bas-reliefs of the New Kingdom; many have retained their original colour. After the death of his father, Ramses II (1279–1213 BC) built his own temple to the north of Seti's temple. Although only partially intact, it is noted for its hieroglyphs.

Entrance to the temple is gained via the first hypostyle hall. The temple's highlights include the bas-relief scenes in the second hypostyle hall, which show Seti I with the gods Osiris and Horus. Just beyond, the seven chapels dedicated to a deified Seti I and the gods Ptah, Ra-Harakhty, Amun, Osiris, Isis and Horus are remarkable for their coloured reliefs and delicate decoration. Each chapel contained the statue and barque of the relevant god and would be served daily by the high priests. Behind the temple, Seti had built the Osirieon (the tomb of Osiris) from huge blocks of stone. Today it is partly underwater.

The Red Monastery near Sohag, founded by the Coptic saint Bishoi

❽ Dendara

Dendara, where Hathor supposedly gave birth to Horus's child, the god Ihy, was Hathor's cult centre from pre-Dynastic times. Buried under sand until the 19th century, the vast Temple of Hathor remains remarkably intact. The current temple is Graeco-Roman but its design imitates typical Pharaonic temple architecture – a series of large hypostyle halls leading to a sanctuary, surrounded by storerooms, chapels and crypts. Other buildings include two *mammisi* (birth houses) and a Coptic basilica.

★ **Astronomical Ceiling**
In this detail from the ceiling, the sun-god Ra is shown sailing his sacred barque across the sky.

Temple Façade
The façade shows Tiberius and Claudius making offerings to Horus and Hathor.

★ **Hathor-headed Columns**
Hathor is shown in her human form with cow's ears at the head of the 18 columns in the hypostyle hall.

Entrance to temple

KEY

① **Dendara Zodiac** A copy of the famous zodiac ceiling is located in one of the rooftop sanctuaries. The original was removed in 1820 and is now in the Louvre, Paris.

② **The east staircase** led back down into the temple.

③ **The open-air kiosk** was the focus of the New Year celebrations. It may have had a light wooden cover that was removed to expose the statues to the sun.

④ **The New Year Chapel** is where rituals were performed before Hathor's statue was taken up to the roof. The ceiling shows Nut giving birth to the sun.

⑤ **Elaborate bas-reliefs depicting offerings to Hathor**

Cult of Hathor

Hathor was the goddess of pleasure and love, and wet nurse and lover of Horus. Every year she was carried on a barque to Edfu *(see p208)* to be reunited with Horus. The Festival of Drunkenness, celebrating the divine union, followed. On New Year's Day, Hathor's statue was carried up the decorated west staircase of the temple to the open-air kiosk on the roof, where it was revitalized by the sun.

Hathor with the sun-disk and cow horns

Cleopatra and Caesarion
A huge relief on the southern exterior wall shows Cleopatra making offerings to Hathor. Caesarion, her son by Julius Caesar, stands in front of her burning incense.

Temple of Hathor Reconstruction
The intricate carved reliefs that adorn the temple were originally painted in vivid colours.

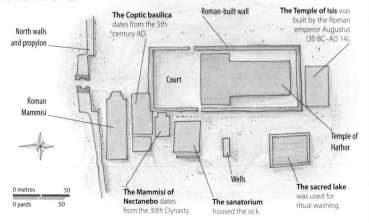

Roman Mammisi
This small temple celebrated the divine birth of Hathor's son. The southern wall has some exquisite reliefs on its exterior.

Dendara Site Plan

The Coptic basilica dates from the 5th century AD.

Roman-built wall

The Temple of Isis was built by the Roman emperor Augustus (30 BC–AD 14).

North walls and propylon

Court

Roman Mammisi

Temple of Hathor

0 metres 50
0 yards 50

The Mammisi of Nectanebo dates from the 30th Dynasty.

The sanatorium housed the sick.

Wells

The sacred lake was used for ritual washing.

❾ Luxor and Thebes

Modern Luxor grew out of the ruins of Thebes, once the capital of ancient Egypt's New Kingdom (1550–1069 BC). The monumental temples at Luxor and Karnak were famed throughout the ancient world and have attracted tourists since Greek and Roman times. Across the Nile, on the West Bank, lies the Theban necropolis, perhaps the world's richest archaeological site. To foil thieves, the Theban kings hid their tombs deep in the surrounding hills, away from their mortuary temples on the flood plain. Visiting the Luxor monuments is straightforward, but due to the number of sights and the distances involved, some planning is needed to get the most out of a visit to the West Bank.

⑦ **Medinet Habu**
Second only to Karnak in size, the Mortuary Temple of Ramses III was modelled on the Ramesseum.

Luxor and Thebes

① Luxor Temple (pp190–91)
② Luxor Museum (p191)
③ Karnak Temple (pp192–4)
④ Valley of the Kings (pp196–8)
⑤ Tombs of the Nobles (p199)
⑥ Hatshepsut Temple (pp200–1)
⑦ Medinet Habu (pp202–3)
⑧ Valley of the Queens (p203)
⑨ The Ramesseum (pp204–5)
⑩ Colossi of Memnon (p206)
⑪ Temple of Merneptah (p206)
⑫ Deir al-Medina (pp206–7)
⑬ Temple of Seti I (p207)
⑭ Howard Carter's house (p207)
⑮ New Gurna (p207)

Key

☐ Town area

0 kilometres   1
0 miles   0.5

THEBES

GE

⑥ **Hatshepsut Temple**
Discovered only in the mid-19th century, and still being restored by the Polish Mission, the Mortuary Temple of Hatshepsut rises out of the desert in a series of terraces that merge with the sheer limestone cliffs behind.

◀ Giant statues of Ramses in the Luxor Temple

Getting Around

Luxor Temple is in the centre of town and easily accessible on foot; Karnak Temple can be reached by minibus, bicycle, taxi or *caleche*. Most Luxor hotels offer tours to the West Bank including the services of a guide. Alternatively, you can cross by ferry from Luxor Temple and hire a taxi in Gezira village, on the other side of the river. Bicycles can be hired from Luxor for the day and taken across on the ferry.

⑨ The Ramesseum
Built to perpetuate the pharaoh's glory, the Mortuary Temple of Ramses II was part of a large complex that included a royal palace and a great many granaries and storerooms. Both pylons are decorated with scenes from the Battle of Qadesh.

Tips for Visitors

- Do not try and see everything at once. Limit yourself to two or three major sights per day.
- To avoid the post-midday heat, most people visit the area early in the day, although late afternoons can be less crowded.
- All ticket kiosks are open 6am–4pm (till 5pm summer). Tickets are valid only on the day of purchase.
- Tickets for the valleys of the Kings and Queens and for Hatshepsut Temple can all be purchased on site.
- Holders of a valid ISIC card are entitled to a 50 per cent reduction in admission prices.
- Photography and guides are prohibited inside all tombs.
- Always carry plenty of water and maybe a snack, as facilities are limited and expensive.

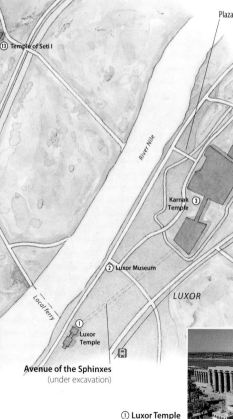

⑭ Howard Carter's House

Plaza

⑬ Temple of Seti I

River Nile

Karnak Temple ③

② Luxor Museum

Local ferry

LUXOR

①
Luxor Temple

Avenue of the Sphinxes
(under excavation)

③ Karnak Temple
The Karnak complex was known as *"Ipet-Isut"* ("the most perfect of places") to the ancient Egyptians.

① Luxor Temple
Founded by Amenhotep III, Luxor Temple was dedicated to the Theban triad of Amun, Mut and Khonsu, who are celebrated at the annual Festival of Opet *(see p194).*

For keys to symbols *see back flap*

Street-by-Street: Luxor

Built on the site of the New Kingdom capital city of Thebes, Luxor has returned to prominence as the tourist mecca of the Nile Valley. The exciting excavations that were led by European archaeologists in the 19th and early 20th centuries, especially the discovery of Tutankhamun's tomb, aroused international interest in the town and visitors have been coming to marvel at the amazing concentration of ruins here ever since. Today the livelihood of Luxor's resident population depends almost entirely on tourism and visitors can expect to be approached by salesmen and touts at every turn. The bustling town is centred around the magnificent Luxor Temple, an enduring symbol of its glorious past.

Sharia Souk
Gated and paved, the market may have lost some charm, but good local products are still available.

Post office

Train station

The Corniche
The riverside Corniche, which leads from Luxor to Karnak, is one of the busiest streets. Most visitors stick to the stretch between the Winter Palace and the Luxor Museum.

★ **Luxor Museum**
Located on the Corniche, halfway between Luxor and Karnak, the museum has a collection of statues and funerary goods, including this fine relief of Tuthmosis III *(see p191).*

SHARIA SOUK

SHARIA AL-KARNAK

Avenue of sphinxes

Luxor Museum and Karnak ✗

Key

— Suggested route

0 metres 100
0 yards 100

Winter Palace Hotel
Founded in 1887, the most famous of Luxor's hotels has played host to celebrities such as Agatha Christie and Noel Coward.

VISITORS' CHECKLIST

Practical Information
Luxor Governorate, 674 km (419 miles) S of Cairo. 360,000. Opposite Luxor railway station (095) 2372 188. daily. Moulid of Abu al-Haggag, two weeks before Ramadan.

Transport

Felucca on the Nile at Luxor

Corniche

★ Luxor Temple
With its grand colonnades, Luxor Temple is one of the most impressive ancient monuments in Egypt. It is situated on the waterfront in the heart of modern Luxor and looks particularly beautiful when illuminated at night (see pp190–91).

Public ferry

The Abu al-Haggag Mosque stands amid the ruins of Luxor Temple.

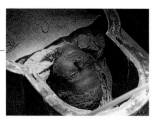

★ Mummification Museum
The ancient Egyptian practice of mummification is explained in detail in this fascinating museum close to the river (see p191).

Exploring Luxor

Spread out along the east bank of the Nile, Luxor today is a bustling town of some 360,000 inhabitants. The main tourist attractions are concentrated in the heart of town between Sharia al-Karnak and the Corniche. Luxor Museum is a short distance away on the Corniche in the direction of Karnak. Walking around town is a great way to soak up the atmosphere though it can also be fun to ride through the streets in a *caleche* (carriage).

The first pylon, built by Ramses II, forming the façade of Luxor Temple

Luxor Temple

Corniche el-Nil. **Open** 6am–9pm daily (10pm in summer).

Dominating the banks of the Nile in the centre of town, Luxor Temple is an elegant example of Pharaonic temple architecture. Dedicated to the Theban triad of Amun, Mut and Khonsu, the temple was largely completed by the 18th-Dynasty pharaoh Amenhotep III and added to during the reign of Ramses II in the 19th Dynasty. Although the temple was further modified by later rulers, including Alexander the Great, its design remained strikingly coherent in contrast to the sprawling complex that developed at nearby Karnak. In the 3rd century AD the temple was occupied by a Roman camp and the site was subsequently abandoned. Over the centuries it was engulfed in sand and silt, and a village grew up within the temple walls. Then in 1881 archaeologist Gaston Maspero rediscovered the temple in remarkably good condition, but before excavation work could begin the village had to be removed. Only the **Abu al-Haggag Mosque**, built by the Arabs in the 13th century, was left intact, standing high on the layers of silt accumulated over

the years. An avenue of sphinxes, which stretched all the way from Luxor to Karnak, almost 2 km (1.2 miles) away, is being excavated, and will link the two temples once more. Fronting the entrance to the temple, the gigantic first pylon is decorated with scenes of Ramses II's victory over the Hittites in the battle of Qadesh. Two enormous seated colossi of Ramses and a huge 25-m (82-ft) high pink granite obelisk flank the gateway to the temple. The obelisk was originally one of a pair; the other was removed

The Abu al-Haggag Mosque in Luxor Temple

in the early 19th century and re-erected in the Place de la Concorde in Paris, a gift from the Egyptian ruler Mohammed Ali to the people of France.

Beyond the first pylon lies the Court of Ramses II, with the Abu al-Haggag Mosque towering over the courtyard to the east. The height of the mosque above the stone floor demonstrates the depth of debris that once buried the entire temple. The western corner of the court incorporates an earlier barque shrine (to house the gods' sacred boats) dedicated to the Theban triad. A double row of papyrus-bud columns encircles the court, interspersed with huge standing colossi of Ramses II.

More giant black granite statues of Ramses guard the entrance to the original part of the temple, which begins with the majestic Colonnade of Amenhotep III, with its avenue of 14 columns. The walls here were embellished during the reign of Tutankhamun and depict the annual Opet festival, when the images of Amun, Mut and Khonsu were taken in procession from Karnak to Luxor (*see p194*). The western wall shows the outward journey to Luxor and the eastern wall the return journey to Karnak. The colonnade leads to the superb Court of Amenhotep III, which is noted for its double rows of towering papyrus columns, the best preserved

The avenue of sphinxes leading to the entrance of Luxor Temple

Colonnade of Amenhotep III with its lofty papyrus columns

and most elegant in the temple. In 1989, work here on the foundations of the court led to the discovery of 22 New Kingdom statues, now on display in the Luxor Museum.

The hypostyle hall on the southern side of the court served as a vestibule to the main temple. It has 32 papyrus columns in four rows of eight, bearing the later cartouches of Ramses II, Ramses IV, Ramses VI and Seti I. The antechamber beyond was converted into a church by the Romans in the 4th century AD, its Pharaonic reliefs being plastered over and covered with Christian paintings.

A second, smaller ante-chamber, the offerings chapel, leads on to another columned hall with the Sanctuary of the Sacred Barque in the centre. Rebuilt by Alexander the Great, this granite shrine was where Amun's barque ended its journey from Karnak in the Opet festival (see p194). It is decorated with scenes of Alexander making offerings to the Theban triad. The birth room to the east has reliefs depicting the divine birth of Amenhotep III, intended to validate his claim to be the son of Amun. Finally, behind the Sanctuary of the Sacred Barque, another hall leads to a small, damaged sanctuary that once housed a golden statue of Amun.

Pink granite obelisk

Mummification Museum

Corniche el-Nil, opposite Mena Palace Hotel. **Tel** (095) 2370 062. **Open** 9am–3pm daily. 🖼 🔲 📷

This small museum on the banks of the Nile houses a fascinating display describing the process of mummification performed by the ancient Egyptians (see pp32–3). Instruments for removing internal organs, substances to treat the body and items needed by the mummy on its journey to the afterlife are all displayed here. The intact mummy of Maseharti, a 21st-Dynasty high priest and general, was found at Deir el-Bahri along with Maseharti's painted coffin. A mummified cat, the symbol of the goddess Bastet, and a mummified ram, the symbol of the god Khnum, are among the other exhibits. Among the informative items on display is a cross-section of a mummified skull, stuffed with material where the brain has been removed. There is also a piece of a mummified toe.

Sharia Souk

Sharia Souk, opposite Luxor train station. **Open** 24 hours daily.

Sharia Souk is a street market that has been cleaned up in an attempt to appeal to tourists. What was an authentic market street has been paved over but the stalls still sell the usual market wares, such as fabrics, pottery, spices and food. There are also cafés, restaurants and hotels alongside it. The market is kept swept and cleaned all night long, but tourists may prefer to shop at the stalls in the dusty, more characterful streets north of Sharia Souq.

Luxor Museum

Corniche el-Nil, Luxor. **Tel** (010) 0670 3638. **Open** 9am–3pm daily. 🖼 ♿

Situated on the Corniche halfway between Luxor Temple and Karnak, this well-designed museum has an excellent

Statue of Tuthmosis III in the Luxor Museum

collection of statues and artifacts found in temples and tombs in the Luxor area. Near the entrance is a stunning gilded head of Hathor, the cow-goddess, discovered in the tomb of Tutankhamun in the Valley of the Kings. Also on the ground floor look out for the large pink granite head of Amenhotep III and the beautiful carved figure of a youthful Tuthmosis III.

On the first floor, further exhibits from Tutankhamun's tomb include a funerary bed and two model barques. Also exhibited here are three busts of Amenhotep IV (Akhenaten) and a reconstructed wall made up of 283 sandstone blocks from Akhenaten's temple at Karnak. The relief scenes depict daily life during Akhenaten's reign and show the heretical pharaoh and his wife Queen Nefertiti making offerings to the sun-god Aten.

The spectacular lower hall near the entrance on the ground floor is a highlight. It displays a collection of beautifully preserved New Kingdom statues, discovered at Luxor Temple in 1989. The pieces include a near-perfect 2.5-m (8-ft) high statue of Amenhotep III and a statue of the gods Mut and Amun.

Two mummies, Ahmes I and (possibly) Ramses I, are on display in the Thebes Glory wing.

Painted relief from Akhenaten's Karnak Temple in Luxor Museum

Karnak: Temple of Amun

At the heart of the immense Karnak complex lies the
Temple of Amun, dedicated to the king of the gods. With
its endless courts, halls and colossi and huge sacred lake,
the scale and complexity of this sprawling temple is
overwhelming. From its modest 11th-Dynasty beginnings,
pharaoh after pharaoh added to and changed the existing
buildings, seeking to make their mark on the country's
most important temple. No expense was spared and
during the 19th Dynasty some 80,000 men worked in the
temple as labourers, guards, priests and servants. The
temple lay buried under sand for more than 1,000 years
before excavation work began in the mid-19th century.
Today, the huge task of restoration continues.

★ Great Hypostyle Hall
The glorious highlight of Karnak,
this cavernous hall was supported
by 134 gigantic columns.

★ Colossus of Ramses II
An imposing granite statue
of Ramses II, with one of his
daughters at his feet, stands
in front of the entrance to
the Great Hypostyle Hall.

Reconstruction of the Temple of Amun

*The temple's brightly
coloured exterior is visible
in this reconstruction,
which shows how the
temple would have
looked in around 1000 BC.*

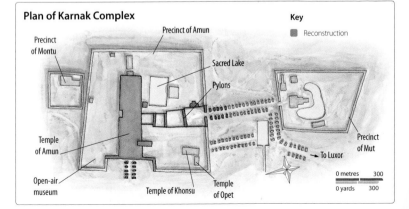

Plan of Karnak Complex

Key

▪ Reconstruction

Precinct
of Montu

Precinct of Amun

Sacred Lake

Pylons

Temple
of Amun

To Luxor

Precinct
of Mut

Open-air
museum

Temple of Khonsu

Temple
of Opet

0 metres   300

0 yards   300

Botanic Gardens
Part of the temple built by Tuthmosis III, this roofless enclosure lies behind the Great Festival Temple. It is decorated with reliefs of exotic flora and fauna, brought back to Egypt by the pharaoh during his campaign in Syria.

★ Great Festival Temple
The central hall of this temple built by Tuthmosis III was supposedly designed to resemble the tent in which he lived while on campaign.

KEY

① **A row of sphinxes** led to the Nile.

② **Tomb of Seti II** dedicated to the Theban triad.

③ **Temple of Ramses III**

④ **Eighth Pylon**

⑤ **The Ninth Pylon** was built by Horemheb using blocks from the demolished Aten temple.

⑥ **Flagpoles**

⑦ **Row of sphinxes**

To Precinct of Mut

Sacred Lake
Priests purified themselves in the holy water of the Sacred Lake before performing rituals in the temple. North of the lake is a huge stone scarab of Khepri, built by Amenhotep III.

Exploring Karnak

After the Pyramids of Giza, Karnak is Egypt's most important Pharaonic site. Excavations over the years have gradually uncovered the original structure of the temple complex, which was built over a 1,300-year period and covers a vast area just north of Luxor. As well as the colossal Temple of Amun, the site comprises a fantastic array of temples, chapels, pylons and obelisks, all testifying to the importance of Thebes.

Statues of the lioness-goddess Sekhmet line up in the Precinct of Mut

🚩 Temples of Khonsu and Opet

Dedicated to the son of Amun and Mut, the well-preserved Temple of Khonsu was built largely during the reigns of Ramses III and IV. The main entrance is via a magnificent gateway, built by Ptolemy III, which is still virtually intact.

Close by is the smaller Temple of Opet (the goddess thought to be the mother of Osiris). It contains some finely decorated reliefs dating from Ptolemaic and Roman times, but is closed for excavation.

🏛 Open-air Museum

Located to the northwest of the Precinct of Amun, the open-air museum contains a fine collection of monuments that were discovered during an excavation of the Third Pylon. Among the museum's main attractions is the lovely, reconstructed, 12th-Dynasty White Chapel of Senusret I. This has delicate carvings of the king making offerings to Amun. The restored 18th-Dynasty Red Chapel of Hatshepsut can also be seen here; the chapel served as a shrine for the barque of Amun. Other attractions include the Alabaster Chapel of Amenhotep I and the Shrine of Tuthmosis III.

A separate ticket for the museum must be purchased before entering the complex.

🚩 Precinct of Mut

Built by Amenhotep III, the precinct contains the ruins of a temple dedicated to Amun's consort Mut. Huge, black granite statues of the lioness-goddess Sekhmet line the temple courts. To the west of the sacred lake surrounding the temple is the ruined 20th-Dynasty Temple of Ramses III. Relics of the Temple of Amenhotep III, dedicated to Amun, lie to the northeast.

🚩 Precinct of Montu

The Precinct of Montu is just north of the Temple of Amun. Montu, the warrior-god, was the original deity of Thebes and was still worshipped after Amun rose to pre-eminence. The precinct contains Amenhotep III's Temple of Montu and the Temple of Amun, which was added during the 20th Dynasty. Both are closed to the public at present.

Sound and Light

The sheer size of the Karnak complex means that one visit is seldom enough to take it all in. A good way to revisit the site is to attend the spectacular Sound and Light Show, which helps to unravel the complex 1,500-year history of the building of the Temple of Karnak. The shows are performed in various languages, and there are three shows each evening. Check with Luxor Tourist Office or at www.soundandlight.com.eg for details of times and prices.

Ram-headed sphinxes lit up at Karnak

The Festival of Opet at Karnak

Amun was the principal god of Thebes who, along with his consort Mut and their son Khonsu, was worshipped as part of the Theban triad. Once a year, during the flood season, the Festival of Opet celebrated the king's rebirth as the son of Amun. Accompanied by priests and revellers in a riotous festival, the images of Amun, Mut and Khonsu were carried on decorated barques to the Nile and then to Luxor Temple. Even today, elements of the Opet festival live on in the Islamic Moulid of Abu al-Haggag, a five-day event preceding Ramadan. Luxor occasionally stages a re-creation of the festival for tourists on 4 November, the anniversary of the discovery of Tutankhamun's tomb.

Priests carrying the image of Amun in his barque during the Opet festival

Cruising the Nile

Along with the Grand Tour of Europe, a trip to Egypt was one of the most exciting journeys available to the 19th-century traveller. Having disembarked at Alexandria, wealthy European and American tourists were transported to Cairo – in the early days by boat, later by train. After several days visiting the sights of Cairo, often staying at the world-famous Shepheard's Hotel, passengers would board a *dahabiya* (large sail boat) or steamer, and set off for a trip up the Nile. The pace was languid: a steamer took three weeks to reach Aswan, while a sailing boat could take six to twelve weeks. Slow days on deck alternated with treks through the desert to marvel at the newly found secrets of ancient Egypt. It was not uncommon for tourists to come across or even fall into hitherto undiscovered tombs. Expeditions were led by local guides, while servants carried supplies of food and drink for picnics amid the ruins.

Thomas Cook, the founder of modern tourism, played a dominant role in the development of Egyptian travel. He once owned all the steamers plying the Nile.

Florence Nightingale described her 1848 trip up the Nile in a series of letters. Other writers inspired by the trip include Agatha Christie, who wrote *Death on the Nile*.

The highlight of a trip to Egypt for 19th-century travellers was then, as now, a visit to the Great Pyramids and the Sphinx at Giza. As seen in this illustration, these sites had yet to be fully excavated.

Shepheard's Hotel was the focus of European life in Egypt from its founding in 1841 until it was burned down in 1952.

Exciting new discoveries from Egypt's ancient past provided an added thrill for early visitors to the country. Each year new finds were made.

Thebes: Valley of the Kings

The remote, barren Valley of the Kings was the necropolis of the New Kingdom pharaohs. By digging their tombs deep into the Theban Hills, pharaohs from Tuthmosis I (1504–1492 BC) hoped to stop robbers stealing the priceless possessions buried with them. It was an unsuccessful strategy. Despite their hidden locations, every burial chamber was raided except for those of Yuya and Tuya *(see p81)*, and Tutankhamun, discovered by Howard Carter in 1922, its glorious treasures still intact *(see p81)*. But for all that, the structures themselves remain, their dramatic corridors and burial chambers stunningly adorned with symbolic accounts of the journey through the underworld and ritual paintings to assist the pharaohs in the afterlife.

Tomb of Horemheb (No. 57) Horemheb was the final pharaoh of the 18th Dynasty. His tomb departs from the usual style of 18th-Dynasty tombs in that it consists of a single straight corridor with side chambers. It is decorated with reliefs from the Book of Amduat.

Valley of the Kings, chosen as a burial ground because of its secluded location amid limestone hills

Tomb of Tuthmosis III (No. 34) Dug 30 m (98 ft) above ground in a vain attempt to stop thieves, today the tomb is reached by a metal staircase. The walls are painted with figures portraying the Book of Amduat (funerary text used for pharaohs), and a red granite sarcophagus is the sole remaining artifact.

The Valley Tombs

Sixty-three tombs have been found in the Valley of the Kings and 62 are numbered on the map in the order of their discovery. The most significant tombs, some of which are described on p198, are marked with a red bullet. Of all the tombs, only about 11 are open at any one time.

KEY

① Ticket kiosk for Tombs of Tutankhamun and Ramses VI

② Visitor centre and ticket office

Tomb of Seti I (No. 17)
Finely carved bas-reliefs and gilded paintings decorate this stunning tomb. The burial chamber is particularly remarkable with its astronomical ceiling. The tomb is currently closed.

VISITORS' CHECKLIST

Practical Information
2 km (1 mile) N of West Bank ticket kiosk. **Open** 6am–4pm daily (5pm in summer).
Visitor centre ticket office; ticket valid for three tombs only. Separate tickets are needed for tombs of Tutankhamun and Ramses VI, payable at Valley of the Kings ticket kiosk.

Tomb of Ramses VI (No. 9)
Originally built for his predecessor Ramses V, this large tomb was expanded by Ramses VI. Among its most striking features are the vaulted astronomical ceiling and the inner sarcophagus of the pharaoh.

| 0 metres | 75 |
| 0 yards | 75 |

Tomb of Tutankhamun (No. 62)
Tutankhamun's tomb is small with parts undecorated. Yet the burial chamber, whose walls depict the "Opening of the Mouth" ceremony *(see p33)*, is unique in that it still contains the king's body inside the gilded coffin.

Tomb of Ramses IV (No. 2)

Although Greek and Coptic graffiti mar the walls of this 20th-Dynasty tomb, there are some beautiful, vividly coloured scenes from the Book of the Dead. In the burial chamber, the goddess Nut stretches across the blue ceiling. The enormous pink granite sarcophagus is covered with magical texts and carvings of Isis and Nephthys, designed to protect Ramses's mummy from danger.

Tomb of Ramses IX (No. 6)

This typical late Ramesside tomb is long and steep, with interesting scenes on the sloping corridor walls taken from the Litanies of Ra, a religious work celebrating the solar deity's nightly journey. A four-pillared room precedes the burial chamber, which has an impressive astronomical ceiling, featuring the goddess Nut surrounded by sacred barques full of stars. Gods and demons are painted on the dark walls. Only the mark of the sarcophagus remains on the floor.

Tomb of Merneptah (No. 8)

The tomb of 19th-Dynasty pharaoh Merneptah, son of Ramses II, was excavated by Howard Carter in 1903. Reliefs of Isis and Nephthys worshipping the solar disc decorate the tomb's entrance. From here the corridor descends steeply to the burial chamber, where the sarcophagus still lies. A false burial chamber did not fool robbers, who escaped with treasures but dropped the heavy sarcophagus lid in one of the corridors.

Tomb of Ramses III (No. 11)

Discovered by the Scottish traveller James Bruce in 1768, the tomb of Ramses III is known as the "Tomb of the Harpists" after the bas-relief of two blind musicians in one of the side chambers. It is beautifully preserved and, unusually for a royal tomb, its colourful reliefs include scenes taken from everyday Egyptian life.

Tomb of Queen Tawsert/ Sethnakht (No. 14)

Originally built for the wife of Seti II, Queen Tawsert, this tomb was appropriated by 20th-Dynasty pharaoh Sethnakhte after he ran into difficulties building his own tomb. The well-preserved wall paintings include depictions of the "Opening of the Mouth" ceremony and, in the burial chamber, the gods greeting Sethnakhte.

Tomb of Ramses I (No. 16)

The tomb of Ramses I, founder of the 19th Dynasty, is small but exquisitely decorated. Discovered in 1817 by the Italian explorer Giovanni Battista Belzoni, the walls are painted with scenes relating to the Book of Gates. A large granite sarcophagus remains in the burial chamber.

Tomb of Amenhotep II (No. 35)

This is one of the deepest tombs in the valley, with 90 steps leading down to different levels. Although thieves made off with the treasure, Amenhotep's mummy was still in its decorative sarcophagus when the tomb was discovered by Victor Loret in 1898. Nine other royal mummies, hidden in the

Colourful wall painting from the well-preserved Tomb of Siptah

tomb by priests, were also found. The pillared burial chamber is decorated with illustrations and texts from the Book of Amduat.

Tomb of Siptah (No. 47)

The Tomb of Siptah, who reigned briefly at the end of the 19th Dynasty, is one of the longest in the valley, stretching 106 m (350 ft) into the rock. Lightly coloured bas-reliefs decorate the walls and the ceiling is painted with a procession of vultures whose wings spread the width of the corridor.

A hallway in KV5 being examined

KV5

In 1994 the American archaeologist Kent Weeks began excavating a tomb that had previously been considered unimportant by Egyptologists. What he found is the largest and most complex tomb in the Valley of the Kings. Known as KV5, the tomb is believed to be the burial site for Ramses II's sons. A 16-pillared entrance hall and more than 121 corridors and chambers have so far been discovered and although no treasure has been found, thousands of important artifacts have been recovered from the rubble. The tomb is currently still undergoing excavation.

Amenhotep II's burial chamber, containing the pharaoh's sarcophagus

Thebes: Tombs of the Nobles

Extending over a large area to the south of the Valley of the Kings, the Tombs of the Nobles is made up of more than 400 tombs of Theban nobles and high officials, mainly from the New Kingdom. The tombs lie close to the surface of the hills overlooking the Nile. Because of the poor quality of the limestone here, the tombs are painted and there are few carved reliefs. Vivid artworks cover the walls, providing an invaluable insight into daily life in the New Kingdom. The Sheikh Abd al-Gurna Tombs are clustered around the village of Old Gurna. Further east, tombs at the necropolises of Khokha, Assasif and Abu al-Naga are now open to the public. Of all the tombs, only a few open at any one time.

VISITORS' CHECKLIST

Practical Information
Thebes/Luxor, West Bank (follow signs for Sheikh Abd al-Gurna Tombs). **Open** 6am–4pm daily (5pm in summer). 🚌 go to West Bank ticket kiosk; for Assasif Tombs, go to Hatshepsut Temple ticket kiosk.

Richly detailed paintings of life in ancient Egypt in the Tomb of Sennefer

Sheikh Abd al-Gurna Tombs

All the tombs here date from the 18th Dynasty. The **Tomb of Sennefer (No. 96)**, mayor of Thebes and overseer of the gardens of Amun under Amenhotep II, is one of the best preserved. The ceiling is covered with brightly coloured paintings of vines, and Sennefer is shown with his family and making offerings to the gods. The **Tomb of Rekhmire (No. 100)**, a vizier during the reigns of Tuthmosis III and Amenhotep II, shows servants at work and Rekhmire collecting taxes and receiving gifts from foreign lands.

Treading grapes – Tomb of Nakht

The **Tomb of Nakht (No. 52)** is decorated with scenes of rural life, such as fishing, harvesting and hunting in the Nile Delta. Nakht was the scribe and astronomer of Tuthmosis IV. The well-preserved **Tomb of Menna (No. 69)**, an inspector of estates, shows Menna and his wife making offerings to the gods. It contains a detailed harvest scene and paintings of fishing and hunting.

The **Tomb of Ramose (No. 55)**, governor of Thebes before and during Akhenaten's reign, has reliefs showing both the old style of worship and the worship of Aten imposed by the heretic pharaoh. The **Tomb of Userhat (No. 56)** has detailed scenes of everyday life, including a trip to the barber's. Userhat was one of Amenhotep II's scribes.

The **Tomb of Khonsu (No. 31)**, an adviser to Tuthmosis III, is painted with colourful scenes of the Festival of Montu, while the **Tomb of Benia (No. 343)** has vignettes of daily life and statues of the deceased and both his parents.

Khokha Tombs

Three tombs, discovered here in 1915, were opened for the first time in 1995. The **Tomb of**

Djehuty-Mes (No. 295) shows this 18th-Dynasty priest with his wife and family. The **Tomb of Neferronpet (No. 178)**, a scribe during the reign of Ramses II, contains a painting of the scribe and his wife before Osiris. The **Tomb of Nefersekheru (No. 296)**, another 19th-Dynasty scribe, shows a similar scene.

Assasif Tombs

The **Tomb of Kheruef (No. 192)**, steward to Queen Tiy, contains scenes of the queen and 18th-Dynasty pharaoh Amenhotep III watching a dance in their honour. The nearby **Tomb of Anchhor (No. 414)**, overseer of the priests of Amun, is an elaborate structure, but the decoration is not well preserved. The **Tomb of Pabasa (No. 279)**, a 26th-Dynasty official, is noted for the pillared first court with its very detailed fishing, bee-keeping, wine-making and fruit-picking scenes.

Abu al-Naga Tombs

The first tombs in this area opened in 1999. The **Tomb of Roy**, a steward in the 18th Dynasty, and the **Tomb of Shuroy**, an 18th-Dynasty official, both have colourful tableaux of daily life.

Recording the harvest scene, Tomb of Menna

Thebes: Hatshepsut Temple

Against its stark mountainous backdrop, the partly rock-hewn Mortuary Temple of Hatshepsut at Deir al-Bahri is a breathtaking sight. It was designed by Queen Hatshepsut's architect Senenmut in the 18th Dynasty and is an extraordinary monument which rises from the desert plain in a series of imposing terraces. The temple was damaged by Ramses II and his successors, and Christians later turned it into a monastery (hence the name Deir al-Bahri, which means "Northern Monastery"). However, the ongoing excavation of the site by the Polish mission continues to reveal much exquisite decoration. Adjacent to the main temple are the ruins of the much older Temple of Montuhotep II, the ruler of the 11th Dynasty who managed to unite Egypt, and the 18th-Dynasty Temple of Tuthmosis III.

Temple of Montuhotep II
The prototype for Hatshepsut's Temple, the older Temple of Montuhotep II now lies in ruins.

The imposing Hatshepsut Temple, in its stunning setting at the foot of a sheer limestone cliff face

Reconstruction of the Temples at Deir Al-Bahri

This reconstruction shows the Temples of Montuhotep II, Tuthmosis III and Hatshepsut as they would have looked during the reign of Tuthmosis III in the 18th Dynasty. Partly rock-cut and partly freestanding, the three temples are set into a natural amphitheatre and are given added majesty by the dramatic cliffs behind them.

KEY

① **Temple of Tuthmosis III**

② **The Shrine of Amun** was dug into the cliff behind the temple.

③ **Sanctuary of the Sun**

④ **Myrrh trees** planted in the gardens yielded a gum that was burnt as incense.

⑤ **Avenue of sphinxes** led off in the direction of the temple complex at Karnak.

★ **Chapel of Hathor**
This chapel is noted for its Hathor-headed columns. The walls have retained much original colouring, including this relief of the *ankh* and *djed* pillar, symbols of life and stability.

★ **Statues of Hatshepsut**
The columns of the portico around the upper terrace were decorated with Osiride statues of Hatshepsut, characteristically represented as a male king with a beard. Although many statues were destroyed by later pharaohs, several have been reconstructed from their fragments.

VISITORS' CHECKLIST

Practical Information
2 km (1 mile) NE of West Bank ticket kiosk. **Open** 6am–4pm daily (5pm in summer).

Transport
T or on foot or bike from other sites.

Chapel of Anubis
This chapel contains brightly coloured murals, including a relief of Tuthmosis III making offerings to the sun-god Ra-Harakhty.

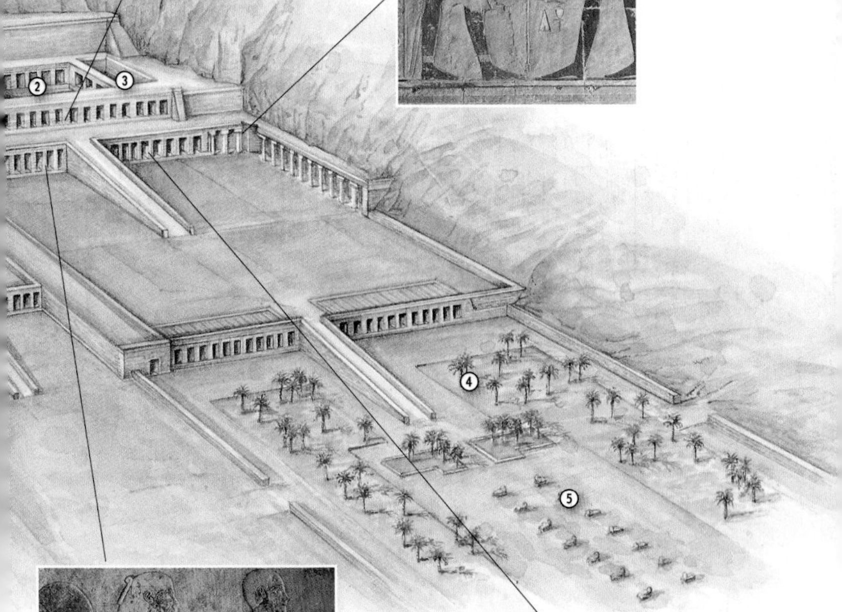

★ **Reliefs of Punt Expedition**
Faded reliefs relate Hatshepsut's journey to the Land of Punt (Somalia). The king of Punt is seen here with his wife Ati (left), who is depicted suffering from obesity.

Birth Colonnade
Scenes along the Birth Colonnade portray the divine birth of Hatshepsut, designed to legitimize the queen's claim to the throne. On the right, the young queen is shown in the arms of the goddess Neith.

Thebes: Medinet Habu

Second only to Karnak in size and detail, the magnificent precinct of Medinet Habu is one of the less-visited sights in Thebes. The mortuary temple of the early 20th Dynasty pharaoh Ramses III was first excavated in 1859 and remains the focal point of the complex. However the area was a sacred sight prior to his reign and even today is considered magical among local farmers, the *fellaheen*. The enclosure walls provided refuge for the entire population of Thebes during invasions later in the 20th Dynasty. Later still, the temple was appropriated by the Coptic Church, ironically preserving some remarkable polychrome reliefs, which the Christians had covered in mud.

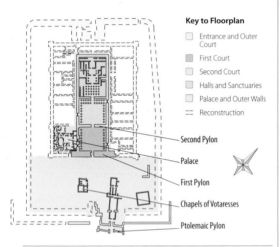

Key to Floorplan

☐ Entrance and Outer Court

◼ First Court

☐ Second Court

☐ Halls and Sanctuaries

☐ Palace and Outer Walls

= = Reconstruction

Second Pylon

Palace

First Pylon

Chapels of Votaresses

Ptolemaic Pylon

his chariot and scribes tallying vanquished foes by the traditional counting of severed hands and genitals. Osiride statues of Ramses III line the First Court. The Window of Appearances on the left provided a view of the king in his adjacent palace.

Imposing Osiride columns featuring Ramses III line the First Court

The Second Court

The second pylon, which is approached via a ramp, is etched with further scenes of Ramses's god-given victories over the Sea Peoples, including the Philistines, and over Asia Minor. The ceiling of the pylon gateway merits attention for its painted winged cobras and sun-disks. The citizens of the Coptic settlement of Djeme removed the Osiride columns to build a church within the Second Court. They have been returned but are still damaged; however, the beautifully coloured reliefs were preserved when Christians covered their sacrilegious content with mud.

Entrance and Outer Court

The complex is still accessed, as Ramses intended, via the Migdol Gate, which lies adjacent to the 3rd century BC Ptolemaic Pylon. The three-storey gatehouse is modelled on a Syrian fortress. The second floor holds a suite where the pharaoh frolicked with his harem. It is decorated appropriately with reliefs of scantily clad women. As you enter the outer courtyard the small temple called Djeser Set, or "Holy is the Place", is dedicated to Amun. It was built by Hatshepsut around 1490 BC and later added to by Tuthmosis III and successive pharaohs. The Chapels of the Votaresses (priestesses of Amun) were built during the Nubian-led 25th Dynasty. Excellent reliefs are

found in the chapel forecourt and in the shrine of Amenirdis, sister of King Shabaqo. Sadly, access to the roof, where the views are excellent, is no longer permitted.

The First Court

The temple itself is a slightly smaller replica of the nearby Ramesseum (see pp204–5) built by Ramses II, but the pylons at Medinet Habu are the most imposing of any temple in Egypt. Massive reliefs on the first pylon, which reaches 27 m (89 ft), show Ramses defeating the Nubians on the left and the Syrians on the right, although he fought neither. The inner pylon reliefs depict actual events and show an oversized Ramses scattering Libyans from

The Halls and Sanctuaries

The Hypostyle Hall is similar in style and scope to that of Karnak. Archaeologists assume that the damage to this part of the temple was caused by the earthquake of 27 BC. The roof and the eight-columned central aisle are no more, and all that remains of the 24 pillars are their hieroglyphic-covered bases. To the right are locked rooms, presumed to have been treasuries, as their reliefs depict the weighing of items such as myrrh, gold and lapis. Opposite is a series of chapels dedicated to Ramses, his namesake Ramses II and to the gods Ptah, Osiris and Sokar. Approaching the holy sanctuaries to the Theban triad (Mut, Amun and Khonsu) are two pillared halls holding the funerary chamber of Ramses III to the left, and an altar to Re to the right.

Hieroglyphic-covered pillar bases in the Hypostyle Hall

The Palace and Outer Walls

The now-ruined mudbrick Palace is too small to have been a long-term residence for the pharaoh, but he did grace his favourites with gifts from the Window of Appearances during visits. A rugged walk along the exterior of the outer walls provides the highlight of Medinet Habu: a series of detailed and unique reliefs. A royal hunt covers the first pylon, the dying bulls and antelope having been depicted with great empathy. As you continue, the reliefs show a Calendar of Festivals on the short axis of the enclosure walls, followed by the Nubian and Libyan Wars, and then an assessment of the captives as you turn the corner. Further along Ramses charges the Libyans then battles the Sea Peoples (Sardinians, Philistines and Cretans); this is Egypt's sole relief of a naval battle. The fighting is broken up by another hunting scene to extol Ramses's courage.

Thebes: Valley of the Queens

Named by Champollion, the Valley of the Queens lies to the southwest of the Valley of the Kings and holds the tombs of many royal wives and children. Although it was used as a burial site in the 18th Dynasty, it was only from the reign of the 19th-Dynasty pharaoh Ramses I that royal wives were laid to rest here. Of the nearly 80 tombs populating the valley, the most famous is that of Queen Nefertari and only a few are open to the public at any one time.

Tomb of Amunherkhepshep (No. 55)

The elegant, well-preserved tomb of Prince Amunherk-hepshep (Amun), son of Ramses III, is the highlight of the Valley of the Queens, unless you can afford the VIP entrance to Nefertari's tomb *(see box, below)*. Amun would have succeeded his father as pharaoh but he died when he was a child and was buried in this royal tomb.

Steps lead down to the tomb hall, which contains beautiful, brightly coloured wall paintings of Ramses accompanying his young son on a visit to pay homage to the gods of the underworld. Amun is easily recognizable because he is wearing the characteristic braided hairstyle of a prince. From here, a corridor decorated with the Keepers of the Gates leads to the burial chamber, where the skeleton of a five-month-old foetus is on display in a glass cabinet. Foetuses have been found in other burial chambers and may have been placed there as part of the ritual of rebirth.

Tomb of Queen Titi (No. 52)

Queen Titi was married to one of the Ramesside pharaohs of the 20th Dynasty, although it is unclear which one. Her tomb is small and damaged in parts, but certain sections have particularly colourful paintings. Some of the best scenes are in the burial chamber, where Hathor appears in both bovine and human form.

Tomb of Prince Khaemweset (No. 44)

This is the tomb of another of Ramses III's sons who died in infancy. Its intricate reliefs have preserved much of their colour. Ramses is shown introducing his son to the different deities and making offerings to them. The goddesses Isis, Nephthys, Neith and Selket are also depicted.

Repairing Queen Nefertari's Tomb

Queen Nefertari wearing a white gown and jewels

Regarded as the most beautiful in Egypt, Queen Nefertari's tomb (No. 66) was first discovered in 1904. Carved from poor-quality limestone, its reliefs have sustained damage over time and despite a restoration project that began in 1986 the tomb remains extremely fragile. Access can be gained only by applying to the Secretary General of the Supreme Council of Antiquities and payment of a LE 20,000 fee.

Thebes: The Ramesseum

Pharaoh Ramses II, ruler of Egypt for 67 years in the 19th Dynasty, built his mortuary temple, the Ramesseum, as a statement of his eternal greatness and to impress his subjects. The huge complex, which took more than 20 years to complete, now lies largely in ruins. Dedicated to Amun, it once boasted an 18-m (60-ft) high, 1,000-tonne colossus of Ramses, parts of which lie scattered at the site. The complex also included a smaller temple dedicated to Ramses's mother Tuya and his wife Nefertari, as well as a royal palace and storehouses.

★ **Osiride Columns**
Statues of Ramses as Osiris, god of the underworld, face into the second court. These figures, arms crossed bearing the crook and flail, signal the funerary nature of the temple.

★ **Head of the Colossus of Ramses**
The shattered head and shoulders of the immense colossus of Ramses now lie in the second court. An image of this evocative sight inspired Percy Bysshe Shelley to write his famous poem "Ozymandias".

Reconstruction of the Ramesseum

This reconstruction shows how the Ramesseum would have looked when it was completed in around 1250 BC. The flooding of the Nile and earthquakes later took their toll, leaving today's atmospheric ruins.

KEY

① **Landing stage** provided mooring for boats from the Nile.

② **Royal palace**

③ **Vestibules** led to the sanctuary.

④ **Huge mudbrick walls** protected the entire temple complex.

First Pylon
The imposing first pylon was decorated with scenes of Ramses in battle. Sadly, an earthquake badly damaged the pylon, and the gateway to the first court is now supported by concrete.

Hypostyle Hall Plant Capital
The hypostyle hall roof is supported by tall columns. The still-colourful patterns of papyrus and lotus plants symbolize the union of Lower and Upper Egypt.

Mudbrick Stores
Innumerable vaulted mudbrick magazines once surrounded the temple, used as storerooms, workshops and living quarters.

Foundations of the Temple of Tuya
A small temple dedicated to Ramses's mother Tuya and his wife Nefertari stood to the north of the hypostyle hall.

Battle of Qadesh

Ramses II portrayed himself as a warrior pharaoh of great bravery and military prowess. Around 1275 BC, he led the Egyptian army into battle against the Hittites at Qadesh, an important trading town in the Orontes Valley in Syria. Although the battle was really a draw, Ramses paraded it as a victory on the walls of several of his great temples, including the Ramesseum. Ramses is depicted firing arrows at the fleeing Hittites and, in traditional pose, holding his enemy's head, about to inflict the fatal blow.

Wall relief on the inner face of the second pylon, depicting Hittites slain at the Battle of Qadesh

Exploring Other Sites in Thebes

Scattered amid the wadis and hills of the West Bank are several other sites well worth a visit. Often bypassed in favour of the more famous Theban attractions, these additional sites can be visited in relative peace, well away from the tourist hordes. Deir al-Medina provides a rare insight into the lives of ordinary people in ancient Egypt, as well as containing some exquisite tombs. The Temple of Merneptah hosts some outstanding reliefs and is complemented by a well laid out and informative museum.

The awesome Colossi of Memnon on the flat desert plain of the West Bank

🔟 Colossi of Memnon

500 m (0.3 mile) E of West Bank ticket kiosk.

Soaring 18 m (60 ft) into the sky, the two enthroned statues of Amenhotep III are the first monuments most visitors see on arriving in the West Bank. They originally guarded Amenhotep's mortuary temple – thought to have been the largest ever built in Egypt – which was plundered for building material by later pharaohs and gradually destroyed by the annual floods. However, ongoing excavations are revealing a wealth of immense statues that have been buried in the silt for millennia. The area is out of bounds, but the finds can be viewed from the roadside.

During the Roman period the northernmost statue became a popular tourist attraction as it was heard to "sing" at sunrise. Prominent visitors to the site to hear this included the Emperor Hadrian, and the colossi are mentioned by classical authors such as Strabo and Pliny. The Greeks had attributed the sound to Memnon greeting his mother Eos, the goddess of dawn, with a sigh. In fact, the statue had been badly damaged in an earthquake in 27 BC and its musical talent probably had a purely physical cause related to the damage it had sustained. Whatever the reason, once the statue had been repaired in AD 199 by the Roman emperor Septimius Severus, the singing stopped.

🔟 Temple of Merneptah

NE of West Bank ticket kiosk. **Open** 6am–4pm daily (5pm in summer). 🏛

Merneptah was the 13th of Ramses II's 52 sons and became his successor in 1213 BC only because he outlived his 12 older brothers. He ascended to the throne at the age of 50, ruling for just 10 years. In design, Merneptah's temple is a smaller version of his father's Ramesseum (*see pp204–5*). Merneptah located his temple on the same floodplain as the inundated temple of Amenhotep III, from where he plundered most of his building materials and statuary. Not surprisingly, it was similarly washed away. British archaeologist William Matthew Flinders Petrie examined the site in the 1890s but the temple was then forgotten until the 1970s.

There are no massive pylons here, but an excellent museum displays some small detailed works and fragments of a colossal limestone sphinx. A series of polychrome reliefs of Amenhotep III, discovered and displayed here, are probably the finest examples known in Egyptian art history.

🔟 Deir al-Medina

1 km (0.6 mile) NW of West Bank kiosk. **Open** 6am–4pm daily (5pm in summer). 🏛 separate ticket required for Tomb of Pashedu.

The craftsmen, servants and labourers who worked on the royal tombs lived in the village of Deir al-Medina, also known as the Workmen's Village, to the south of the Valley of the

Painted relief from the Ptolemaic temple at Deir al-Medina

Sennedjem and his wife worshipping gods in his tomb at Deir al-Medina

Queens. They were buried in the nearby necropolis, in tombs that were intricately decorated and surmounted by a small pyramid. One of the most beautiful is the **Tomb of Sennedjem (No. 1)**, a 19th-Dynasty servant. Discovered in 1886, its yellow ochre walls are in perfect condition; they show Sennedjem and his wife, Iyneferti, worshipping different gods and working in the fields of the underworld. The adjacent **Tomb of Inherkhau (No. 359)**, the "foreman of the mayor of the Two Lands", is equally beautifully decorated with memorable scenes, including the Cat of Heliopolis killing the serpent Apophis under the holy tree. The small size of these tombs means that only 10 people are allowed in them at one time. The **Tomb of Pashedu (No. 3)**, a servant during the Ramesside era, is renowned for its delicate paintings and for a famous scene of Pashedu crouching next to a stream under a palm tree.

To the north of the village is a small Ptolemaic temple, dedicated to the goddesses Hathor and Maat. During the Coptic period it was turned into a monastery, which led to the site being named Deir al-Medina or "City Monastery".

🏛 Temple of Seti I
3 km (2 miles) E of West Bank ticket kiosk. **Open** 6am–4pm daily (5pm in summer). 🖼

Away from the popular tourist trail, the 19th-Dynasty mortuary Temple of Seti I, the northernmost of all the temples of Thebes, is dedicated to

Amun and to the cult of Seti's father, Ramses I. After Seti's death, his son Ramses II completed the temple. Although the pylons and surrounding buildings are in ruins, the sanctuary, halls and antechambers of the main sandstone temple are well preserved and there are some interesting, high-quality reliefs, including those showing Seti and Ramses II making offerings to Amun. Part of the roof, featuring vultures and the winged sun-disk, is still intact. The German Archaeological Institute is in the process of restoring the site.

🏛 Howard Carter's house
3 km (2 miles) E of West Bank ticket kiosk. **Open** 9am–4pm daily (5pm in summer). 🖼

British archaeologist Howard Carter, best known for his discovery of the tomb of Tutankhamun in 1922 (see p24), lived for many years in this domed house north of the Temple of Seti I. In 2010, the house opened as a museum displaying pictures of Carter's discoveries, copies of letters to

his patron Lord Carnarvon, and a short 3D film that brings his character to life.

The Villages of Gurna
Built on and around the Tombs of the Nobles (see p199), Old Gurna, with its brightly painted mudbrick houses, was long considered a threat to the tombs. In the 1940s, New Gurna was built to rehouse residents. Designed by architect Hassan Fathy, it was inspired by traditional Nubian architecture, yet it failed to lure the Old Gurna residents who believed they should safeguard both the monuments and tourists. A Palace of Culture is being developed in New Gurna.

Today most of Old Gurna has been demolished and the government has moved residents to purpose-built housing in Tarfa and Gabawy to the northeast. Only a few examples of the old villages remain, with their decorations of pilgrimages to Mecca, on the hillside near Medinet Habu; however, the villages are now empty.

Part of a village near Old Gurna, in the foothills of the Theban Hills

🏛 New Gurna
2 km (1 mile) SE of West Bank ticket kiosk.

🏛 Gurna
500 m (0.3 mile) N of West Bank ticket kiosk.

The domed house of British archaeologist Howard Carter

Detail of the Temple of Khnum's astronomical ceiling at Esna

⑩ Esna

Qena governorate, 54 km (33 miles) S of Luxor. 🚶 55,000. 🚌 🚊 🚇 🚆 from Luxor or Aswan.

The sleepy farming town of Esna lies on the western bank of the Nile, just south of a sandstone dam across the river, built in 1906. Known as Latopolis by the ancient Greeks because the Nile perch (*lates* in Greek) was worshipped here, Esna is today best known for the **Temple of Khnum**. This Graeco-Roman structure was designed to resemble a much earlier temple on the site, built by 18th-Dynasty pharaoh Tuthmosis III (*see p53*). Both temples were dedicated to the ram-headed god Khnum, who, according to one of the Egyptian creation myths, fashioned mankind out of Nile clay using a potter's wheel.

Gradually, repeated flooding by the Nile buried the Graeco-Roman structure under layers of silt and mud, and the modern town of Esna was built on top of it. Excavation work on the site began in the 1860s but this has only cleared one part of the temple, the Roman hypostyle hall, which was built during the reign of the Roman emperor Claudius (AD 41–54). Today this well-preserved hall stands in a huge excavation ditch 10 m (33 ft) below street level in the centre of town. Its roof, which remarkably is still intact, is on the same level as the foundations of the surrounding houses. The façade of the hall is inscribed with the cartouches of Roman emperors Claudius, Vespasian (AD 69–79) and Titus (AD 79–81). Inside the hall the last emperor mentioned is Decius, who died as late as AD 249. The roof is supported by 24 columns inscribed with hieroglyphs and fascinating texts describing the sacred festivals of Esna and recording hymns to the god Khnum. The colours of the astronomical ceiling have been blackened by smoke but it is still possible to make out the zodiac register, remarkable for its subtlety and detail.

🏛 **Temple of Khnum**
Open 6am–4pm daily (5pm in summer). 🎟

⑪ Edfu

Aswan governorate, 115 km (71 miles) S of Luxor; 104 km (65 miles) N of Aswan. 🚶 56,000. 🚌 🚊 🚇 🚆 from Luxor or Aswan.

Edfu stands beside the Nile almost exactly halfway between Luxor and Aswan. It was an important sacred site to the Egyptians because, according to ancient myth, this was where the falcon-god Horus fought a fierce battle with his uncle Seth, who had cruelly murdered Horus's father Osiris (*see p30*).

The **Temple of Horus** at Edfu, which was buried under sand and silt for nearly 2,000 years, is the largest and best-preserved Ptolemaic temple in Egypt. Construction of the temple began under Ptolemy III Euergetes in 237 BC and the main temple complex took 25 years to complete. However, construction continued up to the time of Ptolemy XII Neos Dionysus (80–51 BC).

Despite its relatively recent construction, the temple is of great interest to Egyptologists because it closely imitates much older Pharaonic designs. The imposing 36-m (118-ft) high first pylon is typically decorated with Pharaonic scenes of Ptolemy XII defeating his enemies in front of Horus and Hathor. Two elegant black granite statues of Horus flank the entrance to the pylon, which leads to a large colonnaded court and the first hypostyle hall. Behind this lies a second, smaller hypostyle hall with chambers off to the side. Gifts for the gods were stored in these rooms before being taken into the hall of offerings beyond. Stairs lead from the hall of offerings to the roof, which is inaccessible; however the staircase walls are beautifully decorated with scenes from the New Year festival, a ritual celebrated in temples all over Egypt. On the first day of the

Granite statue of the falcon-god Horus

Pylon of the Temple of Horus in Edfu with reliefs showing pharaoh Ptolemy XII

year, in each temple, a procession of priests carried the statue of the temple god up to the roof to be revitalized by the sun. Beyond the hall of offerings is the sanctuary of Horus with its black granite shrine which contains a model of Horus's sacred barque. Several chapels with excellent reliefs surround the sanctuary.

Southwest of the temple lie the remains of Horus's birth house. This was the focus of the annual Coronation Festival, a ritual celebrating the birth of Horus and his incarnation as the reigning pharaoh.

🏛 Temple of Horus

Open 7am–6pm daily (7pm in summer). 🎵 Sound & Light Show: 8pm, 9pm, 10pm. 🎵
🌐 soundandlight.com.eg

Postcard of Bedouin and camels – both at home in the desert

Ships of the Desert

The *Camelus dromedarius* or one-humped Arabian camel has been an essential part of life in Egypt for thousands of years. Used primarily for transporting goods, the camel also provides milk, wool and meat. Contrary to myth, the camel's hump is not filled with water; it contains fat which allows the camel to survive for up to a week without food. Camels are ideally suited to desert life with their third, transparent eyelid that allows them to see in sand storms, nostrils that close between breaths and their unique body thermostat that minimizes unnecessary water loss through sweating. When they walk, camels move both legs on one side and then both legs on the other. This creates a rolling motion, hence their nickname "ships of the desert".

Relief of Sobek, the crocodile-god, in the temple of Kom Ombo

⑫ Temple of Kom Ombo

40 km (25 miles) N of Aswan. 🚌 🚕 🚃 🚂 from Aswan or Luxor. **Open** 7am–7pm daily (9pm in summer). 🎵

Surrounded by fields of sugar cane and corn, Kom Ombo is a pleasant agricultural town, home to many Nubians displaced by the creation of Lake Nasser *(see p214)*. The town's ruined yet imposing Graeco-Roman temple is in a particularly beautiful setting overlooking the Nile. The temple building is totally symmetrical with two

entrances, two halls and two sanctuaries. This unusual structure is the result of the temple's dedication to two gods – the left side to the falcon-god Haroeris (Horus the Elder) and the right side to Sobek, the local crocodile-god. The construction of the temple was begun by Ptolemy VI Philometer in the 2nd century BC and mostly completed by Ptolemy XII Neos Dionysus during the 1st century BC. Finally the Roman emperor Augustus added the entrance pylon in around 30 BC. From the largely ruined forecourt, two doors lead to the hypostyle hall, which contains scenes relating to Haroeris on the left wall and Sobek on the right. The many columns are carved with the lotus or lily of Upper Egypt and the papyrus of the Delta. A series of halls and vestibules leads through to the sanctuaries of Haroeris and Sobek.

A museum near the exit of the temple houses 40 crocodile mummies from the nearby crocodile necropolis.

⑬ Daraw

8 km (5 miles) S of Kom Ombo. 🏔 31,000. 🚕 from Kom Ombo. 🛒 Tue.

Travellers sometimes combine a trip to Kom Ombo with a visit to the nearby village of Daraw for the famous Tuesday camel market, when hundreds of camels are up for sale. Most of the camels have been brought from Sudan on a month-long journey along "The Forty Days Road", an ancient droving route and former slave trail. The market is chaotic, colourful and noisy. Traders travel from Cairo to haggle for camels to sell at the famous Birqash camel market *(see p172)*, while locals come in search of a bargain.

Camels for sale in the famous Daraw camel market, held every Tuesday

⑭ Aswan

Situated downriver from the First Nile Cataract, Aswan is Egypt's southernmost city. From Old Kingdom times, this strategically important garrison town guarded Egypt's southern frontier and was a base for military incursions into Nubia and Sudan. Located at the crossroads of ancient trade routes between Egypt, Africa and India, the town was also a prosperous marketplace, where exotic goods were traded. Aswan stands on the most enchanting part of the Nile, where the desert comes right down to the water's edge and the river is dotted with islands. It is home to a large Nubian community, and the town's laid-back atmosphere makes it one of the more relaxing places in Egypt to visit.

The imposing Hotel Sofitel Legend Old Cataract Aswan, overlooking the Nile

🏨 Hotel Sofitel Legend Old Cataract Aswan

Corniche el-Nil. **Tel** (097) 231 6000.
The English crime-writer Agatha Christie penned part of her best-selling novel *Death on the Nile* in this impressive Moorish-style hotel, which opened in 1899. Set in beautiful gardens, with superb views over the Nile and Elephantine Island, it is one of the most famous hotels in Egypt. Past guests include the German Field Marshal Rommel, Sir Winston Churchill and King Farouk. Soak up Aswan's romantic atmosphere while sipping afternoon tea on the verandah.

🏛 Nubian Museum

Off road to Aswan Dam, 1 km (0.6 mile) S of Aswan. **Tel** (097) 231 9 222. **Open** 9am–1pm, 4–9pm daily.
This well laidout museum traces life in Nubia – the area between Aswan in Egypt and Khartoum in Sudan – from the earliest settlements to the present day. Nubian crafts such as basket making and pottery are featured and there is a fascinating display about the UNESCO-backed projects to save Nubian monuments from submergence under Lake Nasser (*see p214*). The garden contains a reconstructed cave with prehistoric rock carvings, a Nubian house and a water feature showing the Nile's course and cataracts.

🏛 Unfinished Obelisk

1.5 km (1 mile) S of Aswan, next to Fatimid Cemetery. **Open** 7am–4pm daily (5pm in summer).
A gigantic obelisk, dating from the New Kingdom, lies semifinished in an ancient granite quarry just south of Aswan. Had it been completed, it would have weighed a staggering 1,085 tonnes (1,197 tons) and stood 41 m (134 ft) high. Three sides of the shaft were quarried before a flaw was discovered in the stone and the obelisk had to be abandoned, still partly attached to the parent rock.

To the west of the quarry, the Fatimid cemetery contains several hundred mudbrick Islamic tombs, built between the 8th and 12th centuries.

🛒 Souq

Sharia as-Souq. **Open** daily.
From embroidered *galabiyyas* and coloured caps to aromatic spices, live chickens and fresh vegetables, there is a vast array of goods on sale in Aswan's lively and extensive market. Renovations have eroded some of the narrow alleyways and chaotic atmosphere but this is still a fascinating place to take in the exotic and colourful environment. The market runs parallel to the Nile and becomes noticeably less tourist-orientated further inland from the busy main street, Sharia as-Souq.

🏛 Elephantine Island

Aswan.
Known as Yebu (meaning "elephant") during the Old Kingdom, Elephantine Island is the oldest inhabited part of Aswan. It is not known whether the island was named after the huge granite boulders at the

Spices on Sharia as-Souq, the main street through Aswan's famous market

◀ The Ramesseum at sunrise, Thebes

A Nubian village on the banks of Elephantine Island

southern end of the island, which resemble bathing elephants, or because it was a major ivory trading post.

In ancient times, the island was the cult centre of the ram-headed god Khnum, creator of humankind and god of the Nile flood. Among the ruins of the ancient fortress town that once stood on the southern end of the island are the ruins of the **Temple of Khnum**, built by Nectanebo in the 4th century BC. An impressive gateway, added in the 1st century BC, showing Ptolemy XI worshipping Khnum, can be seen on the west side of the temple. Immediately to the north is the Graeco-Roman **Necropolis of the Sacred Rams**,

and to the east, the **Temples of Satet**, built by Queen Hatshepsut. This area is being excavated by German archaeologists and some areas are out of bounds.

In the middle of the island, two traditional Nubian villages are distinguished by their brightly coloured homes.

🏛 Nilometer

Elephantine Island. **Open** 8am–4pm daily (5pm in summer). 🖼

The steep Nilometer steps descend into the river. The walls were calibrated to record the height of the annual flood and so indicate the likely crop yield for the next year. Dating from Pharaonic times, the Nilometer was briefly put back into use after its discovery in 1822.

🏛 Aswan Museum

Elephantine Island. **Open** 8am–4pm daily (5pm in summer). **Closed** due to ongoing renovations

The Aswan Museum is set among pleasant, subtropical

VISITORS' CHECKLIST

Practical Information
Aswan governorate, 215 km (133 miles) S of Luxor; 900 km (560 miles) S of Cairo. 🚉 220,000.
ℹ️ Located outside railway station (097) 231 2811.
🚢 daily.

Transport
✈️ 25 km (15 miles) SW of town.
🚉 🚌

Calibration on walls of Nilometer

gardens near the southern end of Elephantine Island. It is home to a collection of artifacts found on digs in and around Aswan and Elephantine Island. Exhibits range from prehistoric weapons to Graeco-Roman mummies and are labelled in chronological order. An annexe displays finds from the island, including jewellery discovered at the Temple of Satet and a marriage contract dating from 350 BC.

Aswan

1. Hotel Sofitel Legend Old Cataract Aswan
2. Nubian Museum
3. Unfinished Obelisk
4. Souq
5. Elephantine Island
6. Nilometer
7. Aswan Museum
8. Kitchener's Island
9. Aga Khan Mausoleum
10. Monastery of St Simeon
11. Tombs of the Nobles

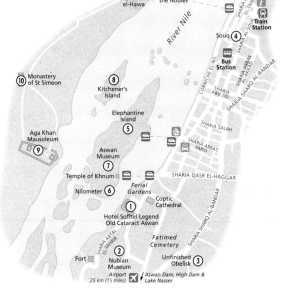

0 metres 750
0 yards 750

For keys to symbols see back flap

Lush botanical gardens stocked with plants from all parts of the world on Kitchener's Island, Aswan

Kitchener's Island

Aswan. 🚌 🚤 **Open** 7am–5pm daily (6pm in summer). 🎫

Situated in the Nile, west of Elephantine Island, the smaller Kitchener's Island (also known as the Island of Plants) is one of the most delightful places in Aswan. The lush botanical gardens that cover the island make it an ideal place to go for a peaceful stroll or simply relax in the shade of the trees.

The British general Horatio Kitchener was presented with the island in the 1890s as a reward for leading the Egyptian army's successful campaigns in Sudan. He made the island his home and indulged his passion for beautiful flowers by covering it with exotic plants imported from all around the world.

The huge sycamore trees, coconut palms and date palms that tower towards the sky are filled with colourful birds and

egrets, and as the sun begins to go down the entire island rings out with the sound of their calls.

🕌 Aga Khan Mausoleum

West bank, on the road to the Monastery of St Simeon. **Closed** to the public.

Standing on a barren hillside on the west bank of the Nile, opposite Aswan, is the Aga Khan Mausoleum. Aga Khan III (1877–1957), the 48th Imam, or leader, of the Ismaili sect of Shiite Muslims, fell in love with Aswan, where he spent the winter every year. After his death in 1957, his widow, the Begum, erected a mausoleum in his honour on the hillside behind their villa.

The domed and turreted sandstone construction is outwardly modelled on Cairo's Fatimid tombs (see pp98–9). Inside, there is a marble shrine and the Aga Khan's sarcophagus, inscribed with texts from the Quran. Until her

death in 2000, the Begum spent part of each year in the villa and would visit the mausoleum daily to place a red rose on her husband's sarcophagus.

Lake Nasser, an enormous blue expanse in the desert

Lake Nasser

Stretching south more than 500 km (310 miles) from the High Dam and reaching depths of over 180 m (590 ft), Lake Nasser is the world's largest artificial lake. It was created by the construction of the High Dam and holds Egypt's only wild crocodiles. The lake flooded a huge expanse of land between Aswan and Abu Simbel, homeland of the Nubians since before Pharaonic times. About 800,000 Nubians were displaced, many settling in Aswan, and dozens of ancient temples had to be carefully relocated (see p25).

Mausoleum of the Aga Khan on a barren hillside opposite Aswan

For hotels and restaurants in this region see p274 and pp287–9

The imposing fortifications of the Monastery of St Simeon, Aswan

🏛 Monastery of St Simeon

West bank. 🚤 🐪 then by camel or on foot. **Open** 8am–4pm daily (5pm in summer). 🎫

The desert Monastery of St Simeon, on the west bank of the Nile, was built in the 7th century AD. Once home to a community of around 300 monks, it was abandoned in the late 12th century after an attack by the famous Arab leader Salah ad-Din.

The monastery was built as a fortress and, though the main buildings now lie largely in ruins, the imposing fortification walls remain. The lower levels of the complex, which comprised a church, living areas for the monks, stables and work quarters, are made of stone, while the upper levels are made of brick. In the roofless basilica, frescoes of the apostles are still visible, their faces scratched out by Muslims. In the evening, the monastery offers fantastic views of the sun setting over the desert.

The Tombs of the Nobles in the cliffs on the west bank of the Nile near Aswan

Harnessing the Power of the Nile

The Aswan Dam was built to regulate the flow of the Nile and so increase Egypt's cultivable land and provide hydroelectric power. However, it soon proved too small to control the river's unpredictable floods. President Nasser's solution was the construction of the High Dam and the creation of Lake Nasser. The resultant increases in agricultural production and hydro-electricity have arguably saved Egypt from famine, but there have been environmental consequences. The rising water table is destroying ancient monuments and silt, previously deposited in the Delta, is retained in Lake Nasser, forcing Egypt's farmers to use potentially harmful chemicals.

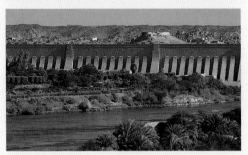

The Aswan Dam, built by the British to regulate the flow of the Nile

🏛 Tombs of the Nobles

Qubbet al-Hawwa, West bank. 🚤 🐪 then by camel or on foot. **Open** 7am–4pm daily (5pm in summer). 🎫

The hills on the west bank of the Nile, north of Kitchener's Island, are pockmarked with the rock-hewn Tombs of the Nobles. Dating from the Old and Middle Kingdoms, many of the tombs are decorated with scenes of everyday life. The largest and best-preserved tomb is that of Prince Sarenput II (No. 31), governor of southern Egypt during the 12th Dynasty. The burial chamber is decorated with statues of the prince and paintings of him and his son hunting and fishing. The tombs of Mekhu (No. 25), a noble from the 6th Dynasty who was murdered while on a military expedition in Nubia, and his son Sabni (No. 26), are crudely decorated with funeral and family scenes. Only one tomb may be open at any one time however, probably that of Sarenput II. The ancient necropolis is spotlit at night and looks particularly magical when viewed from across the river in Aswan.

🏙 Aswan Dam

11 km (7 miles) S of Aswan. 🚉 Stretching across the Nile, just beyond the First Cataract, the Aswan Dam was built by the British between 1898 and 1902. At the time of its construction it was the largest dam in the world, and its height was twice raised again in an effort to control the river. The roads to Abu Simbel and the airport cross the dam and the views over the river and islands are stunning.

🏙 High Dam

6 km (4 miles) S of Aswan Dam. 🚉 🅿 🎫 🖼 Built between 1960 and 1971, the immense High Dam measures 3,830 m (12,562 ft) across, 111 m (364 ft) high and 980 m (3,214 ft) wide at its base. At the eastern end of the dam there is a visitors' pavilion detailing the construction of the dam and at the western end there is a lotus-shaped tower, built to commemorate the Soviet Union's support in the building of the dam.

The Temple of Kalabsha, dominating the shores of Lake Nasser close to the High Dam

⑮ Temple of Philae

Agilika Island, S of Aswan Dam.
🚆 from Aswan to Shellal then 🚌
Open 7am–4pm daily (5pm in
summer). 🎆 Sound and Light Show:
6:30pm, 7:45pm, 9pm daily. 🎆 See
🌐 **soundandlight.com.eg** for
language and time details.

As the centre of the cult
of Isis, the island of
Philae was an important
place of pilgrimage for
worshippers until long
into the Christian era.
From Philae, Isis was said
to watch over the
sacred island of Biga,
one of the mythical
burial sites of her
husband Osiris.

After the building
of the Aswan Dam
(1898–1902), the
island's temples were partly
submerged in water and visitors
peered at the remains from
rowing boats. With the building
of the High Dam (1960–71), the
monuments were relocated
to the nearby island of Agilika.
The UNESCO-led project lasted
until 1980, by which time
Agilika had been landscaped
to look like Philae.

Boats now drop visitors at
the southern end of Agilika, near
the oldest building on the island,
the **Kiosk of Nectanebo II**, which
dates from the 4th century BC.
From here, a long courtyard,
flanked by colonnades, leads to
the magnificent **Temple of Isis**,
the main building in the Philae
temple complex. Built in the
late Ptolemaic and early Roman
periods, the huge temple
combines ancient Egyptian and
Graeco-Roman architecture.

Ptolemy XII Neos Dionysos built
the first pylon, which has scenes
of him massacring his enemies,
watched by Isis, Horus and
Hathor. The birth house, built by
Ptolemy VI and altered by later
rulers, is dedicated to Isis's son
Horus. To the west of the temple
lies the **Gate of Hadrian**, which
was inscribed, on 24 August
AD 394, with Egypt's last
hieroglyphics. On the
eastern side of the island,
the small **Temple of
Hathor** contains reliefs
of musicians, among
them Bes, the god
of singing. Further
south, close to the
edge of the water,
is the 14-columned
Kiosk of Trajan,
which has scenes
of the Roman
emperor burning incense in
front of Osiris and Isis. At the
northern end of the island,
Temple of Augustus and **Gate
of Diocletian** lie in ruins.

Lion in the Temple
of Isis, Philae

⑯ Temple of Kalabsha

W of High Dam. 🚆 from Aswan.
Open 7am–4pm daily (5pm in
summer). 🎆

The imposing temple of
Kalabsha was built under
Emperor Augustus in the 1st
century AD on the site of earlier
buildings by Amenhotep II and
Ptolemy IX. Dedicated to the
fertility god Marul (known as
Mandulis by the Greeks), it was
moved 50 km (31 miles) north
of its original location in 1970
in a German-funded rescue
operation following the
flooding of Nubia. The temple
now dominates a stretch of
Lake Nasser's shore, just west of
the High Dam. The land here
often forms an island due to the
changing water levels.

From the water's edge an
imposing causeway leads to the
temple's first pylon, beyond
which there is a colonnaded

The well-preserved western colonnade leading to Philae's Temple of Isis

court. The roofless hypostyle hall is noted for its ornate column capitals and its reliefs, which include Amenhotep offering wine to Marul.

Environs
Moved at the same time as Kalabsha Temple, the battered remains of the Roman **Kiosk of Qertassi** lie to the northwest. Two Hathor-headed columns mark the entrance to this small kiosk, which commands fine views of Lake Nasser. The nearby **Temple of Beit al-Wali**, also relocated from Nubia, was built during the reign of Ramses II. Its walls depict Ramses's great battles, notably against the Nubians.

Avenue of sphinxes leading to the Temple of Wadi as-Sebua

⓱ Temple of Wadi as-Sebua

140 km (87 miles) S of High Dam. 🚌 🚂 from Aswan. **Open** 7am–4pm daily (5pm in summer). 📷

Approached by the remains of an avenue of sphinxes, this temple was built by Ramses II and dedicated to the deified pharaoh Amun-Ra and Ra-Harakhty. In the early 1960s the temple was moved a short distance west to its current site. Two colossi and statues of Ramses adorn the temple, which is partly carved directly into the rock. The inner sanctuary was converted into a Christian church and faint images of saints can be seen over the ancient reliefs.

Environs
Just to the north, the **Temple of Dakka** was begun by the Ethiopian king Arkamani in the

3rd century BC and added to in the Ptolemaic and Roman eras. Dedicated to the god Thoth, it was originally 40 km (25 miles) further north. The huge pylon is still in good condition. Also relocated here, the **Temple of Maharraka** dates from Roman times. The best remains are in the hypostyle hall.

⓲ Temple of Amada

185 km (115 miles) S of High Dam. 🚌 🚂 from Aswan. **Open** 7am–4pm daily (5pm in summer). 📷

Dedicated to Amun-Ra and Ra-Harakhty, the Temple of Amada was constructed by Tuthmosis III and Amenhotep II, and added to by Tuthmosis IV. Moved just 3 km (2 miles) from its original site, it is the oldest surviving Nubian temple. It also has some of the best-preserved Nubian reliefs, including those on the sanctuary's back wall, which depict Amenhotep killing his Syrian prisoners of war.

Environs
A short distance across the desert is the relocated **Temple of Derr**. Built under Ramses II, it was later converted into a church. Although badly damaged, some colourful reliefs remain, particularly in the second pillared hall, where the pharaoh is seen presenting offerings to the gods. The nearby rock-cut **Tomb of Pennout**, viceroy of northern Nubia under Ramses VI, used to be 40 km (25 miles) south of Amada in a necropolis of Old and New Kingdom tombs at Aniba. The tomb is decorated with scenes of Pennout and his family, and the "weighing of the heart" ceremony *(see p33)*.

Finely preserved relief from the tomb of the Nubian viceroy Pennout, near Amada

⓳ Qasr Ibrim

60 km (37 miles) N of Abu Simbel. 🚌 **Open** 7am–4pm daily (5pm in summer).

This ruined fortress is on its original site, although the flooding of the region means that, whereas it once stood on a high plateau overlooking a valley, it is now close to the water's edge. It is believed there was a fort here as far back as 1000 BC. By Roman times, seven temples stood within the fortified walls, including a temple dedicated to Isis and a 7th-century BC temple built by the Nubian king Taharaqo. One of the last strongholds of paganism, Qasr Ibrim finally submitted to Christianity and a cathedral was built here in the 10th century AD. It resisted Islam until the 16th century, when Bosnians invaded the fort on orders from the Ottoman sultan and the cathedral was turned into a mosque. Still under excavation, the fort can only be visited by cruise boats on the lake.

The ruined fortress of Qasr Ibrim on the shores of Lake Nasser

⓴ Abu Simbel

Hewn out of a solid cliff in the 13th century BC, the Great Temple of Abu Simbel and the smaller Temple of Hathor are a breathtaking sight. Although dedicated to the patron deities of Egypt's great cities – Amun of Thebes, Ptah of Memphis and Ra-Harakhty of Heliopolis – the Great Temple was built to honour Ramses II. Its 33-m (108-ft) high façade, with four colossal enthroned statues of Ramses II wearing the double crown of Upper and Lower Egypt, was intended to impress and frighten, while the interior revealed the union of god and king.

★ Temple Façade
Buried in sand for centuries, the façade was discovered in 1813 by Swiss explorer Jean-Louis Burckhardt.

Relocated Temples at Abu Simbel
In the 1960s, as Lake Nasser threatened to engulf the temples, UNESCO cut them from the mountain and moved them to an artificial cliff 210 m (688 ft) back from and 65 m (213 ft) above their original position.

Ramses II Colossi
Accompanied by carved images of captives from the north and south, the four colossi on the temple façade boast of a unified Egypt. Ramses's names adorn the thrones in cartouche form.

KEY

① **The broken colossus** lost its head in an earthquake in 27 BC.

② **Statue of Ra-Harakhty**

③ **Baboons greeting the rising sun**

④ **Storerooms**, located off the vestibule and Hypostyle Hall, held offerings to the gods and ritual items.

⑤ **10-m (33-ft) high statue of Ramses as Osiris**

⑥ **The vestibule** is adorned with scenes of Ramses and Nefertari making offerings to Amun and Ra-Harakhty.

Entrance to temple

★ **Inner Sanctuary**
Ramses II sits with Amun-Ra, Ptah and Ra-Harakhty. On two days of the year the sun's rays reach the once gold-covered statues.

VISITORS' CHECKLIST

Practical Information
Aswan governorate, 280 km (174 miles) S of Aswan. **Open** 7am–4pm (5pm in summer; later when there are evening flights). Sound and Light Show: 6pm, 7pm, 8pm, 9pm in winter; 8pm, 9pm, 10pm in summer.
W soundandlight.com.eg

Transport

Battle of Qadesh
Reliefs inside the hypostyle hall show Ramses II defeating Egypt's enemies including, on the right-hand wall, the defeat of the Hittites in the Battle of Qadesh c.1275 BC.

Temple of Hathor

Dedicated to the goddess Hathor, the smaller temple at Abu Simbel was built by Ramses II to honour his favourite wife, Nefertari. The hypostyle hall has Hathor-headed pillars and is decorated with scenes of Ramses slaying Egypt's enemies, watched by Nefertari. The vestibule shows the royal couple making offerings to the gods, and the inner sanctuary holds a statue of Hathor in the form of a cow.

★ **Hypostyle Hall**
In Osiride form – carrying crook and flail – the colossi on the southern pillars wear the Upper Egypt crown, while the northern ones wear the double crown of Upper and Lower Egypt. The walls show Ramses II making offerings to his deified self.

Statues of Nefertari as goddess Hathor alternate with Ramses II on the façade of Queen Nefertari's Temple

SINAI AND THE RED SEA COAST

Treasured in Pharaonic times for its turquoise, copper and gold quarries, the region today is a magnet for tourists, attracted by the white, sandy beaches and fantastic marine life. Sinai is an area of great religious significance; its rugged interior was the setting for many important events in the Bible and remains a holy place for Jews, Muslims and Christians alike.

Wedged between Africa and Asia, the Sinai peninsula is bordered by the Mediterranean Sea, the gulfs of Aqaba and Suez, and Egypt's Suez Canal zone. The area has been plagued by conflict, most recently between 1967 and 1982 when it was occupied by Israel before being returned to Egypt in the Camp David peace treaty. However, since the late 1980s tourism has boomed along Sinai's eastern coast with resorts such as Sharm el-Sheikh becoming popular holiday destinations. Besides the dry, sunny climate, the main attraction of the region is the underwater world – the Red Sea coral reefs and teeming marine life make this area one of the world's richest dive sites. Yet despite the rapid growth of tourism, much of Sinai's stunning mountainous interior, inhabited by the nomadic, tribal Bedouin people, remains unexplored.

Egypt's Red Sea Coast stretches more than 1,250 km (777 miles) from the Suez Canal to the Sudanese border. Separated from the Nile Valley by the hills of the Eastern Desert, the coastline is famed for its brilliant turquoise waters. The area around the diving resort of Hurghada has developed massively as many more new resorts and hotels have been built here.

The Suez Canal, a phenomenal feat of engineering when it opened in 1869, separates Sinai from mainland Egypt. In the past it was a cause of conflict; today it is one of Egypt's most important sources of revenue.

Shopping for fruit and vegetables in the Red Sea diving resort of Hurghada

◀ Exquisitely coloured coral reef in the warm waters of the Red Sea

Exploring Sinai and the Red Sea Coast

With its combination of mountains and sea, the natural beauty
of the Sinai peninsula is awe-inspiring. Most visitors head for the
sea, where there is a string of tourist resorts from Taba to Sharm
el-Sheikh. St Catherine's Monastery in the interior can be visited
as a day trip. On the western Red Sea Coast, Hurghada is the
main resort and from here the monasteries of St Anthony and
St Paul make interesting excursions. The Suez Canal to the north
is hardly picturesque, but the canal town of Ismailia is pretty and
Port Said has good duty-free shopping.

Monastery of St Anthony, inland from the western Red Sea Coast

Key

═══ Motorway
──── Major road
──── Minor road
──── Scenic route
– – Track
── Main railway
── Minor railway
▬▬ International border
■ ■ Disputed border
△ Summit

0 kilometres 100
0 miles 50

Luxury resorts and diving centres around Naama Bay, to the north
of Sharm el-Sheikh

Sights at a Glance

For hotels and restaurants in this region see pp274–5 and pp289–91

Camels and their Bedouin keepers at Assalah, to the north of Dahab, where camel treks into the interior can be arranged

Getting There

The coastal roads of the Sinai peninsula are good and the main resorts can be reached by bus, car or service taxi. Exploring the interior is best done on organized trips with jeeps or camels and a Bedouin guide. Although there is a bus service to St Catherine's Monastery from Cairo at 11am each day, there is no bus service to here from towns on the East Sinai coast. There is a good coastal road on the western Red Sea to Hurghada and Port Safaga, and also from Port Said to Suez. Inland sites are best visited on organized day trips or by taxi. A ferry service operates between Sharm el-Sheikh and Hurghada; check with the tourist office for service updates *(see p236)*.

Due to continuing insurgent activity all roads to Northern Sinai are closed. If you are travelling to the north of the Sinai region, please check with the foreign office to ensure it is safe to do so.

Ain Musa's springs, reputedly made drinkable when Moses, guided by God, threw in a branch

For keys to symbols *see back flap*

A fishing boat dwarfed by a cruise ship in the Suez Canal

❶ Suez

134 km (83 miles) E of Cairo.
👥 490,000. ℹ️ Sharia Suez Canal
(062) 3191 141. 🚌 🚆 🚕

Situated at the southern end of the canal, Suez was a prosperous port in medieval times. In the 18th century, it was used by the British as a staging post on the route to India. Following the opening of the Suez Canal in 1869, it expanded further, but was severely damaged during the 1967 and 1973 wars with Israel. Thanks to money from Gulf states, however, Suez has been rebuilt and it is one of Egypt's most important ports and a major industrial centre. Suez holds little of interest for the tourist but those travelling to or from Sinai use the Ahmed Hamdi Tunnel, 12 km (7 miles) to the north of town or the bridge at Al-Qantara.

❷ Ismailia

120 km (74 miles) NE of Cairo.
👥 600,000. 🚌 🚆 🚕

Named after its founder Khedive Ismail, who ruled Egypt from 1863 to 1879, Ismailia was developed for foreign engineers and labourers working on the Suez Canal in the 1860s.
It is the prettiest and most populous of the canal towns. South of the railway line, huge European-style villas with lush gardens line the wide boulevards. On Mohammed Ali Quay, the house of Ferdinand de Lesseps, director of the Suez Canal Company and French vice-consul to Egypt at the time of its construction, is an impressive example of these grand houses. It now serves as a hotel for guests of the Suez Canal Authority.

The **Ismailia Museum** nearby is home to a small collection of Pharaonic and Graeco-Roman artifacts, of which the highlight is a 4th-century mosaic floor. To visit the nearby Garden of Stelae and its Pharaonic remains, permission is needed from the museum.

The Sweetwater Canal, built to bring fresh water from the Nile to the canal workers, leads to Lake Timsah (Crocodile Lake), which has some pleasant beaches. A ferry from Ismailia runs to the east bank of the canal, where Egypt launched its celebrated attack on Israeli forces in 1973.

🏛️ **Ismailia Museum**
Sharia Salah Salem. **Tel** (064) 3912 749. **Open** 9am–4pm daily.
Closed 11:30am–1:30pm Fri. 🈲 🈳

A sphinx outside the Ismailia Museum

❸ Port Said

225 km (139 miles) NE of Cairo.
👥 526,000. ℹ️ 8 Sharia Palestine
(066) 3235 289. 🚌 🚆 🚕

On the coast where the Suez Canal meets the Mediterranean, Port Said was founded in 1859 by Khedive Said Pasha to house workers on the canal. For years, the city was associated with drugs and smuggling but it has now shaken off its seedy past and is today mostly renowned as a tax-free shopping zone and minor beach resort.

Port Said, which is largely built on land reclaimed from Lake Manzila, is surrounded by water. It was heavily bombed during the 1956 Suez crisis and during the conflicts with Israel in 1967 and 1973, but most of the damage has since been repaired. The distinctive green domes of the Suez Canal Building, built in 1869 on Sharia Palestine, are one of the city's important landmarks.

Nearby, **Port Said National Museum** covers Egyptian history from ancient times; exhibits include Coptic antiquities and Pharaonic mummies. It is currently closed for restoration.

The **Military Museum** on Sharia 23rd July presents a vivid account of the various conflicts that have chequered the history of the canal.

A 19th-century colonial-style villa in Ismailia

View across the Suez Canal from Port Said to Port Fuad

🏛 **Port Said National Museum**
Sharia Palestine. **Closed** for
restoration. 🖼

🏛 **Military Museum**
Sharia 23rd July. **Tel** (066) 3224 657.
Open 9am–2pm & 6–9pm daily
(9am–3pm & 6–10pm in summer;
9am–2pm & 8–11pm during
Ramadan). 🖼

❹ Ain Musa

25 km (15 miles) SE of Ahmed Hamdi
Tunnel. 🚌 from Cairo or Port Said.

Also known as the Springs of
Moses, Ain Musa lies to the
southeast of the Ahmed Hamdi
Tunnel, which runs under the
Suez Canal near its junction
with the Gulf of Suez. According
to the Old Testament, it was
here that Moses, after leading
the Israelites across the Red
Sea, turned a bitter spring into
sweet drinking water by
throwing a branch into it, as
instructed by God.
 Although Ain Musa was a
main source of fresh water for
the local town until the 1860s,
only one of the 12 springs
mentioned in the Book of
Exodus remains today. It was
used as a strategic stronghold
by the Israeli army during their
occupation of Sinai from 1967,
but was recaptured by Egyptian
forces in 1973.
 Just over 3 km (2 miles) north
of the springs is the Military
Touristic Memorial of Ain Musa,
a small museum dedicated to
the achievements of the
Egyptian army.

❺ Serabit al-Khadim

32 km (20 miles) E of Abu Zneima, Sinai.

Built during the 12th Dynasty,
the rock temple of Serabit
el-Khadim (Heights of the
Slave) is perched on a 755-m
(2,500-ft) summit to the east of
the petroleum-industry town
of Abu Zneima. In Pharaonic
times the area was rich in
copper
and turquoise and thousands
worked in the mines. The
temple was dedicated to
Hathor, goddess of love and
"Mistress of the Turquoise".
Some jeep safaris from Naama
Bay (near Sinai's southern tip)
include Serabit al-Khadim in
their tours of this beautiful part
of Sinai's rugged interior. Hiring
a four-wheel-drive vehicle is an
alternative, as is a camel safari,
accompanied by a local guide.

❻ Wadi Feiran

60 km (37 miles) W of St Catherine's
Monastery, Sinai. 🏔 650.

Lying halfway between
St Catherine's Monastery and
the Red Sea Coast, at the foot
of the 2,000-m (6,560-ft) high
Mount Serbal, Wadi Feiran is
the largest oasis in south Sinai.
A winding valley, thick with
shady palms, tamarisks and
orchards, the oasis is believed
to be the *Rephidim* mentioned
in Exodus – the last place of rest
for the weary Israelites before
they reached Mount Sinai.
 An early Christian community
flourished here and, in AD 451,
it became the seat of a
bishopric that governed St
Catherine's Monastery (*see
pp226–9*). The bishop's palace
and convent were destroyed
in the 7th century, but a small
convent was rebuilt on the
site with stone from the
original Byzantine buildings.
Today, the oasis belongs to
the Tawarah tribes.

Palms flourishing in the oasis of Wadi Feiran, south Sinai

❼ St Catherine's Monastery

Nestling at the foot of Mount Sinai, the Greek Orthodox monastery of St Catherine is thought to be the oldest continuously inhabited Christian monastery in the world. Founded in AD 527 by Emperor Justinian, it replaced a chapel built by the Empress Helena in AD 337 on the site where it is believed that Moses saw the Burning Bush. The monastery was renamed St Catherine in the 9th or 10th century after monks claimed to have found the intact body of the saint on a nearby mountain.

Library
The collection of priceless early Christian manuscripts is one of the most important in the world.

★ Museum Icon Collection
The monastery holds 2,000 icons, including this of St Peter. A selection is on view, along with treasures gifted over the years.

The Burning Bush
This evergreen is said to be from the same stock as the bush from which God instructed Moses to lead his people out of Egypt to the Promised Land.

KEY

① **The Chapel of the Burning Bush**, where the miraculous bush supposedly grew, is the most sacred part of the monastery.

② **The Walls of Justinian**, dating from the 6th century, are part of the complex's original structure.

③ **St Stephen's Well**

④ **Dispensary**

⑤ **The Mosque** was built in 1106 by converting a chapel originally dedicated to St Basil. Its creation was an attempt to placate local Muslim rulers.

⑥ **Monks' quarters**

⑦ **The elevated entrance**, reached by a pulley system, used to be the only access.

⑧ **The underground cistern** was dug to store fresh water from the monastery's springs.

★ Basilica of the Transfiguration
This richly decorated church owes its name to a rare 6th-century Mosaic of the Transfiguration in the apse. The mosaic is located behind the gilded 17th-century iconostasis.

Bell Tower
Built in 1871, the tower houses nine bells donated by Tsar Alexander II of Russia. They are only rung on religious festivals.

VISITORS' CHECKLIST

Practical Information
Sinai, 90 km (56 miles) W of Dahab and Nuweiba. **Tel** (069) 3470 353. **Open** 9am–11:45am Mon–Thu & Sat, 11am–noon Fri. **Closed** Sun, Greek Orthodox holidays. 🖼 (museum).

Transport
✈ 10 km (6 miles) NE of monastery. 🚌 one bus per day from Cairo to St Catherine's village (Al-Milga), then taxi 3 km (2 miles). Most visitors come with a tour. Petrol available at the monastery.

Monastery Gardens
A cemetery is located in the orchard from where monks' bones are periodically exhumed and taken to the Charnel House.

Charnel House & Guesthouse

Visitors' entrance

Well of Moses
Inside the outer wall lies the monastery's main water source where Moses is said to have met his future wife, Zipporah, Jethro's daughter.

St Catherine of Alexandria

St Catherine was one of the most popular early Christian saints. Supposedly born into a wealthy Alexandrian family in the early 4th century, she was tortured for her beliefs, first spun on a spiked wheel (hence Catherine wheel) and then beheaded by the pagan emperor. A marble sarcophagus in the monastery's Church of St Catherine contains two silver caskets said to hold part of her remains, found by monks 600 years after her death.

Detail of St Catherine from clerical vestments

Exploring St Catherine's Monastery

Completely isolated for many years, and surrounded by red granite mountains, the monastery is now on the main tourist trail and busloads of visitors arrive each day. Around 20 or so monks (mostly from Greece) still live in the monastery, and hence its opening times are strictly controlled. The surrounding mountains are incredibly beautiful and most visitors climb the well-worn path to the top of Mount Sinai – where Moses is said to have received the Ten Commandments – to enjoy the spectacular view over this setting of profound biblical significance.

Ornately carved wooden inner door to the 6th-century basilica

Inside the monastery

Entry is through a small postern or gateway in the northeastern wall. The elevated entrance above it contains a pulley and used to be the only way into the monastery after the main gate was blocked as a defence against raiders in the Middle Ages. Parts of the huge granite walls date from the 6th century although they have been substantially rebuilt over the years – firstly, after an earthquake in the 14th century and again in 1800 when Napoleon sent masons from Cairo to restore the stonework.

The monastery's main church, or basilica, built by Emperor Justinian's architect Stephanos Ailisios in AD 527, is known as the Basilica of the Transfiguration. It is one of the few remaining churches in the region which survive from this period. Massive 11th-century wooden doors open onto the narthex (porch). Beyond is another door, carved with reliefs of animals, birds and

flowers, which is believed to be the original from Justinian's church. The central nave is flanked by six pillars bearing Byzantine icons of saints worshipped in each month of the year. The marble floor and coffered ceiling are 18th century. A gilded iconostasis, painted in the early 17th century, separates the nave from the altar. Behind this, the roof of the apse is decorated with a superb 6th-century mosaic of the Transfiguration. Beyond the altar lies the Chapel of the Burning Bush, the holiest place of the monastery, which is closed to the public. The thorny, evergreen bush, reputedly a descendant of the original Burning Bush from which Moses heard the Lord speak, is of a species found nowhere else in Sinai.

The monastery's library, with over 3,000 ancient manuscripts in Greek and other languages, is second in importance only

to that of the Vatican. One of the highlights is the *Codex Syriacus*, a 5th-century Syriac version of the New Testament. The priceless icons, dating from the early Byzantine period, are among the only survivors from the Iconoclast era (726–843) when such images were held to be heretical. They include a *St Peter* (5th–6th century), and the 7th-century *Christ in Majesty* and *Ladder of Paradise*. A selection of icons and manuscripts are on display in the excellent museum near the entrance to the monastery.

In the garden, dense with olive and apricot trees, is the monastery cemetery and the Chapel of St Triphonius. The latter's crypt holds the Charnel House, which contains the bones of monks who have died here over the centuries. The monastery guesthouse is set near the lovely orchards and gardens, and has a good courtyard café.

Monks' skulls inside the Charnel House

Environs

Rising to a height of 2,286 m (7,500 ft), **Mount Sinai** is held to be the Biblical Mount Horeb (Exodus 24) where Moses spent 40 days and nights before receiving the Ten Commandments. There are two paths to the top, both starting behind the monastery. The more gentle "Camel Path", created by Abbas Hilmi I, Pasha of Egypt from 1849–54, is the usual route up. Camels can be hired from the foot of the mountain, though the last 700

Chapel of the Burning Bush, viewable only by special dispensation

View of St Catherine's Monastery from path leading to Mount Sinai

steps have to be undertaken on foot. The 3,700 steps of the "Stairs of Repentance" is a steeper route. Along it are several votive sites, including Moses' Spring, which gushes from a small cave, and St Stephen's Gate. Most visitors climb at night to reach the summit in time for sunrise.

Around 700 steps below the summit is **Elijah's Basin**, a sandy plain dotted with cypress trees, one of which is estimated to be 1,000 years old. This is where those who accompanied Moses are said to have waited while he climbed to the summit alone. Camping here, rather than at the summit, is recommended for those wanting to spend the night on the mountain.

At the summit, where God is believed to have spoken to Moses from a fiery cloud, is a 12th-century mosque and the small **Chapel of the Holy Trinity**, built in 1934 on the site of a 6th-century church. Neither of these is currently open to the public.

To the southwest of Mount Sinai, **Mount Catherine**, Egypt's highest mountain at 2,642 m (8,666 ft), offers a steep but picturesque climb. At the summit there is a small chapel containing many icons, and a truly outstanding view, taking in the gulfs of Aqaba and Suez and the mountains of both Africa and Saudi Arabia.

St Catherine's Protectorate

Formally established in 1996, the Protectorate covers an area of 4,350 sq km (1,672 sq miles) around Mount Sinai. Its aim is to protect the area's plant and animal life and conserve historic and religious sites. A Trekkers' Code urges visitors to avoid leaving litter, removing rocks or plants and writing or carving graffiti.

A series of guides produced by the Protectorate details various hikes in the area along **Wadi Arbaein** and **Wadi Shrayj**,

taking in cultural sites and beauty spots. One describes the climb up **Abbas pasha Mountain**, which leads to an incomplete 19th-century palace at 2,383 m (7,816 ft) – intended as a sanatorium for the sick Pasha. The books can be purchased and guides organized (walkers must be accompanied by a Bedouin guide) from the Visitors' Centre near the monastery and at the Protectorate Management Office in St Catherine's village.

The Bedouin of the Sinai Peninsula

The Bedouin of the Sinai, descendants of tribes from the Arabian peninsula, have lived a nomadic lifestyle in harsh arid regions for centuries, depending on sheep, goats and camels for a livelihood and sleeping in tents made of goatskin. Their name derives from the Arabic word *bedu*, meaning "desert dwellers". The Bedouin are distinctive in their traditional garb: the women don black garments with sequinned veils and the men wear long white robes. Their tightly wrapped figures invariably accompany images of bleak, sandswept landscapes. But life is rapidly changing for these denizens of the desert. With government resettlement programmes and tourism encroaching all over the Sinai, the old ways are under threat. TV aerials protrude from concrete houses and children are increasingly dressed in Western-style clothes. While some Bedouin are still nomadic livestock breeders, many now work with jeeps not camels, and make a living from the tourist trade.

Bedouin woman in traditional dress

Naama Bay, a popular resort area in Sharm el-Sheikh

❽ Sharm el-Sheikh

300 km (187 miles) SE of Suez.
🚌 35,000. ✈ 🚌 🚌 👔 (069)
3664 721. **Open** 8am–3pm daily.

The popular resort of Sharm el-Sheikh, north of Ras Mohammed, stretches over 20 km (12 miles) along the coast and is a renowned diving and snorkelling destination.

Sharm, as it is known to visitors, is divided into two main parts – the town and port to the south and **Naama Bay**, the upmarket tourist enclave 7 km (4 miles) to the north. Om El Sid (El Hadaba) sits on the cliff between them.

After it was captured in the 1967 war, the port was developed by the Israelis, who began to build hotels along the coast. The development that began in the late 1980s is still booming.

With diving schools and hotels lining the Corniche, Naama is far removed from the traditional Bedouin way of life. Nevertheless the water here is beautiful and there are many accessible dive sites along the coast – both for beginners and more experienced wreck divers.

After a rare spate of shark attacks in 2010, beach controls have been put in place, such as designated swimming spots and lookout towers.

Environs
Around 10 km (6 miles) north of Naama is **Shark's Bay**, a quieter but expanding resort area. The coral gardens and tropical fish here are beautiful and despite its name, there are no sharks. North of Shark's Bay, where the Red Sea meets the Gulf of Aqaba, lie the Tiran Straits. Diving trips to **Tiran** and **Sanafir Island** leave from Naama, Sharm and Shark's Bay. Further up the coast is the **Nabq National Park**, which has also been developed into a resort area. It remains popular, however, with bird-watchers as the most northerly mangrove forests in the world are home to many birds such as grey and white herons, ospreys and storks. Animals suited to the arid conditions, such as gazelles, rock hyraxes and desert foxes, live inland.

Turtle swimming in the Red Sea

🐢 **Nabq National Park**
29 km (18 miles) N of Sharm el-Sheikh.
🚕 🚌 **Open** daily. 🏞 🏊

❾ Ras Mohammed National Park

20 km (12 miles) S of Sharm el-Sheikh.
✈ 🚌 to Sharm el-Sheikh, then taxi.
👔 Visitors' Centre (069) 3660 559.
Open daily. 🏞 🏊

Covering the southernmost tip of the Sinai peninsula, Ras Mohammed became Egypt's first Marine National Park in 1989. The wealth of underwater life and extensive reefs dotted with brilliant corals and sponges make it one of the best places for diving and snorkelling in the world. Over 1,000 species of colourful fish populate the clear waters and barracuda, reef sharks, turtles and manta rays are among the more unusual creatures to look out for. Above water, the park is home to ibexes, gazelles and a wide range of birdlife. The mangrove forests here grow in a shallow channel south of the peninsula and are an important breeding area for birds. A visitors' centre in the park shows videos about the area and also offers a map of the colour-coded tracks which lead to the different beaches. Although thousands of tourists visit the park each year, considerable effort is made to protect the area from serious damage by not allowing any hotels to be built and carefully restricting the number of dive boats.

One of Sharm el-Sheikh's many diving centres

Coral Reefs of the Red Sea

Coral reefs are one of the richest ecosystems on earth. Coral is made up of colonies of tiny animals called polyps that need precise environmental conditions to grow. There are two types of coral: hard corals, which form hard outer skeletons for themselves, and soft corals, that do not. Most reefs are built over thousands of years from the accumulated skeletons of dead hard corals. In places, the Red Sea reefs form sheer walls covered with exotically shaped corals of pastel pink, yellow and red. Scuba diving in the Red Sea is the highlight of many visitors' holidays and the area is well served for dive centres *(see pp308–13)*. However, if using an aqualung does not appeal, then the shallow lagoons that the reefs create are perfect for exploring with a snorkel. These beautiful, calm lagoons serve as nurseries for schools of smaller fish. A word of caution: although the reefs seem robust, they are an extremely fragile environment and swimmers should look but not touch.

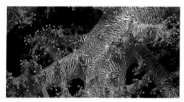

Soft corals require salty, clear water and warm, gentle currents to bring them their food. At night the coral polyps use their fine tentacles to sting and capture plankton as it swims past.

The jewel grouper favours shady areas of the reef, for in the dim light this hunter's stunning colouring becomes surprisingly good camouflage as it waits for its smaller prey to swim past.

Sea anemones look like colourful plants but they are in fact animal predators. They use their stinging tentacles to stun their prey and feed it to their centrally located mouth.

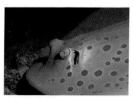

Blue-spotted rays glide across the sea floor scooping up snails, worms and crabs before crushing them with special flattened teeth.

Reef walls plunge to depths of 80 m (260 ft) or more and provide a home for over 1,000 species of fish and more than 150 types of coral.

Camels and their Bedouin keepers near Dahab

⑩ Dahab

100 km (62 miles) N of Sharm el-Sheikh. 🚌

The word *dahab* means gold in Arabic, and the name of this popular resort derives from its tawny golden beaches. The resort grew up around the Bedouin village of Assalah, to the north of the town, where the beach huts, hotels, restaurants, dive centres and market stalls lining the waterfront cater mostly for independent young travellers on tight budgets.

To the south of the town, in Dahab "city", the scene is distinctly upmarket, with luxury holiday resorts attracting a very different clientele. For all tourists, however, the sea is the main attraction, and the coral reef, with its immensely rich marine life, is close to shore. A popular dive site is the **Blue Hole**, to the north of Dahab accesible by 4WD on an unpaved road. This is almost entirely surrounded by coral reefs and drops to a depth of 80 m (260 ft) just a few metres from the shore. The Blue Hole and the nearby Canyon can be dangerous for inexperienced divers and lives have been lost here in the past. A safe alternative is to use snorkelling equipment to admire the reef.

Jeep and camel safaris into the mountains can be easily arranged from Dahab. These are a great way to explore Sinai's beautiful, rugged interior and to see something of the Bedouin way of life.

Environs

About 15 km (9 miles) to the north of Dahab is **Ras Abu Galum**, a beautiful and secluded protectorate. This remote area, a prime destination for dive safaris, can be reached by foot or by camel from the Blue Hole via a coastal path. Inland from Ras Abu Galum's lovely deserted beaches is a maze of wadis teeming with plants and wildlife, including desert foxes, ibexes and hyraxes. The crystal-clear waters are wonderful for scuba diving or snorkelling. There are many outfits that offer dive safaris and provide diving equipment. Ras Abu Galum is easily accessible as a day trip from Dahab and it is also a popular destination for those wanting to experience a night under the stars, sleeping on the beach with food provided by hosts from the Bedouin settlement nearby.

Windsurfer on the Gulf of Aqaba, Dahab

Situated 8 km (5 miles) north of Ras Abu Galum is another stunning and even more remote spot, the **Blue Lagoon**. This is well-known for its tranquility and clear blue water

⑪ Nuweiba

85 km (53 miles) N of Dahab. 🚌 🚢 from Aqaba (Jordan).

Located midway along the Gulf of Aqaba coast, Nuweiba is divided into three areas, spread over a 10-km (6-mile) stretch. To the north is the Bedouin settlement of Tarabeen, where camp sites with bamboo and concrete huts are flanked by a couple of hotels. In the village are the restored ruins of a 16th-century fortress, which was built by the Mamluk sultan Ashraf al-Ghouri. About 1 km (half a mile) south of Tarabeen, reasonable but not particularly luxurious resort accommodation can be found in Nuweiba City. There are also a few hotels in the unattractive port of Nuweiba, 8 km (5 miles) further south, which are convenient if you are planning to catch the ferry to Aqaba.

All along the coast around Nuweiba, hotels and camp sites are being built, offering a choice of 5-star and budget accommodation. The setting is particularly beautiful with the Sinai Mountains providing a hazy backdrop and those of Saudi Arabia clearly visible across the water.

Nuweiba is a quiet resort offering magnificent beaches

A resort near Nuweiba, with Saudi Arabia visible across the sea

◀ St Catherine's Monastery located in a valley at the foot of Mount Sinai

Crusader castle on Pharaoh's Island, south of Taba, in the Gulf of Aqaba

and a chance to unwind. Accessible snorkelling off the beaches provides an easy way to explore the spectacular coral reefs and marine life.

Also popular is a trip to the ancient city of Petra, taking the catamaran from Nuweiba port to Aqaba. This spectacular metropolis, 96 km (60 miles) north of Aqaba, was carved out of desert rock between the 3rd century BC and 1st century AD.

Environs
Nuweiba is a good base for exploring the interior, and jeep and camel trips are easily arranged. The **Coloured Canyon**, about 30 km (19 miles) inland from Nuweiba, is a popular destination. It is reached via the oasis of Ain al-Furtaga, usually by four-wheel-drive vehicle, though it is possible to get there (more slowly) by camel. The narrow gorge gets its name from the pink, brown, green and yellow layers caused by the oxidation of minerals.

⓬ Pharaoh's Island

7 km (4 miles) S of Taba. Ⓣ
🚌 then ferry.

Surrounded by fabulous reefs, Pharaoh's Island (known as Coral Island by Israelis) is popular with divers. The island is just 250 m (820 ft) from the shore, close to

the border with Israel, and boats leave from the Salah ad-Din Hotel on the coastal road opposite the island.

Worth exploring are the restored ruins of a 12th-century Crusader castle, strategically placed to ensure the safety of pilgrims to the Holy Land. The castle was captured by Salah ad-Din in 1170 and used as an Arab stronghold against the Crusaders until 1183, when it was eventually abandoned.

⓭ Taba

70 km (43 miles) N of Nuweiba. 🚌

On the border with Israel, Taba was only returned to Egypt in 1989 after international intervention. Egypt was

determined to reclaim all its land from Israel and the dispute over this area lasted for seven years after the rest of Sinai had been recovered.

There are a few high-end hotels and local eateries at Taba, but most visitors are just crossing between the two countries. The 70-km (43-mile) stretch between Taba and Nuweiba has been dubbed the "Egyptian Riviera" by the government. There are a few beach camps along this beautiful stretch of coastline.

If you are leaving Egypt at Taba, note that an Israeli stamp in your passport means that entry into some Arab countries, notably Lebanon and Syria, will be denied. Ask to have a separate piece of paper stamped.

The Coloured Canyon near Nuweiba

For hotels and restaurants in this region see pp274–5 and pp289–91

The distinctive façade of the Monastery of St Anthony with the Red Sea Mountains in the background

⓮ Monastery of St Anthony

47 km (29 miles) W of Zafarana.
🚉 from Cairo, Suez or Hurghada.
Open daily.

Isolated in the Red Sea Mountains, St Anthony's Monastery (AD 361–3), marked the beginning of the monastic tradition. It is the oldest Coptic monastery in Egypt. Legend has it that Anthony, orphaned at 18, retreated to the mountains to serve God. His disciples built the monastery on the site of his grave.

The monastery complex has retained much of its original appearance, despite attacks from Bedouin tribes in the 8th and 9th centuries, from Muslims in the 11th century and a murderous revolt by Bedouin servants in the 15th century. It is the largest in the country, with several churches and chapels and extensive living quarters, but only 25 resident monks. On the interior walls of the Church of St Anthony are some vivid 13th-century murals. Two kilometres (just over one mile) to the northeast of the monastery is the cave where St Anthony is said to have spent his last years.

⓯ Monastery of St Paul

80 km (50 miles) SE of St Anthony's Monastery. 🚉 from Cairo, Suez or Hurghada. **Open** daily.

A winding road leads to the Monastery of St Paul, hidden behind lofty walls. St Paul (AD 228–348) was from a wealthy Alexandrian family but became the earliest known hermit when he retreated to the Eastern Desert aged 16. The monastery's turreted walls were built around the cave where he lived for decades. The main Church of St Paul is painted with murals representing the Virgin and Child, and the archangels. The chapels contain scores of icons while

Two of the monks at the Monastery of St Paul

ostrich eggs, a symbol of the Resurrection, hang from the ceiling. A five-storey keep behind the church, supplied with water from a hidden canal, was used to protect the monks from Bedouin raids.

⓰ Hurghada

320 km (200 miles) S of Suez.
🏙 180,000. ✈ 🚌 🚉 ⛴ catamaran and ferry services temporarily suspended. Check with tourist office for updates. ℹ Sharia Banque Misr (065) 344 4420.

Hurghada, on the Red Sea Coast, has undergone a complete transformation since the early 1990s when it was little more than a fishing village. Now a sprawling tourist town with resorts stretching all along the coast, it is famous for its dive centres which offer scuba and snorkel trips to view the fantastic Red Sea marine life. There is a wide choice of accommodation; cheaper lodgings are centred around Ad-Dahar, at the northern end of town, while Sigala to

Windsurfer at Sindbad Beach in Hurghada on the Red Sea Coast

the south is more upmarket. Some hotels have good private beaches, and a variety of offshore excursions are on offer, including day trips to **Giftun Island**. For those who wish to enjoy the wonders of the deep without getting wet, submarine tours are available from Sindbad Submarine or trips in a glass-bottomed boat can be arranged through most hotels. There is an **Aquarium** on the corniche and a **Marine Museum** north of town. In response to environmentalists' fears that the influx of tourists was damaging marine life, the Hurghada Environmental Protection and Conservation Association was set up in 1992 to raise awareness and preserve the reef.

Aquarium
Al-Corniche. **Tel** (011) 1618 1111.
Open 9am–7pm daily. ⬚

Marine Museum
7 km (4 miles) N of Hurghada. **Tel** (0114) 989 8445. **Open** 10am–7pm daily. ⬚

Environs
Just 30 km (19 miles) north of Hurghada, **El-Gouna** is a luxurious resort and ever-expanding town. Set on a beautiful strip of coastline, the dome-roofed hotels and villas have a distinct Nubian theme.

Soma Bay, 45 km (28 miles) to the south of Hurghada, is another sprawling tourist development with an 18-hole golf course, a marina, and upmarket hotels and villas.

Remains of two Roman quarries in the Red Sea Mountains are accessible on day trips from Hurghada and the coast. **Mons Porphyrites**, 60 km (37 miles) north of town, was the site of ancient porphyry quarries. The pinky-purple stone was mined by the Romans for building and sent throughout the Empire. Parts of the Roman mining town are still in evidence. The mines at **Mons Claudianus**, around 50 km (31 miles) southeast of Hurghada, supplied the Romans with black granite columns – some of which still support the Pantheon in Rome today. Ruins of the fort and of the Roman town can also be visited.

Traditional shipbuilding at Port Safaga

⓱ Port Safaga

58 km (36 miles) S of Hurghada.
🏙 33,500. 🚉 🚌

Just to the south of several upmarket resorts, Port Safaga is within easy range of some stunning reefs. Local weather conditions are ideal for wind-surfing and in 1993 the World Windsurfing Championships were held here. Apart from tourism, Port Safaga's principal activities are exporting locally mined phosphates and ferrying travellers to Saudi Arabia.

Colourful house in a street of the Red Sea port of Al-Quseir

⓲ Al-Quseir

80 km (50 miles) S of Port Safaga.
🏙 20,500. 🚉 🚌

The small town of Al-Quseir has a distinguished history. Queen Hatshepsut left from here on her famous expedition to the Land of Punt *(see p201)*. Known in Ptolemaic times as *Leukos Limen* (White Harbour), it was the largest Red Sea port until the 10th century, popular with pilgrims travelling to Mecca. After the opening of the Suez Canal in 1869, Al-Quseir declined and today is little more than a quiet fishing village. The 16th-century Ottoman fortress of Sultan Selim still overlooks the town.

As a relatively late starter, development has arrived with a little more environmental awareness. Regular dive trips are offered to the islands of Big Brother and Little Brother, 67 km (42 miles) northeast of Al-Quseir. For those who prefer to sample more of the local life, however, the town has a traditional souk, and a Bedouin community. An ancient caravan trail to Qift in the Nile Valley leads from the town through the mountains, passing several Pharaonic and Roman sites on the way.

⓳ Marsa Alam

132 km (82 miles) S of Al-Quseir.
🏙 6,000. 🚉 🚌

With the completion of the airport north of Marsa Alam, this most southerly section of the Red Sea Coast is being developed into large resorts as well as more rustic ecolodges. The diving is excellent and secluded here, close to the Sudanese border. Head further south to Berenice and Elphinstone Reef. Berenice lies 250 km (155 miles) south of Marsa Alam and is similarly being developed. It is linked by road to Aswan.

THE DELTA AND THE NORTH COAST

Fanning out between the two main branches of the Nile, the Delta is a green triangle in a desert landscape. Several Pharaonic dynasties ruled from here but, apart from the ruins of Bubastis and Tanis, most sites have long disappeared. The resorts of the North Coast are popular with Egyptians seeking relief from the summer heat.

The Nile Delta, Egypt's most fertile and densely populated region, produces the bulk of the country's crops, helping to feed the rapidly increasing population. To the east of the Delta, beyond the Suez Canal, lies the Sinai peninsula; to the west is the legendary city of Alexandria and a sandy coastline that stretches for over 500 km (310 miles) to the Libyan border.

Although the North Coast between Alexandria and Libya enjoys clear seas and beautiful beaches, many stretches are inaccessible because of landmines left over from World War II. However, there are dozens of holiday villages along the route to Marsa Matruh and more are planned.

Most visitors to Lower Egypt, as the north of the country is called, head straight for Alexandria, Egypt's cosmopolitan second city. Its rich history, links with Cleopatra's reign, moderate climate and pleasant beaches, make Alexandria the region's key attraction.

Although usually ignored by tourists, the Delta itself is worth exploring. This is the rural heart of the country: crisscrossed by irrigation canals, the flat land is rich with cotton, maize, sugar cane and vegetables. Buffalo plough the fields, donkeys pull carts, and mudbrick pigeon huts punctuate the picturesque landscape.

The lakes in the northeast attract an amazing variety of birdlife, especially during the annual winter migration south. Off the tourist trail, Rosetta's rich Ottoman architecture is one of the highlights of the area. Another is the cycle of lively *moulids* (religious festivals) that begin in October and transform the Nile Delta into a joyful place of celebration.

Colourful river taxis at Rosetta, where a branch of the Nile flows into the Mediterranean

◄ Men pulling sail boats along a canal, Nile Delta

Exploring the Delta and the North Coast

Annual flooding and plundering over the centuries have ensured that little remains to testify to the role of the Delta in ancient Egyptian history. However, the ruins at Tanis and near Zagazig hint at the area's importance in ancient times. Damietta and Rosetta have fine examples of Ottoman architecture, while Alexandria retains the faded grandeur of 19th-century colonial architecture and offers glimpses of its greatness as the Graeco-Roman capital of Egypt. Along the Mediterranean coast are a growing number of resorts, while the cemeteries at El- Alamein serve as reminders of the World War II battles that were fought here.

One of three sphinxes from a tomb near Pompey's Pillar, Alexandria

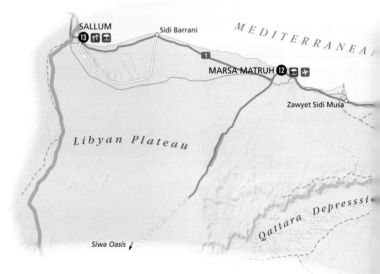

Street scene in Marsa Matruh, a resort to the west of Alexandria

Getting Around

Alexandria has an international airport, with daily flights to and from Cairo. Trains run regularly between the two cities, and the desert road linking them makes car and bus travel easy. Other towns in the Delta are served by buses, minibuses, service taxis and trains. A frequent bus service runs along the North Coast road to the Libyan border, and a very slow train runs between Alexandria and Marsa Matruh in summertime. The latter is also served by a domestic airport.

For hotels and restaurants see p276 and pp291–2

Sights at a Glance

1. Damietta (Dumyat)
2. Zagazig
3. Tanta
4. Tanis
5. Rosetta (Rashid)
6. *Alexandria pp244–51*
7. Montazah Palace
8. Abu Qir
9. Agami
10. Abu Mina
11. El-Alamein
12. Marsa Matruh
13. Sallum

Fort Qaitbey, dating from the 1480s and occupying the site of the Pharos – Alexandria's legendary lighthouse

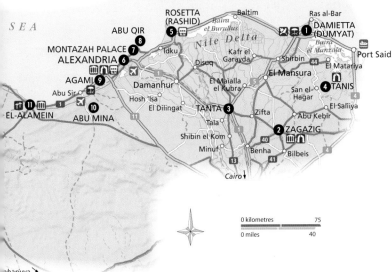

Key

▬ Motorway
▬ Major road
▬ Minor road
▬ Scenic route
- - Track
▬ Main railway
▬ Minor railway
▬ International border

Sidi Abdel Rahman, near the El-Alamein battlefield memorials

For keys to symbols *see back flap*

Detail of building in Damietta old town, illustrating Delta-style architecture

❶ Damietta

210 km (131 miles) NE of Cairo.
🏔 78,000. 🚌 🛈 🚇

Damietta (or Dumyat) is an industrial port known for its furniture, textiles, sweets and fishing, that lies on Egypt's North Coast, next to the eastern branch of the Nile. A wealthy port in the Middle Ages, the town was attacked by the Byzantines, occupied twice by Christian forces then completely destroyed in 1250 by the Mamluks. Damietta was rebuilt by the Ottomans (though sadly few of their "Delta-style" villas can still be seen today) and its importance as a port was restored. The completion of the Suez Canal in 1869, and the subsequent growth of Port Said to the east, however, seriously undermined Damietta's prosperity, although the building of a new port in 1987 resulted in an economic revival.

There is not a great deal to do here, though the restoration of three of the city's ancient mosques is a potential draw. To the east of Damietta, the huge expanse of **Lake Manzila** – a saltwater lagoon separated from the sea by a narrow peninsula – is a popular destination for bird-watchers who come to observe the migrating flamingos, herons, pelicans and storks that stop here. Egypt is on one of the major migration routes for many species, and millions of birds pass through this region every autumn and spring.

To the north of Damietta is the small beach resort of **Ras al-Bar**, which has numerous restaurants, hotels and tea houses.

❷ Zagazig

80 km (50 miles) NE of Cairo.
🏔 268,000. 🚌 🛈 🚇

Built in the 1830s to house workers on the Nile Barrages (see p173), Zagazig's main claim to fame is as the birthplace of Colonel Ahmed Orabi, the nationalist who led the 1882 revolt against British rule, and whose statue stands outside the railway station. The town has a small museum that displays archaeological finds from the region.

Just to the southeast of Zagazig are the sparse ruins of **Bubastis**, capital of ancient Egypt in the 22nd and 23rd Dynasties and cult centre of the cat-goddess Bastet. It is believed that huge festivals in her honour were held at Bubastis and attracted

thousands of revellers. The events involved dancing, vast quantities of alcohol and sacrifices to the goddess. Work began on the Temple of Bastet at

Bronze sculpture of Bastet in the form of a cat

Bubastis during the 6th Dynasty and, for nearly 1,500 years, it was regularly added to; now, all that remains to be seen are scattered stones. Nearby, in the underground galleries of a cat cemetery where mummified cats were buried, bronze statues of the sacred animal have been discovered. A museum now stands on the site.

Moulids

Meaning "birth" in Arabic, a *moulid* commemorates the birthday of a local saint or holy person. Celebrated by Muslims and Christians alike, the *moulid* probably has its roots in the customs of ancient Egypt when, on festival days, a statue of the local god was paraded in a boat. Nowadays, big *moulids* in Cairo, Luxor and Tanta draw millions of people, allowing everyone a release from everyday concerns. After visiting the tomb or church, revellers might attend a *zikr*, a ritual chanting of Allah's name to induce a trance-like state. *Tartours* (cone-shaped hats) and *fawanees* (lanterns) are sold, while traditional entertainment such as puppet shows and stick dancing take place alongside more modern funfair attractions. Usually lasting a week, *moulids* climax on the Great Night or *Leila al-Kebira*.

Reeds of Lake Manzila (Damietta) providing cover for migrating birds

❸ Tanta

94 km (58 miles) N of Cairo.
🗺 373,000. 🆃 🚉

Tanta, Egypt's fifth largest city and an important university town, is best known for its eight-day festival, or *moulid*, which is held each year after the October cotton harvest. Up to two million people take part in the event, which honours Sayyid Ahmed al-Badawi, the 13th-century founder of one of the largest Sufi brotherhoods in Egypt. Groups of Sufis from throughout Egypt camp in makeshift lodgings around the city and hold *zikrs* – lengthy sessions of chanting, singing and swaying, intended to achieve unity with Allah. A procession led by the current sheikh closes the *moulid* on the eighth morning, but in recent years officials have toned down this event.

Although fundamentally a spiritual occasion, this annual festival is also an important social event, allowing young Egyptians to let off steam in the boisterous atmosphere.

Panelled wall in the Ottoman House of Amasyali in Rosetta

21st- and 22nd-Dynasty tombs at the royal necropolis at Tanis

❹ Tanis

70 km (43 miles) NE of Zagazig. 🆃

Near the modern village of San el-Hagar, to the northeast of Zagazig, lie the jumbled ruins of the ancient Egyptian city of Djanet, known by the Greeks as Tanis. For several centuries, Tanis was one of the largest cities in the Delta and became the capital of Egypt during the 21st Dynasty. Flooding led to its decline, however, and by the 14th century the area was practically deserted. San el-Hagar grew up on reclaimed land during the 1820s. Excavations at Tanis have revealed ruins dating back to the 6th Dynasty: huge blocks and fragments of statues from the Ramessid Temple of Amun, as well as the foundations of many other temples, are among the remains on site. Several intact 21st- and 22nd-Dynasty tombs, including those of Psusennes I and Sheshonq III, were discovered at the royal necropolis, which lies to the south of the temple. The breath-taking treasures can be seen at the Egyptian Museum in Cairo *(see pp78–81)*.

❺ Rosetta (Rashid)

65 km (40 miles) E of Alexandria.
🗺 58,000. 🚌 🆃

Founded in the 9th century by Ibn Tulun, the Muslim governor of Egypt, Rosetta (which is also known by the modern name of Rashid) became one of Egypt's most important ports, reaching its heyday during the 17th and 18th centuries. With Alexandria's revival in the 19th century, however, Rosetta fell into decline and today it is little more than an attractive fishing village surrounded by palm and orange groves.

Many beautiful Ottoman houses and mosques – reminders of Rosetta's more glorious past – can still be seen around the town and a few are open to visitors. Among the most beautiful are the House of Amasyali on Sharia Amasyali and the Kili House on Midan al-Gumhuriyya, which is now a small museum. Next to the House of Amasyali is the well-preserved Abu Shahim Mill, and to the south of town is the ornate 18th-century Azouz *hammam* (public baths).

Rosetta is best known for the famous Rosetta stone *(see p26)*, which was discovered here by French soldiers in 1799. Part of a black basalt stele dating from the 2nd century BC, the stone was carved with a decree by Ptolemy V, written in ancient hieroglyphics, Greek and demotic Egyptian. From these inscriptions, French professor Jean-François Champollion was able, in 1822, to formulate a system for deciphering hieroglyphics – a feat that was to unlock much of ancient Egyptian history.

Conceded to the British in 1801, the Rosetta stone remains on display at the British Museum in London.

Palm trees bordering the Rosetta branch of the Nile Delta

⑥ Alexandria

Stretching 20 km (12 miles) along the coast, Alexandria is Egypt's second largest city. Founded in 332 BC by Alexander the Great, the city grew to rival Rome before falling into decline in the 4th century AD. In the 19th century, the Pasha Mohammed Ali revived Alexandria's fortunes as a port by linking it to the Nile. This prosperity drew many Europeans, who fostered the decadent atmosphere chronicled by writers such as Lawrence Durrell and Constantine Cavafy. This era ended in the 1950s as the foreigners fled Nasser's revolution. Little remains of the city's ancient magnificence, but it is hoped that excavations will reveal the tombs of Cleopatra and Mark Antony.

Colourful fishing boats in Alexandria Harbour

🏛 Midan Saad Zaghloul
Situated on the seafront, Midan Saad Zaghloul is at the heart of modern Alexandria. From this square, a statue of Egyptian nationalist leader Zaghloul (1860–1927) *(see p66)* watches over the eastern harbour and the busy tram and bus stations in the adjacent Midan Ramla.

Sadly, nothing remains of the Caesareum, a magnificent temple built on the site more than 2,000 years ago. Begun by Cleopatra VII for Mark Antony and finished by Octavian after their deaths in 30 BC *(see pp58–9)*, only two obelisks survived its destruction in 912. Known as Cleopatra's Needles, they were relocated to London and New York in the 1800s.

Today the square consists of shops, hotels and three 1920s Art Deco cafés, Athineos, Délices and Trianon. South is Sharia Nabi Daniel, believed to be the ancient Street of Soma – a marble road lined with columns. It is now lined with street vendors, and its glory has faded.

🏛 Bibliotheca Alexandrina
Shatbi. **Tel** (03) 483 9999. **Open** 10am–4pm Sun–Thu (9am–3pm during Ramadan). 🚭

Founded in the 3rd century BC, the Bibliotheca Alexandrina was the greatest library in the ancient world, attracting the best international scholars. The library and cultural centre was re-inaugurated in October 2002, more than two millennia after the original building was destroyed by fire.

The Bibliotheca Alexandrina is striking in its architecture and also contains a Planetarium and four interesting museums. The main library is encased in a giant cylindrical building at the far northern end of the corniche. The circular outer wall is made of Aswan granite engraved with letters from world alphabets. The partly glazed roof which tilts towards the sea is designed to angle sunlight on to the desks of the seven-tier 2,000-seat reading rooms. Eventually, the library will contain 8 million volumes.

🏛 Steigenberger Cecil Hotel
16 Midan Saad Zaghloul. **Tel** (03) 487 7173.

One of the more obvious landmarks of Midan Saad Zaghloul is the Moorish-style Steigenberger Cecil Hotel, which featured in Lawrence Durrell's *Alexandria Quartet*. Opened in 1929, it is reputed to be built on the site where Cleopatra VII committed suicide after her Egyptian fleet was defeated by Octavian in the Battle of Actium in 31 BC.

During World War II the hotel was used by the British Secret Service and later played host to politicians and writers such as Winston Churchill, Somerset Maugham and Noel Coward. Though restoration has not quite captured its past grandeur, the roof garden is a pleasant place to enjoy a drink.

🏛 Cavafy Museum
4 Sharia Sharm el-Sheikh, off Sharia Nabi Daniel. **Open** 10am–5pm Tue–Sun. 🚭

The poet Constantine Cavafy (1863–1933) was born to Greek parents but spent most of his life in Alexandria. This small museum is housed in the flat where he spent the last 25 years of his life. Some of the rooms are arranged as they would have been when

Façade of the Steigenberger Cecil Hotel

Marble benches capable of seating up to 800 Romans in the Amphitheatre at Kom al-Dikka

he lived here – the display of possessions includes his bed, desk, death mask, rare editions of his books and some of his letters. Cavafy is buried in the Greek Cemetery nearby.

Another room in the small museum is devoted to one of Cavafy's students, the Greek writer Stratis Tsirkas (1911–81).

🕿 Roman Amphitheatre at Kom al-Dikka

Sharia Yousef. **Open** 9am–5pm daily. 🗭

In 1965, a semicircular Roman amphitheatre was discovered under what was known as Kom al-Dikka (Mound of Rubble) after the remains of a Napoleonic fort were levelled for a housing project. The 13 tiered rows of marble seats, excavated by Polish archaeologists aided by the Graeco-Roman Museum, date from the 2nd century AD. Originally a small theatre, the building was altered over time and served as an assembly hall. A couple of sections of the original mosaic floor are on view in front of the theatre.

Other excavations are still under way. To the north lie the brick ruins of a Roman bathing complex. A series of basins and channels reveal how water would have passed through the heating system to the marble-covered baths. To the east lie the ruins of a residential area dating from

Roman mosaic at Kom al-Dikka

the 1st century AD, where the Villa of the Birds, a beautifully colourful nine-panelled mosaic, has been uncovered.

Some items found at an underwater excavation near Fort Qaitbey, including part of an obelisk from the era of Seti I and a weather-beaten sphinx, are on show in the amphitheatre grounds.

VISITORS' CHECKLIST

Practical Information
Alexandria governorate. 🗺 4 million. 🛈 23 Sharia El Mina El Sharqeya, Raml Station (03) 485 1556; Masr Station (03) 424 9427.

Transport
✈ 5 km (3 miles) SE of the city. 🚇 Masr Station, Midan al-Gumhuriyya; Sidi Gaber Station. 🚌 Muharram Bey Bus Station.

Alexandria City Centre

① Midan Saad Zaghloul
② Bibliotheca Alexandrina
③ Steigenberger Cecil Hotel
④ Cavafy Museum
⑤ Roman Amphitheatre at Kom al-Dikka
⑥ Graeco-Roman Museum
⑦ National Museum of Alexandria
⑧ Attarine Mosque
⑨ Midan Tahrir
⑩ Ottoman District (Anfushi)
⑪ Fort Qaitbey
⑫ Necropolis of Anfushi
⑬ Ras el-Tin Palace
⑭ Pompey's Pillar
⑮ Catacombs of Kom ash-Shuqqafa
⑯ Fine Arts Museum
⑰ Mahmoud Said Museum Centre
⑱ Royal Jewellery Museum

For keys to symbols *see back flap*

Alexandria: Graeco-Roman Museum

Situated in the heart of modern Alexandria, the Graeco-Roman Museum contains around 40,000 artifacts, mostly covering around 1,000 years of history from the founding of the city in 331 BC to the Arab conquest in AD 640. The museum was established in 1892 by Khedive Abbas II. Its 25 rooms and central gardens are crammed with items found in Alexandria and the surrounding areas, including a large mosaic from the 3rd century BC. The vast collection of artifacts from ancient Egyptian, Classical and Christian cultures testifies to the city's complex history. The museum is currently closed for major renovations.

Museum Gardens
In the museum's central gardens, among a wealth of tombs, statues and other artifacts, sits the head of a once huge statue of Mark Anthony.

Statue of Aphrodite
(2nd century AD)

Tomb Painting
Two oxen driving a waterwheel (an invention of Alexandrian scientists) are depicted in this tomb fresco dating from the 2nd century AD.

White Marble Sarcophagus
A bas-relief from the 2nd century AD depicts Dionysus and his retinue as they find Ariadne asleep on the island of Naxos before she was abandoned by her lover, Theseus.

Sacred Crocodile
This mummified crocodile was carried in processions honouring Sobek, the crocodile-god.

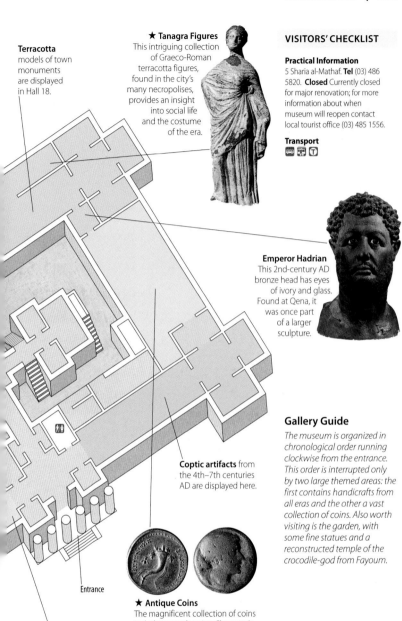

Terracotta models of town monuments are displayed in Hall 18.

★ Tanagra Figures This intriguing collection of Graeco-Roman terracotta figures, found in the city's many necropolises, provides an insight into social life and the costume of the era.

VISITORS' CHECKLIST

Practical Information
5 Sharia al-Mathaf. **Tel** (03) 486 5820. **Closed** Currently closed for major renovation; for more information about when museum will reopen contact local tourist office (03) 485 1556.

Transport

Emperor Hadrian This 2nd-century AD bronze head has eyes of ivory and glass. Found at Qena, it was once part of a larger sculpture.

Gallery Guide

The museum is organized in chronological order running clockwise from the entrance. This order is interrupted only by two large themed areas: the first contains handicrafts from all eras and the other a vast collection of coins. Also worth visiting is the garden, with some fine statues and a reconstructed temple of the crocodile-god from Fayoum.

Coptic artifacts from the 4th–7th centuries AD are displayed here.

Entrance

★ Antique Coins The magnificent collection of coins includes some bearing Cleopatra's profile (above right).

Alexander the Great (356–323 BC) Sculpted from marble, this head of Alexander the Great is one of several portraits of the leader in the museum. He became the object of a cult worship that spread throughout the ancient world.

Key

- Coptic
- Ptolemaic
- Pharaonic
- Graeco-Roman
- Handicrafts (all periods)
- Coins
- Non-exhibition space

The Italianate National Museum of Alexandria

🏛 National Museum of Alexandria

110 Sharia Horreya. **Tel** (03) 483 5519.
Open 9am–4:30pm daily. 🖼

Over 1,800 artifacts, many in ingenious hanging diagonal glass showcases, are on display in this museum. It is located in a restored three-storey Italianate building, which dates from 1929 and is set in a large garden of rare trees and plants.

Most of the museum's treasures were excavated in and around the city itself. The basement spans pre-dynastic and ancient Egyptian artifacts, featuring a replica of a tomb similar to those found in the Valley of the Kings. The first floor has Graeco-Roman finds, including several beautifully painted terracotta Tanagra figurines.

A black basalt statue of a high priest of the goddess Isis, excavated from the seabed in 1998, is a star exhibit of the Coptic and Islamic collection.

🕌 Attarine Mosque

Sharia Attarine.

Topped by a pretty minaret, the Attarine Mosque lies just

Midan Tahrir at the centre of Alexandria

south of Midan Tahrir. It was built on the site of the fabled Mosque of a Thousand Columns, which itself stood on the site of a church dedicated to St Athanasius in AD 370.

Napoleon's men removed a 7-ton sarcophagus from the mosque, believing it to be Alexander's. Handed over to the British it was found to be the sarcophagus of Nectanebo II, the last Egyptian pharaoh.

Around the Attarine Mosque, the sprawling antiques district begins. Shops piled high with European furniture, and trinkets dating back to Napoleonic times, fill the backstreets. Here also, the intriguing belongings of many Europeans who fled the 1952 revolution are up for sale. However, the area is well known by international antiques dealers and genuine bargains can be hard to find.

🕌 Midan Tahrir

Originally known as Place des Consuls, the square was the centrepiece of Pasha Mohammed Ali's new Alexandria in the 1830s. In 1873 his equestrian statue was set in its place on a high plinth and the square was thereafter known as Midan Mohammed Ali. After the destruction brought about by the British bombardment in 1882 *(see p63)*, the area was rebuilt as Midan Mansheiyya, before Nasser's revolution in 1952 renamed the square Midan Tahrir.

It was here that an assassination attempt was made on President Nasser as he

gave a speech in 1954. This gave him the opportunity to remove any opposition to his rule. Two years later, in 1956, it was from Midan Tahrir that Nasser shocked the Western world and announced the nationalization of the Suez Canal.

To the north is Midan Orabi, a major transport hub with tram, minibus and bus depots. The grand Neo-Classical Monument to the Unknown Soldier, designed by the Italian architect Verucci and erected in 1937, stands on the corniche, facing out to the sea.

Detail of Andalusian-styled Mosque of Abu al-Abbas Mursi in Anfushi

🕌 Ottoman District (Anfushi)

The peninsula leading to Fort Qaitbey was home to the inhabitants of Alexandria in Ottoman times (1517–1914). The atmosphere here differs from the rest of the city and it is best experienced on foot. To the south, lively souqs sell medicinal herbs and perfume while Turkish-style houses overhang the narrow streets.

Ottoman mosques are also dotted throughout the area, with the El-Shorbagi Mosque Complex at the heart of the district. Built in the mid-18th century, it has a distinctive gallery on the first floor with shops below. The Terbana Mosque on Faransa Street was originally built in 1685 and two antique columns, taken from another site, support the minaret. Further north, in Midan El-Gawamaa is a mosque

Pharos Lighthouse

Built in the 3rd century BC on an island in the eastern harbour, the Pharos Lighthouse stood up to 150 m (492 ft) high and was one of the Seven Wonders of the ancient world. Built mainly of limestone to the design of the Asiatic Greek architect Sostratus, the lighthouse had three differently-shaped storeys. The base was square and used as lodgings for mechanics and for storing fuel. The second storey was octagonal and the third, which contained the lantern mechanism, was circular and topped with a huge bronze statue of Poseidon, god of the sea. Used for nearly 1,000 years, the lighthouse was neglected during the Arab occupation. The lantern collapsed in AD 700 and the lighthouse was later destroyed by a series of earthquakes in the 12th and 14th centuries. Underwater excavation has discovered blocks of stone believed to be from the Pharos Lighthouse and a temple dedicated to Isis (see p30) which stood nearby.

Reconstruction of the Pharos Lighthouse

dedicated to the 13th-century Andalusian, Sidi Abu al-Abbas Mursi, the city's patron saint of fishermen. The current structure was designed in 1945 by Italian architect Mario Rossi. The octagonal-shaped building has a 73-m (240-ft) minaret.

Fort Qaitbey

Corniche. 🚌 15. **Open** 9am–4pm daily. 🖼

Although the turretted Fort Qaitbey situated on the tip of the Eastern Harbour looks like some kind of toy castle from the corniche, up close it is an imposing building. The fort was built in the 1480s by Sultan Qaitbey (1468–96) on the site of the Pharos Lighthouse, using stones from the dilapidated building. Within the keep there is a small mosque – the oldest in Alexandria – and a Naval Museum displaying relics from ships sunk nearby, the result of Roman and Napoleonic sea battles. These include bottles of wine and astronomical instruments retrieved from the French ship *L'Orient*. The fort was badly damaged by the British bombardment in 1882 when the mosque's minaret was blown clean off. From its elevated position, set back from the corniche, the fort has fantastic views of Alexandria and out to sea.

🏛 Necropolis of Anfushi

Sharia Ras el-Tin, Anfushi.
Open 9am–4pm daily. 🖼

The five rock tombs in the Necropolis of Anfushi date from around 250 BC and were discovered in 1901 and 1921. Cut into limestone, the tombs consist of a stairway leading down to a central courtyard with individual burial sites located off to the side. Tomb No. 2 is the most interesting and best preserved. The stairway walls are decorated with paintings of Osiris, Horus and Isis with the deceased as well as scenes of daily life and even an example of ancient Greek graffiti. The wall paintings and decoration are significant as they combine features of Greek and Egyptian art. There are also two vestibules with burial chambers; the one to the northeast is painted with black and white squares to resemble more expensive alabaster and marble tiling. The door to the burial chamber is flanked by two small stone sphinxes on stands, keeping watch over the tomb.

Fort Qaitbey from across the Eastern Harbour, built by recycling the stones from the Pharos Lighthouse

🏛 Ras el-Tin Palace

Sharia Ras el-Tin, Bahari. 🔲 🔳

Overlooking Alexandria's
Western Harbour, Ras el-Tin
Palace is surrounded by elegant,
formal gardens. The palace was
built originally by Ottoman
Pasha Mohammed Ali (1805–48)
so that he could keep watch on
his new fleet. Under King Fuad I
(1917–36), it was redesigned by
Italian architects and served as
the government's summer seat.

During the 1952 revolution,
the palace was besieged by
Nasser's men and King Farouk
was forced to abdicate and
flee to Italy. The palace is now
Admiralty headquarters and
is reserved for state guests;
however its pleasant gardens
are open to the public.

🏛 Pompey's Pillar

Sharia Amoud al-Saweiri, Karmous.
🔳 16. **Open** 9am–4pm daily. 🖼

To the southwest of the city, in
the impoverished district of
Karmous, Pompey's Pillar is a
striking sight. Made of red
Aswan granite, the 27-m (89-ft)
high pillar was erected around
AD 297 in tribute to the Roman
emperor Diocletian. On its base
is written in Greek "To the most
just of emperors, the divine
protector of Alexandria,
Diocletian the invincible:
Postumus, prefect of Egypt."

The monument's popular
name may have come from
medieval travellers who thought
that the Roman general Pompey,
murdered in Egypt in 48 BC, was
buried here; in fact, the pillar
came from the Serapeum
complex or Temple of Serapis,
which was built in the mid-3rd
century BC. (Serapis was an
Egyptian deity, very popular in
the Graeco-Roman period, who
combined aspects of the gods
Osiris and Apis.) The pillar would
have been freestanding and is all
that remains of the temple
which was once an important
repository of religious texts
and the "daughter library" of
that of Alexandria.

Enlarged by the Emperor
Hadrian in the 2nd century AD,
when it was described as
second only to the Capitol in
Rome, the temple was

Pompey's Pillar, once part of the beautiful
Temple of Serapis

destroyed by Christians in
AD 391. Nearby there are
some underground galleries,
where the sacred Apis bulls
(see p168) were buried, as
well as several statues of the
Sphinx that originally stood
at Heliopolis.

🏛 Catacombs of Kom ash-Shuqqafa

Sharia al-Nasserieh. 🔳 16.
Open 9am–4:30pm daily (3pm
during Ramadan). 🖼

Dating from the 2nd century
AD, the catacomb complex of
Kom ash-Shuqqafa (Mound of
Shards) just south of Pompey's
Pillar is the largest Graeco-
Roman necropolis in Egypt.
Dug into the rock to a depth
of about 35 m (115 ft), the
complex has three levels.
However, flooding has made
the lowest level inaccessible.

The catacombs are reached
via a spiral staircase encircling
a shaft down which bodies of
the deceased were lowered.

On the first level there is a
central rotunda and a large
banquet hall, the Triclinium,
where friends and relatives
of the deceased gathered to
pay their last respects.

To the east of the rotunda
is the Caracalla Hall, an older
burial complex that became
accessible from the main
chamber when tomb robbers
broke through the wall. This
area is dedicated to Nemesis,
the goddess of sport.

From the central rotunda,
stairs lead down to a second
storey with a vestibule and
burial chamber. Here the
decorated sarcophagi and wall
reliefs display a mixture of
Egyptian, Roman and Greek
styles: by the doorway, Anubis,
the god of the dead, is shown
as a Roman legionary with a
dragon's tail. On either side of
the burial chamber, below
heads of Medusa, are carved
two giant serpents, wearing
the double crown of Egypt.

From the burial chamber,
eerie passages lead off in all
directions to rooms containing
more than 300 loculi – small
chambers for bodies.

Back above the ground,
the enclosure is strewn with
sarcophagi and the broken
remains of several sphinxes. The
surrounding area of Karmouz is
worth a visit to see the colourful
markets and vibrant local life,
where foreign tourists rarely visit.

🏛 Fine Arts Museum

18 Sharia Menasce. **Tel** (03) 393 6616.
Open 9am–3pm daily. 🖼

A short distance to the
southeast of Masr station, the
Fine Arts Museum is housed in
a beautiful villa that was

Relief of Anubis presiding over a mummification at Kom ash-Shuqqafa

donated in 1954 to the city of Alexandria by the wealthy Jewish Menasce family. The museum is used mainly for frequently changing exhibitions of contemporary foreign and Egyptian artists. The museum is also known for hosting the Alexandrian Biennial, a showcase for art from Mediterranean countries.

A statue by Mahmoud Mokhtar (1891–1934), who has been acclaimed as the first sculptor in the modern Egyptian art movement, stands in the gardens outside.

🏛 Mahmoud Said Museum Centre

6 Sharia Said Pasha, Gianaclis. 🕐 🚇 2. **Tel** (03) 582 1688. **Open** 10am–2pm daily. 🖼

An Alexandrian aristocrat, Mahmoud Said (1897–1967) was one of Egypt's most important modern artists. The museum that bears his name is housed in what was the family villa.

Said trained originally as a lawyer and worked as a judge, but painting was his passion and in 1947 he gave up law to dedicate himself to art. His work combines Western techniques with Egyptian and Pharaonic themes to produce stunning, sensuous paintings. His 1924 self-portrait echoes a haunting Fayoum mummy portrait (see p173).

The first floor of the museum contains works by the prolific Alexandrian ,painters, the Wanly brothers, Seif (1906–79) and Adham (1911–59). The eclectic choice of paintings includes portraits, landscapes, and even a few cartoons.

The lower floor of the museum is also worthy of a visit. Here a small modern art gallery displays the works of other Egyptian artists.

Elsewhere in the museum, portraits of the royal family adorn the walls alongside period light fittings, which are works of art in themselves. The gorgeous inlaid wooden floors, considered too beautiful to walk on, are protected by raised walkways in places.

Montazah Palace, an eclectic mix of Turkish and Florentine architecture

🏛 Royal Jewellery Museum

27 Sharia Ahmed Yehia Pasha, Gleem. 🕐 🚇 2. **Tel** (03) 586 8348. **Open** 9am–2:15pm & 5–6:15pm daily (but call ahead of your visit). 🖼

This building was originally constructed for Mohammed Ali's granddaughter, Princess Fatima el-Zaharaa (1903–83), and later used as a palace by King Farouk. The museum has an extensive collection of jewels dating from Pasha Mohammed Ali's rule in the early 19th century to the end of King Farouk's reign in 1952.

Key pieces include a gold snuff box with Mohammed Ali's name spelled out in diamonds, King Farouk's gold- and diamond-studded chess set, Prince Youssef Kamal's gold desk inlaid with 166 diamonds, and a fabulous platinum crown glittering with well over 2,000 diamonds.

The palace is lavishly, if not always tastefully, decorated with stained-glass vignettes of life in 18th-century France. The two bathrooms, the ladies' tiled with scenes of nymphs bathing in Alpine surrounds and the men's with pictures of French fishermen and seagulls, should not be missed. The museum has undergone an impressive renovation programme and is now a real highlight of Alexandria's numerous attractions. There is also a pleasant café in the garden which makes a good place to relax after a tour of the jewels.

❼ Montazah Palace

18 km (11 miles) E of Alexandria. 🕐 🚌 **Tel** (03) 547 7153. **Open** 7am–11pm daily. 🖼

Montazah Palace is set in extensive gardens and overlooks a truly beautiful stretch of coast. Built at the beginning of the 20th century by Khedive Abbas II, a relative of King Farouk, the palace mixes Turkish and Florentine architecture: the central tower was inspired by the Palazzo Vecchio in Florence. Although the palace itself is closed to the public, the lush park and the semiprivate beach are popular places to relax.

To the east lies the private beach resort of **Mamoura**. It has a more relaxed dress code than public beaches and the sand is relatively clean.

🚌 Mamoura

Sharia Abu Qir. 🖼

The elegant gardens and groves of Montazah Palace, Alexandria

❽ Abu Qir

24 km (15 miles) E of Alexandria.
🏙 33,000. 🚉 🚌

The small fishing town of Abu Qir, on the coast to the east of Alexandria, is renowned for two reasons: historic battles and excellent fish restaurants. It was at Abu Qir Bay that Admiral Nelson destroyed the French fleet in the dramatic Battle of the Nile in 1798. With the loss of his ships and army, Napoleon's plans for an eastern empire were effectively ruined. A year later the tables were turned slightly when Napoleon's troops repulsed a landing attempt by a British contingent of 15,000 Turkish soldiers and many thousands drowned.

Since 1998, underwater excavation work by teams of French and Egyptian divers has uncovered many artifacts from the sunken warships including gold coins, cannons and plenty of everyday items. There are plans to build a new museum to display these finds.

Although the beach at Abu Qir is not suitable for bathing, at the weekend the streets are filled with Alexandrians who come to savour the delights of a small seaside town. These include eating in one of the many seafront restaurants that serve delicious seafood. Sitting right on the beach, the Zephyrion (see p291) – the ancient Greek name for Abu Qir – is reputed to be one of the best restaurants in Egypt.

Brightly painted fishing boats at Abu Qir

❾ Agami

20 km (12 miles) W of Alexandria. 🚌

Agami was traditionally the summer resort of the Cairene and Alexandrian elite during the 1950s. Known then as the Egyptian St Tropez, it is far less exclusive these days. The semiprivate beaches are less conservative and less crowded than in Alexandria, and the nightlife is livelier. High-rise apartment blocks have replaced most of the original resort architecture. Exceptions include the **Beit al-Halawa**, designed in 1975 by Abd el-Wahid el-Wakil and the extreme angular lines of **Villa Lashin**, built in 1962 by the architect Ali Azzam.

Environs

Other popular resorts nearby include the small village of **Hannoville**, 1 km (half a mile) to the west, notable for its inexpensive accommodation,

and the private beach resort of **Sidi Krear**, which lies 14 km (8.5 miles) further west along the coast.

❿ Abu Mina

63 km (39 miles) SW of Alexandria. 🚌

To the west of Alexandria, 15 km (9 miles) inland from Abu Sir on the coast, lies the Coptic Monastery of Abu Mina (Deir Mari Mina). St Mina was an Alexandrian-born Roman legionary who was tortured and killed in Phrygia (Asia Minor) at the end of the 3rd century for his Christian beliefs. His body is said to have been buried here after a camel carrying it home refused to go any further. Legend has it that a spring with miraculous powers immediately started flowing nearby and a church and basilica were built around the tomb. After the Emperor of Byzantium's daughter was cured by the waters in the 4th century its fame spread. The water was exported throughout Christendom and Abu Mina became a busy pilgrim town. However, after repeated sackings by the Bedouin, the town fell into decay as the water source dried up.

Today a modern monastery dominates the site and there are few impressive remains to see, although there are plans for a museum and archaeological park. The area is still important to pilgrims who visit the monastery, especially on 11 November, St Mina's day.

Monastery at Abu Mina built in 1959 on the site of a much older basilica

◀ The imposing Fort Qaitbey on the Eastern Harbour, Alexandria

⑪ El-Alamein

105 km (65 miles) W of Alexandria.
⚏ 1,800. 🚐

El-Alamein, a small village on the coast to the west of Alexandria, was the site of a World War II battle which changed the course of the North Africa campaign in the Allies' favour. On 23 October 1942, the British General Montgomery's Eighth Army attacked Field Marshal Rommel's German-Italian Afrika Korps at El-Alamein. After 11 days of fierce fighting, Rommel's troops retreated to Tunis to surrender six months later. More than 11,000 soldiers died and at least 70,000 were injured in the battle.

The **War Museum** to the west of town shows the stages of the North Africa campaign using electronic displays and many World War II mementoes, uniforms and photographs. Tanks and artillery used during the battle are on display in the grounds. The **Commonwealth War Cemetery** to the east, where row upon row of Allied graves lie surrounded by the desert, is a chilling testimony to the war. A memorial here also lists the names of over 11,000 men whose bodies were never found. On the coast, 4 km (2.5 miles) west, lies the **German Cemetery**. This imposing fortress of a

Gravestones at the Commonwealth War Cemetery at El-Alamein

Sherman tank outside the War Museum

memorial overlooking the sea honours the 22,000 Germans who died in the North Africa campaign. The **Italian Cemetery** is just 3 km (2 miles) further west along the coast, with a marble tower in honour of the 22,000 Italian soldiers killed in the fighting. Further west, a string of resort villages line the coast. One with a particularly stunning beach is the upmarket and unspoiled resort at **Sidi Abdel Rahman**, 23 km (14 miles) west of El-Alamein.

🏛 **El-Alamein War Museum**
Tel (046) 410 0021. **Open** 9am–4pm daily (Phone ahead to check, as opening hours sometimes vary). ♿

⑫ Marsa Matruh

290 km (180 miles) W of Alexandria.
⚏ 52,000. 🚆 🚐 ℹ Governorate Building, Al-Corniche (046) 493 1841.

The coastal town of Marsa Matruh is a very popular summer resort for Egyptians. However, although the coast is beautiful, the town itself and its beaches are pretty tatty and the resort lacks appeal for most tourists.

The town has a historical pedigree and was founded by Alexander on his way to the oracle at Siwa; later it served as a port for Anthony and Cleopatra's doomed fleet and this link is reflected in many of the place names.

West of town the sea is gorgeous. **Cleopatra Beach** is 7 km (4 miles) west, though rocks and a sudden drop in the seabed make this a difficult place to swim. The royal queen herself is said to have bathed at Cleopatra's Bath nearby. The best place to swim is **Agibah Beach**, 28 km (17 miles) west on the coastal road. A steep path leads down to a cove where rock shelves make ideal platforms for diving into the sea.

⑬ Sallum

222 km (137 miles) W of Marsa Matruh. ⚏ 6,000. 🚐

Sallum is the last Egyptian town before Libya and an important trading centre for the Bedouin. The town sits high up on a cliff looking out to sea, with a small harbour down below. This was the ancient Roman port of Baranis, and there are still some Roman wells in the area.

Sallum is not traditionally a tourist area, and although the beaches in town can be dirty, to the east there are stretches of golden sand and crystal waters that permit relatively secluded swimming. Visitors should check with the local Tourist Police first that bathing is allowed as some areas and beaches are out of bounds.

There is also a small **Allied War Cemetery** where soldiers killed fighting with Rommel's Afrika Korps lie buried.

Waves crashing into the rocks at Cleopatra's Beach, Marsa Matruh

For hotels and restaurants in this region see p276 and pp291–2

THE WESTERN DESERT

Egypt's vast Western Desert stretches over nearly 3 million sq km (1.2 million sq miles), from the west bank of the Nile to Libya, and from Sudan towards the Mediterranean Sea. Despite covering over two-thirds of Egypt's total land area, the desert is virtually uninhabited, except for the fertile oases where communities and crops flourish amid barren desert surroundings.

There are five oases in the Western Desert: Siwa, Kharga, Dakhla, Farafra and Bahariyya. Except for Siwa, the oases have been under the control of the rulers of the Nile Valley since Pharaonic times, when they were crucial stopping points on the busy caravan trading routes from Africa. The Ptolemaic temples and Roman forts dotted around the oases bear witness to their past importance and ongoing archaeological work is continually uncovering new finds.

Each of the Western Desert oases has its own unique character. While the main settlements of Bahariyya and Farafra are little more than villages, those of Dakhla and Kharga are towns, surrounded by fascinating historical sites. In Siwa, isolated near the Libyan border, the inhabitants retain their own language and distinct culture.

In the late 1950s a plan was made to reclaim part of the desert and relocate thousands of people there from the crowded Nile Delta and Valley. The area, covering Bahariyya, Farafra, Dakhla and Kharga oases, was named the New Valley. Although some building began, very few people moved, and financial constraints together with the questionable sustainability of the water supply meant that the project was virtually abandoned.

The Western Desert today remains one of the few places in the world where travellers can experience a feeling of total isolation. Its sheer scale is overwhelming. From huge dunes to fantastical rock formations, the landscape varies dramatically and camping out overnight in such astonishing surroundings can be one of the highlights of a trip to Egypt.

Taking a break during the heat of the day in Dakhla, one of the Western Desert oases

◀ Mud building at the Siwa Oasis with a lake and the desert in the background

Exploring the Western Desert

The Western Desert offers visitors the chance to escape the crowded sites of Cairo and the Nile Valley and sample the peace and tranquillity of the empty desert and its green oases. In the northwest, the remote Siwa is the perfect place to relax. Further east, Bahariyya is a picturesque oasis within easy reach of Cairo. The road leading on to Farafra, the least developed of the oases, passes through the Black Desert and the incredible White Desert, with its mysterious, wind-eroded rock formations. Pockets of fertile land growing fruit, rice and peanuts are dotted among the sand dunes between Farafra and the beautiful Dakhla oasis. For lovers of ancient monuments, Dakhla and the more built-up Kharga have the most to offer.

Marsa Matruh

Qa

SIWA OASIS
Siwa ⑤

Wester
Desert

Great Sand Se

Dakhla Oasis near Al-Qasr, showing the striking contrast between the fertile soil and the barren, inhospitable desert

Getting Around

Travelling in the Western Desert is much easier than it used to be. Roads link the main oases and buses run fairly frequently. Siwa Oasis is best reached by bus from Marsa Matruh. Bahariyya and Farafra can be visited from Cairo, and Dakhla and Kharga can be reached quite easily from Asyut. There are airports at Dakhla and Kharga but flights are only once per week. Depending on time pressure and your sense of adventure, the 1,000-km (620-mile) Great Desert Circuit of Bahariyya, Farafra, Dakhla and Kharga is an option. Usually starting at Cairo and ending at Luxor or Asyut, the trip can be taken either with an organized tour, hired transport or by bus. It is also now possible to cross the desert track between Siwa and Bahariyya by 4WD. Your tour operator can organize permits.

Siwa Oasis, with the salt lake Birket Siwa visible in the distance, viewed from the Mountain of the Dead

For hotels and restaurants in this region see p277 and p293

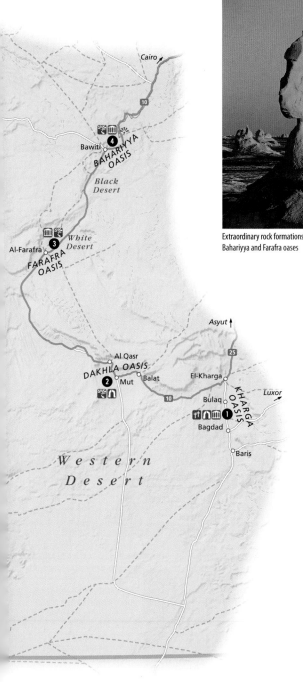

Extraordinary rock formations in the White Desert between Bahariyya and Farafra oases

0 kilometres 100
0 miles 50

Sights at a Glance

❶ Kharga Oasis
❷ Dakhla Oasis
❸ Farafra Oasis
❹ Bahariyya Oasis
❺ Siwa Oasis

Key

— Major road

═ Minor road

— Minor railway

– – Track

▬ International border

For keys to symbols *see back flap*

Lush date groves surrounding the fertile fields of Dakhla, the prettiest of the Western Desert oases

❶ Kharga Oasis

233 km (144 miles) SW of Asyut. ⛰ 65,000. ✈ 5 km (3 miles) N of El-Kharga. 🚍 *i* Government building, Midan Nasser, El-Kharga (092) 792 1206.

Kharga, the largest of the oases, rose to prominence as the penultimate stop on "The Forty Days Road", the infamous slave-trade route between Sudan and Egypt. Today the modern, sprawling city of El-Kharga is capital of the New Valley governorate, which covers Kharga, Dakhla and Farafra oases. The city lacks charm, but its **Antiquities Museum** displays impressive archaeological finds from Kharga and Dakhla.

Standing in palm groves just north of the city, the **Temple of Hibis**, built by Persian emperor Darius I in the 6th century BC, is the only sizeable Persian temple left in Egypt. Also north of the city is the **Necropolis of al-Bagawat**. This Christian cemetery contains hundreds of domed, mudbrick tombs decorated

with Coptic murals, dating from around the 4th to 6th centuries AD. The best-preserved paintings are in the Chapel of the Exodus and portray Moses leading the Jews out of Egypt, away from Pharaoh's pursuing troops.

Environs
Perched on a hill on the road south to Baris are the ruins of the 25th-Dynasty **Qasr al-Ghueita** hilltop fortress and temple. Further south, Nasser and Bulaq are known for their thermal springs, reputed to treat rheumatism.

🏛 **Antiquities Museum**
Sharia Gamal Abdel Nasser.
Open 8am–5pm daily. 🖼

🏯 **Temple of Hibis**
2 km (1 mile) N of El-Kharga. **Open** 8am–4pm daily (5pm in summer). 🖼

🏯 **Necropolis of al-Bagawat**
3 km (2 miles) N of El-Kharga. **Open** 8am–4pm daily (5pm in summer). 🖼

🏯 **Qasr al-Ghueita**
18 km (11 miles) S of El-Kharga. **Open** 8am–4pm daily (5pm in summer). 🖼

❷ Dakhla Oasis

190 km (118 miles) W of Kharga. ⛰ 70,000. ✈ 10 km (6 miles) SW of Mut. 🚍 *i* Sharia as-Sawra al-Khadra, Mut (092) 782 1686.

With many springs set in a lush landscape, Dakhla is regarded as the prettiest of the oases. A long band of pinkish rock sits along the northern horizon, and olives, dates, wheat and rice thrive on the fertile land. In the capital, Mut, the **Traditional Museum** displays figures sculpted by Mabrouk, a local artist.

Dakhla's ancient sites are situated in the outlying parts of the oasis. They can easily be reached by hiring a pick-up truck from Mut.

Environs
With its narrow, winding streets and mudbrick houses, **Al-Qasr**, 27 km (17 miles) northwest of Mut, retains a strong medieval feel. The town has a museum, a 12th-century mosque and a 10th-century *madrassa* (school), with superb rooftop views. Care is needed, however, as the roof is dilapidated. The **Al-Muzawaka tombs** date from Pharaonic times. The two best are those of Petosiris and Petubastis, which have vivid coloured reliefs, but are currently closed for restoration. Just 10 km (6 miles) to the west, the remnants of **Deir al-Hagar** temple, built in the first century AD, stand isolated in the desert. **Balat**, a medieval village on the site of an Old Kingdom settlement, lies 35 km (22 miles) east of Mut.

Mudbrick tombs in the Necropolis of al-Bagawat, Kharga Oasis

🏛 Traditional Museum
Sharia as-Salem. Tel (092) 782 1311.
Open by prior arrangement.

🏛 Al-Muzawaka tombs
5 km (3 miles) W of Al-Qasr. **Open**
8am–4pm daily (5pm in summer).

🏛 Deir al-Hagar
12 km (7 miles) W of Al-Qasr. **Open**
8am–4pm daily (5pm in summer).

❸ Farafra Oasis

310 km (192 miles) NW of Dakhla.
🚗 2,800. 🚌

The most isolated and least
populous of the New Valley
oases, Farafra is an extremely
peaceful place to visit. Its mainly
Bedouin inhabitants are well
known for their strong traditions
and religious piety. The largest
settlement, Al-Farafra, is built like
the other oasis towns around a
ruined fortress, where villagers
would shelter from attacks.
Though the traditional mudbrick houses remain, concrete
developments have sprung up

Golden Mummies

Since 1996, around 250
Graeco-Roman mummies
have been unearthed near
Bahariyya, about 3 km (2 miles)
south of the Temple of
Alexander the Great. Most of
the mummies remain in situ in
their tombs within the "Valley
of the Golden Mummies", but
five gilded mummies have
been removed and are
currently on display at the
Antiquities Inspectorate
Museum in Bawiti (open
8am–4pm daily). One ticket
purchased here allows entry to
most of the cultural treasures
at Bawiti and Bahariyya.
Archaeologists have ceased
excavations of the mummies
for the moment, but work is
continuing at an extensive
26th-Dynasty site known as
the Sheikh Subi Tombs.

Bizarre rock formations caused by wind erosion in the White Desert, near Farafra Oasis

in an effort to attract outsiders
to the area. The curious little
Badr's Museum displays
sculptures by local artists.

Environs
The **White Desert** is located
41 km (25 miles) from Al-Farafra
on the road to Bahariyya.
Named after its bright-white
rock formations, the White
Desert resembles a haunting
lunar landscape.

❹ Bahariyya Oasis

185 km (115 miles) NE of Farafra.
🚗 33,000. 🚌 ℹ️ Town council
building, Bawiti (0122) 373 6567.

This oasis, a key agricultural
centre in Pharaonic times, is
famed for its honey, dates and
olives. Bawiti, the charming
main village, is surrounded by
palm groves. The **Oasis
Heritage Museum** has clay
figures by local artist
Mohammed Eed. Hot and cold
springs encircle the oasis; just
west of Bawiti a hot spring, **Ain
Bishmu**, is used by the villagers
for washing and swimming.
Further afield, a few ruins of the
Temple of Alexander the Great,
built in 332 BC, lie just north of

the discovery of the Golden
Mummies. The nearby
26th-Dynasty **Temple of Ain
al-Muftela** is better preserved.
Bahariyya is surrounded by
hills, and the **Black Mountain**,
7 km (4 miles) northeast of
Bawiti, is worth a visit. Also
called the "English Mountain", it
is crowned with an old World
War I British outpost. Climbing
to the top takes about an hour,
but the view is very rewarding.

Environs
The **Black Desert**, created by
wind eroding the dark, rocky
outcrops, begins 20 km (12 miles)
south of Bahariyya. Further
south are the mainly quartz rock
formations of **Crystal Mountain**.

🏛 Oasis Heritage Museum
1 km (0.6 mile) N of Bawiti.
Open 8am–4pm daily. includes
entry to both temples (below).

🏛 Temple of Alexander the Great
6 km (4 miles) SW of Bawiti. **Open**
8am–4pm daily (5pm in summer).
includes entry to Oasis Heritage
Museum and Temple of Ain al-Muftela.

🏛 Temple of Ain al-Muftela
5 km (3 miles) W of Bawiti. **Open** 8am–
4pm daily (5pm in summer). includes entry to Oasis Heritage Museum
and Temple of Alexander the Great.

Clay figures in the Oasis Heritage Museum, Bahariyya Oasis

A blue-painted mudbrick dwelling in Siwa Oasis

❺ Siwa Oasis

550 km (341 miles) W of Cairo, 305 km (189 miles) SW of Marsa Matruh. 30,000. Opposite Arous al-Waha, road to Marsa Matruh (0100) 546 1992.

Siwa Oasis seems to spring out of nowhere, its lush, green orchards glistening like a mirage in the surrounding barren and inhospitable desert. More than 300 freshwater springs and streams sustain this remote desert oasis, feeding 300,000 date palms and 70,000 olive trees. Huge saltwater lakes add to the spectacular scenery. Isolated on the edge of the Great Sand Sea, Siwa remained unchanged and largely unvisited for centuries. In the 1980s, a road was built to Siwa from Marsa Matruh, bringing an influx of tourists to the area. Another rough road heading southeast to Bahariyya is only passable by 4WD, but makes a memorable journey through the empty desert.

The ruins of the ancient mudbrick town of **Shali** tower above modern Siwa's main square. Built in 1203 to house the 40 survivors of a tribal attack on the nearby settlement of Aghurmi, this walled, hilltop town protected the entire Siwan population for centuries. Though the houses were abandoned in 1926 after heavy rain, the steep maze of streets can still be explored, and several buildings have been rebuilt and restored.

Close to Siwa's town centre, the **House of Siwa Museum** displays a collection of typical Siwan clothing, jewellery and handicrafts. The museum was the brainchild of a Canadian ambassador who feared the threat posed by tourism to Siwa's traditional way of life. A short distance north of the town, the limestone **Mountain of the Dead**, or Jebel al-Mawta, is riddled with tombs from the 26th Dynasty, Ptolemaic period and Roman era. When fighting spread to Siwa during World War II, the Siwans sheltered in

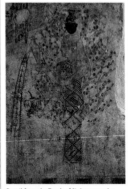
Detail from the Tomb of Si-Amun on the Mountain of the Dead, Siwa

the tombs from bombing attacks. The 3rd-century BC **Tomb of Si-Amun** contains scenes depicting the deceased – a Siwan of Greek origins – with his family and the gods.

About 3 km (2 miles) east of Siwa, the **Temple of the Oracle**, built between 663 and 525 BC, stands on a rock that was once at the heart of the ancient settlement of Aghurmi. The Oracle's fame was widespread and Alexander the Great came here to consult it in 332 BC after liberating Egypt from Persian rule. The steep climb to the top is worthwhile for the stunning views it affords over the palm trees and lakes below.

A short distance away is **Cleopatra's Pool**. Despite the name, Cleopatra never bathed here, but many people do venture into the circular pool for a swim, undeterred by algae floating on the surface of the water and onlookers watching from the path.

A better place for swimming can be found on **Fatnis Island** (also known as Fantasy Island), on the salt lake Birket Siwa, 6 km (4 miles) west of the town. A narrow causeway leads to the island, which is covered in palm trees and has a freshwater pool in the centre.

A day trip can be organized to the remote oasis of Qara, 125 km (78 miles) northeast of Siwa.

🏛 **House of Siwa Museum**
Siwa. **Open** 9am–2pm Sun–Thu.

🏠 **Mountain of the Dead**
1 km (0.6 mile) N of Siwa.
Open 9am–5pm daily.

Siwan Culture

Far removed from the rest of Egypt, Siwans have their own distinct culture and way of life, although these are increasingly threatened by tourism. Siwi, a Berber language, is spoken alongside Arabic, and Siwan women, who are rarely seen in public, dress in costumes decorated with coins. The oasis is renowned for its silver jewellery and hand-woven baskets. Siwans are very conservative and visitors should dress modestly.

Traditional hand-woven Siwan basket

Oases in the Egyptian Deserts

A welcome sight for tired and weary travellers, oases have sufficient water to allow permanent plant growth and human settlement. The major depressions beneath Egypt's Western Desert give rise to a chain of oases west of the Nile, for here the water table is near the earth's surface. The oasis of Siwa, for example, lies 18 m (59 ft) below sea level. Oases vary considerably in size and can be anything from just a few palms around a spring to large expanses of water capable of sustaining cities. As well as supporting a human population, they also offer ideal conditions for many species of wildlife, such as the striped hyena, the Egyptian mongoose and the little green bee-eater. However, the combination of a growing population and increasingly intensive farming is threatening the water supply. The oasis of Fayoum *(see p172)* now has to channel water from the Nile to supplement its inadequate natural resources.

Saltwater lakes are formed over thousands of years by evaporation. As the water evaporates dissolved minerals are left behind and the salinity of the lake slowly increases.

Human settlements have developed around many oases. These isolated, self-sufficient communities are typically surrounded by green patches of cultivation and separated from each other by areas of dry desert.

Agriculture thrives on the fertile land of the oases. Rice, wheat, olives, dates, figs, mangoes and apricots are some of the crops grown.

Date palms have always been a multipurpose crop, providing food, timber and leaves for thatching.

The Formation of Oases

Rain falling a long way from the oasis seeps into porous rocks, known as aquifers, through which it slowly flows. This water emerges at an oasis, either where the water table is at or near the surface, or where pressure created by the flow of water in the aquifer forces it up through a fault in the rock.

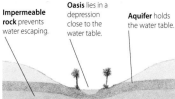

Impermeable rock prevents water escaping.

Oasis lies in a depression close to the water table.

Aquifer holds the water table.

Fault allows water to escape upwards.

Oasis

Water flows down the porous aquifer, creating pressure.

Oasis formed by a natural depression

Oasis resulting from a fault in the rock layers

TRAVELLERS' NEEDS

WHERE TO STAY

In colloquial Egyptian, the word for hotel (funduq) derives from a verb meaning "to leave wide open" – as in leaving a door ajar – and this phrase reflects the traditional Egyptian sense of hospitality. Visitors will find "open doors" throughout the country, with hotels offering accommodation at a wide range of prices and an even wider range of quality. At the top end are grand old colonial hotels in Cairo, Luxor and Aswan, along with an array of modern, four- and five-star high-rises and resort complexes,

especially in the Red Sea coastal regions. Even at such expensive places, Egyptian hospitality doesn't always translate into good service, but hotel managers and tourism officials are aware of this and standards are improving. At the other end of the scale, cheap doesn't have to mean squalid: you can still find simple but clean accommodation in some of the country's most picturesque settings. However, always look closely at what you are getting before handing over your money.

Where to Look

Tourism has long been a major industry in Egypt and, as a result, you will find hotels just about everywhere. In Cairo, the luxury hotels are clustered in three main areas, catering to the different purposes and needs of visitors to the city. Several are situated to the northeast of the city, around the airport and the suburb of Heliopolis, making them convenient for air travel but rather far away from the city's major tourist attractions. Then there are the downtown luxury hotels, which are found mainly along the banks of the Nile. These offer great views and are a more convenient base for getting around the city sights, but they leave the traveller right in the thick of downtown Cairo, which can be a daunting

A sumptuous suite at the Maritim Jolie Ville Kings Island, Luxor *(see p274)*

prospect. Finally, there are hotels around the Pyramids in Giza. For many visitors, staying right next to what they consider to be Egypt's biggest tourist attraction may outweigh the disadvantage of being further away from other sights in central and Islamic Cairo, such as the Egyptian Museum and Khan al-Khalili.

Alternatively, you can find smaller and cheaper hotels throughout the city. Many low-budget, backpacker hotels are located in the downtown area near Midan Talaat Harb and Midan Tahrir. The leafy island of Zamalek has a few pleasant mid-range hotels and, though the area has few sights of its own, it is good for nightlife and is handy for accessing the rest of the city.

The same general pattern can be found in most towns in Egypt, with large five-star hotels in the town centre, low-budget places clustered around the train station and mid-range options

scattered throughout the rest of the town. Except for the most important tourist destinations, most towns in Upper Egypt and the Delta do not have any five-star hotels at all.

Hotel Touts

The newly arrived traveller in Cairo may fall prey to hotel touts who attach themselves to the unwary, using every trick in the book to get them to the hotel for which they are hustling. Some taxi-drivers are part of the scam, earning a commission from the hotels to which they take their fares. To avoid being taken in by these tricksters, be alert to their strategies and be very firm about your plans. If possible, book a room in advance and don't be diverted from going there, whatever claims are made. If a taxi-driver says he hasn't heard of your hotel, don't get in his cab. Never let anyone go into the hotel with you.

One of the domed accommodation buildings at the Bawiti Oasis Resort *(see p277)*

◄ Vareity of goods on sale in Khan al-Khalili, Cairo

Booking a Room

Higher-category hotels follow standard international procedures for reservations, with customers often being asked to give their credit card number as confirmation of a booking. Hotels lower down the scale may do the same, but with slightly less reliable results. The more popular inexpensive hotels sometimes operate on a first-come, first-served basis but most now accept reservations by phone or email.

Hotel Grading and Facilities

Egyptian hotels are graded on a star-rating system with up to five stars, which are allocated by the government. Large, internationally run chain hotels generally get into the four- and five-star class, while locally owned premises fill out the middle and lower ranges.

Hotel gradings can appear a little arbitrary at times and, in many cases, seem to owe more to influence than to actual quality and service. Sometimes the only tangible difference between two stars and no stars is price – and five-star hotels are certainly not all equal in the facilities or service offered. A five-star hotel will, however, always include several restaurants, a bar and some form of nightclub or disco. There will also always be a swimming pool and health-club facilities. Five-star hotels at resorts are likely to include facilities such as riding stables, diving centres, tennis courts and similar amenities.

The pool area at Basma has lovely views over Aswan *(see p274)*

A four-star hotel will usually have a coffee shop, restaurant, a bar of sorts and usually a smaller swimming pool that is good enough for a cooling dip.

Hotels at the lower end also usually have some kind of eating establishment, but alcohol will rarely be served in such premises. It is rare to find telephones in the rooms of smaller establishments, but most will have a telephone at the front desk and internet or Wi-Fi.

Hidden Extras

Apart from some of the Red Sea resorts, which are all-inclusive, normal practice is to pay for extras as you use them. Up to 25 per cent tax may be added to your hotel bill, along with charges for phone calls and other services. In smaller, two- and three-star hotels, check exactly what is included: you may be charged extra for breakfast and for having a fridge, air-conditioning and TV

in your room. Tipping (*baksheesh*) is a way of life in Egypt: many hotel workers survive on the tips they get for carrying out minor tasks for guests, such as carrying bags or flagging taxis. A couple of Egyptian pounds is sufficient.

Discounts

Discounts on hotel rooms are rarely offered and are available only through travel companies. In low season (July–September) in Upper Egypt, however, it may be possible to bargain down room prices, especially in hotels in the lower price categories. Egyptians and foreigners with residence permits, however, qualify for vastly cheaper rates.

Chain Hotels

The familiar international chain hotel names can all be found in Egypt: Hilton, Sheraton, Marriott, Sofitel, Meridien, Mövenpick, Swissôtel, Four Seasons, Sonesta and Hyatt are all present, especially in Cairo where they dominate the hotel scene. The big chain hotels are the most luxurious and the most expensive in the market and they generally offer a dependable level of service, despite the occasional variation from international standards.

There is no established chain of cheap or budget hotels in Egypt: the vast number of mid-level and inexpensive hotels in the country are usually family owned and independently run.

The spectacular entrance hall of a luxury hotel in Alexandria

The Sofitel, Four Seasons and Grand Nile Tower *(see p272)* hotels in Cairo

Smaller Hotels

The choice of mid-range hotels and amenities in Egypt is continuously expanding across all destinations and so travellers are no longer limited to just five-star hotels or budget backpacker accommodation.

Every major destination in Egypt has a wide selection of small, cheap hotels catering for the young traveller. For those willing to forsake private bathrooms and air-conditioning, the price can be amazingly low. Many small hotels offer a variety of rooms, including those with or without bathrooms and air-conditioning. All have the option of more than one bed in the room. In Cairo and Alexandria, most small hotels are located on the upper floors of old apartment buildings, which can provide an intimate setting that is full of character. At most places, the price includes a simple continental breakfast.

Two- and three-star hotels are more likely to take up a whole building. Such establishments often include a coffee shop and a small restaurant, and their rooms always have bathrooms and air-conditioning; they also increasingly have a small swimming pool. Quality varies widely and, while some mid-range hotels are excellent and quite charming, others are not even remotely worth the price. When negotiating for a room in a one- or two-star hotel, check the room to see whether facilities such as hot water and clean bed linen are provided, and confirm with the proprietor whether breakfast is included in the price.

Business Travellers

Cairo is rapidly turning into a major business centre and its hotels are adapting to the new market. New, ultra-luxurious, five-star hotels are springing up with the requirements of the travelling business executive in mind, distinguishing themselves by the extra services and facilities that such clients expect. Well-trained concierges and an efficient, well-equipped 24-hour business service are becoming standard in Cairo's resort hotels, from the Four Seasons hotels, one on each bank of the Nile, to the Conrad on the Corniche. These have rooms furnished with computers, fax, voicemail, and internet connections. Well-equipped meeting rooms and conference facilities are available, as are chauffeur-driven limousines to ferry guests to and from Cairo's international airport.

The luxurious Churchill Suite at Mena House, Cairo *(see p273)*

Disabled Travellers

Egypt is not the easiest destination for the disabled visitor. With many cheaper hotels located on the fairly inaccessible upper storeys of tall buildings, wheelchair-bound travellers are usually restricted to the modern five-star hotels. Even many of those still have stairs instead of ramps at vital places, though that is starting to change. What Egypt does have in its favour, however, is friendly people for whom disability carries no alarm and who will be more than ready to assist travellers with extra needs with a minimum of fuss.

Children

Egyptians love children and consider them a blessing, so bringing them should not present any particular problems. This is not to say that Egyptian hotels make any special provisions in terms of extra activities – the exception being some of the luxury resort hotels, which organize daily programmes for children. Even if you are not staying at a four- or five-star hotel, either in Cairo or at a resort, many of the bigger hotels have swimming pools that they allow nonresidents to use, often without charge for children, and this can provide an excellent way of soothing frazzled youngsters when the heat and bustle get too much.

Budget Options

Egypt can be a paradise for travellers on low budgets, as witnessed by the generations of young backpackers who visit the country, whether seeking Pharaonic ruins, exotic culture, or a bit of sun and surf in the Sinai peninsula.

No matter where you are in Egypt, there will always be hotels offering fairly decent accommodation at fairly low prices. Youth hostels exist, but comparing their poor quality with the other available options, they are best avoided: why settle for a three-tier bunk bed when a clean room can be found closer to the city centre for only a few pounds more? In any case, most of Egypt's cheaper hotels, which are not by any means frequented only by young backpackers, offer the camaraderie familiar in youth hostels worldwide.

Camping in Egypt is a little more problematic and is not particularly recommended in most towns. Camp sites can be found in Luxor and some of the other southern cities, but the facilities are rudimentary at best.

Rather better opportunities exist for camping elsewhere in the country, however. There are some beautiful places in the Sinai, including the Ras Mohammed National Park, near Sharm el-Sheikh, and a night under the stars in the Western Desert is an experience not to be missed.

Safaris, consisting of a guide with a large 4WD, can be organized out of any of the oasis towns. It should be borne in mind that camping in the

Comfortable room at Al Tarfa Desert Sanctuary, Dakhla Oasis *(see p277)*

YHA sign at youth hostel in Aswan

Western Desert is mainly a winter activity, and that the nights can be cold. Desert camping is not recommended during high summer and, in fact, very few guides will be interested in venturing out during that time. Wherever you camp, follow common-sense rules and keep all your valuables with you. Litter is a problem in Egypt so be sure to remove yours when leaving a camp.

Recommended Hotels

The hotels in this section have been chosen to reflect their quality and amenities within the themes of luxury, boutique, historic, value for money, eco and resort, although it is fair to say that some establishments will fall into more than one category. Egypt has a large number of luxury hotels, especially in Cairo, with a wealth of amenities like gourmet restaurants and wellness centres, and the listings include some of the best. Similarly, many hotels offer an ultra-modern boutique-style decor, which we have categorized accordingly. Others are historic or offer good value for money. Desert establishments are often, although not always, ecofriendly with conservation projects in place and built using local materials. Resorts offer family amenities like playgrounds and children's clubs, and for this reason may be ideal for families.

The DK Choice hotels are extra special. They may have above-average standards and amenities or a breathtaking location, or simply have a charm that sets them apart.

DIRECTORY

Hotels Offering Central Booking

Hilton Hotels
Tel 08705 909090 (UK).
Tel 1-800 445 8667 (US).
w hilton.com

InterContinental Hotels
Tel 0800 1800 1800 (UK).
Tel 1-800 465 4329 (US).
w ihg.com

Marriott Hotels
Tel 0800 1927 1927 (UK).
Tel 1-888 236 2427 (US).
w marriott.com

Sheraton Hotels
Tel 0800 3253 5353 (UK).
Tel 1-800 325 3535 (US).
w starwoodhotels. com/sheraton

Sonesta
Tel (02) 2264 1211 (Cairo).
Tel 1-800 766 3782 (US).
w sonesta.com

Finding a Hotel

Egyptian State Tourist Office
170 Piccadilly,
London W1V 9DD.
Tel (020) 7493 5283.
w egypt.travel

MISR Travel
(State-run tourist company) 1 Sharia Talaat Harb, Cairo.
Tel (02) 2393 0010.
w misrtraveleg.net

Tourist Office Alexandria
Sharia El Mina Sharqia, Raml Station, Alexandria.
Tel (03) 485 1556.
Open 8am–8pm daily.
Train Station Tourism Office, MISR Train Station, Alexandria.
Tel (03) 392 5985.
Open 8am–8pm daily.

Tourist Office Cairo
5 Sharia Adly, Cairo.
Tel (02) 2391 3454.
Open 8am–8pm daily.
Cairo Tourism Office, Cairo Airport, Cairo. **Tel** (02) 2265 5000/1. **Open** 8am–8pm daily. Giza Tourism Office, Giza Pyramids, Giza, Cairo.
Tel (02) 3383 8823.
Open 8am–8pm daily.

Tourist Office Hurghada
Resort Strip, Hurghada.
Tel (065) 346 3221.
Open 8am–8pm daily.

Tourist Office Luxor
Corniche El Nil, Luxor.
Tel (095) 2280 902.
Open 8am–8pm daily.

Tourist Office Sharm el-Sheikh
Corniche Sharm el-Sheikh.
Tel (069) 366 4721.
Open 8am–8pm daily.

Disabled Travellers

Disability Action Group
Portside Business Park, 189 Airport Rd West, Belfast BT3 9ED. **Tel** (028) 9029 7880.
w disabilityaction.org

Disability Rights UK
Ground Floor, CAN Messanine, 49–51 East Road, London N1 6AH.
Tel (020) 7250 8181

Youth Hostels

Egyptian Youth Hostels Association
1 Sharia El Ibrahimy, Garden City, Cairo.
Tel (02) 2796 1448.

Youth Hostels Association
Trevelyan House, Dimple Road, Matlock, Derbyshire DE4 3YH. **Tel** (01629) 592700. **w** yha.org.uk

Where to Stay

Cairo

Central Cairo

Berlin £
Value for money **Map** 5 C3
2 Sharia El-Shawarby, Kasr el-Nil
Tel *(02) 2395 7502*
Located a few minutes' walk from the Nile, the Berlin is something of a haven in busy Cairo. Guest rooms are bright but traditional in decor, and have private balconies.

Lotus £
Historic **Map** 5 B3
12 Sharia Talaat Harb
Tel *(02) 2575 0966*
W lotushotel.com
Step back in time at the Lotus where an authentic Art Deco interior is coupled with elegant furnishings. The bar is popular with the artsy downtown crowd. Family-run. Central city location.

Mayfair £
Value for money **Map** 1 A3
9 Sharia Aziz Osman, Zamalek
Tel *(02) 2735 7315*
W mayfaircairo.com
The Mayfair looks out over lush consulate grounds in upmarket Zamalek. Its sunny breakfast terrace maximizes the view. Rooms are well presented. Free Wi-Fi on the terrace.

Odeon Palace £
Value for money **Map** 5 C2
6 Sharia Abdel Hamid Said
Tel *(02) 2577 6637*
W hodeon.com
This place offers panoramic views of the city from its rooftop bar, along with cosy guest rooms and a restaurant decorated in Arabic style. Central location.

Pension Roma £
Value for money **Map** 6 D2
169 Sharia Mohammed Farid, Downtown
Tel *(02) 2391 1340*
W pensionroma.com.eg
Housed in a Neo-Classical building, the charming Pension Roma has a reputation for impeccable cleanliness. Antique furniture and traditional decor. Good location.

The President £
Value for money **Map** 1 A1
22 Sharia Taha Hussein, Zamalek
Tel *(02) 2737 2780*
W presidenthotelcairo.com
A popular hotel with amenities that include an upmarket restaurant and pastry shop, cellar bar and upper-level cocktail lounge with city views.

Cosmopolitan ££
Historic **Map** 5 C3
1 Sharia Ibn Taalab
Tel *(02) 2392 3845*
Occupying a prime spot near major sights, this is a good base for sightseeing. Decor is old-world colonial with antique furniture. Rooms with private balcony.

DK Choice

Hotel Longchamps ££
Boutique **Map** 1 A3
21 Sharia Ismail Mohamed, Zamalek
Tel *(02) 2735 2311*
W hotellongchamps.com
Plush en-suite rooms, quiet garden terraces, a vibrantly coloured breakfast restaurant plus top-notch service have helped make this an award-winning hotel. Family-run since the 1950s, Longchamps is located on Zamalek island near upmarket shops and restaurants.

DK Choice

Windsor House ££
Historic **Map** 6 D2
19 Sharia Alfi Bei
Tel *(02) 2591 5810*
W windsorcairo.com
This landmark hotel was built around 1900 for the Egyptian royal family and retains a sense of grandeur. Full of character, it has provided a backdrop to many Egyptian and international films. Its Barrel Bar and Windsor Lounge are popular with locals. Elegant rooms, roof garden and an à la carte restaurant.

Price Guide

Prices are based on one night's stay in a standard double room, inclusive of breakfast, service charges and taxes.

£	up to 500 EGP
££	500–1000 EGP
£££	over 1000 EGP

Cairo Marriott £££
Luxury **Map** 1 B3
16 Sharia Saray al-Gezira, Zamalek
Tel *(02) 2728 3000*
W marriott.com
Set in a large garden, this is one of the city's top hotels. It has luxurious rooms and suites, 15 themed restaurants, bars, a casino and a health suite. It was originally built for the opening of the Suez Canal in 1869.

Conrad £££
Luxury **Map** 1 B3
1191 Corniche el-Nil
Tel *(02) 2580 8000*
W conradhotels.com
This award-winning hotel has lavish rooms, most with Nile views. The hotel also boasts a spa and upmarket restaurants.

Grand Nile Tower £££
Luxury **Map** 3 B1
Corniche el-Nil, Garden City
Tel *(02) 2365 1234*
W grandniletower.com
This Rhoda Island hotel, complete with a revolving restaurant, is a landmark on the Cairo skyline. The plush rooms have Nile views. It has a spa and its own yacht. However, the hotel is not licensed to serve alcohol.

Kempinski Nile £££
Boutique **Map** 5 A5
12 Sharia Ahmed Ragheb, Garden City
Tel *(02) 2798 0000*
W kempinski.com
Traditional decor is given a modern twist at this hotel. Its amenities range from a jazz bar and chocolate lounge to lavish rooms.

Semiramis InterContinental £££
Luxury **Map** 5 A4
Corniche el-Nil, Garden City
Tel *(02) 2798 8000*
W intercontinental.com
Low energy, carbon and water usage is a top priority at this landmark hotel. Amenities include 12 restaurants, a fitness centre and a spa. Most of its luxury rooms and suites look straight out over the Nile.

Elegant furnishings in the Salon Royal, Cairo Marriott

Premier pyramid view room at Mena House

Islamic Cairo

Talisman Hotel de Charme ££
Boutique
39 Sharia Talaat Harb
Tel *(02) 2393 9431*
W talismanhotelcairo.com
Lavish guest rooms, restaurant
and library lounge, all decorated
with authentic upmarket
furniture, set this hotel apart.

Giza and Heliopolis

Baron Heliopolis ££
Historic
Sharia Maahad Al Saharaa, Heliopolis
Tel *(02) 2291 5757*
W baronhotels.com
This hotel overlooks the historic
Baron Empain Palace. Amenities
include glamorous rooms, a night-
club and its own shopping mall.

**Le Riad – Tell a Story Boutique
Hotel** ££
Boutique
*1 Sharia Al Mosheer Ahmed Ismail,
Heliopolis*
Tel *(02) 2267 6807*
W leriadhotel.com
This collection of luxury suites is
presented in rich colours with
Fatimid-inspired fabrics. Tabeekh
cooking is a speciality in its
rooftop restaurant.

Concorde el Salam £££
Luxury
65 Sharia Abdel Hamid Badawi
Tel *(02) 2293 1111*
W concorde-hotels.com
This lavish hotel has seven fine
restaurants and bars, including a
sushi bar. Attractive rooms with
pool or garden views.

Gabriel £££
Boutique
*Sun City Mall, Autostrade Road,
Heliopolis*
Tel *(02) 2696 0700*
W thegabrielhotel.com
A beautiful award-winning hotel
where attention to detail is

evident throughout, from the
chic guest rooms to the glitzy
restaurant, blues bar, nightclub
and library.

DK Choice

Mena House £££
Luxury
Sharia Al-Ahram, Giza
Tel *(02) 3377 3222*
W menahousehotel.com
Overlooking the Pyramids and
set in richly planted gardens,
the Mena House is a landmark
hotel in Giza. It has hosted
royalty and celebs since it
opened its doors in 1869.
Today, it offers pure luxury.
Rooms, suites and spa are
contemporary, while its
restaurants are exotic Egyptian.
Golf course.

Around Cairo

**6TH OF OCTOBER CITY:
Novotel Cairo** ££
Boutique
Sharia 26 July
Tel *(011) 2233 8884*
W novotel.com
Contemporary styling in its
rooms and suites, international
restaurants and lounges is the
deal at the Novotel. Amenities
include a fitness centre complete
with a hammam.

**6TH OF OCTOBER CITY: Swiss
Inn Pyramids Golf Resort** ££
Luxury
Dreamland
Tel *(02) 3855 3308*
W swissinn.net
Located on the Dreamland golf
course and offering a gym and
spa, the Swiss Inn is ideal for
those who like activity breaks.
Elegant rooms and restaurants
complete the package.

**6TH OF OCTOBER CITY:
Mövenpick Hotel & Casino** £££
Boutique
Media City
Tel *(02) 3855 5013*
W moevenpick-hotels.com
This hotel is located next to the
Media City Studios. From luxury
rooms, restaurants and spa to
business suites, it caters to all.
The rooms either overlook the
pool or the lush gardens.

BANI SUWAYF: Green House £
Historic
*Sharia Abd Elsalam Aref,
Zeraeen Square*
Tel *(082) 236 0800*
A traditional hotel that has
embraced modernity with flat-
screen TVs, air-conditioning and
free Wi-Fi. Ideal for visiting Fayoum
and the Pyramid of Meidum.

FAYOUM OASIS: El Moalemeen £
Value for Money
Sharia El Nadi El Riyadi
Tel *(084) 637 6444*
Located in the ancient city of
Fayoum, within easy reach of the
souks, El Moalemeen is a good
base for experiencing the oasis.
Traditional decor.

FAYOUM OASIS: Oasis Resort £
Boutique/Eco
Qarun Lake, Shakshut
Tel *(010) 1313 1328*
With views of the lake, gardens
to wander in and surrounded
by desert, this resort has a
tranquil feel. It offers tasteful
air-conditioned rooms, pool
and children's playground.

**FAYOUM OASIS: Helnan
Auberge Fayoum** ££
Historic
Qarun Lake, Shakshut
Tel *(084) 698 1205*
W helnan.com
Housed in the former hunting
lodge of King Farouk, this luxurious
retreat is a popular haunt of royalty
and celebs. Lavish decor.

DK Choice

**MAADI: Villa Belle
Epoque** £££
Boutique
61 Sharia 13
Tel *(02) 2358 0265*
W villabelleepoque.com
Located in Maadi, a fashionable
suburb of outer Cairo, this
1920s-built mansion has been
transformed into a stylish hotel.
Colonial styling has been
retained throughout. Sun
terraces circle a swimming pool,
around which citrus trees grow.

For more information on types of hotels *see pages 269–71*

The Nile Valley

ABU SIMBEL: Nefertari ££
Value for Money
Abu Simbel El Seyahy
Tel *(02) 2683 1677*
🌐 nefertarihotelabusimble.net
Overlooking Lake Nasser and minutes from the great temples of Abu Simbel, this plush four-star hotel is in its own gardens. Some rooms have views over the lake.

ASWAN: Keylany £
Value for Money
25 Sharia Keylany
Tel *(097) 231 7332*
🌐 keylanyhotel.com
A charming hotel, the Keylany offers simple but well-kept rooms and a rooftop café with city views. Close to Aswan's attractions.

ASWAN: Basma ££
Value for Money
Sharia El Fanadek
Tel *(097) 231 0909*
🌐 basmahotel.com
Set in gardens on top of Aswan's highest hill and with art adorning its walls, the Basma is a chic hotel. Rooms are elegantly furnished.

ASWAN: Mövenpick Resort Elephantine Island £££
Luxury
Elephantine Island
Tel *(097) 230 3455*
🌐 moevenpick-hotels.com
Set amid tropical gardens, this resort offers every amenity from 360-degree views of the river to plush rooms and suites.

DK Choice

ASWAN: Sofitel Legend Old Cataract £££
Historic
Sharia Abdal El Tahrir
Tel *(090) 231 6000*
🌐 sofitel.com
Housed in a glorious 19th-century Nile-side palace, this luxurious hotel is legendary thanks to Agatha Christie's famous novel, *Death on the Nile*. On offer is every modern amenity expected of a five-star hotel, yet it still retains its historic character. Lavish throughout.

LUXOR: Amon Hotel £
Value for Money
Gezira El Bairet, West Bank
Tel *(095) 231 0912*
🌐 amonhotel.com
A delightful hotel in tropical gardens amid the bustle of Luxor. It offers a roof terrace, restaurant and rooms with air-conditioning.

Stylish interiors of Movenpick Resort Elephantine Island, Aswan

DK Choice

LUXOR: Marsam £
Value for Money
Al-Gurna, West Bank
Tel *(095) 237 2403*
🌐 marsamluxor.com
Housed in what is believed to be the oldest resthouse on the West Bank, this atmospheric mudbrick-style hotel has all mod cons. All rooms are en suite. The hotel has its own camels for riding.

LUXOR: Merryland Hotel £
Value for Money
Sharia Nefertiti, East Bank
Tel *(095) 237 6903*
The Merryland is located just minutes from the Luxor Temple. It offers pleasing rooms with balconies overlooking the Nile.

LUXOR: Maritim Jolie Ville Kings Island ££
Luxury
Sharia Awameya, Kings Island
Tel *(095) 227 4855*
🌐 jolieville-hotels.com
This resort appears like an oasis where tropical gardens surround stylish, bungalow-style rooms and suites. The shuttle bus and boat provide transport to Luxor centre.

LUXOR: Luxor Hilton £££
Luxury
Sharia Karnak
Tel *(095) 237 4933*
🌐 hilton.com
While deep pockets may be required to stay at this upmarket hotel, its luxurious rooms, endless amenities and location near the attractions make up for it.

MINYA: King Akhenaton £
Historic
Corniche el-Nil
Tel *(086) 236 5918*
🌐 kingakhenaton.com
Nestled on the west banks of the Nile, the Akhenaten is a landmark hotel in the centre of Minya. It is a small hotel that provides a comfortable base.

MINYA: Grand Aton £££
Boutique
Corniche el-Nil
Tel *(010) 0030 8020*
🌐 grandatonhotel.com
Housed in a traditional-style complex, the Grand Aton has tasteful, well-equipped rooms. There is also an outdoor pool and tropical gardens.

Sinai and the Red Sea Coast

DAHAB: Bishbishi Camp £
Eco
Sharia Mashraba, Mashraba
Tel *(069) 364 0727*
🌐 bishbishi.com
This delightful camp comprises simple but stylish chalets with fans, screened windows and the option of a private bathroom. Diving packages offered.

DAHAB: Dahab Resort ££
Luxury
Dahab Bay
Tel *(069) 364 0051*
🌐 dahabresorteg.com
With its tastefully designed buildings set around a pool, this resort is a landmark in Dahab Bay. Dive and windsurfing centres.

DAHAB: Jasmine Pension ££
Value for Money
Sharia Mashraba, Mashraba
Tel *(069) 364 0852*
🌐 jasminepension.com
Housed in a charming, timber-framed building, the beachside Jasmine offers a rooftop lounge, restaurant and en-suite rooms, Wi-Fi and air-conditioning.

EL GOUNA: Club Paradiso ££
Resort
El Gouna Resort
Tel *(065) 354 7934*
🌐 clubparadisio.elgouna.com
A beachside resort, with chic decor, that is popular with families. Leisure amenities range from golf to good restaurants.

EL GOUNA: Sheraton Miramar Resort ££
Luxury
El Gouna Resort
Tel (065) 354 5606
w sheratonmiramarresort.com
This Egyptian-style resort blends with the landscape and is built over nine islands and offers villas and apartments. There is a marina and diving and scuba facilities.

EL QUESIR: Mövenpick Quesir-Sirena Beach £££
Resort
Sirena Beach
Tel (065) 335 0417
w moevenpick-hotels.com
Built in a traditional Nubian bungalow style, this resort stands beside the sea. Reef and diving centre, plus themed beach events.

HURGHADA: Arabella Azur Resort ££
Resort
Sharia El Corniche
Tel (065) 354 5086
w azur.travel
The Arabella Azur combines tasteful Nubian-style domed rooms with an array of amenities – tennis courts, spa, restaurants and dive centre among them.

HURGHADA: Sheraton Soma Bay £££
Luxury
Soma Bay, Red Sea
Tel (065) 356 2584
w sheraton-somabay.com
A thalassic spa, fine dining, championship golf course and diving are all on offer at this beach resort. Its architecture resembles an Egyptian temple.

ISMALIA: Mercure Forsan Islands ££
Eco
Gezirat al-Forsan
Tel (064) 391 6316
w mercure.com
Overlooking Temsah Lake in the centre of Ismalia, this is a popular

city landmark. Ecofriendly hotel, offering a private beach, pools, restaurant and watersports.

DK Choice

MARSA ALAM: Red Sea Diving Safari £
Eco
Marsa Shagra, Marsa Nakari and Wadi Lahami villages
Tel (065) 337 1833
w redsea-divingsafari.com
This environmental and sustainable tourism project has three beachside centres. Simple tents and chalets on the beach, some with private bathrooms. The PADI dive programme is outstanding. Snorkelling, kitesurfing and nature treks offered.

MARSA ALAM: Coraya Beach Resort £££
Resort
Madinat Coraya, km 67 Al Quseir, Sharia Marsa Alam
Tel (065) 375 0000
w iberotel.de
This resort is an adults-only hotel standing in gardens. Guest rooms are modern and stylish. On site is a wellness suite and sports.

NUWEIBA: La Sirene ££
Value for Money
Corniche
Tel (069) 350 0701
w nuweibabeach.com
Set right on the beach, La Sirene has rooms and bungalows that are well equipped. Its leisure amenities are few but do include diving and a restaurant.

NUWEIBA: Hilton Coral Resort £££
Luxury
Nuweiba City
Tel (069) 352 0320
Overlooking the Gulf of Aqaba and located on a private beach, this resort has tasteful rooms featuring

a balcony or patio to make the most of the view. The many amenities, include five restaurants, a watersports centre, children's club and tennis courts. Hammocks on the beach are provided.

PORT SAID: Grand Albatros ££
Luxury
Corniche
Tel (066) 333 2211
w pickalbatros.com
This elegant hotel is close to the Suez Canal and one of the best in Port Said. Almost every room looks out over the Mediterranean. There is even a bakery on site.

PORT SAID: Resta Port Said ££
Resort
Sharia Sultan Hussein
Tel (066) 332 5511
w restaresorts.com
The Resta is a large place right at the entrance to the Suez Canal. Contemporary rooms. There is a choice of restaurants, a shopping centre and gym.

SHARM EL-SHEIKH: Four Seasons £££
Resort
Four Seasons Boulevard
Tel (069) 360 3555
w fourseasons.com
Plush rooms and suites, fine dining, sports and a spa are just some of the luxury features of this five-star hotel. It is situated in landscaped gardens and within easy reach of sights.

DK Choice

SHARM EL-SHEIKH: Rixos Sharm el-Sheikh £££
Luxury
Nabq Bay
Tel (069) 371 0210
w rixos.com
Oozing glamour, this luxurious hotel sits in gardens that, literally, meet the beach. Fashioned as an Egyptian village, it offers elegant rooms, 10 fine dining restaurants and an excellent spa. Entertainment takes the form of shows, plus there are children's pools and a club, as well as sport facilities.

TABA: Miramar Resort Taba Heights ££
Resort
Taba and Nuweiba Highway
Tel (069) 358 0234
w miramar.tabaheights.com
This sprawling resort of orange-hued buildings sits beside a beach. There are restaurants, a casino, a variety of sports amenities and a children's club.

Beach frontroom at Sheraton Miramar Resort, El Gouna

For more information on types of hotels *see pages 269–71*

The Delta and the North Coast

ALEXANDRIA: Mecca £££
Value for Money
44 Sharia Kamb Shezar
Tel *(03) 592 3925*
W meccaalex.com
Housed in an imposing building in a prime spot beside the beach, the Mecca offers rooms that all have sea views, a buffet restaurant and a fitness centre.

ALEXANDRIA: Mercure Alexandria Romance £££
Boutique
303 Tareek El Gueish Saba Pasha
Tel *(03) 584 0911*
W mercure.com
Two restaurants, one French and other Egyptian, are among the delights offered at this modern hotel just off the corniche. Suites and rooms all have sea views.

ALEXANDRIA: Four Seasons £££
Luxury
399 Sharia El Geish, San Stefano
Tel *(03) 581 8000*
W fourseasons.com
The 19-storey Four Seasons is an architectural landmark with most rooms affording fabulous sea views. There's a spa and fitness centre, squash courts and swimming pools. Stylish rooms. Children's programme offered. Private beach.

DK Choice

ALEXANDRIA: Helnan Palestine £££
Historic
El Montaza Palace
Tel *(03) 547 3500*
W helnan.com
Surrounded by tropical gardens, this is one of the most exclusive hotels in Alexandria. A host of sports and leisure facilities are offered, along with luxurious rooms. Known for its spa. There is a children's play area and jogging tracks in the beachside gardens.

ALEXANDRIA: Steigenberger Cecil £££
Historic
16 Saad Zagloul Square, Rami Station
Tel *(03) 487 7173*
W steigenberger.com
Overlooking picturesque Fort Qaitbay and the harbour, this hotel has luxurious rooms and communal spaces, and is housed in one of the city's most imposing period mansions.

ALEXANDRIA: Tolip £££
Luxury
252 Moustafa Kamel, Corniche Roshdy
Tel *(03) 545 5456*
W tolipalexandria.com
From the lavish fabrics and furnishings to the amenities available to guests, luxury is the byword at the Tolip. It has nine restaurants, lovely rooms and a spa complex.

EL ALAMEIN: Aida Beach £££
Value for Money
Alexandria to Matruh Road
Tel *(03) 484 9017*
W aidagroup.com
Set beside a private beach outside the city, the Aida is a smart hotel where guests' relaxation is key. Activities major on swimming, squash and tennis, plus children have their own play area. Lovely rooms and a choice of restaurants.

DK Choice

EL ALAMEIN: Porto Marina Resort & Spa £££
Luxury
Alexandria to Matruh Road
Tel *(046) 4451 9156*
W portoworldhotels.com
Housed in a mighty red-brick building beside a marina full of yachts, this resort has every amenity expected of an upmarket place. A gymnasium and spa, tennis courts and even gondolas are available, plus there is a cinema and children's club. Rooms are built over the resort's restaurants, shops and its own Grand Canal.

MARSA MATRUH: Gardenia £
Resort
Sharia El Awam
Tel *(012) 0880 8879*
Located minutes from the beach and offering pleasing self-catering apartments with the

benefit of an open-air garden restaurant and children's play area, the Gardenia is a gem.

MARSA MATRUH: Beau Site £££
Resort
Corniche
Tel *(02) 2259 9480*
W beausitehotel.com
Beau Site is steps from the beach and certainly lives up to its name. A resort-style hotel, it offers modern sea-view guest rooms with balconies, along with two restaurants and gardens.

MARSA MATRUH: Negresco £££
Value for Money
Corniche
Tel *(046) 493 4492*
An elegant, cared-for hotel, the Negresco overlooks the sea in the heart of Marsa Matruh. It has a French-style bistro, buffet restaurant and guest rooms with elaborate balconies.

MARSA MATRUH: Jaz Crystal £££
Resort
Almaza Bay, km 37 east of Marsa Matruh
Tel *(046) 436 0020*
W jaz.travel
Plush guest rooms around a lagoon pool, fine dining, sports and a spa are just some of the luxury features of this five-star resort. Sits in landscaped gardens beside a private beach.

MARSA MATRUH: Omneya Le Mirage Bay Front Resort £££
Boutique
Sidi Henish, km 45 east of Marsa Matruh
Tel *(02) 2670 5026*
W lemiragehotels-resorts.com
This upmarket boutique-style hotel hugs the beach in the select Sidi Henish area. Refined amenities include an à la carte restaurant, nightclub and wellness suite.

Panoramic view of Porto Marina Resort & Spa, El Alamein

The Western Desert

BAHARIYYA OASIS: Badr's Sahara Camp   £
Eco
El Bawiti
Tel *(010) 0745 9591*
W badrysaharacamp.com
Badr's Safari Camp is a charming collection of tents, lounge areas and a restaurant serving Bedouin dishes, all constructed from natural materials. Hot water and bathrooms.

BAHARIYYA OASIS: Bawiti Oasis Resort   £
Eco
Sharia Bir Al-Matar, El Bawiti
Tel *(010) 772 4942*
W egyptvacations.eu
Relax at this resort where beautifully presented rooms are contained within domed buildings. On-site facilities include a restaurant, a barbecue area and a natural hot spring bath, plus Wi-Fi.

BAHARIYYA OASIS: Desert Rose Eco Lodge   £
Eco
Sharia Bir Al-Matar, El Bawiti
Tel *(012) 2823 3731*
W desertrose-ecolodge.com
Desert Rose is an ecolodge constructed using natural clay for coolness. It stands in a garden of organic orchards and olive groves, with a restaurant and tasteful guest rooms.

DK Choice

BAHARIYYA OASIS: Bedouin Castle   ££
Eco
Sharia Ain Muftella, El Bedawi
Tel *(010) 0404 6240*
W bedouincastle.com
Housed in a building that combines Nubian and Islamic design, the Bedouin Castle is an upmarket hotel and restaurant. All rooms have lake views and a private bathroom. The hotel is owned by an archaeologist and tours of sites, along with desert safaris, can be arranged.

DAKHLA OASIS: Badawiya Hotel   £
Eco
El Qasr, El Wadi El Gadid
Tel *(092) 751 0060*
W badawiya.com
This hotel provides the rare chance to live with a Bedouin family; they own the property. It is a gorgeous place with elegant en-suite rooms, a pool and terrace, and a restaurant.

Interesting decor at Al Tarfa Desert Sanctuary, Dakhla Oasis

DK Choice

DAKHLA OASIS: Al Tarfa Desert Sanctuary   £££
Eco
Al Mansura
Tel *(010) 0100 1109*
W altarfa.net
Al Tarfa is a luxurious lodge, with an eco and social responsibility ethos, providing a serene environment in a classic oasis-style property. There are chic rooms, a gourmet restaurant, a sauna and spa complex, gardens with a pool and a lounge. Tours and treks available.

DAKHLA OASIS: Desert Lodge   £££
Eco
El Qasr
Tel *(092) 690 5240*
W desertlodge.net
Housed in a Nubian-style property, this upmarket lodge offers bright rooms, elegant eateries and a sun terrace around a mineral spring pool. Art workshops and safaris available.

EL KHARGA OASIS: Sol Y Mar Pioneers Hotel   ££
Eco
Sharia Gamal Abdel Nasser
Tel *(092) 792 9751*
W jaz.travel
This collection of pretty mudbrick bungalows house elegant en-suite rooms and suites. Gardens surround the pool and there is a children's play area.

FARAFRA: Badawiya Hotel   ££
Eco
Sharia Gamal Abdel Nasser, El Wadi El Gadid
Tel *(092) 751 0060*
W badawiya.com
Like its sister hotel in Dakhla, this traditionally built lodge offers cosy and elegant rooms, an organic restaurant and leisure amenities that include a safari programme.

SIWA: Dream Lodge   £
Eco
Gabal El Mawta
Tel *(010) 0099 9255*
W siwadreamlodgehotel.com
Dream Lodge is housed in a stone-built house, complete with a pool terrace garden. Rooms have exposed stone walls and Siwan furnishings. There is a restaurant on site.

SIWA: Palm Trees Hotel   £
Value for Money
Siwa
Tel *(046) 460 1703*
W siwaoasis.com
A rooftop garden with panoramic views of ancient Shali, a restaurant and Siwan-style guest bungalows set in landscaped gardens are the highlights of Palm Trees.

SIWA: Siwa Gardens Hotel   ££
Historic
Sharia Ayn Al Arias, Siwa
Tel *(046) 460 2801*
W siwagardens.com
Set in Siwa's historic palm garden, this family-run hotel is traditional in style with chic rooms set around a spring-fed pool. Domed restaurant and a tea garden.

DK Choice

SIWA: Siwa Shali Resort   ££
Eco
Gabal El Dakror
Tel *(046) 921 0064*
W siwashaliresort.com
Comprising "islands" with tastefully decorated mud-rendered chalets, this resort is picture-postcard pretty. The large swimming pool meanders through the resort. The restaurant focuses on organic produce. There is also a wellness complex that offers everything from a hammam to beauty treatments and a gym.

For more information on types of hotels *see pages 269–71*

WHERE TO EAT AND DRINK

According to an Egyptian proverb, "the best food is that which fills the belly". Traditional Egyptian cooking combines Arabic and Turkish with European and African influences. The result is sometimes described as bland, but this is unjust. Hearty main dishes are usually accompanied by a selection of pickles and dips, so you can spice up or cool down your meal as you wish. The cuisine is dominated by semna (clarified butter), which ensures a rich taste and a heavy impact on the arteries. Egyptians often say no meal is complete without meat, yet *fuul* (mashed fava beans), *taamiyya* (deep-fried patties filled with fava bean paste and green herbs, otherwise known as falafel) and *koshari*

(a mixture of noodles, rice, lentils and onions) – the meatless staples of the poor – are consumed by all classes. The restaurant scene throughout Egypt is continually evolving and, while most large Egyptian towns have a few old-fashioned European-style restaurants, the country is seeing a growing number of fast-food outlets, pizzerias and restaurants serving a wide range of ethnic cuisines, such as Japanese, Chinese, Indian and Lebanese, along with Mediterranean. In Cairo, there is a notable number of Korean restaurants opening. Egyptian cuisine still dominates, however, and restaurants serve a wide variety of traditional local dishes.

Restaurants and Bars

In much of Egypt, other than in the more cosmopolitan cities, the idea of dining out is quite new. As a result, the wide range of dishes that Egyptians eat at home is simply not available in restaurants. Their delicious meat and vegetable stews, for example, are hard to find in a restaurant, except during the month of Ramadan. There is, however, a distinct Egyptian cuisine that adapts remarkably well to modern demands for fast food. *Fuul* sandwiches or roasted chicken (*firakh*), for example, are likely to be sold in any settlement bigger than a hamlet. Most towns have at least one *kebabgi*, offering a selection of kebabs and a choice of several salads. These are often accompanied by dips such as *tahina* (made from sesame paste) and *babaghanoush* (grilled aubergine and *tahina*). Quality varies, but eating out

Lively night-time café culture in Cairo

at a good kebab place is an experience not to be missed. Pigeon is another popular dish in Egypt. It is stuffed with rice and spices and roasted, or cooked in a stew (*tagine*) with onions and tomatoes.

The culture of dining out is most deeply rooted in the cosmopolitan Mediterranean city of Alexandria, where a number of Greek, Italian and French restaurants and cafés still thrive. Alexandria is also rightly famous for its seafood, which can be eaten at an open-air grill or in one of the town's restaurants. Either way it will be fresh and delicious.

In Cairo, the foreign embassy community alone is enough to keep several old European-style restaurants in business. Younger expatriates and upper-class

Egyptians tend to frequent Cairo's trendier restaurant-bars, with flashy decor, loud music and variations on nouvelle Mediterranean fare. More and more ethnic restaurants are opening, and now it is possible to get a full range of Asian food, from Korean and Chinese to Thai and Indonesian.

Many fashionable restaurants double as bars, so going for an evening meal can easily turn into a full-scale night out. Cairo has the remnants of a colonial café scene and some of these places, such as Café Riche, are enjoying a revival. Cairo also has a few traditional-style pubs, which often provide some form of food. Bars usually display signs stating a minimum drinking age of 21, but this guideline is not applied very strictly.

Modern Mediterranean dining at Maison Thomas, Cairo *(see p284)*

Relaxed dining area at Sofra, Luxor (see p289)

Opening Hours

Street stalls selling snacks of *fuul* and *taamiyya* open at the crack of dawn for a basic breakfast. Juice bars are usually open from 8am–10pm, serving freshly squeezed juice. *Koshari* restaurants and shops selling *baladi* sandwiches (*baladi* is a flat, round, country bread) open around 10am. Most other restaurants, unless specifically serving breakfast, open at midday. Very few establishments open before 1pm on Fridays, except those that cater specifically for foreign visitors.

Egyptians tend to eat their main meal in the afternoon, and most restaurants close around 11pm to 1am.

Prices and Paying

In Egyptian restaurants, dishes are usually ordered individually rather than as fixed combinations. In many establishments, *mezzes (see pp282–3)* will be brought to your table, whether or not you order them. These will be charged for, so send them back if you do not want them and make sure that they are not included on your bill.

A service charge of 12 per cent is added automatically to every restaurant bill, but customers are expected to pay a small tip as well – usually an additional 10 per cent, but not more than LE 10. So once the sales tax of 10 per cent is added on, diners are paying more than 25 per cent over the price of their food.

Booking

Reservations are required only at the most upmarket restaurants. Such places will have a telephone, and most of them will have at least some staff who speak English. Attempts to book a table at less upmarket establishments can prove frustrating, however, and it is likely that there will be no record of your call when you arrive at the restaurant. Nevertheless, the staff will probably be most accommodating and make every effort to find you a table.

Etiquette

As is the case generally in Egypt, shorts and short skirts are not appropriate attire for restaurants. Other than that, however, most places are quite relaxed as far as dress code is concerned. Egyptians like to dress smartly when going out – including visits to fast-food outlets, which are considered trendy by young Egyptians. It is not unusual to see women dressed in cocktail dresses, especially late in the evenings. Foreign visitors can usually get away with wearing fairly casual clothing, but in more upmarket establishments a shirt with a collar, and shoes rather than sandals, would be advisable.

In Egypt, smoking either by use of cigarettes or a *shisha* water-pipe is inescapable in bars and pervasive in restaurants. Some of the more expensive restaurants in Cairo have established no-smoking sections, but these areas tend to be small and are often tucked away in a corner, surrounded by smoking tables. Fast-food establishments are now smoke free, thanks to a campaign by the environment ministry.

Children

Children are welcome in most restaurants and cafés before about 11pm, though it would not be appropriate to bring them along to places that are primarily drinking establishments. Some restaurants have gardens with play equipment. The Felfela and Andrea chains, for example, have several child-friendly branches, including those on the Corniche and in the Pyramids area.

The contemporary bar area at Bordiehn's B's at Marina, Hurghada (see p290)

Le Pacha 1901, which has a number of enticing restaurants *(see p285)*

Disabled Customers

Few Egyptian establishments have facilities for disabled customers, such as wheelchair access, though staff will be willing to help customers overcome any obstacles. Public toilets with wheelchair access are unheard of, but at least the traditional hole-in-the-floor type is almost extinct.

Fast-Food Outlets

While there has been some form of international fast food in Egypt since the 1970s, the last few years have seen a proliferation of international brand names.

In addition, Egypt has its own indigenous fast-food tradition. Street stalls sell bread (*aish*) stuffed with *fuul* and *taamiyya*, while *koshari*, a mixture of rice, noodles and crispy fried onions

Cairo's Café Riche – a reminder of Egypt's colonial café scene *(see p284)*

in a spicy tomato sauce, is sold at stand-up stalls and sit-down restaurants. More expensive, café-like establishments, known as *fatatri*, specialize in *fatir*, a cross between pancakes and pizzas, made from filo pastry with sweet or savoury fillings.

Vegetarian Food

Vegetarianism is extremely rare in Egypt and, as a result, vegetarian restaurants are almost unheard of – L'Aubergine in Zamalek *(see p285)* is one of the few exceptions. However, many Egyptian dishes contain no meat, and restaurants in the cheaper range frequently serve only meatless dishes. More expensive restaurants will usually have a few vegetarian dishes on the menu. Strict vegans could have a harder time, but staples such as *fuul*, *taamiyya* and *koshari* should be acceptable to almost anyone. Obviously, places to avoid are those specializing in *kofta* and kebab or rotisserie chicken.

Koshari **served at Abou Tarek**

Hygiene

Suffering some degree of gastric ailment in Egypt seems to be fairly inevitable for anyone spending more than a few days

there, but experienced travellers have come up with a few rules of thumb. Some suggest you avoid raw vegetables and salads, particularly lettuce, because these are often not properly washed. Others believe that the real problem is with the meat. Although it might seem that eating only at the more expensive restaurants would minimize the risk, there are stories of people getting sick everywhere. In major towns and cities, tap water is safe to drink though heavy chlorination does little for the taste. New arrivals should stick to mineral water (*mayya maadaniyya*), which is readily available. When buying bottles of mineral water, always check that the seal is intact. One notable scam in Egypt is street-sellers, especially those around tourist attractions, offering resealed bottles containing tap water. *(See also pp326–7.)*

Ramadan

Ramadan is an interesting (though also potentially frustrating) time to be in Egypt. The ninth month of the Islamic calendar, Ramadan is a period akin to Lent in the Christian Church, with a fast that involves abstention from food, drink and smoking during daylight hours.

The fast is strictly observed and days revolve around waiting for sunset. Then the sunset call to prayer is made, lamps are lit on the minarets and everyone gets down to eating the first meal of the day and enjoying the night-time celebrations.

During Ramadan, restaurants may be open during the day, but only tourists will be eating and fewer options will be available. Travellers may prefer to postpone their meal until after sunset, especially since the cooks making the food and the waiters serving it will not have eaten all day. At sunset, most restaurants are packed, and many set up huge tents so they can fit in as many customers as possible. These feasts provide a good opportunity to get to meet a cross-section of Egyptian society. Everyone sits together at long tables and will probably be quite friendly – once they've eaten.

A wider, more interesting range of traditional dishes will be available during Ramadan, and restaurants will be open throughout the night, in order to serve *sohour*, the last meal before sunrise. In addition, certain food and drinks, such as apricot juice (*amar el din*), are specific to this time of the Islamic calendar.

A cook prepares kebabs, a Middle East staple food, on a sidewalk grill in Cairo

Mint tea

Entertainment

If you are keen to combine dining out with some form of entertainment, then your best bet is to book a table at one of Cairo's five-star hotels. Most of these have nightclubs where a flat charge covers an excellent four-course meal and a floor show featuring some of Egypt's most popular dancers and traditional musicians. Smart dress and reservations are required at these venues.

For a variation on this idea, you might like to try one of Cairo's floating restaurants. Many of these offer cruises on the Nile, during which lunch or dinner is served to the accompaniment of live Egyptian music or a floor show complete with belly dancers and band. In Zamalek and Giza there are also luxury Nile Cruisers from a bygone era that remain moored, serving food in opulent surroundings. These restaurants often also have live entertainment.

If five-star hotels are beyond your means, you could try one of the less expensive nightclubs, where dinner is served and entertainment is provided – though both food and performances are likely to be of variable standard. Several of these clubs are located on the Pyramids Road and Downtown.

Remember that nightlife in Cairo doesn't really begin until after midnight, with the floor shows going on as late as 3 or 4am.

Recommended Restaurants

The restaurants in this section have been chosen to reflect their quality, amenities and variety of cuisine. Egypt has a large number of restaurants serving local cuisine and the listings include those that offer the most authentic Egyptian experience. Similarly, the country has a choice of restaurants serving international cuisine, especially in Cairo where Korean, Lebanese, Japanese, Chinese, Indian and Mediterranean dishes are especially popular. Cities like Alexandria and Luxor, along with the Red Sea resorts, also have a growing number of such eateries. Egypt is a multi-cultural destination and the establishments listed reflect this. Egypt also has cafés and fish restaurants and a small number of eateries specializing in vegetarian dishes; almost all restaurants will have vegetable dishes on their menu.

The restaurants highlighted as DK Choice offer something extra special such as historical charm, especially high standards or an stunning location. These establishments offer a truly memorable experience.

Felfela restaurant in Cairo offers tasty Egyptian dishes *(see p284)*

The Flavours of Egypt

Egypt shares many dishes with its Mediterranean and Middle Eastern neighbours. The cuisine leans heavily towards earthy pulses, brightly coloured vegetables, gamey meats and hearty stews, with the use of spices and simmering cooking methods infusing dishes with warmth. Cooking techniques from the time of the pharaohs are still in existence today and the food in this part of North Africa excels in both freshness and flavour. If you are invited to an Egyptian home then you could expect to enjoy soup, some meat and a vegetable-based stew with bread and salad. Desserts are not as rich as those of many other Arab countries.

Fresh figs

Spices sit alongside coloured dyes on a market stall

Meat, Poultry & Game

Egyptian families view meat as a luxury and it is often served in small amounts or combined with rice and vegetables, such as in stuffed vine leaves, to make it go further. As a result, whenever meat is to be served as a main dish it is prepared with a great deal of care and attention. Poultry is usually roasted, and lamb, mutton and veal are also popular, although beef isn't typically eaten. Meat and poultry may be stuffed with fruit, nuts and rice. Try the traditional delicacy that is pigeon (hamaam). These birds are raised throughout the country and are stuffed with seasoned rice before being grilled. But be warned – some chefs serve the head of the bird, buried in the stuffing.

Fish & Seafood

Ever since ancient times, Egyptians have enjoyed fish fresh from the Nile, salted or dried by being hung out in the strong sun to bake. Today Egyptians serve both freshwater and sea fish under the general term of samak. The best sea fish come from shallow coastal waters and the best freshwater ones are found at Aswan, where they are caught

Babaghanoush · Egyptian salad · Olives · Falafel · Aish · Hummus · Fuul · Sabanikhiyat · Stuffed vine leaves

Some of the many dishes that make up typical Egyptian *mezzes*

Egyptian Dishes and Specialities

Koshari is the rich, hearty dish of pasta, pulses and vegetables that has long been considered part of the Egyptian identity, eaten both at home and at market. Another classic dish is *molokiya* – the best versions of this herby green soup are found in Aswan and Luxor, although variations are found throughout the land. The waters of the Red Sea teem with some of the country's finest perch and tuna, and *sayyaddia* (fish with rice) features on many an Egyptian menu. A *mezze* is an easy way to enjoy a whole range of bite-sized Egyptian delicacies such as *sabanikhiyat* (spinach turnovers), *kofta* (meatballs), *babaghanoush* (a smoky aubergine/eggplant purée), hummus and *fuul* (a lemony broad/fava bean dip). Bread (*aish*), in particular the flat *baladi* bread, accompanies dips.

Chickpeas (garbanzos)

Molokiya soup is named for the muculaginous green mallow leaves that flavour it. It may be served without meat.

Goods piled high in palm-leaf baskets at a village grocer's shop

from Lake Nasser. Common bass and sole feature frequently but so do shrimps, squid, scallops and eel. Eel can be sampled, deep-fried, at markets.

Vegetables & Fruit

Robust root vegetables such as garlic and onion are vital to much of Egypt's cooking and are also cherished for their health benefits. Peas and beans are sometimes eaten on their own with a plain oil and vinegar dressing. Potatoes (*bataatis*) are often fried but can also be boiled or stuffed. Dried vegetables are also used a great deal. Egyptian salads (*salata*) feature lettuce, tomatoes, cucumber, potatoes, olives or eggs and sometimes even beans and yogurt. Fruit is eaten after a meal, with juicy plums and pomegranates

joining dates for a rich choice in sweetness. Figs have been hugely popular since ancient times. Fresh, dried or as a syrup, they appear in savoury dishes and breads as well as in sweets.

Waiter bringing a tray of mint teas at a Cairo café

Dairy Produce

Egyptian cheese, known as *gibna*, comes in two varieties. White, fresh *gibna beida* has a salty, clean taste similar to Greek feta, while *gibna rumy* is a sharper-tasting cheese with a pale yellow colour. They are most often found in salads and sandwiches. *Bbouzat haleeb*, or ice cream, shares little in common with its rich Western namesake. It has a fresh, light texture that even stretches a little as you scoop it. Egyptian yogurt (*laban zabadi*) is fresh and unflavoured but is usually served sweetened with such things as honey, jam, preserves, nuts, figs or dates.

WHAT TO DRINK

Despite Egypt being a Muslim country, alcohol is widely available in restaurants and bars. The local Stella and Sakkara lagers are good and the quality of Egyptian wines has improved greatly in recent years. Hot drinks include *chai* (mint tea) and *ahwa* (Arabic coffee) which is strong and either *ziyada* (sweet), *mazboota* (medium) or *saada* (bitter). *Karkade*, an infusion made from hibiscus leaves, is served hot or cold. Freshly squeezed fruit juices, including delicious and unusual ones such as apricot, are widely available and are very refreshing, as is *asab*, a sweet, light-green drink with a foamy head, made from pressed sugar cane.

Koshari combines pasta, rice, lentils and pulses with a spicy tomato sauce and crispy onions.

Sayyaddia is simply a whole fresh fried fish such as sole, flounder, trout or bass, served with rice and lemon.

Mahallabiyaa is a delicately rosewater-flavoured ground rice dessert, topped with toasted nuts and cinnamon.

Where to Eat and Drink

Cairo

Central Cairo

Koshari Lux £
Egyptian   **Map** 3 B2
68 Sharia Kasr El Einy, Garden City
Tel *(02) 2794 1140*
Specializing in *koshari*, an age-old Egyptian staple of rice, macaroni and lentils topped with tomato and chickpeas, this cosy eaterie minutes from the Nile is popular with Cairenes.

Café Riche ££
Café   **Map** 5 C3
17 Sharia Talaat Harb
Tel *(02) 2391 8873*
Housed in a historic building with photos of celeb customers on the walls, Café Riche has a lively atmosphere. It serves coffees and teas as well as beer and wine, salads, grills and platters.

Didos Al-Dente ££
Italian   **Map** 1 A2
26 Sharia Bahgat Ali, Zamalek
Tel *(02) 2735 9117*
A whole host of home-made pasta dishes for which Didos Al-Dente is renowned, along with pizza with an array of toppings, is the deal at this lunch through to late-night place.

Don Quichotte ££
European/French   **Map** 1 A2
9A Sharia Ahmed Hashmet, Zamalek
Tel *(02) 2735 5496*
Perfect for a romantic dinner, the dishes here incorporate classic French flavours. Try the lamb stewed in eggplants. Well-stocked bar. Reservations recommended.

Delicious spread of dishes at Terrace Café

Eish & Malh ££
Italian   **Map** 5 C2
20 Sharia Adley
Tel *(010) 0302 5346*
Pizzas, pastas, sandwiches and light snacks as well as salads, beverages and a wide range of desserts are on the menu. *Shishas* available. Popular with the downtown artsy crowd.

DK Choice

El Nil ££
Fish & Seafood   **Map** 5 C3
25 Sharia al-Bustan
Tel *(02) 2794 0336*
One of just a few fish and seafood eateries in Cairo, and certainly one of the best, El Nil offers a menu that includes red snapper and shrimps sold by the kilo. Fish is grilled on a large open grill in the centre of the restaurant and served with fresh *baladi* bread. Popular with residents who live in this downtown part of Cairo around the Bab al-Louq.

Estoril ££
Egyptian   **Map** 5 B3
12 Sharia Talaat Harb
Tel *(02) 2574 3102*
Famed for its *mezzes*, which typically comprise its signature garlic-rich dip *tomeya* served with *baladi* bread, as well as vegetarian choices such as spinach-stuffed cannelloni, Estoril is a relaxed eaterie.

Felfela ££
Egyptian   **Map** 5 C3
15 Sharia Hoda Shaarawi
Tel *(02) 2391 6846*
Dining on courses of authentic Egyptian fare is the promise at Felfela. Try the tomato and okra *bamiyya*, *fuul eskanderani* and grilled, succulent quails.

Le Grillon ££
French   **Map** 5 B3
8 Sharia Kasr el-Nil
Tel *(02) 2574 3114*
Le Grillon offers the chance to dine alfresco in its atrium garden, complete with waterfalls and shrubs, or inside in its red-orange decorated dining hall.

Il Divono Pizzeria ££
Italian   **Map** 1 A2
5 Sharia Abul Feda, Zamalek
Tel *(02) 2737 2551*
This two-storey pizzeria is a favourite with the city's trendy set who seem to adore the

Price Guide

Prices are based on a three-course meal for one, inclusive of coffee, tax and service.

£	up to 70 EGP
££	70 to 150 EGP
£££	over 150 EGP

imaginative pizzas, desserts and gourmet coffee. Focal point is a wood-fired oven.

Maison Thomas ££
Café   **Map** 1 A3
157 Sharia 26 July, Zamalek
Tel *(02) 2735 7057*
Housed in an atmospheric Zamalek building complete with a brick and brass interior, the upmarket Maison Thomas is famed for its gourmet pizzas with ham toppings, bistro sandwiches and light snacks. Open round-the-clock.

Naguib Mahfouz Café ££
Egyptian   **Map** 1 5F
5 El Baddistan Lane, Khan el-Khalili
Tel *(02) 2590 3788*
Run by the Oberoi Group, this café serves stuffed pigeon and mixed grills, and has a good selection of *mezzes*. Stop by for the *shishas*. Efficient service.

Taboula ££
Lebanese   **Map** 5 B4
1 Sharia Amerika al-Latineya, Garden City
Tel *(02) 2792 5261*
Classic Lebanese dishes *fattoush*, *taboula* and fried *kebbah* to start, and mains of fish *tajine*, are menu staples at Taboula. One of several branches.

Terrace Café ££
Café   **Map** 5 A2
1115 Corniche el-Nil
Tel *(02) 2577 7444*
Located within the Ramses Hilton hotel and overlooking the Nile, this café offers everything from continental breakfast to soup, sandwiches and cakes to evening dining. Vegetarian options, too.

Asia Bar £££
Asian/Indian   **Map** 1 B5
9 Sharia Saraya al-Gezira, Zamalek
Tel *(02) 2735 3114*
Located on the top deck of the Blue Nile Boat moored at Zamalek. Authentic and high-quality Chinese, Japanese and Indian cuisine is the deal here. Sizzling platters and its famous chocolate fondant dessert are signature offerings.

DK Choice

L'Asiatique £££
Asian   Map 1 B4
Le Pacha 1901, moored off Sharia Saray al-Gezira, Zamalek
Tel *(02) 2735 6730*
L'Asiatique is a stylish place where gourmet sushi and Asian dishes reign. Signature dishes include the chicken lemongrass and Thai red curry, both served with glass noodles. Crisp linens, crystal, an elegant decor and uniformed waiters are the deal here. Located in Le Pacha 1901 boat on the Nile.

L'Aubergine £££
Egyptian   Map 1 A3
5 Sharia Al-Sayyid al-Bakri, Zamalek
Tel *(02) 2738 0080*
A favoured haunt of business types, L'Aubergine serves an especially good vegetarian selection, along with gourmet-style Egyptian and international dishes.

Il Piccolo Mondo £££
Italian   Map 1 B4
Le Pacha 1901, moored off Sharia Saray al-Gezira, Zamalek
Tel *(02) 2735 6730*
Il Piccolo Mondo is one of several restaurants in Le Pacha 1901, a boat moored on the Nile. The decor is inspired by Italy's piazzas, complete with stone archways. A buffet of antipasti precedes the mains and home-made desserts.

Jayda Lounge £££
Lebanese   Map 1 B2
1191 Corniche el-Nil
Tel *(02) 2580 8017*
Located within the Conrad Cairo Hotel, Jayda Lounge is a stylish place known for its gourmet meat, fish and seafood dishes fresh from the roasting oven, grill or oak-smoker. Signature Scandinavian-style breads and superb desserts.

Kandahar £££
Indian
3 Sharia Gamaat El Dawal El Arabiyya, Mohandiseen
Tel *(02) 3303 0615*
Located just off Midan Sphinx, this cosy eatery with traditional decor is a city favourite. It serves Far Eastern food, especially Indian dishes. *Murgh makhani* (butter chicken) is the signature dish.

Kebabgy £££
Egyptian   Map 3 A1
Sofitel Cairo El Gezirah, 3 Sharia El Thawra Council, Zamalek
Tel *(02) 2737 3737*
Select from the à la carte menu, watch your meat being

Beautifully lit interiors of Le Steak restaurant

barbecued and choose from 25 different *shishas* flavours.

DK Choice

Sequoia £££
Egyptian/Lebanese   Map 1 A1
53 Sharia Abou El Feda, Zamalek
Tel *(02) 2735 0014*
Savour 360-degree views of the Nile from this popular outdoor restaurant located on the tip of Gezira Island. Egyptian and Lebanese cuisine is offered, and sushi is also on the menu. Try the cocktails and *shishas*. Reserve in advance, especially on weekends.

Le Steak £££
French   Map 1 B4
Le Pacha 1901, moored off Sharia al-Gezira, Zamalek
Tel *(02) 2735 6730*
Located in La Pacha 1901, Le Steak has a distinctive French-inspired ambience and menu. Along with classic French dishes, this eatery excels when it comes to steak topped with creamy sauces like bearnaise or Roquefort. Fine wines and great views.

Giza and Heliopolis

Kalmangi £
Café
Sun City Mall, Sharia Autostrade, Heliopolis
Tel *(010) 1559 5666*
Since it opened a year or two ago, this Leventine and *shisha* eatery inside the Sun City Mall has earned itself a reputation for fine food at inexpensive prices. Always busy with Cairenes as well as tourists.

Koshary Hind £
Egyptian
5 Sharia Thawra, Heliopolis
Tel *(010) 9992 0373*
Koshary Hind is the go-to place for authentic *koshari*. Its mix of

chickpeas, pasta and rice, with tomato sauce and crispy fried onions served as a side, is legendary. Central location near the sights.

Asmak Al Sherif ££
Fish & Seafood
42 Sharia Anqara, Heliopolis
Tel *(02) 2267 7458*
Tilapia, mullet, shrimp and calamari are among the fish and seafood cooked fresh to order, to eat in or take away, at this Cairenes' favourite. Fish is served with arugula leaves and lemon. Accommodates customers who wish to bring their own seafood and get it cooked.

Car Café ££
Café
26 Sharia el-Nile, Giza
Tel *(02) 3336 1776*
With its Pop Art exterior and racetrack-inspired interior, this characterful eatery is a landmark in Giza. Popular with youngsters, it serves smoothies and iced teas, burgers, grills and an assortment of salads.

El Mashrabia ££
Egyptian
4 Sharia Ahmed Nessim, Giza
Tel *(02) 3748 3501*
If you enjoy good honest Egyptian cuisine then El Mashrabia is the place to go. Typically, the menu offers *mombar* (stuffed sheep intestines) followed by rabbit *molokhiyya* with lashings of hummus.

Schatz ££
Italian
55 Sharia Al Shheed Abdel Moneim Hafez, Heliopolis
Tel *(02) 2290 3170*
Schatz has earned a reputation for its fine *shisha* and gourmet coffee selection, plus a seemingly endless selection of pizza and pasta dishes. The specialty is *frutti di mare* pasta (seafood pasta).

DK Choice

Le Chantilly £££
Swiss/French
11 Sharia Baghdad, Heliopolis
Tel *(02) 2290 5213*
Swiss and French cuisine is the deal at La Chantilly, a romantic restaurant with uniformed waiters. The signature dish is *veau à la zurichoise* (veal cooked Zurich-style). For dessert, don't miss the home-made strawberry ice cream. Open for breakfast through to dinner.

Le Chateau £££
Swiss
Sharia El Nasr Building el-Nile, Giza
Tel *(02) 3748 6270*
Le Chateau takes its inspiration from Switzerland for its fine wine list, exquisite menu selection and desserts that include a chocolate fondue. It is open for breakfast, daytime dining and dinner.

Shogun £££
Japanese
Intercontinental Citystars Cairo, Sharia Omar Ibn El Khattab, Heliopolis
Tel *(02) 2480 0100*
Sushi, sashimi and *teppanyaki* cooked at live cooking stations is the promise at Shogun, a stylish hotel-restaurant that has gained a reputation for creating an authentic Japanese dining experience. Fine wine list and decor with an exotic fish tank.

La Sirena £££
Fish & Seafood
115 Sharia Othman Ibn Affan, Heliopolis
Tel *(02) 2415 8714*
Compact La Sirena is one of Cairo's smallest and finest seafood restaurants, with specials that include imaginative fish *tajines* and large, artfully plated platters. Good wine list. Cosy decor.

Around Cairo

6TH OF OCTOBER CITY: Cote Jardin ££
European/Lebanese
Sharia 26 of July, 6th of October City
Tel *(011) 2233 8884*
A menu of French, Italian and Lebanese dishes at this trendy restaurant in the Novotel hotel. Dine inside or on the terrace.

6TH OF OCTOBER CITY: Paul ££
Café
Mall of Arabia, Juhayna Square, 6th of October City
Tel *(011) 1994 6002*
A popular French chain, Paul is known for desserts such as tartelettes, macaroons and eclairs. Wide range of coffees and juices. Serves excellent soups, salads and mains as well.

6TH OF OCTOBER CITY: Saraya ££
Grill
Bonne Vie, Near Dreamland, 6th of October City
Tel *(012) 7017 4444*
A tastefully decorated à la carte restaurant, the Saraya is housed within the Bonne Vie hotel. Grills and sauces are the specialty.

6TH OF OCTOBER CITY: Indigo £££
European/Arabian
Al Yasmin Mall, 6th of October City
Tel *(012) 0278 1278* **Closed** *Mon*
A decor of deep purple with accent lighting sets the scene for intimate dining at this lounge bar. Wide choice of cocktails.

6TH OF OCTOBER CITY: Leila £££
Lebanese
Mall of Arabia, Juhayna Square, 6th of October City
Tel *(010) 9090 4967*
Mezzes of dips like *muhammara* (pepper) and *babaghanoush* (spicy eggplant), followed by classic mains and honey-rich desserts.

EL MA'ADI: Ma7ali £
Café
10b Sharia 11
Tel *(011) 4848 2448*
Ma7Ali is an organic eaterie with an informal café and deli section, and a garden dining area complete with a *forn baladi* (bakery). Grab a sandwich or opt for a three-course meal.

EL MA'ADI: Crust ££
Italian
12 Sharia Mostafa Kamel
Tel *(02) 2380 3001*
Crust is an elegant pizzeria with an outside patio. Inspired salads precede pizzas served hot from the wood-fired oven. Speciality toppings include calamari and three cheeses.

EL MA'ADI: Kahwet Leila ££
Café
Sharia Corniche el-Nil
Tel *(010) 2717 8882*
Refined yet informal, Kahwet Leila is located right on the banks of the Nile. This Lebanese *shisha* café serves traditional dishes like *fuul* made with vegetables, falafel and *mfarakeh*.

EL MA'ADI: Lan Yuan ££
Chinese
84 Sharia 9
Tel *(02) 2378 2702* **Closed** *Sun*
Lan Yuan has an attractive Oriental decor, soft music plays and the menu options are extensive – a good combination. All the classics are here, such as spring rolls and sweet and sour dishes.

EL MA'ADI: Casa Lingo £££
International
6 Sharia 4
Tel *(02) 2358 2150*
Casa Lingo is a stylish place with a courtyard for dining alfresco. The cuisine is gourmet with Oriental platters, Indian curries and steaks all artfully plated.

EL MA'ADI: Gaya £££
Korean
41 Sharia 218
Tel *(02) 2519 7769*
Gaya is famed for its authentic Korean cuisine, and in particular the rich miso made from seaweed and tofu, and the *kimchi* (spicy vegetables). Chic decor.

EL MA'ADI: Maharani £££
Indian
Sharia 6
Tel *(02) 2359 7777*
Biryanis, *saag gosht* curry and kashmiri *pulao*, along with flavoured *naan* bread, all served with a gourmet flourish are what makes this restaurant special.

Outdoor seating at Crust, a pizzeria in El Ma'adi

DK Choice

EL MA'ADI: San Marino £££
Korean
29 Sharia 263, New Maadi
Tel *(02) 2519 2451*
San Marino is one of the best Korean restaurants in Cairo. Vegetables, chicken, beef and pork are cooked to authentic recipes and artfully plated. The signature dishes are stir-fries with imaginative sauces and the Korean barbecue where meals are cooked over coals at diners' tables. Good wine list.

FAYOUM OASIS:
El Moalemeen £
Egyptian
Sharia El Nadi El Riyadi
Tel *(084) 637 6444*
A cosy restaurant housed within the El Moalemeen hotel, this eaterie serves traditional cuisine with an emphasis on organic ingredients. It can be found near the souks.

FAYOUM OASIS: Kamariat
El Mandara £
Egyptian
Tunis, Lake Qarun, Izbat an Namus
Tel *(010) 6883 3081*
Specializing in Oriental food, the tastefully presented à la carte restaurant of the Kamariat El Mandara hotel looks out over Lake Qarun and the wilderness beyond.

DK Choice

FAYOUM OASIS: Helnan
Auberge Fayoum £££
European
Lake Qarun, Shakshut
Tel *(084) 698 1300*
The elegant restaurant of the Helnan Auberge, with its burgundy and cream decor and atmospheric lighting, is a pleasing place to dine on dishes influenced by French, Italian and Oriental cuisine. Smart dress is required. It is part of the former hunting lodge of King Farouk and enjoys a location on the shores of Lake Qarun.

SHEIKH ZAYAD: Baladina ££
Egyptian
Arkan Mall
Tel *(011) 2220 8887*
Egyptian classics like *kishk* (cheese) with *baladi* bread, followed by a meat or vegetable *tagine*, can be found on the menu at Baladina. A trendy yet village-style eaterie inside the mall.

DK Choice

SHEIKH ZAYAD: La
Gourmandise ££
Mediterranean
Arkan Mall
Tel *(010) 0126 0401*
Big comfy sofas and art on the walls combine to give La Gourmandise an edgy feel. It specializes in gourmet-style snacks like smoked salmon and capers on fresh baguettes, as well as pizzas with imaginative toppings. The display of French pastries and cakes, including the signature hot chocolate cake, is outstanding.

SHEIKH ZAYAD: Olive & Oil ££
Lebanese
Arkan Mall
Tel *(011) 1000 8608*
A contemporary eaterie on Arkan Mall's plaza, Olive & Oil takes Lebanese food to a new level. Staples like *manakeesh*, chicken *fattah* and the highly recommended *shish tawook* are made trendy with creative flavours.

SHEIKH ZAYAD: Charwood's £££
Steakhouse
Zayad 2000 Village
Tel *(010) 1920 3120*
Charwood's has long been a city centre favourite, and has now opened this branch in Sheikh Zayad. It can usually be found full of locals. Steaks cooked to perfection and dishes like chicken brochettes served with creative salads are what makes this place special. Also offers a selection of international wines.

The Nile Valley

ASWAN: Al-Masry £
Egyptian
Sharia Al-Matar
Tel *(097) 230 2576*
Al-Masry is a cosy restaurant with a varied selection of Egyptian and European-style cuisine, including grilled chicken and fish. Lengthy choice of desserts.

ASWAN: Biti £
Italian
Midan al-Mahatta
Tel *(097) 230 0949*
Occupying a three-storey property complete with roof terrace, the Biti is a buzzy place famed for its sweet and savoury *fatir* (Egyptian pizza) selection. Try the dessert *fatir* filled with coconut and bananas, dusted with powdered sugar.

Relaxed seating on the terrace at Baladina, Sheikh Zayad

ASWAN: Aswan Moon ££
Egyptian
Felucca Quay, Corniche el-Nil
Tel *(097) 231 6108*
Serving *mezzes, koshari* and grills, the Aswan Moon combines good food with views. It can be found right on the riverside Felucca Quay. Good choice of fish and vegetarian dishes.

ASWAN: Emy ££
Egyptian
Corniche el-Nil
Tel *(097) 230 4349*
Emy is a floating restaurant moored on the corniche with views of Elephantine Island. The high-quality menu includes the popular fresh grilled fish.

ASWAN: Makka ££
Egyptian
Sharia Abtal El-Tahrir
Tel *(097) 230 3232*
Makka, an air-conditioned restaurant, is like a breath of fresh air when the sun is at its hottest. Here, tour groups come to refresh and dine on delicacies like stuffed pigeon with an array of salads.

DK Choice

ASWAN: Nubian ££
Egyptian
Essa Island
Tel *(097) 910 8000*
Nubian is a stylish little place set on Essa Island in the Nile. It provides a free ferry boat from the dockside opposite EgyptAir's Aswan office. Popular with tour groups and tourists, it serves a good selection of international and Egyptian food, along with wine and beer. The Nile perch and *shish tawook* are recommended. Hosts a live folkloric show most nights.

For more information on types of restaurants *see pages 278–81*

ASWAN: Panorama ££
Egyptian
Corniche el-Nil
Tel *(097) 231 6169*
Panorama lives up to its name with views over Lake Nasser from the terrace. It specializes in upper Nubian cuisine, with a signature dish of rich local *molokhiyya*.

ASWAN: Sayhida Nafisa ££
Egyptian
Sharia Ahmed Maher
Tel *(097) 231 7152*
A central location and with a covered terrace for eating alfresco, the Sayhida Nafisa is a popular place, especially in summer. The menu focuses on Egyptian specialities.

ASWAN: Chef Khalil £££
Fish & Seafood
Sharia as-Souq
Tel *(097) 231 0142*
This pleasing little place uses fish and seafood, either caught from nearby Lake Nasser or sourced from further afield, prepared with herbs and lemon, baked or grilled, and served with flair. Price is by weight. The signature dish is lobster, with *tahina*, salad and rice. Located near the souk.

ASWAN: Nefertay £££
French/Italian
Isis Island
Tel *(097) 231 7400*
Located within the luxurious Pyramida Isis hotel, Nefertay is a tasteful restaurant with an extensive menu. Fine wine list.

ASWAN: Orangerie £££
Egyptian
Elephantine Island
Tel *(097) 230 3455*
The Orangerie is the large, bright restaurant of the Mövenpick Hotel; open for buffet-style breakfast through to dinner. À la carte menu of international and Egyptian dishes.

DK Choice

ASWAN: Terrace £££
European
Sharia Abdul El Tehrir
Tel *(097) 231 6000*
With stunning views over the Khnum Temple and Elephantine Island, the Terrace is a lovely place to dine. Oriental, French and Italian cuisine is showcased on the international gourmet menu. Extensive fine wine list. Located within the Sofitel Legend Old Cataract hotel that featured in Agatha Christie's novel, *Death on the Nile*.

Pretty rooftop terrace at Al Gezira, Luxor

ASYUT: Al Watania Palace ££
Egyptian
Sharia al-Gomhuriyya
Tel *(088) 228 7981*
Bamiyya and *molokhiyya* stews and grills are among the offerings at this tasteful rooftop hotel-restaurant in the heart of Asyut.

LUXOR: Al Gezira £
Egyptian
Geziret El Beirat
Tel *(095) 231 2505*
Enjoy a family atmosphere, fine local cuisine and traditional Egyptian music in the rooftop restaurant of the Al Gezira hotel. Views of Luxor by night while dining are mesmerizing.

LUXOR: Al Sahaby Lane £
Café
Sharia Al Sahaby
Tel *(095) 225 6086*
Al Sahaby Lane is famous for its meat and fish *tajines* cooked to authentic Bedouin recipes. Choice of vegetarian dishes. Enjoy views of the Luxor Temple.

LUXOR: Oasis £
Café
Sharia El Madina
Tel *(095) 336 7121*
With a cool ambience and soft jazz playing in the background, Oasis lives up to its name. It is a place to escape from the bustle and heat of Luxor. It serves a range of dishes, including grills, pasta and vegetarian options.

LUXOR: Pizza Roma It £
Italian
Sharia El Mahdi
Tel *(011) 1879 9559*
Pizza Roma is a brightly decorated little eaterie with a faithful following of locals drawn by its excellent pizzas. Authentic Italian pasta creations are menu favourites too. Beer and wine on request.

DK Choice

LUXOR: Wenkie's German Ice Cream & Iced Coffee Parlour £
Café
Sharia El Gawazat
Tel *(012) 8894 7380* **Closed** *Fri*
Wenkie's serves fresh ice cream made from water buffalo milk and flavoured with such goodies as doum palm dates, local lemons, fresh mint, nuts and spices. The specials also include waffles smothered with sauce, milkshakes and iced coffee. All ingredients are 100 per cent natural.

LUXOR: Gerda's Garden ££
Egyptian/German
Sharia Fondouk Al Nile Helton
Tel *(095) 235 8688*
Perfect for an informal dinner, Gerda's Garden serves delicious fillet steak, grilled duck and fish *tagine*. German specialities such as *frikadeller* (meat dumplings) and local Egyptian favourites are on the menu. Excellent service.

LUXOR: Jewel of the Nile ££
British
Sharia al Roada al Sharyfa, off Medina Street
Tel *(010) 6252 2394*
Enjoy British classics such as cottage pie, Sunday roast and apple crumble with custard. The owners Laura, Mamoud and their staff are always ready to welcome customers with a smile.

LUXOR: King's Head Pub ££
Mediterranean
Sharia Khalid Ebn El Walid
Tel *(095) 228 0489*
Creative cocktails, beers, spirits and wines, plus big-screen TVs and pool tables, are found at the popular King's Head Pub. Dine on salads followed by shish kebab, steaks, fish and seafood, or pizza baked in an Italian-style oven.

LUXOR: The Lantern ££
British
Sharia al Roda al Sharifa
Tel *(010) 0395 2215*
Specializing in English cuisine, The Lantern is a cozy place where you will find expats enjoying home-made soup, roasts and grills, seafood and Sunday specials. Thursday is Egyptian theme night.

LUXOR: A Taste of India ££
Indian
Sharia St Joseph
Tel *(010) 9373 2727*
As its name suggests, this restaurant specializes in Indian cuisine. Kormas, curries and masalas all feature on the menu, along with a few international and vegetarian dishes. Popular with locals.

DK Choice

LUXOR: 1886 Restaurant £££
French
Corniche el-Nil
Tel *(095) 238 0422*
Super-elegant and serving gourmet French cuisine, the 1886 is where locals go to celebrate. Dine by candlelight to live guitar music. Highlights include pressed duck and crayfish risotto. Fine wine list. Dress code is smart. Located inside the Sofitel Winter Palace Hotel right beside the Nile.

LUXOR: La Fleur £££
French
Kings Island
Tel *(095) 2274 855*
With its wood and cream decor and crisp linens, La Fleur is the stylish French à la carte restaurant of the Jolie Ville hotel on Kings Island. Here, smart waiters serve fine wines and artful creations from the kitchen.

LUXOR: Luxor Grill £££
Asian/European
Corner Sharia El Mahdi and Sharia El Madina
Tel *(010) 1305 0405*
Luxor Grill is a stylish place to unwind, with its tasteful decor, crisp white linens and accent lighting, the. The menu varies from gourmet-style burgers to a full Asian and European fusion menu. Good choice of vegetarian dishes.

LUXOR: Sofra £££
Egyptian
90 Sharia Mohamed Farid
Tel *(095) 235 9752*
Sofra is as Egyptian as it gets, from the traditional, upmarket decor

with antique furniture, mirrors and copper chandeliers, to the menu of classic dishes like *kamonia* (veal) and *saniyet kofta* (lamb). This is where diners come to eat good authentic cuisine. It is housed in a characterful 1930s property.

MINYA: King Akhenaton £
Egyptian
Corniche el-Nil
Tel *(086) 236 5918*
The restaurant of the King Akhenaton has panoramic views out across the Nile. It serves a fusion of Egyptian, Oriental and European cuisines buffet-style.

MINYA: MG Nefertiti ££
Egyptian
Corniche el-Nil
Tel *(086) 234 1515*
Serving Egyptian dishes like kebabs with *babaghanoush* followed by stuffed pigeon is the draw at this rooftop restaurant. Great views of the Nile.

MINYA: Grand Aton £££
Egyptian
Corniche el-Nil
Tel *(010) 0030 8020*
The restaurant of the Grand Aton is a tasteful place with a menu of international as well as Egyptian dishes.

Sinai and the Red Sea Coast

DAHAB: Bedouin £
Egyptian
Bedouin Lodge Hotel, El Mashraba
Tel *(069) 364 1125*
Serving authentic Bedouin cuisine, along with international dishes, this atmospheric restaurant has an emphasis on local produce. There's a selection

Beautiful and elegant dining room at 1886 Restaurant, Luxor

of meat grills, vegetarian dishes and fruit juices. Diners sit on Bedouin-style striped cushions with locals, right next to the Arabian sea. Live local music.

DAHAB: Inmo £
Middle Eastern
Inmo Divers Home, Mashraba Beach
Tel *(069) 364 0370*
This excellent beachside restaurant has pure Bedouin decor, while the cuisine focuses on Middle Eastern dishes like *mansaf* (lamb) and *maglubeh* (chicken), and international grills. Breakfast through to evening dining. Good vegetarian options.

DK Choice

DAHAB: South North Tea Garden £
Café
Sharia Mashraba
Tel *(010) 0404 0179*
This lovely place set in gardens of palms has curved seating and contemporary furnishings. It serves light snacks and a whole host of beverages. The speciality is tea – choose from Pina Colada, goji berry and wadi lemon, or Egyptian teas flavoured with hibiscus or cinnamon, to name just a few. Gourmet coffees, milkshakes and *shishas*.

DAHAB: Bride of the Sea ££
Fish & Seafood
Sharia Mashraba
Tel *(069) 364 1878*
Choose from the catch of the day downstairs and then head upstairs for a beautiful meal. The seafood soup is highly recommended. Bring your own alcohol.

DAHAB: Carm Inn ££
Vegetarian
Masbat (Lighthouse) Bay
Tel *(012) 2227 0443*
This rustic place along the promenade offers a diverse menu of vegetarian dishes. Save room for the banana sundae. A favourite for over a decade; Mondays witness a live band performance. Inviting ambience.

DAHAB: Nesima £££
Mediterranean
Nesima Hotel, Mashraba Asilah
Tel *(069) 364 0320*
Nesima is an intimate eatery with an à la carte menu. Typically, home-made soups and pasta dishes precede upmarket mains of fish *tajines* and platters, sautéed veal, steaks with French-inspired sauces, and heavenly desserts.

For more information on types of restaurants *see pages 278–81*

HURGHADA: The Lodge £
Egyptian
Hurghada Marina
Tel *(012) 2416 3912*
Known for its good food and water-
side location. The menu focuses
on Egyptian classics, along with the
famed fish platters and cocktails.

DK Choice

HURGHADA: SubZero Ice Bar £
Mediterranean
Sharia Sheraton
Tel *(010) 0503 7249*
SubZero is one of Hurghada's
top fun venues. The walls, bar,
tables and glasses in which
drinks are served are, literally,
made of ice. The temperature is
kept at -5°C and visitors wear
cloaks while inside. Enjoy tapas,
pizzas, pasta dishes and grills.
Menu of shots and cocktails.

HURGHADA: Asia House ££
Asian
Sharia Sheraton
Tel *(010) 1154 3008*
This stylish Oriental-themed
restaurant offers an Asian fusion
menu featuring classic Chinese,
Thai and Indian dishes. Also has
a British bistro menu.

HURGHADA: Moby Dick ££
Fish & Seafood
Sharia Sheraton
Tel *(065) 344 0050*
Housed in an elegant building in
the heart of Hurghada, Moby Dick
is known for top-quality steaks
and innovative fresh fish dishes.

**HURGHADA: Bordiehn's B's
at Marina** £££
Steakhouse
New Marina Boulevard
Tel *(010) 0123 2354*
This waterfront eaterie is the haunt
of trendy locals and is known for
its innovative gourmet-style menu.
Themed meals include platters of
camel steak with chocolate sauce,
complete with side dishes and a
drink pairing. Open for breakfast.

HURGHADA: Granada £££
Italian
Sharia Sheraton
Tel *(010) 0102 3107*
Overlooking the bay, this stylish
restaurant has a relaxed vibe. It
specializes in Italian cuisine. The
wine selection is sourced from Italy.

HURGHADA: Heaven £££
Fish & Seafood
Hurghada Marina
Tel *(012) 2242 8204*
Heaven is a tastefully decorated
place where fish and seafood

platters and steaks are served as
works of art. Located in the marina.

**HURGHADA:
Little Buddha** £££
Japanese
Sharia Hurghada
Tel *(012) 2021 1221*
If upmarket Japanese sushi and
seafood in French and Asian-
inspired sauces is a passion then
Little Buddha is likely to impress.
It has an opulent interior, music
and a discerning clientele.

NUWEIBA: Cleopatra ££
Fish & Seafood
Main Square
Tel *(012) 745 4282*
Cleopatra is in Nuweiba's main
square where the aroma of
seafood and skewered fish
cooking over coals tempts
passers-by. Creative selection
of salad and kebabs.

NUWEIBA: Oasis ££
Egyptian
Helnan Nuweiba Bay
Tel *(069) 350 0401*
With a panoramic view over the
pool and the beach beyond,
the Oasis is a light, bright restau-
rant with dining inside and out.
The cuisine is international with
the emphasis on Egyptian.

NUWEIBA: Blue Blue £££
Italian/Egyptian
Hilton Nuweiba Coral Resort
Tel *(069) 352 0320*
A menu of international dishes,
along with Italian and Egyptian
corners, is the deal at Blue Blue.
This elegant restaurant is great
for evening dining when
lighting highlights the palm
tree gardens.

Thai red snapper curry served with a
bowl of rice

**PORT SAFAGA:
Coral Garden** ££
Asian/Egyptian
Coral Garden Resort, Gassous Bay
Tel *(010) 0669 4153*
The Coral Garden is the elegant
restaurant of this dive resort
complex on the beach. The
selection of dishes are served
buffet-style. Weekly barbecue
evenings on the terrace. Diners
can enjoy panoramic views of
the pool and the sea beyond.

PORT SAID: Gianola £
Café
Sharia al-Gumhuriyya
Tel *(066) 324 0002*
This attractive little pastry shop
and bakery tempts with the aroma
of freshly ground coffee and its
window displays. It is known for
lavish cake creations, but serves
light savoury snacks too.

PORT SAID: Pizza Pino ££
Italian
*Corner Sharia 23rd of July and Sharia
al-Gumhuriyya*
Tel *(066) 332 4812*
A lively eaterie with art on the
walls and a loyal clientele, Pizza
Pino serves breakfast through to
evening meals. It offers a
seemingly endless selection of
pizzas, but also pasta, grills and
seafood. Great place to people-
watch from the outside tables.

PORT SAID: El Borg £££
Fish & Seafood
Sharia Tarh El Bahr, El Manakh
Tel *(066) 332 3442*
Located in the Beach Plaza
complex, this spacious restaurant
is always buzzing with locals. They
come for the excellent selection
of octopus, lobster and other
seafood cooked to perfection.
Specials include stuffed calamari
and *molokhiyya* with shrimps.
Shishas and drinks available.
Dine on the seafront terrace.

DK Choice

**SHARM EL-SHEIKH: Farsha
Chill Out Café** £
Café
Umm El Sid Hill
Tel *(069) 360 1391*
With its location perched on a
cliff with panoramic views to
the sea, and with big comfy
sofas, colourful cushions and
atmospheric lighting everywhere, the Farsha lives up to its
name as a chill-out place. Along
with drinks, a menu of creative
cocktails and flavoured *shishas*,
the café serves a menu of finger-
food-style dishes and pizzas.

Key to Price Guide *see page 284*

SHARM EL-SHEIKH:
Camel Bar ££
European/Indian
Camel Hotel, Naama Bay
Tel *(069) 360 0700*
This trio of bars serves colourful cocktails, as well as a full dinner menu featuring Indian, Italian and British cuisine. Rooftop *shisha* terrace. Sports screens. Central location.

SHARM EL-SHEIKH:
El Fanar ££
Italian
Ras Umm El Sidd Beach
Tel *(069) 366 2218*
Serving some of the town's finest Italian cuisine, elegant El Fanar is where locals go to celebrate. Prides itself on using fresh Italian produce. Located on the beach below the lighthouse. Good wine list.

SHARM EL-SHEIKH:
The Lounge ££
English
Mall 6, Naama Bay
Tel *(010) 6491 8425*
This elegant wood-panelled lounge bar is an ideal place to relax over coffee or a cocktail, or to enjoy a full English meal. Sunday roasts a specialty. Entertainment most evenings.

SHARM EL-SHEIKH:
La Luna ££
Italian
Sharia El Fanar
Tel *(010) 9902 0031*
La Luna is run by an Italian couple who provide authentic cuisine from the regions of Italy. Try the potato gnocchi and home-made pasta. Fine wines. Good location surrounded by gardens.

SHARM EL-SHEIKH:
Blue Fountain £££
Mediterranean
1 Market Square, Naama Bay
Tel *(010) 9993 4746* **Closed** *Fri*
Creole curries, gourmet burgers and steaks, along with sizzling platters, are among the dishes cooked fresh to order at the Blue Fountain. Cocktails. Artful presentation and decor.

SHARM EL-SHEIKH:
Fairuz £££
Lebanese
Naama Centre, Sharia King of Bahrain, Naama Bay
Tel *(012) 8802 1418*
Fairuz is one of Sharm's best-kept secrets. Locals know it for its authentic Lebanese cuisine, which is creatively plated and delicious. Try the huge seafood platter. Fine wine list. Mall location.

Mombar mahshy (stuffed beef sausage), a traditional Egyptian dish

DK Choice
SHARM EL-SHEIKH:
Fish Market £££
Fish & Seafood
Sultan Gardens Resort, Shark's Bay
Tel *(069) 360 2130*
A locals' favourite, the award-winning Fish Market serves fresh fish and seafood according to weight and what has been caught earlier in the day. It also has an à la carte menu and hosts a hugely popular weekly seafood barbecue evenings and "all you can eat" shrimp nights. Dine inside or on the terrace with views of the Red Sea. Open for breakfast.

SHARM EL-SHEIKH: Rangoli £££
Indian
Movenpick Resort Naama Bay, Coast Road
Tel *(069) 360 0081*
Considered one of the best Indian restaurants in town, Rangoli combines meat and seafood fresh from the tandoor embers with a stunning view of Naama Bay.

The Delta and the North Coast

DK Choice
ABU QIR: Seven Seas ££
Fish & Seafood
30 Sharia Alkaid Gohar
Tel *(03) 563 5314*
Located on the beach, Seven Seas is popular with the locals. Eat inside or alfresco. Diners can sink their feet in the sand while feasting on the freshest seafood cooked and presented in a number of creative ways. Skewered shrimps, towers of white fish and seafood-filled wraps plated with salads or sauces are among the menu options.

ABU QIR: Zephyrion ££
Egyptian
Abu Qir
Tel *(03) 562 1319*
Zephyrion might be in the middle of nowhere, but it has great views from the terrace and a faithful clientele due to the wholesome meat and seafood dishes it's been serving for decades.

ALEXANDRIA: Fuul Mohamed Ahmed £
Egyptian
17 Sharia Shakour
Tel *(03) 487 3576*
Founded in 1957, this traditional little restaurant has earned itself a reputation for authentic *fuul*, the Egyptian dish made from fava beans. It offers different varieties. A popular haunt for locals.

ALEXANDRIA: Gad £
Egyptian
Sharia Gamila Bouhraid, Midan El Saah
Tel *(03) 526 6588*
Gad is a small chain of eateries known for authentic Egyptian *fuul*, *fatir* (puff-style pizza) and falafel patties. This branch is central and ideal for a quick meal while sightseeing.

ALEXANDRIA: Taverna £
Egyptian
Sharia Zaghloul, Midan Ramla
Tel *(03) 487 8591*
Taverna is known among locals as the place to go for fresh *fatirs* (Egyptian pies), *shawerma* (kebabs) and home-made *babaghanoush* (aubergine dip). Authentic cuisine in a cosy setting.

ALEXANDRIA: Balbaa Village ££
Egyptian
Sharia Malk Hifny
Tel *(03) 202 3446*
If you wish to dine in an authentic Egyptian eaterie with dishes cooked to age-old recipes then this is the place to come. Traditional dips precede mains like *koshari* and grills.

ALEXANDRIA: Chez Gaby   ££
Italian
22 Sharia al-Horreya
Tel *(03) 487 4404*
Chez Gaby is a cosy place complete with wooden ceiling beams and knick-knacks on the walls. The team's talent lies in producing pizzas and pasta dishes from authentic Italian recipes. Founded in 1979. Beer available.

ALEXANDRIA: Delices   ££
Café
46 Sharia Zaghloul
Tel *(03) 486 1432*
This branch of Delices is a bit of a landmark. It's a popular place largely because of its over-the-top desserts which can be enjoyed with a gourmet coffee. Full breakfast, lunch and dinner menu too.

ALEXANDRIA: Fish Market   ££
Fish & Seafood
Sharia El Corniche
Tel *(03) 480 5114*
As its name suggests, this eaterie specializes in all types of fish and seafood, which it does extremely well. Tasteful place with a panoramic sea view.

ALEXANDRIA: Ole Café Espaniol   ££
Mediterranean
3 Sharia Kafr Abdou and Mirage Mall
Tel *(010) 6679 3999*
Ole's contemporary look is as refreshing as the lengthy choice of juices, cocktails and upmarket coffees. The menu is creative yet simple with breakfasts through to evening tapas.

DK Choice

ALEXANDRIA: Roastery   ££
Italian
38 Sharia Adb El Kada Ragab
Tel *(03) 542 8262*
From sandwiches with fillings like Mexican grill, steak and salmon, right through to full three-course dinners, the meals at Roastery are huge, creative and plated with flair. The huge menu has soups and starters, mains comprising meat, fish and pasta platters, and desserts to challenge the diet.

ALEXANDRIA: Byblos   £££
Middle Eastern
399 Sharia El Geish
Tel *(03) 581 8000*
Byblos is the lavish gold-themed restaurant of the Four Seasons Hotel, and where locals go to celebrate. The menu is gourmet Middle Eastern cuisine. Sea views.

Interesting decor at Roastery, Alexandria

ALEXANDRIA: China House   £££
Chinese
16 Midan Saad Zaghloul
Tel *(03) 487 7173*
Located on the rooftop of the Steigenberger Cecil Hotel, China House combines a fabulous sea view with gourmet-style Chinese food. Sizzling meat and seafood plates are signature dishes.

DK Choice

ALEXANDRIA: Greek Club   £££
Fish & Seafood
Sharia Qaitbey, Anfushi
Tel *(03) 480 2690*
Platters of octopus, lobster and calamari are among the fresh fish and seafood dishes on the menu at Greek Club. This nautical-themed place is elegant, with tables outside on a terrace to make the most of the views of Alexandria across the water. Greek music adds to its charm.

ALEXANDRIA: Samakmak   £££
Fish & Seafood
42 Sharia Kasr Ras El Tin, Anfushi
Tel *(03) 481 1560*
Known for its excellent service, this delightful restaurant across the boat builder's beach has a fresh selection of fish, squid, crabs, mussels and shrimps. The seafood soup is highly recommended.

DAMIETTA: Caviar   ££
Fish & Seafood
Sharia Corniche el-Nil
Tel *(057) 225 0738*
One of Damietta's most popular restaurants, Caviar is popular with locals. It serves fish. Squid, tuna and sea bass all appear on the menu, and are caught fresh daily.

DK Choice

DAMIETTA: Tuscany Pasta Grill   ££
Italian
Sharia El Seidi, New Damietta City
Tel *(010) 227 8773*
A selection of pizzas and pasta dishes, plus succulent steaks, salmon with its own lemon cream and grills are all offered at Tuscany Pasta Grill. The signature dish is country-grilled ribeye marinated in rosemary and Tuscan spices. Classic Italian desserts like tiramisu.

MARSA MATRUH: Corallo   ££
Fish & Seafood
Jaz Crystal Resort, Almaza Bay
Tel *(046) 436 0020*
With its elegant blue decor and outside seaview terrace, both with candlelit tables, the Corallo is a romantic restaurant. Fine wine list.

MARSA MATRUH: Morgana   ££
Mediterranean
Jaz Almaza Beach Resort, Almaza Bay
Tel *(046) 436 0000*
Morgana is a large, bright restaurant overlooking the beach. Dine on fish and pizzas on a terrace surrounded by gardens.

DK Choice

MARSA MATRUH: Makai Tukai   £££
Asian
Jaz Oriental Club, Almaza Bay
Tel *(046) 436 0040*
This stylish restaurant has an Asian fusion menu that encompasses authentic Thai, *teppanyaki*, sashimi and sushi dishes. It is popular with locals and visitors. Pre-dinner drinks and *shishas* can be enjoyed in the Jaz Oriental's Mazagy Roof Bar.

The Western Desert

BAHARIYYA OASIS: Bawiti Oasis Resort £
Egyptian
Sharia Bir Al-Matar, El Bawiti
Tel *(010) 772 4942*
The Bawiti Oasis restaurant caters for most diets: there's a lengthy vegetarian selection and halal meat. Fish is delivered daily from Cairo. Bright decor.

BAHARIYYA OASIS: Bedouin Castle £
Egyptian
Sharia Ain Muftella, El Bedawi
Tel *(010) 0404 6240*
The Bedouin Castle is a hotel-restaurant housed in a gorgeous Nubian-style building. Serves hearty meals like *molokhiyya* with meat, stuffed vegetables and lamb.

BAHARIYYA OASIS: Desert Rose Eco Lodge ££
Middle Eastern
Sharia Bir Al-Matar, El Bawiti
Tel *(012) 2823 3731*
Food cooked in traditional clay pots with herbs is the speciality of this ecolodge restaurant. Set in a garden that includes a small orchard and an olive grove.

DAKHLA OASIS: Ahmed Hamdy £
Egyptian
Sharia as-Sawra al-Khadra, Mut
Tel *(092) 794 0767*
Spicy stuffed chicken and *koshari* top the menu favourites at Ahmed Hamdy, a traditional place on Mut's main approach road.

DAKHLA OASIS: Abu Ballas ££
Egyptian
Desert Lodge, El Qasr
Tel *(02) 2690 5240*
A glorious, bright restaurant with a high vaulted ceiling and stained-glass windows, the Abu Ballas serves Egyptian dishes and fine wines. Its organic farm provides most of the ingredients.

DK Choice

DAKHLA OASIS: Qasr Al Mansura £££
Egyptian
Al Tarfa Desert Sanctuary, Al Mansura
Tel *(010) 0100 1109*
Imaginative gourmet-style Egyptian dishes accompanied by fine wine are offered at this elegant restaurant that's part of an up-market lodge and spa complex. The ingredients used are either grown in the lodge's farm or sourced from local villages.

EL KHARGA OASIS: Palm £
Egyptian
Sol Y Mar Pioneers Hotel, Sharia Gamal Abdel Nasser
Tel *(092) 792 9751*
Live cooking stations are the focal point of this hotel-restaurant, part of a traditional mudbrick hotel complex. The emphasis is on locally sourced ingredients.

FARAFRA OASIS: Badawiya ££
Egyptian
Sharia Gamal Abdel Nasser, El Wadi El Gadid
Tel *(092) 751 0060*
The restaurant of the Badawiya Hotel, a mudbrick lodge built to a Bedouin style, specializes in using organic produce. Tastefully decorated in cream and red with a vaulted ceiling.

SIWA OASIS: Campione £
Café
Market Square
Tel *(010) 6661 0807*
Campione is a great place to relax over a gourmet-style coffee and *taamiyya* (home-made patties), and people-watch from the terrace overlooking the market square.

SIWA OASIS: Dream Lodge £
Egyptian
Gabal El Mawta
Tel *(010) 0099 9255*
Dine alfresco around the pool of this attractive complex, or inside in the cosy dining space with exposed stone walls and a fire for chilly evenings. Egyptian *molokhiyya* is the specialty.

SIWA OASIS: Nour El Waha Garden £
Egyptian
Sharia El Seboukha
Tel *(046) 460 0293*
This pretty garden restaurant is set among palm trees. The menu changes daily and typically features kebabs and *tajines*.

SIWA OASIS: Palm Trees £
Egyptian
Siwa
Tel *(046) 460 1703*
Palm Trees is an elegant little place with a menu comprising pure Egyptian classics, including *bamiyya* and *koshari*. Drinks can be enjoyed in the rooftop garden with panoramic views of ancient Shali.

SIWA OASIS: Tanta Waa £
Café
Cleopatra Springs
Tel *(010) 1508 4294*
Tanta Waa is a lively place serving morning coffee, smoothies and fresh fruit juices, right through to a feast of Egyptian dishes for lunch or dinner. Located at the springs.

SIWA OASIS: Siwa Gardens ££
Egyptian
Sharia Ayn Al Arias, Siwa
Tel *(046) 460 2801*
Tea available all day culminates in an evening feast of Egyptian dishes in the Siwa Gardens, a lovely domed restaurant complete with antique lamps and tasteful decor.

DK Choice

SIWA OASIS: Siwa Shali £££
Egyptian/Italian
Gabal El Dakror
Tel *(046) 921 0064*
The Siwa Shali is a stylish restaurant with atmospheric dining spaces and a terrace for a romantic alfresco candlelight dinner. The à la carte menu focuses on Egyptian and Italian cuisine, along with a specialist detox and low-calorie selection. Produce is grown in its organic garden, while fish is flown in from the Mediterranean.

Rustic charm of Bawiti Oasis Resort, Bahariyya Oasis

For more information on types of restaurants *see pages 278–81*

SHOPPING IN EGYPT

When it comes to shopping, the souqs and bazaars are undoubtedly Egypt's main attraction. The biggest and most famous is Cairo's Khan al-Khalili *(see pp92–4)*, a 500-year-old maze of commerce at the heart of the old Islamic city. While on first encounter it can seem to cater excessively to tourism, explore deeper and the narrow alleys become a bustling hive of small workshops turning out attractive jewellery, glass, copper and brassware. Here you can buy direct from the artisans and cut out the middleman. Most other towns and cities throughout the country also have souqs, with particularly good ones in Alexandria, Aswan and Port Said. For visitors intending to shop in these places it is essential to become acquainted with the art of bargaining. In contrast to the traditional nature of the souq, larger cities, such as Cairo and Alexandria, also possess modern shopping precincts, as well as shopping centres filled with globally recognized brand names.

Opening Hours

There are no strictly defined opening hours in Egypt – it depends on each individual proprietor. Generally, however, except for local grocery stores, which open early, business activity begins at around 9 or 10am. Businesses tend to close for a siesta from around 2 to 5pm, except in Cairo, where shops remain open all day. They then typically stay open until 9pm or later. In summer, in busy commercial areas, and especially Khan al-Khalili, the shutters often do not come down until 10 or 11pm, as people prefer to shop when it is cooler. Other souqs keep shorter hours, with stalls and businesses packing up around sunset. Friday is the official day off, although in Cairo many shops are open seven days a week. Those open on Friday may still close for a couple of hours in the middle of the day for noon prayers. Businesses owned by Christians may close on Sunday. During Ramadan shops close 30 minutes before sunset but reopen a couple of hours later. The whole country shuts down on major feasts, which include Moulid an-Nabi, Eid al-Fitr and Eid al-Adha *(see p43)*.

How to Pay

Although their use as a form of payment is increasing, credit cards are typically still only accepted at larger or tourist-oriented shops, such as those found in hotel complexes or shopping malls. Likewise, travellers' cheques are hardly accepted anywhere. In most places, it is necessary to pay in cash. Egyptian pounds are the country's only legal currency and purchases cannot usually be made in dollars.

Souqs and Markets

Besides Khan al-Khalili there are numerous other souqs and markets in Cairo, many worth a visit irrespective of whether you intend to buy anything. Fruit and vegetables are sold at the many street markets scattered throughout the city. Every neighbourhood has one. In central Cairo there is the Tawfiqiyya market, one block north of Sharia 26 July, open so late that many stallholders don't bother going home; they simply sleep beside their carts. On the east bank of the Nile,

Cairo's Downtown bookshops are excellent for books on Egypt

opposite Zamalek, again just north of Sharia 26 July, is Bulaq market selling textiles, second-hand clothing, car parts and military surplus. An even stranger mix is presented at the weekly Souq al-Gomaa, or Friday market, held just south of the Citadel, where the trade is in bric-a-brac and animals. It must be one of the few markets where you can buy both a set of 1930s crockery and a squawking cockatoo. Next to Ataba Metro station, just north of Midan Opera, is Al-Azbakiyya Gardens. Here, second-hand books and magazines, many of them in English, are sold from a collection of cabins.

In Alexandria, Attarine is not so much a market as a maze of narrow alleyways lined with antique shops that spill their goods out on to the street. Al-Arish in northern Sinai also has a colourful Thursday morning market frequented by local Bedouin who sell embroidered dresses and distinctive, hand-crafted jewellery.

Stacked merchandise in one of Cairo's markets

Examining the brass- and copperware in Khan al-Khalili

Shopping Centres

Cairo – and Alexandria to a lesser extent – has a rapidly growing number of large shopping centres. These are filled with standard arcade-type outlets that sell everything from greetings cards to electrical goods, most of which are US and European imports. They also usually incorporate fast-food outlets and multiscreen cinemas. **Nile City Towers**, in Rhod al-Farag, is a modern mall with international brands and excellent dining options, as is **Dandy Mall**, which also has a Carrefour hypermarket. The **Mall of Arabia**, on the outskirts of Cairo, has a 4-D cinema and is a popular destination for families. For a chic shopping destination, head to the **First Residence Mall** in Giza, which overlooks the zoo and forms part of an accommodation complex for the rich. The **Ramses Hilton Mall**, adjacent to the Ramses Hilton hotel in the city centre, is more family friendly and offers value-for-money shoes and clothing. On the top floor is a cinema and a snooker hall. Out in Nasr City, the vast **Citystars Centre** has shops galore, an excellent food court and a cinema, making it a popular hangout for local kids.

Buying Antiques

Most antiquities offered to visitors are anything but antique. "Old" papyrus may well have been painted just last week and probably not on papyrus (which has all but vanished) but on dried banana leaves. Similarly, so-called ancient scarabs are often made by carving them from old bone and then feeding them to turkeys – the birds' gastric juices create a realistic ageing effect. However, in some respects this is all just as well because genuine antiquities (in general, anything over 100 years old) can only be exported with a licence from the Department of Antiquities.

How to Bargain

Buying and selling in Egypt is traditionally a highly ritualized affair, in which bargaining is far more than just haggling for a cheap price. The aim of the exercise is to establish a fair price that both vendor and buyer are happy with. As part of the process, a shop-owner may well invite you to have a cup of tea or coffee and may literally turn the place upside down to show something. You should not feel obliged to buy because of this, as it is a common sales practice and all part of the ritual.

Bargaining even happens in city-centre shops over goods which appear to have a fixed price. It is in the souq, however, that it becomes a necessity if you want to avoid paying greatly over the odds.

Once you have identified an article that interests you, especially if it is an expensive one, be brave enough to offer half the price quoted by the shop-owner. Don't be put off by feigned indignation or mockery on the shop-keeper's part, and only raise your next offer by a small amount. Through a process of offer and counter-offer you should eventually arrive at a mutually agreeable price. If you don't reach a price you think is fair then simply say thank you and leave. Making to walk away can often have the effect of bringing the price tumbling down.

In theory, although you may feel uncomfortable, no one gets cheated. You, the buyer, have set the price yourself, so it follows that you are happy with what you have agreed to pay. The shop-keeper, for his part, will never sell at a loss, so he will certainly have made a profit on the deal.

The brightly lit Citystars Centre in Nasr City, Cairo

Where to Shop in Egypt

Cairo's Khan al-Khalili *(see pp92–4)* is the first place to look for Egyptian souvenirs, while city-centre shopping focuses on the triangle of Sharia Talaat Harb, 26 July and Qasr el-Nil. The island suburb of Zamalek is a great hunting ground for boutiques specializing in ethnic crafts, designer wear and antiques. Elsewhere in Egypt, there is less choice for shopaholics; local specialities include colourful textiles and spices in Aswan and pottery and jewellery in the oases.

Souvenirs

Khan al-Khalili in Cairo and other tourist bazaars in Upper Egypt are crammed with incredibly kitsch items, such as Nefertiti reading lamps, alabaster pyramids, stuffed leather camels and Tutankhamun baseball caps.

There are more worthwhile items to be found, however: attractive backgammon boards, like those used in Egyptian coffee houses, at least have a practical purpose. Or you could buy your own *shisha* (waterpipe), though you will also need to stock up on the special tobacco and the small clay pots that the tobacco is stuffed into. Small boxes inlaid with mother-of-pearl are pretty and very inexpensive. Inlaid chessboards are also popular buys. Almost everyone visiting Egypt picks up some "papyrus" – often cheap and poor quality, shoddily painted with scenes copied from Pharaonic wall paintings. For better quality work, visit the **Dr Ragab's Papyrus Institute**, a museum with a shop where you can get the genuine article, which will not crack or have the paint flake off when it is rolled.

Souvenir figure of Anubis

Brass and Copperware

Plates, coffee pots and trays of brass and copper are made in the workshops around Khan al-Khalili. For good examples, have a look at the Coppersmiths' Market (Souq an-Nahassin) in Sharia al-Muizz li-Din Allah, south of the great mosques on Bein al-Qasreen.

Stallholder selling leather belts in Midan Ataba

Handicrafts

Different parts of Egypt are associated with their own particular crafts, but much of the best of this work makes its way to Cairo. For example, **Oum el Duniya**, meaning "Mother of the World" *(see p145)* is a quirky, little shop located just off Midan Tahrir. It carries a full range of high-quality yet reasonably priced locally produced crafts such as ceramics from Fayoum, bags, jewellery and glassware, as well as books on Egypt in English and French. Opposite the entrance to the Mosque of Ibn Tulun, in Islamic Cairo, **Khan Misr Touloun** is a beautiful gallery selling local handicrafts from the villages and oases of Egypt. These include wooden chests, bowls and plates, blown glass, clay figurines, scarves and woven clothing. Based in Zamalek, **Fair Trade Egypt** has Bedouin rugs and embroidery from Sinai and the northern Western Desert, hand-made paper from Muqattam and shawls from Upper Egypt. Also in Zamalek, **Nomad** specializes in jewellery and traditional Bedouin crafts and costumes and **Al-Qahira** sells wrought-iron furniture, wall hangings, glass-ware and locally made leather goods. For crafts, lights and other home furnishings there is the shop **Caravanserai**.

Carpets and Rugs

Unlike Morocco, Turkey or Iran, Egypt is not a big carpet producer. What you will find, however, are hard-wearing, brown-and-beige striped, camel-hair rugs of Bedouin origin. The biggest selection is to be found in the Haret al-Fahhamin, a tight maze of alleys behind the Mosque of Al-Ghouri, across the road from Khan al-Khalili in Islamic Cairo. Many of the places mentioned in the Handicrafts section also stock Bedouin rugs. Connoisseurs might want to visit the weekly markets at Al-Arish, in northern Sinai, and in Dahab. In the area of the

Coppersmith's workshop in Sharia al-Muizz li-Din Allah

Locals gather at one of Cairo's colourful carpet bazaars

Pyramids, just off the road to Saqqara, the **Wissa Wassef Art Centre** specializes in very distinctive woollen rugs and wall hangings depicting rural and folkloric scenes. These can also be bought at **Senouhi**, a fascinating little shop on the fifth floor of an apartment block in Downtown Cairo. Senouhi also sells quality jewellery, antiques, Bedouin rugs and art.

Cloth and Textiles

Cotton is Egypt's biggest cash crop, and department and clothing stores in central Cairo and Alexandria carry excellent quality, plain cotton shirts, T-shirts and underwear. Look out, in particular, for **Nagada** and for branches of Mobaco Cottons, found in all the big malls and in some hotel shopping complexes. Down in Middle Egypt, just across the Nile from Sohag, the village of Akhmim is the centre of an ancient weaving tradition. Legend has it that pharaohs were buried in shrouds of Akhmim silk. Still in production, but now in factories rather than the local workshops, the cloth comes in deep, rich colours, with elaborate floral and paisley-style patterns. It is extremely beautiful, but hard to find. The best bet is to go direct to the factories; otherwise some of the hotel shops in Luxor carry a small selection.

Belly-dancing Costumes

Sequinned bras, beaded hip-bands, veils and flimsy skirts are sold in a couple of specialist shops in Khan al-Khalili. One is in the small passageway leading from Muski to Fishawi's coffee house. Serious practitioners should pay a visit to the studio of **Amira al-Khattan** in Mohandiseen, who tailors costumes to order.

Jewellery

Egypt's gold and silver shops are concentrated in the centre of Khan al-Khalili. Jewellery is sold by weight, with a little extra added for workmanship. The current gold prices are listed each day in the *Egyptian Gazette*. The most popular souvenirs are gold or silver cartouches with a given name engraved in hieroglyphics. Most of the shops in Khan al-Khalili can arrange to have this done.

Spices and Herbs

Khan al-Khalili in Cairo and the souk in Aswan are both excellent for spices. Generally these are fresher and of better quality than any of the packaged variety sold in the West. They are also much cheaper, especially saffron. The stalls that sell spices often also have heaps of purplish, dried hibiscus leaves. When boiled up, strained and sugared, these make *karkade*, the excellent deep-red, iced drink served in coffee houses. Some of the shop owners in the Spice Bazaar are also herbalists, who prepare traditional remedies for a variety of ailments.

A colourful display of aromatic spices in the Spice Bazaar

What to Buy in Egypt

Egypt's magical souqs and bazaars offer the visitor an eclectic mix of trinkets and souvenirs. The quality can vary greatly so always inspect the items closely and be prepared to haggle over the price *(see p295)*. *Shishas* (waterpipes), backgammon boards, decorative boxes and an array of kitsch paraphernalia fill the market stalls alongside traditional handicrafts often made by local artisans. Egyptian copperware and Muski glass are produced in Cairo's Khan al-Khalili *(see pp92–3)*, while Bedouin jewellery traditionally comes from Sinai. The best hand-woven silk and cotton is made in Akhmim in Middle Egypt, famous for the quality of its weaving.

Shishas
A fixture in every coffee house, a waterpipe makes an excellent gift. Decorated with stainless steel or brass fittings, the pipes use a special fragrant tobacco loosely packed into a clay pot.

Backgammon Board
Backgammon and chess are popular pastimes in Egypt. Sets of varying quality are readily available with the cheaper boards being crudely made and with little inlay. The better sets are made out of hard woods and inlaid with intricate designs of mother-of-pearl, bone or ivory.

Sandals
Reasonably priced leather items such as bags, wallets and hand-crafted sandals are sold in most bazaars.

Glass and Pottery
Hand-blown, blue Muski glass is uniquely Egyptian and fashioned into plates, vases, glasses and candle-holders. Good handmade pots, like this sculpted alabaster vase, are also easily found.

Perfume Bottles
These delicate glass perfume bottles are fashioned into intricate shapes. They come in various sizes and make wonderful gifts.

Bedouin Jewellery
Bedouin jewellery traditionally comes from Sinai and Siwa Oasis, and often features coins in its designs. While truly authentic Bedouin jewellery is hard to find, its styles have been widely imitated. Other popular designs include those based on Pharaonic, Islamic and Nubian motifs.

Copperware
A wide range of copper and brass goods is sold throughout Egypt but the Cairo souqs and workshops offer the widest selection. Typical buys include Arabic coffee pots, trays and hanging lamps as well as decorative pieces such as plates embossed with classic arabesques.

Clothes and Textiles

Cotton is one of Egypt's major crops and cotton clothes are popular. Plain and embroidered cotton shirts, trousers and *galabiyyas* (loose, all-in-one robes) are usually of high quality and good value. The brightly coloured fabrics are excellent as scarves, cushion covers, wall hangings and throws. Garish belly-dancing outfits are also popular purchases.

Embroidered cotton shirts

Brightly coloured woven scarf

Sequinned belly-dancing costume

Tourist Souvenirs

A myriad of kitsch reproductions of Pharaonic art, alabaster pyramids, stuffed leather camels, busts of Nefertiti and sheets of papyrus painted with scenes from temples or tombs are sold in all tourist areas. These items, along with trinket boxes, ashtrays, chessboards and *shishas* make popular and inexpensive gifts.

Stuffed leather camel

Papyrus with Pharaonic scenes

Bust of Nefertiti

Carved figurines of ancient gods

Alabaster ashtray

Egyptian Music

The easiest way to re-create the Egyptian experience is to buy some Egyptian CDs. The choice ranges from traditional folk music and the mournful sounds of Umm Kolthum (*see p129*) to modern, bouncy Egyptian pop.

Spices and Flavourings

Colourful and fragrant, Egyptian spices can be located easily in the bazaars. Spices are sold loose by weight and are often far cheaper, fresher and of better quality than the pre-packaged ones sold in the West. One word of caution, however, Egyptian saffron is very cheap but it may not be top quality.

Carob

Cinnamon

Cloves

Chillies

Turmeric

Cayenne pepper

Cardamon pods

Saffron threads

ENTERTAINMENT IN EGYPT

Most people find that the range of entertainment options in Egypt, especially outside Cairo, is surprisingly limited. Locals tend to fill their free time with visits to friends or family, or, in the case of the menfolk, whiling away the hours in a coffee house. A few major, well-attended cultural events punctuate the calendar, notably the Cairo International Book Fair in January and the Cairo International Film Festival in November and December *(see p45)*. Otherwise the annual high spots are tied into religion – the feast days of Eid al-Adha and Eid al-Fitr *(see p43)*, and the holy month of Ramadan. On these occasions, temporary fairgrounds are often set up in main squares, and there are plenty of performances of traditional music and folk dancing. Old Ottoman houses in Islamic Cairo are often the venue for free concerts, so look out for posters in the area which advertise events.

Cairo by night, its bright lights reflected in the calm waters of the Nile

Information

There is no shortage of entertainment guides in Egypt. Each month a glossy magazine called *Egypt Today* is published and includes extensive coverage of artistic and cultural events taking place throughout the country. It is available from bookstands and newsagents everywhere. The weekly English-language newspapers *Al-Ahram Weekly* and *The Middle East Times* also carry good listings information on what is showing at cinemas, galleries and the theatre, although their coverage is limited solely to Cairo. **Cairo 360** and **Cairo Scene** are online magazines that publish up-to-date news on all sorts of events in the capital.

There is no central booking office for shows and concerts, and it is generally necessary to buy tickets from the relevant theatre or concert hall box office. It is also a sensible precaution to book tickets several days in advance if possible.

Arabic Music

Much of the programming at the **Cairo Opera House** and Alexandria's **Sayed Darwish Theatre** involves live performances of Arabic classical music. In Islamic Cairo, particularly during Ramadan, music evenings and theatre productions are held at the **Beit Zeinab Khatoun** and the **Al-Ghouri Palace for Traditional Culture**, part of the historic Al-Ghouri Complex *(see p96)*. It is worthwhile trying to attend one or more of the performances at the Al-Ghouri Complex even if it is only to savour the atmosphere, as the stories are told in Arabic.

Whirling Dervishes

The Wikala of al-Ghouri in Islamic Cairo stages whirling-dervish performances on Mondays, Wednesdays and Saturdays, from 8:30pm. The shows are free. There is fairly limited seating, so go at 6:30pm to collect an advance ticket. It is permitted to take photos but not to film on video. More dance and musical events are held at the **Al-Sawy Culture Wheel**.

Whirling dervish putting on a spectacular performance in Cairo

Belly Dancing

Despite a heritage that dates back to Pharaonic times, modern-day belly dancing owes more to the European experience of Egypt in the 18th and 19th centuries. The sensual movements of the Egyptian dancers, who blended folk, gypsy and Ottoman dances, fired the imaginations of repressed Europeans. It is largely due to their descriptions that the dancing was associated with prostitution. Even dedicated, professional belly dancers, who prefer the term "oriental dancer", get tarred with this brush. The advent of cinema put belly dancing on the big screen, increasing its popularity and making stars of the performers.

Today, despite its popularity, belly dancing still carries a social stigma which discourages Egyptian women from entering the profession, and the gap is increasingly being filled by foreign dancers.

Dancers played an important part in ancient Egyptian ritual and celebration. Their poses, as shown here, clapping or using castanets, are very similar to modern Egyptian dancing.

Salome, in the Bible, asked Herod for the head of John the Baptist as reward for her dancing. Late 19th-century writers added eroticism to the story, resulting in a series of scantily clad cabaret acts as depicted in this 1909 music sheet cover.

Superstar Amira dances at the Giza Pyramids. Although belly dancing's popularity has been hit by the rise of Islamic fundamentalism, its top stars are among Egypt's highest earners.

Belly dancers at nightclubs in Central Cairo perform before mainly male audiences, who look but most definitely do not touch.

Orientalist painters from America and Europe frequently depicted exotic scenes such as this French 1914 lithograph. However, here they ignored the fact that men would not have been allowed in the harem.

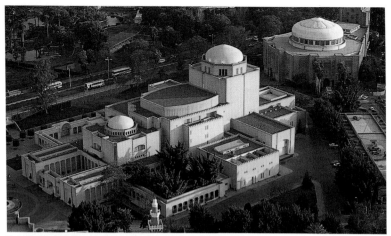

View of the Cairo Opera House from the top of the 185-m (610-ft) Cairo Tower *(see p88)*

Belly Dancing and Folkloric Dance

While the best dancers perform at the nightclubs attached to Cairo's five-star hotels, such as the **Haroun al-Rashid Club** in the Semiramis Hotel, where a seat costs about US $90 a head (buffet included), for pure entertainment visit the much cheaper **Sherherazade** on Sharia Alfy Bey, Downtown. The main act generally does not appear until at least 1am and the band will not call it a night until the sun is rising. Dancers can be seen at most hotels and tourist restaurants in the country. Venues in Luxor and Aswan, such as the **Aswan Cultural Palace**, often feature Egyptian folkloric dance troupes.

Billboards advertising forthcoming cultural events in Cairo

Sound and Light Shows

Every major site in Egypt feels compelled to present a sound and light show. These begin once the sun goes down, and involve the monument being illuminated by coloured floodlights while a recorded voice narrates snippets of history and mythology. The narration often leaves a lot to be desired, but it is worth going just to revisit some of Egypt's

sights by moonlight. The Pyramids at Giza, Luxor, Karnak, Philae, Edfu and Abu Simbel all offer several shows a night in various languages.

Western Classical Music

Egypt's main classical music venue is the **Cairo Opera House** *(see p305)*, on the island of Gezira. Its main hall hosts regular performances from a variety of visiting international artists. On such occasions a jacket and tie is compulsory for men. The small hall has nightly recitals by quartets, soloists and ensembles and is also used by the Cairo Symphony Orchestra, which gives concerts here every Saturday from September to mid-June. The Cairo classical music scene is well covered in *Al-Ahram Weekly*. In Alexandria, both the **Alexandria Conference Hall** and **Sayed Darwish Theatre** host classical concerts organized by the French, Italian or German consulates. Details of what's on are posted in the window of the Elite restaurant. Otherwise, you are unlikely to hear much Western classical music in Egypt.

Opera and Ballet

The premises of the **Cairo Opera House** are shared by both the Cairo Ballet Company and the Cairo Opera Company. The season is limited, and productions are few, although they are sometimes supplemented by visiting companies. There are also occasional dance performances at Cairo's **Gumhuriyya Theatre** *(see p305)*. Almost every year, the Ministry of Culture also mounts a grand production of *Aida*, the opera written in honour of the opening of the Suez Canal *(see pp64–5)*. Previous performances have been held at the temples of Hatshepsut and Karnak in Luxor, but most recently the venue has been the Pyramids. It is a very high-profile occasion, drawing opera-lovers from all over the world. Egypt's overseas tourist offices will be able to provide full details on when the next grand event takes place.

Inside a young and fashionable bar in upmarket Mohandiseen, Cairo

Bars and Discos

Despite being predominantly Islamic, there are plenty of bars in Egypt beyond those in the hotels – look for signs for "cafeterias". Some of the best are to be found in Alexandria, notably the **Spitfire**, one of the city's oldest and most popular bars, which attracts an eclectic crowd. In Cairo, nightlife centres on the upmarket neighbourhoods of Zamalek and Mohandiseen. Bars such as **Deals** and **L'Aubergine** cater mainly for young wealthy Egyptians, as well as the city's large expatriate community. Later on, those with the energy move on to the busy Downtown discos which play hip-hop and dance music.

Red Sea and Sinai resorts such as Sharm el-Sheikh, Naama Bay and Hurghada are also packed full of bars and discos. **Little Buddha** and **Pacha** are the current favourites in Sharm el-Sheikh, while Hurghada now has the very fashionable **Papas Beach Club**.

The resorts along the north Egyptian coast have few good

A hotel disco at Agami, on the North Coast, west of Alexandria

bars or discos, and typically those available are attached to hotels.

Rock, Jazz and Pop

Rock, jazz and pop concerts are virtually unheard of. A handful of artists, such as The Grateful Dead and Shirley Bassey have played the Pyramids, but such events happen very rarely. Egyptian pop stars don't do concerts either. Practically the only place to hear live contemporary music is in hotel lounges and bars like the

Camel Bar at the Camel Hotel in Sharm el-Sheikh. Each Thursday evening this lively bar puts on live bands who play varied styles of music, all good for dancing to. Every major five-star establishment has a resident cabaret singer or jazz quartet, but don't expect to recognize any names. About the only dedicated live venue in the country is the **Cairo Jazz Club**, a small, suitably smoky joint, with a band every night, usually drawn from the tiny but enthusiastic local scene.

DIRECTORY

Information

Cairo 360
W cairo360.com

Cairo Scene
W cairoscene.com

Arabic Music and Whirling Dervishes

Al-Ghouri Palace for Traditional Culture
Sharia al-Muizz li-Din Allah, Cairo.
Map 2 F5.
Tel (011) 5441 8037.

Al-Sawy Culture Wheel
1 Sharia 26 July,
Zamalek, Cairo.
Tel (02) 2736 8881.
W culturewheel.com

Beit Zeinab Khatoun and Beit al-Harawi
Harat al-Azhar, Cairo.
Map 2 F5.
Tel (02) 2510 4174.

Sayed Darwish Theatre
22 Tariq al-Horreyya,
Alexandria.
Tel (03) 486 5106.

Belly Dancing

Aswan Cultural Palace
Corniche, Aswan.
Tel (097) 231 3390.

Haroun al-Rashid Club
Semiramis
InterContinental Hotel,
Corniche el-Nil, Cairo.
Map 5 A4.
Tel (02) 2797 1818.

Sheherazade
Sharia Alfy Bey, Cairo.
Map 2 D4.

Sound and Light Shows

For all sites
Tel (02) 3385 7320.
W soundandlight.
com.eg

Western Classical Music

Alexandria Conference Hall
International Conference
Centre, Shatby,
Alexandria.

Bars and Discos

L'Aubergine
5 Sharia Al-Sayyid al-Bakri,
Zamalek, Cairo. **Map** 1 A3.
Tel (02) 2738 0080.

Deals
1a Sharia al-Sayyid
al-Bakri, Zamalek, Cairo.
Map 1 A3.
Tel (02) 2736 0502.

Little Buddha
Tropitel Naama Bay Hotel,
Sharm el-Sheikh.
Tel (069) 3600 570.

Pacha
Sanafir Hotel,
Sharm el-Sheikh.
Tel (069) 360 0198.

Papas Beach Club
Hurghada Marina
Boulevard,
Hurghada.
Tel (0106) 883 3552.

Spitfire
7 Sharia Old Borsa,
off Sharia Saad
Zaghloul Manshiyya,
Alexandria.
Tel (03) 380 6503.

Rock, Jazz and Pop

Cairo Jazz Club
197 Sharia 26 July,
Mohandiseen,
Cairo.
Tel (02) 3345 9939.
W cairojazzclub.com

Camel Bar
Camel Hotel,
Naama Bay,
Sharm el-Sheikh.
Tel (069) 360 0700.

The Cosmos cinema, one of many local movie houses in Cairo

Cinema

In recent years, cinema in Egypt has had an overhaul. Large, modern multiplexes have been opened in Cairo and Alexandria and old movie houses have been refurbished. Programming is usually split between Arabic films and the latest Hollywood releases, with foreign films screened in their original languages and subtitled in Arabic. All of the films shown suffer censorship except those screened during the Cairo International Film Festival (see p45), where the possibility of seeing exposed flesh on the big screen ensures packed houses.

Colourful advertising for the Diana Palace cinema

A trip to the cinema is an experience in itself. Audiences are always extremely animated, greeting screen events with cheers, boos or applause. In Downtown Cairo, particularly around the Sharia Talaat Harb area, there are many old, single-screen cinemas, several of which, including the **Miami**, **Cosmos** and **Odeon**, show English-language films. Better-equipped cinemas include the **Galaxy** and those located in shopping malls, such as **Stars** in Heliopolis, the **Ramses Hilton** and the **Renaissance**. In Alexandria, the **Amir** is an outstandingly beautiful period cinema, worth a visit for the architecture alone. But by far the most luxurious cinema in Alexandria is the **Renaissance**, attached to the Zahran Mall, to the east of the city centre.

Up-to-date details of all the films currently being screened are published in The Egyptian Gazette, Al-Ahram Weekly and on www.cairo360.com.

Theatre

The numerous local theatres in Cairo are testimony to a strong dramatic tradition in Egypt. Productions are performed in Arabic and are of local fare, typically slapstick comedy with a bit of belly dancing thrown in. Cairo's Downtown area, particularly along Sharia Emad al-Din, is home to several small theatres including the **Gumhuriyya Theatre**. Al-Azhar Park hosts the **Al-Genina Theatre**. Non-Arabic speakers may wish to visit the **Falaki Theatre**. This venue stages a number of plays throughout the year which are performed in English by students of the neighbouring American University in Cairo (see p76). Occasionally, a high-profile theatrical event takes place at the **Cairo Opera House**. In the past, it has received visits from the likes of Britain's Royal Shakespeare Company.

Once a year, the International Experimental Theatre Festival brings in a variety of acting troupes from all around the world to perform at venues throughout Cairo. The Al-Ahram Weekly newspaper is an excellent source of information on all such events. The newspaper also lists details of all the regular theatre performances taking place in Cairo.

Casinos

Many of Egypt's five-star hotels have casinos, open to non-Egyptians only (passports must be shown at the door). All games are conducted in US dollars or other major foreign currencies, with a minimum stake of US $1. The dress code is smart casual. Hotels with casinos include the **Semiramis InterContinental**, the **Cairo Marriott Hotel**, **Conrad Cairo Casino and Hotel** and the **Pyramisa** in Cairo. Note that

Billboard advertising an Arabic theatre production

in Egypt the word "casino" is sometimes used to denote a bar – this is usually the case when it is encountered outside a hotel.

Spectator Sports

Football rules in Egypt. A big match is one of the few times when the country is silent – at least until the final whistle, when the streets fill with flag-waving, horn-honking fans. Footballing life is dominated by Cairo, home to the country's two biggest clubs, Ahly and Zamalek. These clubs, along with Alexandria's Ittihad team, boast players of international standard. Games between Cairo's big clubs are the highlight of the sporting calendar and take place at the **Cairo Stadium** in Medinat Nasr. Tickets for all major games are in high demand and can be difficult to obtain.

Media sports coverage focuses almost entirely on football, even in summer when there are no matches. Of other sports, the most prominent is squash.

Football fans cheering on the Egyptian national soccer team in Cairo

The annual August Al-Ahram International Squash Tournament draws competitors from all over the world to play in glass-enclosed courts set up next to the Pyramids. The Pyramids also feature as the start and finishing point in the annual Pharaoh's Rally, a four-wheel-drive and trail-bike desert race in October. Other spectator sports include rowing races on the Nile every Friday between November and April, and horse racing at the **Gezira Sporting Club** and

the **Alexandria Sporting Club** from October to May. Since the year 2000, there has also been an annual showjumping competition held in the second two weeks of February at the Alexandria Sporting Club. For something more unusual, watch local Bedouin participate in inter-tribe camel-racing as part of the annual Sharm el-Sheikh festival (see p42).

Details of all sporting fixtures are in *The Egyptian Gazette* and *Al-Ahram Weekly*.

DIRECTORY

Cinema

Amir
41 Sharia Horreyya, Alexandria.
Tel (03) 391 7972.

Cosmos
12 Sharia Emad al-Din, Cairo.
Map 2 D3.
Tel (02) 2574 2177.

Galaxy
67 Sharia Abd al-Aziz al-Saud, Al-Manial, Cairo.
Tel (02) 2532 5745.

Miami
38 Talaat Harb, Downtown, Cairo.
Map 5 C2.
Tel (02) 2574 5656.

Odeon
4 Sharia Dr Abdel-Hamid Sayed, Downtown, Cairo.
Map 5 C2.
Tel (02) 2576 5642.

Ramses Hilton
Ramses Hilton Annexe, Sharia al-Galaa, Downtown, Cairo.
Map 5 B2.
Tel (02) 2574 7436.

Renaissance
Nile City, Corniche el-Nil, Bulaq, Cairo.
Map 1 B2.
Tel (02) 2471 9101.
Dandy Mall, Cairo–Alexandria Desert Road, Cairo.
Tel (0100) 002 1215.
Zahran Mall, Semouha, Alexandria.

Stars
Citystars Center, Heliopolis, Cairo.
Tel (02) 2480 2012/2015.

Theatre

Al-Genina Theatre
Al-Azhar Park, Cairo.
Map 2 F5.
Tel (02) 2362 5057.

Cairo Opera House
Sharia at-Tahrir, Gezira, Cairo.
Map 1 A5.
Tel (02) 2739 0144 (info); (02) 2737 0602 (info & box office).
W cairoopera.org

Falaki Theatre
24 Sharia Falaki, Downtown, Cairo.
Map 5 C4.
Tel (012) 8872 1446

Gumhuriyya Theatre
12 Sharia al-Gumhuriyya, Cairo.
Map 6 D3.
Tel (02) 2390 7707.

Casinos

Cairo Marriott Hotel
Saray al-Gezira, Zamalek.
Map 1 A4.
Tel (02) 2728 3000.

Conrad Cairo Casino and Hotel
1191 Corniche el-Nil, Cairo. **Tel** (02) 2580 8000.
W hilton.com

Pyramisa Hotel
60 Sharia el-Giza, Giza, Cairo. **Map** 3 A2.
Tel (02) 3336 7000.

Semiramis InterContinental
Corniche el-Nil, Cairo.
Map 1 B5.
Tel (02) 2795 7171.

Spectator Sports

Alexandria Sporting Club
Mahatet al-Riada, Alexandria.
Tel (03) 542 0435.

Cairo Stadium
Medinat Nasr, Cairo.
Tel (02) 2260 7863.

Gezira Sporting Club
Zamalek, Cairo. **Map** 1 A4.
Tel (02) 2735 2272.

Coffee-House Culture

Found on almost every street corner, the ubiquitous coffee house (*ahwa*) plays an important role in the everyday life of Egyptians. Like the cafés of continental Europe, *ahwas* are social places where Egyptians can meet to talk with friends, idle away an hour reading a newspaper, or watch football on TV. Frequented predominantly by men, coffee houses are busy at all hours of the day and many remain open around the clock. As well as tea (*shai*) and coffee (*ahwa*), most serve fresh lemon juice (*lamoon*), iced *karkade*, a refreshing crimson drink made from boiled hibiscus leaves, *zabaady*, a yogurt drink and *sahleb*, a warm drink made with semolina powder, milk and chopped nuts. No coffee house would be complete without the *shisha* (waterpipe) through which tobacco is smoked.

Chess is common in Egypt and a few coffee houses are venues for fans of the game, including the popular Horreyya situated in Downtown Cairo.

Backgammon and dominoes are the most popular of the coffee-house games with animated players slamming down their pieces.

A typical coffee house, such as Fishawi's in Khan al-Khalili, is often little more than a collection of old tables and chairs placed in a narrow alleyway.

Shishas (waterpipes) are offered in coffee houses as an accompaniment to drinks. The tobacco is soaked in molasses or sometimes apple juice.

Coffee houses are often all-male environments but foreign women are usually welcomed.

Children's Entertainment

When the heat of Cairo becomes too much, **Dr Ragab's Pharaonic Village** can provide a welcome break and keep children thoroughly entertained. The village is an ancient Egypt theme park situated on the southern tip of Al-Qorsaiah Island which lies on the west bank of the Nile, 10 km (6 miles) south of the city centre. Visitors take small boats through the reed beds viewing scenes of Pharaonic daily life re-created by costumed actors. The park also boasts a replica temple.

The **Cairo Puppet Theatre**, just north of Midan Opera, gives performances of traditional tales like Sindbad and Ali Baba. The plays take place most mornings from October to May and although in Arabic, they are highly visual and easy to follow. Another alternative is the **Cairo Zoo** in Giza. The zoo is set in pleasant grounds on the west bank of the Nile opposite Rhoda Island. Although promises have been made regarding improving conditions, some may find the animal enclosures distressing.

On the outskirts of Cairo are several amusement parks. **Dream Park**, northwest of Cairo, has Disney-type rides, go-karts and games arcades, as well as golf and tennis courts. **Aquapark**, 32 km (20 miles) east of Cairo, offers waterchutes, a wave pool and a playground area. The nearby theme park **Gero Land** also has roller-coasters, go-karts and other thrill rides. Elsewhere in Egypt

Children enjoying themselves at the fairground of a local festival

there are few concessions made to children's entertainment. However, activities are often laid on for children during *moulids* (saints' days) and other festivals. At the coast, many of the bigger resort hotels now run activity centres designed to keep younger guests amused.

Coffee Houses

There is an abundance of coffee houses (*ahwas*) in Egypt, each one filling its own niche and frequented by its own particular clientele. Several of the more interesting coffee houses are tucked away down tight alleys and include the Downtown **Shams Gedid**, notable for its garishly painted walls. One of the oldest and most famous of all the coffee houses is **Fishawi's** *(see p90)*. Buried in the narrow lanes of Khan al-Khalili, it is open 24 hours and is as much a must-see sight for visiting

out-of-town Egyptians as it is for foreigners. In Alexandria, coffee houses line the Corniche, while in Aswan and Luxor there are several dotted around the busy souq areas.

Weddings

Thursday night is the end of the Muslim week and the traditional night for weddings in Egypt. Throughout the country celebrations are heralded with drums, tambourines, honking cars and women wailing. Weddings are very public affairs, where musicians, dancing processions and showers of rose petals fill the streets, and foreign spectators are often invited to join the celebrations.

DIRECTORY

Children's Entertainment

Aquapark
Sharia Ismailia.
Tel (02) 2477 2245.

Cairo Puppet Theatre
Al-Azbakiyya Gardens, Cairo.
Map 6 D2. **Tel** (02) 2591 0954.

Cairo Zoo
Sharia al-Giza, Giza, Cairo.
Tel (02) 3570 8895.

Dr Ragab's Pharaonic Village
3 Sharia al-Bahr al-Azam,
Corniche el-Nil, Giza, Cairo.
Tel (02) 3571 8675.
W pharaonicvillage.com

Dream Park
Sharia el-Wahat, 6th October City.
Tel (02) 3855 3191 or 19355.
W dreamparkegypt.com

Gero Land
El-Obour City, Sharia Ismailia.
Tel (02) 4482 8230.

Coffee Houses

Fishawi's
Khan al-Khalili, Cairo. **Map** 2 F5.

Horreyya
Midan al-Falaki, Sharia at-Tahrir,
Cairo. **Map** 5 C3.

Shams Gedid
Souq al-Tawfiqiyya, Cairo.
Map 1 C5, 5 C3.

A young child enjoying the beach at the resort of Dahab

OUTDOOR ACTIVITIES AND SPECIALIST HOLIDAYS

Egypt's varied terrain – from the expansive plains and oases of the Western Desert to the rugged hills of the Sinai, and from the clear waters and colourful coral reefs of the Red Sea to the unique wetlands of the Nile Delta – offers an exciting range of activities for outdoor enthusiasts.

Year-round clement weather makes Egypt the ideal destination for all outdoor sports, and many five-star resorts around Hurghada and Sharm el-Sheikh, as well as several luxury hotels in Cairo, offer world-class golf and tennis facilities. Elsewhere, the choice of activities ranges from scuba diving and water-skiing to hot-air ballooning; from horse and camel riding to four-wheel-drive safaris across the desert.

Hot-air ballooning over the Valley of the Queens, Thebes

Adventure Packages

Specialist holidays can be booked directly with UK tour operators such as **Abercrombie & Kent Travel**, **Explore Worldwide**, **Egypt Uncovered** and **Exodus Travels**, or in the USA, with **Overseas Adventure Travel**. Most adventure holidays can also be arranged on arrival through travel-agency desks at most large hotels, or through local tour operators.

Holidays off the beaten track can be arranged to suit all budgets and comfort zones: from desert safaris, sleeping in tents, to air-conditioned four-wheel-drive journeys with luxury accommodation.

The rugged interior of the Sinai peninsula is popular for climbing and hiking tours, while the extreme environment of the Western Desert offers different type of adventure.

An organized safari is the only way to experience the thrill of desert driving and camping, with experienced English-speaking guides and drivers, as well as a cook to prepare most meals. Trips into the desert from oases such as Kharga or Bahariyya are offered by many hotels and guest-houses in these areas.

The best season for a holiday off the beaten track is winter (Nov–Mar), when temperatures during the day are tolerable and nights are cool, even chilly.

Visitors intending to take an adventure holiday should ensure that their travel insurance offers adequate cover, including emergency medical evacuation.

Ballooning

Hot-air balloon flights over the Valley of the Kings are run by several companies, such as **Sky Cruise**, **Hod Hod Soliman**, **Sindbad** and **Vikings**. Flights generally lift off early in the morning and take in the ancient sites, the surrounding mountains and the Nile. They often end with a champagne picnic at the landing site.

Diving and Snorkelling

Renowned for the clarity of its waters and the variety of its spectacular corals and fish, the Red Sea offers a wide range of submarine habitats – from remote seamounts that attract large open-water species such as sharks and barracuda, to inshore, shallow-water reefs.

All the larger resort on the southern tip of the Sinai peninsula, the Gulf of Aqaba and the coast near Hurghada have dive clubs. As well as short trips to nearby dive sites, specialist dive operators offer live-aboard cruises that allow divers to spend up to two weeks at sea.

An underwater encounter with Lyretail Anthias fish in the Red Sea

Many dive clubs also offer a variety of courses. Before signing up for these, make sure that the dive centre is certified by a reputable international organization such as **PADI** or the **British Sub Aqua Club (BSAC)**. Recommended dive centres can be found on the websites of either of these organizations. Information, availability and reservations for numerous dive centres at all Red Sea resorts can also be found at www.goredsea.com.

The prestigious El Gouna resort complex has nine diving centres offering courses at all levels, including junior open-water diving courses for children.

For non-divers, snorkelling over shallow reefs is a great alternative. Most dive centres rent masks, fins and snorkels, but the masks are often old or leaky; bring your own, or buy a new one on arrival. For more on diving, see pp312–13.

Feluccas gliding lazily on the Nile

Windsurfing lesson at a beach on the Sinai peninsula

Watersports

Both the Mediterranean and the Red Sea coasts offer excellent powered watersports. Water-skiing, jet-skiing and parascending are available at most beaches. All the major resort hotels have their own watersports centres. These may be a little more expensive than independent operations nearby, but they usually offer better-quality, more reliable equipment and trained English-speaking staff.

Wind and water conditions are reliably excellent for windsurfing at the Sinai resorts of Sharm el-Sheikh, Dahab, Taba and Nuweiba, with consistent cross-shore winds, shallow

waters for novices, and larger swells further offshore that allow experts to use their jumping skills. Kiteboarding is also increasingly popular. Equipment for both sports can be rented at all resorts.

Felucca Sailing

The journey down the Nile from Aswan to Edfu by felucca takes two to three days. Boats with crew can be chartered at Aswan, where hundreds of feluccas are based and boat owners eagerly approach visitors to offer their services. In theory, prices are set by the government and the tourist office in Aswan can provide clear guidance as to the cost. In practice, however, many extra charges must also be negotiated.

Felucca travellers must bring necessities such as toilet paper, a torch and batteries, mosquito repellent and/or a mosquito net and alcoholic beverages if required. Boat owners provide food, water and soft drinks for an extra charge, which must also be negotiated. Felucca travellers can sleep on board under the stars or arrange hotel or guesthouse accommodation for each night along the way. For more information, see p316.

Fishing

The huge expanse of Lake Nasser, the world's largest artificial lake, offers anglers some of the best fishing in the world. The catch here is likely to be tiger fish and

the giant Nile perch. Fly-fishing can also be practised, as can bait fishing for catfish, including the giant vundu, one of the world's largest freshwater fish. Boats with crew may be hired in Aswan through **The African Angler**. Equipment can also be hired.

Golf and Tennis

Many five-star resorts around Cairo and on the Red Sea boast superb golf courses, often flanked by floodlit tennis courts. One of the most impressive courses is the 36-hole Karl Litten-designed **Dreamland Golf Course**, at the Dreamland City leisure development on the outskirts of Cairo. It also has floodlit tennis courts for night play. Other golf and tennis resorts around Cairo include **Katameya Heights**, with a 27-hole course and 10 clay courts, and **Mirage City**, part of the JW Marriott, near the airport. Elsewhere, near Naama Bay, the **Maritim Jolie Ville Golf Resort** has a good international course.

The golfing green at Katameya Heights, not far from Cairo

Bird-watching

Egypt is a rich environment for bird-watchers. There are around 150 resident bird species, but these are outnumbered by the 280 or more species that use one of the world's greatest migration corridors, between Eurasia and southern Africa. Millions of migratory birds traverse the Egyptian skies each year, with waves of storks, raptors and other migrants heading north from mid-February until April, and returning southward from August until early November. Organized birding package tours are available through **Sarus Bird Tours** and **Travel Egypt**.

Horse and Camel Riding

Visitors to the Pyramids are usually approached by touts offering rides on mangy camels or flea-bitten nags. These are best avoided. Instead, rent a mount and guide in advance from a reputable livery stable, such as **Sheikh Tarek's AA** or **Recoub Al Sorat**, both in Giza. The latter offers countryside trail rides as well as rides around the Pyramids of Giza and Saqqara. At Sharm el-Sheikh, the Hotel Sofitel has an excellent stable offering desert rides.

A yacht moored at the small harbour of Giftun Island

Spas

Scarlet ibis

Thanks to a boom in luxury resort developments, Egypt now has hotels with deluxe spa, health and beauty facilities to match any in the world. The prime spots for such hotels are Sharm el-Sheikh, which has the **Four Seasons**, the **Ritz-Carlton** and the **Hyatt Regency**; the purpose-built luxury resort of **El Gouna**, with its cluster of world-class hotels; and the international brand hotels of Cairo and its suburbs, such as **Le Meridien Heliopolis** and the **Oberoi Sahl Hasheesh**. The five-star **Angsana Spa** at the Mövenpick Resort & Spa El Gouna, is the first of its kind on the Red Sea. Managed by the award-winning Banyan Tree group, it offers an array of holistic and contemporary spa treatments. El Gouna's lavish golf clubhouse at the El Gouna resort complex also houses a chic spa that offers Thai, Swedish and shiatsu massages, traditional Egyptian body-scrub treatments, a gym, sauna and Turkish baths. Hotels at all Egyptian destinations offer inclusive spa packages, and guests can also book spa, health and beauty treatments on an ad hoc basis on arrival.

Yachting and Motor Cruising

There are large marinas at ports such as Hurghada and El Gouna, where the Abu Tig Marina and Abydos Marina are rated the finest in the Red Sea. Sailing yachts – either crewed or on a bareboat basis – can be chartered at both Hurghada and El Gouna.

Oasis and Desert Safaris

The Western Desert is an exciting destination for four-wheel-drive safaris using specially equipped desert vehicles with long-range fuel tanks, global satellite positioning (GPS), satellite communications equipment and trained drivers. The **Badawiya Expedition Travel** offers four-wheel-drive safaris through the White Desert. Oases easily accessible from the Nile corridor include Bahariyya, Farafra, Dakhla and Kharga, while longer-range desert safaris travel into the Great Sand Sea, and as far west as Siwa, or head for lesser-known oases such as Areg, Bahrein and Ain Della.

Horse riding around the Pyramids at Giza

Walking

Egypt offers walkers several spectacular walking routes. The St Catherine Protectorate region of southern Sinai peninsula is a hiker's paradise of jagged mountains, natural springs and forgotten ruins. Hikers must be accompanied by a local guide.

Sheik Mousa organizes trekking tours led by Bedouins in the mountains of the Sinai. Treks include the well-trodden Mount Sinai, the summit of Jebel Abbas Pasha and gentler walks along dry river beds. Treks can also be arranged at St Catherine's village; for information, visit the Visitors' Centre at St Catherine's Monastery (see pp226–9).

A number of specialist tour operators in the UK, mainland Europe and North America also offer various escorted walking packages.

Another focus for walking holidays is the Bahariyya Oasis in the Western Desert. Several specialist operators such as Badawiya Expedition Travel offer treks with Bedouin guides and accommodation in tents or village guesthouses.

DIRECTORY

Adventure Packages

Abercrombie & Kent Travel
St Georges House, Ambrose Street, Cheltenham, Gloucestershire, UK.
Tel 01242 547 760.
W abercrombiekent.co.uk

Egypt Uncovered
Leigh House, Varley Street, Leeds, West Yorkshire LS28 6AN, UK.
Tel (0800) 088 6002.
W egypt-uncovered.com

Exodus Travels
Grange Mills, Weir Road, London SW12 0NE, UK.
Tel (0845) 287 3751.
W exodus.co.uk

Explore Worldwide
Tel (012) 5288 3918.
W explore.co.uk

Overseas Adventure Travel
1 Mifflin Place, Suite 400, Cambridge, MA 02138, USA. **Tel** 1-800 493 6824.
W oattravel.com

Ballooning

Hod Hod Soliman
Luxor.
Tel (095) 227 0116.

Sindbad
37 Sharia Abd El Hameed El Omda, Luxor.
Tel (010) 0538 5533.

Sky Cruise
Luxor.
Tel (010) 1816 1677.

Vikings
Luxor.
Tel (095) 227 7212.

Diving and Snorkelling

BSAC
W bsac.com

Colona Dive Centre and Live-Aboards
W colona.com

Deep Blue Divers
W divedahab.com

The Dive Connection
W diveconnection.com

Emperor Divers
W emperordivers.com

Euro Divers
W euro-divers.com

Oonas Dive Club
W oonasdiveclub.com

PADI
W padi.com

Sinai Divers
W sinaidivers.com

Fishing

The African Angler
PO Box 191, Aswan.
Tel (097) 230 9748.
W african-angler.co.uk

Golf and Tennis

Dreamland Golf Course
Dreamland City, Alwahat Road, Cairo.
Tel (02) 3855 3164.
W dreamlandgolf.com

Katameya Heights Golf and Tennis Resort
New Cairo City, Cairo.
Tel (02) 2758 0512.
W katameyaheights.com

Maritim Jolie Ville Golf Resort
Um Marikha Bay, Sharm el-Sheikh.
Tel (069) 360 0635.
W maritim.com

Mirage City
JW Marriott Hotel, Ring Road, Cairo. **Tel** (02) 411 5588. W marriott.com

Bird-watching

Sarus Bird Tours
12 Walton Drive, Walmersley, Bury BL9 5JU, UK. **Tel** (0161) 761 7279.
W sarusbirdtours.co.uk

Travel Egypt (World Explorer Tours and Travel)
724 Charlie Smith Sr. Hwy #5010, Saint Marys, GA 31558, USA.
Tel (888) 999 2354.
W travelegypt.com

Horse and Camel Riding

Recoub Al Sorat
Mamouneya Road, Giza.
Tel (0122) 211 8386.
W alsorat.com

Sheikh Tarek's AA
Tarek Abu Aziza, Giza.
Tel (0122) 296 0749.

Spas

Angsana Spa
Mövenpick Resort El Gouna, El Gouna.
Tel (065) 354 4501.
W moevenpick-hotels.com

El Gouna Resorts
Tel (02) 2461 6131.
W elgouna.com

Four Seasons Sharm el-Sheikh
1 Four Seasons Boulevard, Sharm el-Sheikh.
Tel (069) 360 3555.
W fourseasons.com

Hyatt Regency Sharm el-Sheikh Resort
Gardens Bay, Sharm el-Sheikh.
Tel (069) 360 1234.
W sharmelsheikh.regency.hyatt.com

Le Meridien Heliopolis
51 El Orouba Street, Heliopolis, Cairo.
Tel (02) 2290 5055.
W starwoodhotels.com

Oberoi Sahl Hasheesh
Safaga, Red Sea.
Tel (010) 0600 5104.
W oberoihotels.com

Ritz-Carlton Sharm el-Sheikh
Om el-Seed, Sharm el-Sheikh.
Tel (069) 366 1919.
W ritzcarlton.com

Oasis and Desert Safaris

Badawiya Expedition Travel
21 Sharia Youssef El Guindy, Cairo.
Tel (02) 2390 6429.
W badawiya.com

Walking

Sheik Mousa
St Catherine's, Sinai.
Tel (0100) 641 3575 or (0100) 688 0820.
W sheikmousa.com

Scuba Diving and Snorkelling

Clear waters and abundant sea life make the Gulf of Sinai one of the world's finest dive destinations, with something for every skill level: from inshore reefs and submarine canyons to shipwrecks and blue holes. The major resorts – Hurghada, Sharm el-Sheikh, El-Gouna and Dahab – have numerous dive centres where you can rent equipment. Dive centres all offer internationally recognized learn-to-dive courses. Do a little research and ensure that your dive centre of choice is approved by a reputable organization such as PADI or the British Sub Aqua Club (BSAC). Shallow reefs close to the shore, often in only a few metres of water, offer ideal conditions for snorkelling.

The impressive colours of the Red Sea

① **The Thistlegorm wreck at Sha'ab Ali**, probably the Red Sea's most famous wreck site, lies in 20–30 m (65–100 ft) of water, on the bed of the Straits of Gubal. Legendary diver Jacques Cousteau discovered this wartime wreck in the 1950s but kept its location secret, and it was not until 1992 that it was rediscovered.

⑥ **Shaab Umm Qamar**, a sloping reef wall close to a tiny rocky islet not far offshore from Hurghada, is a magnet for marine life, especially schools of pelagic and reef species, all of which are accustomed to divers and very approachable. The wreck of a fishing boat at 25 m (80 ft) is an attractive focus for divers, and there is plentiful coral. Sharks are sometimes seen.

0 kilometres 140
0 miles 60

Gulf of Suez

Hurghada
Safa

Dive-Site Ratings

Dive sites here range from novice-friendly shallow reefs to deep-water dives that should be attempted only by experienced divers with qualified guides.

	Snorkelling	Novice Diving	Advanced Diving	Expert Diving
① Thistlegorm			•	•
② The Bells			•	•
③ The Islands	•	•	•	•
④ The Blue Hole	•	•	•	•
⑤ Shark's Bay	•	•	•	•
⑥ Shaab Umm Qamar	•	•	•	•
⑦ The Brothers	•		•	•
⑧ Safaga	•	•	•	•

⑧ **Safaga (Kilo 32 North)** is a shore-entry dive site south of Port Safaga, where bottlenose dolphins, turtles and a wide variety of reef fish may be seen in depths of 20–35 m (65–115 ft). Reef walls pierced by crannies and caves surround a shallow bay and are covered by large coral heads and soft corals.

② **The Bells** is located north of Dahab in depths from 25–50 m (80–160 ft). This is a site for experienced divers only, who descend into a 5-m (16-ft) wide chimney that extends into the open sea at 30 m (100 ft). As well as plenty of marine life, you are likely to see black-and-white coral, and plate and cabbage coral.

Getting to the Dive Sites

Dive centres offer boat trips to inshore reefs and wrecks, or minibus rides to walk-in dive sites. Some of the Red Sea's best dive sites can be reached only on a live-aboard dive cruise. Currents can be strong, and diving with a guide who knows the area well is highly recommended.

Getting There: Hurghada, Sharm el-Sheikh and Marsa Alam airports receive flights from Europe and Cairo, Luxor and Alexandria. Access to Nuweiba and Dahab is by bus, minibus or taxi from Sharm el-Sheikh; Safaga is reached by road from Hurghada.

④ **The Blue Hole** is a shore-entry dive close to Dahab. On a good day, the 102-m (335-ft) deep hole should yield jacks, barracuda and reef sharks. The outer slope of the reef enclosing the lagoon offers corals, fissures and shoals of numerous fish species. The Blue Hole also attracts snorkellers.

Nuweiba

④
hab

ikh

③ **The Islands**, a shore-entry, shallow-water dive near Dahab, is a great beginners' dive, in depths of 12–16 m (40–50 ft), with superbly preserved coral, spectacular scenery and wide-ranging marine life from turtles to barracuda. One of the most rewarding dives on this coast.

Red

Sea

Snorkelling off the beach at Dahab

⑤ **Shark's Bay**, just north of Na'ama Bay near Sharm el-Sheikh, is a novice-friendly dive in just 20 m (65 ft) of water. Superb soft corals line a sandy underwater canyon haunted by lyre-tail coralfish; eagle rays, barracuda and sharks are sometimes seen in the deeper water. Angelfish, parrot fish, grouper, wrasse and moray eels also inhabit the reef, while rays favour the sandy bottom.

Octopus found off the shores of Sinai

⑦ **The Brothers** is one of Egypt's most impressive dive sites. These two rocky islets are the tops of twin deep-water reefs, covered by magnificent corals, that attract huge numbers of reef and open-water fish, including large sharks. Features include a vertical wall, shallow reefs and two shipwrecks. Accessible only by live-aboard boat, the Brothers is never crowded; some cruises allow up to a week's diving here.

Turtle in a swim-through

NILE CRUISES

Nothing beats sitting on the deck of a slow-moving boat as it glides elegantly along the Nile. Cruising combines transport and accommodation to provide the most relaxing way of exploring the major cultural sites, as well as those that are otherwise difficult to get to. The on-board guides, many of them qualified Egyptologists, are on hand to explain the history of each site and outline their most important architectural features.

The Nile is home to hundreds of cruise boats and feluccas. Many tour operators offer cruises as part of a package holiday to the region. Flights arrive at Luxor and Aswan airports, and direct transfers are laid on to get you to your cruise ship.

View of the Nile from the deck of a cruise ship

When To Go

The best time for a Nile cruise is from November to February, when it is not too hot. However, this means that resorts like Luxor and Aswan tend to become unpleasantly overcrowded. It also means that prices are higher than at other times of the year, and the opportunities for bargains greatly reduced. From March to April and from October to early November, the weather is still pleasant, but there are fewer visitors, and prices drop. From May to October is the hottest season and not the best time to enjoy cruising. Having said that, if you are not bothered by the heat, this is when the best bargains can be found. At this time the Nile is at its lowest level because of the need to conserve water at the Aswan Dam; this can make it difficult for the boats to navigate. If locks on the Nile are closed, operators arrange boats on either side of the locks and you then transfer between them.

Nile Cruising as a Package Deal

Romanticized by countless films and novels, cruising on the Nile has been a popular tourist pastime since the 19th century, when visiting Egypt's ancient sights was a highlight of the Grand Tour. Since then, cruising has developed into a hugely profitable industry, with an incredible selection of boats plying the river between Aswan and Luxor. The simplest way of organizing a Nile cruise is to book an inclusive package holiday

The elegant, luxurious interior of a cruise ship on the Nile

from home. This will include flights to Egypt, where you will join your cruise boat. Trips vary in length and may be one-way or include the return journey.

A typical trip will start in Luxor and Thebes *(see pp186–207)*, with visits to the Luxor Temple and the Temple of Amun at Karnak. Following a night on board the cruise ship, an organized excursion leaves the next morning for the Valley of the Kings and a few of the more famous tombs, including that of Tutankhamun and possibly those of Ramses VI and Tuthmosis III. Some tours may also include a visit to the Ramesseum, the mortuary Temple of Ramses II. On your way back to the boat, you will stop at the two huge statues known as the Colossi of Memnon.

The cruise ship then leaves Luxor heading south towards Aswan and stopping en route to visit various ancient temples and settlements. As the boat sails slowly along the river, you can unwind by sitting under a sun shade on deck, reading a book or joining some of the many activities that are included in the price. Or you can just relax while Egypt moves slowly past you. Fishermen in feluccas, old men on donkeys and small children on the river bank will all wave to you in much the same way as their ancestors would have done to the pharaohs several millennia ago.

Since your accommodation, transport and meals are included in the price – as are on-board entertainment, entrance fees to the sites and the services of professional guides – most trips offer good value for money. There are always some excellent deals available on Nile cruising holidays, and it does pay to shop around. Before booking, check carefully exactly what is included in the price.

Cruises offered as part of package holidays are generally reliable and of a consistent standard. **Sonesta Nile Cruises** is a tried and trusted American-based operator with offices in Cairo. Its modern fleet consists of five ships built between 1989 and 2006, ranging in size from 33 suites to 65 cabins. Depending on which vessel you choose, facilities include swimming pools, lounge bars and restaurants. Evening entertainment is provided in the form of discos, belly dancers and Nubian shows. Air-conditioned cabins are en suite and come with satellite television, video players, minibars and safety deposit boxes. On the more luxurious ships, you might also find a jogging track or a spa with gym, massage, sauna and Jacuzzi, and extras in the cabins like private telephones, wireless internet access with laptop and private dining until midnight.

During your cruise down the Nile, you are likely to visit the Temple of Dendara (see pp182–3) in Qena, the Temple of Horus in Edfu (see p208) and the Temple of Kom Ombo (see

The Temple of Kom Ombo at sunset

p209). In Aswan (see pp212–15) the shore-based itinerary includes visits to the Aga Khan Mausoleum, the High Dam granite quarries and the Temple of Philae (see p216).

Falcon statue at the Temple of Horus, Edfu

For cruising on a more intimate and luxurious scale, **dahabiya** boats hark back to the glory days of the 19th century, when travellers to Egypt spent weeks or months drifting down the Nile. Several companies now offer these wooden boats for trips between Esna and Aswan, hosting small groups of guests and exploring interesting sites along the way. As the boats are smaller than the cruise ships, they can moor in quiet locations and time visits to temples in order to avoid crowds. The decor is often colonial, meals are taken on deck and tranquillity reigns. **Nour el-Nil**'s fleet of four boats has attentive crews

and gorgeous decor and has trips between Esna and Aswan. Another attractive option is the Lake Nasser cruises run by **Belle Epoque**, between Aswan and Abu Simbel, which offer as intimate an atmosphere as a dahabiya but on slightly larger vessels.

Nile Cruising

From the 1980s until 2012, visitors who were based in Cairo but wanted to cruise the Nile had to travel to Luxor or Aswan and join a ship there. The route from Cairo is now open again, and several cruises make the journey to Luxor (10 days) and Aswan (14 days).

River buses travel regularly up and down the Nile and are good for day trips to Qanater (see p173). However, if you are based in Cairo, Alexandria or the Sinai peninsula and want to visit the ancient monuments of the Nile Valley, you may decide that a cruise is the best way of doing this. Because of the proliferation of boats offering such excursions, cruises are easy to arrange through the major hotels, including the Sheraton, Oberoi and Hilton. The best deals, however, are generally found through local agents or by dealing directly with the boatmen in Luxor or Aswan. Prices vary greatly, depending on the level of luxury offered. Shop around and check out the facilities on board before confirming the booking. Always ensure that you know what is included in the fare.

The hustle and bustle of a port on the banks of the Nile

Enjoying a felucca trip on the Nile

Felucca Trips

No holiday in Egypt would be complete without a trip in a felucca, a working boat of a design that has been used by Nile fishermen for hundreds of years. These vessels are available for short trips or longer cruises. Most felucca trips, however, are fairly short and cannot be compared in any way to the luxurious cruises on what are really floating hotels.

Facilities on feluccas range between the primitive and the nonexistent. You won't have a cabin and will have to sleep on the open deck, under the stars. This is an excellent way to get a true appreciation of the Nile.

The most popular felucca trips are between Aswan and Edfu. Travellers can sail from Aswan to Kom Ombo or Edfu, and continue on to Luxor by road. In winter, when the weather is most favourable, the journey to Kom Ombo takes one night, while the trip to Edfu takes at least two nights. Since the journey upstream from Luxor to Aswan depends heavily on the wind, most travellers start the journey in Aswan and travel downstream. To arrange a day trip, simply walk along the banks of the Nile at Aswan and Luxor. You'll be hailed by boat skippers all looking for work. Decide on a felucca you like the look of,

tell the skipper what you want, and then haggle over the price.

Another option in Luxor is to hire a felucca to take you across the Nile and pick up a taxi to tour the sites. The skipper may offer to make a taxi arrangement on your behalf. It is probably best to turn down all such offers politely but firmly – as soon as you dock, you will be besieged by waiting taxi drivers, so you can negotiate your own deal. Do not ask the skipper to wait until you return or to come back for you at a prearranged time, either. That might prove costly, and there are plenty of boats about, or you can take the ferry.

Felucca trips from Aswan are best arranged with the help of the tourist office, who can recommend good captains and

A member of the crew washing up on board a felucca

quote official rates, whereas hotels will add on a commission.

Prices vary according to the season and demand, so these rates should be taken as a starting point for negotiation. Note that, in some cases, "all inclusive" may not guarantee that water, or even food, is included, so always check.

Ensure that your felucca is stocked with the following: a water container (such as a jerry can); a shade awning; a kerosene stove and lamp; utensils and cutlery; and a luggage hold with a lock. Nights are very cold on the river, so make sure that the felucca has plenty of blankets. Better still, take a sleeping bag with you. Also take some water and some back-up food with you just in case. Three litres (5 pints) of drinking water per person per day is the minimum; this does not include water for cooking. To ensure that you have a pleasant experience, hats, sunscreen and insect repellent are also essential.

Hygiene can be a serious issue on feluccas. Treat the Nile water used for washing up with sterilizing tablets and take extra care to wash your hands before handling food. Bear in mind that you will be going to the toilet on the riverbank, so take sufficient supplies of toilet paper for the duration of your trip. It is also wise to take a torch for possible night-time excursions to the riverbank. Burn all rubbish, and bury bodily waste to avoid polluting the banks of the Nile.

You can take a dip in the Nile between Aswan and Luxor, where it is still blue and welcoming, as the only crocodiles are above the High Dam in the waters of Lake Nasser. The Nile is, however, infested with parasitic worms, the larvae of which penetrate the skin causing bilharzia, an infection also known as snail fever or swimmer's itch. The mortality rate is very low, but the disease is debilitating. Locals insist you will be fine in fast-moving waters but the sluggish banks are best avoided.

DIRECTORY

Nile Cruise Tour Operators

IN EGYPT

Abercrombie & Kent
18 Sharia Yusuf al-Gindi, Cairo. **Map** 5 C4.
Tel (02) 2393 6255.
w abercrombiekent. com

Airlink Travel
6A Sharia Fouah, Mohandiseen, Cairo.
Tel (02) 3302 6243/4.
w airlinktravelegypt. com

Belle Epoque Travel Bureau
17 Sharia Tunis, Maadi, Cairo.
Tel (02) 2358 0265.
w dahabiya.com

Blue Sky Travel
44 Sharia Shehab, Mohandiseen, Cairo.
Tel (02) 3305 9797.
w blueskygroup.net

JAZ
Travco Center, 26 July Corridor, Sheikh Zayed City, Giza.
Tel (02) 3854 2020.
w jaz.travel.com

KT Travel
15 Lebanon Street, Mohandiseen, Cairo.
Tel (02) 3302 8486.
w kt-travel.com

Memphis Tours Egypt
24 Sharia Mourad, Midan Giza, Giza, Cairo.
Tel (02) 3571 6050.
w memphistours.net

Nile Melody
3 El Khadrawi Street, El Tahrir Square, Cairo.
Tel (02) 2578 3127.
w egyptmelody.com

Nour el-Nil
w nourelnil.com

Safari Egypt
w safariegypt.com

Select Egypt
Building 10, Ground Floor, Office No. 2, Road 233, Degla, Maadi, Cairo.
Tel (02) 2517 5492.
w selectegypt.com

Sonesta Nile Cruises
3 Sharia El Tayaran, Nasr City, Cairo.
Tel (02) 2264 1211.
w sonesta.com/ nilecruises

Spring Tours
3 Sharia al-Sayed al-Bakry, Zarnalek, Cairo. **Map** 1 A3.
Tel (02) 2736 5972.
w springtours.com

Suneast Tours
8 First May Buildings, El Nasr Road, Nasr City, Cairo. **Tel** (012) 2772 2233.
w suneasttours.com

Thomas Cook/Travel Choice
17 Sharia Mahmoud Bassiouni, Cairo.
Map 5 B3.
Tel 16119//(02) 2574 3776.
w travelchoiceegypt. com

Travcotels
19 Yehia Ibrahim Street, Zamalek, Cairo.
Tel (02) 3854 3222.
w travcotels.com

IN THE UK

Acacia Adventure Holidays Ltd
23A Craven Terrace, Lancaster Gate, London W2 3QH.
Tel (020) 7706 4700.
w acacia-africa.com

Amoun Travel & Tours Ltd
56 Kendal Street, London W2 2BP.
Tel (020) 7402 3100.
w amountravel.com

Archers Direct
Ground Floor, Dale House, Tiviot Dale, Stockport, Cheshire SK1 1TB.
Tel (0800) 223 0179.
w archersdirect.co.uk

Audley Travel
New Mill, New Mill Lane, Witney, Oxfordshire OX29 9SX.
Tel (01993) 838 400.
w audleytravel.com

Bales Worldwide Ltd
Bales House, Junction Road, Dorking, Surrey RH4 3HL.
Tel (0844) 644 9266.
w balesworldwide.com

Blue Water Holidays
The Old Mill, Firth Street, Skipton, North Yorkshire BD23 2PT.
Tel (01756) 701 199.
w bluewaterholidays. com

Cox & Kings Travel Ltd
6th Floor, 30 Millbank, London SW1P 4EE.
Tel (020) 7873 5000.
w coxandkings.co.uk

Discover Egypt
80 Borough High Street, London SE1 1LL.
Tel (020) 7407 2111.
w discoveregypt.co.uk

Exodus Travels Ltd
Grange Mills, Weir Road, London SW12 0NE.
Tel (0845) 287 2130.
w exodus.co.uk

Explore Worldwide Ltd
Nelson House, 55 Victoria Road, Farnborough, Hampshire GU14 7PA.
Tel (01252) 883 639.
w explore.co.uk

Hayes & Jarvis Worldwide
The Atrium, London Road, Crawley RH10 9SR.
Tel (01293) 739 844.
w hayesandjarvis. co.uk

Kuoni
Kuoni House, Dorking, Surrey RH5 4AZ.
Tel (01306) 855 740.
w kuoni.co.uk

Planet Holidays
Castle House, 21 Station Road, New Barnet EN5 1PA. **Tel** (0871) 871 2234.
w planet-holidays. co.uk

Soliman Travel UK
113 Earl's Court Road, London SW5 9RL.
Tel (0207) 244 6855.
w solimantravel.co.uk

Voyages Jules Verne
21 Dorset Square, London NW1 6QG.
Tel (0845) 166 7003.
w vjv.com

IN THE USA

Egypt Tours Specialist
Tel (212) 332 1010 or 1-800 715 2425.
w egypttours specialist.com

Exodus Travels/ Explore Worldwide
Adventure Center, 1311 63rd Street, Suite 200, Emeryville CA 94608.
Tel 1-800 843 4277 or 1-800 228 8747 (toll free).
w exodus.co.uk
w explore.co.uk

Sonesta Nile Cruises
116 Huntington Avenue, Boston, MA 02116.
Tel 1-800 766 3782; UK: (0800) 898 410.
w sonesta.com

Travel2egypt
329 Belleville Avenue, Bloomfield, NJ 07003.
Tel (888) 377 LIVE or (973) 783 3610.
w travel2egypt.com

World Explorer Tours & Travel Egypt
724 Charlie Smith Sr. Hwy #5010, Saint Marys, GA 31558.
Tel toll free (888) 999 2354.
w pharaohsnile.com

SURVIVAL GUIDE

PRACTICAL INFORMATION

Egypt has made significant progress in improving its tourist infrastructure and the provision of services and security to visitors. Nevertheless certain obstacles remain. Major cities usually have adequate signposting, but most of the monuments still lack proper on-site information panels, signs and labelling. One of ancient Egypt's gifts to the world was bureaucracy and modern-day visitors must now contend with a sometimes bewildering and frustrating number of formal and informal procedures. With six millennia of history behind them, Egyptians are not in as much of a hurry as the rest of the world. Problems can often be avoided by allowing extra time for even the most minor tasks – patience and a good sense of humour are definite assets on a trip to Egypt.

A tourist sign providing general information at Saqqara

Passports and Visas

Visitors to Egypt should possess a passport valid for six months beyond their planned date of entry. All North Americans, New Zealanders, Australians and most Europeans need a tourist visa to enter the country. These can be obtained in advance from Egyptian consulates abroad, but can also be bought on arrival at Cairo, Hurghada or Luxor airport. It is worth bringing US$15 with you to pay for the visa. Note that general visas cannot be bought at the overland crossing of Taba, nor can they be obtained at Aswan, Suez or Nuweiba. Check the latest entry requirements with the Egyptian embassy before leaving.

Both the single-visit and multiple-entry types of visa allow visitors to stay in Egypt for one month; multiple-entry visas allow the bearer to go in and out of the country three times during that period.

Visas that are valid only for Sinai can be purchased at the border crossing at Taba, at Sharm el-Sheikh airport and at the ports of Sharm el-Sheikh and Nuweiba. These visas last for only two weeks and restrict visitors to the Aqaba coastline as far as the main resort of Sharm el-Sheikh and the vicinity of St Catherine's Monastery.

Be prepared for individual officials to be generally obstructive. In such an event, try to keep calm and friendly.

Customs and Duty-Free Allowances

If you wish to bring personal supplies of cigarettes and alcohol into Egypt, it is best to purchase them when you arrive at either Cairo or Luxor airport. Both have duty-free shops, before and after the Customs checkpoint. The shops before Customs are generally better stocked and less crowded than those after. Upon arrival, visitors can purchase 4 litres of alcohol, or 3 litres and a case of beer, and 200 cigarettes. If visitors elect not to purchase these items upon arrival, they have 48 hours to get to a duty-free shop elsewhere, where they can purchase 3 litres of alcohol and 200 cigarettes.

There are duty-free shops in Cairo at Tiba Mall, in Nasr City; 16 Sharia 218, in Maadi; 17 Sharia al-Gumhuriyya, in downtown Cairo; and at the end of Sharia Gamiat ad-Dowal al-Arabiyya in Mohandiseen. There are also duty-free shops in the centre of Luxor and Hurghada. Bring your passport, and be aware that you may be approached by Egyptians asking if you will use your passport to buy duty-free items on their behalf.

The allowance for visitors bringing cigarettes or alcohol that have been purchased in another country is 1 litre of alcohol and 200 cigarettes.

If you bring a video camera or computer into Egypt, it must be declared on "Form D" upon arrival. If either of those items is stolen, be sure to obtain a police report. If not, when you leave, it will be assumed that you have sold them and a duty of 100 per cent will be levied.

Language

Most urban and professional Egyptians speak a little English and sometimes some French as well. Egyptians working in the tourist sector are accustomed to visitors who cannot speak Arabic and will speak enough English to take care of your

Semiramis Hotel on the banks of the Nile, Cairo

◀ Boats anchored on the Nile at Aswan

Typical ticket kiosk at Philae – vendors usually understand some English

needs. It is still worth mastering a few Arabic words and phrases. Recognizing Arabic numerals can help in getting around and dealing with money, while being able to convey a polite greeting will inevitably delight the recipient. If you are planning to travel off the beaten tourist track, a little knowledge of basic Arabic can be useful, if not essential.

Public Conveniences

Public toilets are rare in Egypt, although major tourist sites often have some type of provision. Facilities in petrol stations, bus and train terminals and cafés in the poorer quarters are likely to be unpleasant, squat toilets. Toilet paper is unlikely to be provided, so it is a good idea to carry tissues with you. Small packets are

available from kiosks, stores and street vendors everywhere. Better hotels and restaurants usually have flush toilets. These are often staffed by an attendant who will provide toilet paper and turn on the tap for you. *Baksheesh* of 25–50 piastres is customary for this service.

Electrical Adaptors

The electric current is 220V and sockets take two-pin plugs. A travel converter will enable you to use appliances from abroad. Brief power cuts are common, so it is a good idea to carry a torch with you.

Time

Egypt is two hours ahead of the standard GMT, and often uses its own concept of time – what Egyptians and foreigners alike call "IBM" time, which stands for *Inshallah, Bokra, Maalesh*.

Inshallah (God willing) is a way of remembering Allah in every action, but sometimes, in the context of tourism, it suggests that something might or might not happen. *Bokra* literally means "tomorrow", but it might be used to mean two days, two weeks or perhaps never. It definitely means "not today". *Maalesh* means "Never mind, don't worry, forget about it."

Egyptians do not like to say no or disappoint guests, so you must be persistent and good-humoured in trying to establish when, or if, a desired outcome is likely to occur.

Conversion Chart

Imperial to Metric
1 inch = 2.54 centimetres
1 foot = 30 centimetres
1 mile = 1.6 kilometres
1 ounce = 28 grams
1 pound = 454 grams
1 pint = 0.6 litre
1 gallon = 4.6 litres

Metric to Imperial
1 millimetre = 0.04 inch.
1 centimetre = 0.4 inch
1 metre = 3 feet 3 inches
1 kilometre = 0.6 mile
1 gram = 0.04 ounce
1 kilogram = 2.2 pounds
1 litre = 1.8 pints

DIRECTORY

Egyptian Embassies Abroad

Australia
241 Commonwealth Street, Surry Hills, Sydney.
Tel (612) 9281 4844.
W egypt.org.au

United Kingdom
2 Lowndes Street, London
SW1X 9ET.
Tel (020) 7235 9777.
W egyptianconsulate. co.uk

Canada
454 Laurier Avenue East, Ottawa, ON, K1N 6R3.
Tel (613) 234 4931.

Ireland
12 Clyde Road, Ballsbridge, Dublin 4.
Tel (01) 6606 566.

Israel
54 Rehov Basel, Tel Aviv.
Tel (03) 546 4151.
Egyptian Consulate 68 Efroni Street, Eilat.
Tel (972) 637 6882.

Jordan
14 Riyad Mefleh Street, Amman.
Tel (26) 560 5176.
Egyptian Consulate, Western Units, Istiklal Street, Aqaba.
Tel (26) 201 6181.

United States
3521 International Court, NW Washington, DC 20008.
Tel (202) 895 5400.
Egyptian Consulate 1110 Second Avenue, New York, NY 10022.
Tel (212) 759 7120.

Egyptian Tourist Offices

In the UK
170 Piccadilly, London W1V 9DD.
Tel (020) 7493 5283.

In the US
630 Fifth Avenue, Suite 1706, New York, NY 10111.
Tel (212) 332 2570.

In Canada
1253 McGill College Avenue, Suite 250, Montreal, Quebec, H3B 2Y5. **Tel** (514) 861 4420.

Tips for Visitors

Although practical information is sometimes hard to obtain from the Egyptian tourist board, the major offices are worth visiting as some of the staff usually speak good English and are knowledgeable about the sites. Travel agencies and hotel receptionists are often more helpful and can usually offer up-to-date advice on accommodation, transport and other practicalities.

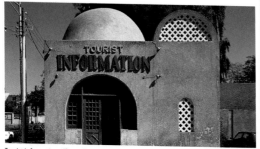

Tourist information office at Aswan with Nubian-style domes

Opening Hours

The major historic sites and museums are open daily from 9am until 5pm (6pm in summer). In Luxor, most monuments open at 6am. During Ramadan, they may open a little later than the advertised time and close around 3pm.

Government and administrative offices generally close on Fridays, while shops and stores sometimes close on Sundays. Most stores are open from 9am until 2 or 3pm, then again from 5 to 9pm. However, shops in tourist areas usually stay open all day and late into the night.

Modestly dressed women visiting a mosque

During Ramadan, offices and shops open later than normal and close around 3pm. They reopen around 8 or 9pm, and remain open until quite late.

Visiting Religious Sites

Egypt generally welcomes non-Muslim visitors to its mosques (see pp36–7). It is, however, advisable to seek permission before visiting any mosque outside Cairo and Alexandria, where residents may be less accustomed to seeing tourists.

With the exception of the mosques of Al-Hussein and Sayyida Zeinab, most religious sites in Cairo are seen as historic monuments, open to non-Muslims from 9am until 4pm. However, tourists should not intrude in any way on worshippers and avoid visiting at prayer times.

Modest dress is essential at all mosques. In some places, women may be asked to cover their hair (a scarf will be provided). You must also remove your shoes before entering the mosque. There is sometimes a shoe custodian (who will expect a small *baksheesh*) or you can leave them outside the door. If you want to climb the minaret, carry your shoes, with the two soles pressed together.

Similar rules apply when visiting monasteries, though you will not have to remove your shoes. With the exception of St Catherine's, which is Greek Orthodox, monasteries in Egypt are Coptic. All the monasteries quite readily admit visitors during the day, except during Lent.

Disabled Travellers

Few tourist sites in Egypt are equipped for disabled visitors. Steep flights of stairs, deep sand and the poor condition of streets combine to make life difficult for those who are less able. On a more positive note, Egyptians are not embarrassed by disability and museum and hotel staff are always willing to help.

The Egyptian national travel company, **Misr Travel**, has tours and accommodation suited for disabled travellers and now has branches worldwide. For those who wish to experience the magic of swimming and diving in the Red Sea, the **Camel Dive Club**, based in Sharm el-Sheikh, has facilities and training geared towards travellers with special needs.

Students

Full-time students can enjoy discounts at museums and historical sites, and reduced air, rail and bus fares with an International Student Identity Card (ISIC). If you arrive in Cairo without one, you can obtain a card at the Egyptian Scientific Centre, 23 Sharia al-Manial on Rhoda Island. A student card can also be purchased at several downtown hotels, but beware of shops offering forgeries.

International Student Identity Card

Etiquette

Egypt is one of the most liberal Muslim countries in the Middle East, and its citizens are justifiably famous for their tolerance, generosity and warmth. However, the presence of five-star hotels, beach resorts, casinos and other trappings of

Visitor about to engage in the ancient art of haggling in Aswan's souk

Western culture, such as mobile phones, luxury cars and bars serving alcohol, may lead the casual observer to conclude that Egypt is more open and liberal than it really is. At its heart, Egypt is still a deeply conservative country and the dominant values are Islamic. To get closer to a truly welcoming people, visitors need to be aware of these values and modify their dress and behaviour accordingly.

Modest dress is essential if one wishes to avoid giving offence or, for women, attracting undue attention. Shorts and swimwear are really only acceptable at beach resorts, primarily along the Aqaba coast on the Red Sea, and the private beaches of certain hotels in Hurghada. In other areas, use your discretion, but remember that, for both sexes, bare shoulders are considered offensive.

Boorish behaviour, such as arrogance or bluntness, can create problems, so remain patient and polite when confronted with bureaucratic hassles or persistent touts. A gentle sense of humour helps to ameliorate difficult circumstances, and is the approach most often deployed by Egyptians themselves.

Egyptians of the same sex frequently hold hands and kiss in public, but open displays of affection between the sexes are rare and can cause deep offence.

If invited to someone's home, a small gift of flowers or sweets is appropriate. For men, sitting with legs crossed and showing the sole of your foot is seen as rude. Shopkeepers will offer tea or soft drinks during negotiations, but this incurs no obligation to buy. When bargaining, however, once you have agreed a price, it is rude to refuse to purchase the item.

Egyptians are aware of their country's weaknesses but do not appreciate it when foreigners point them out. Avoid criticizing religion or the president, and issues such as *baksheesh* or the condition of the streets or buildings.

Photography

Museums and major tourist sites sometimes charge for the use of video and still cameras. The use of a flash is often forbidden. Always ask permission before taking someone's photograph, especially of women or religious figures and in rural areas. Taking photographs that show Egypt as backward or poor may also cause offence. Visitors should remember that it is always forbidden to take pictures of army bases, airports, government buildings, dams, bridges or anything considered vital to security.

Tourists photographing the Sphinx near the Pyramids of Giza

DIRECTORY

Tourist Offices

Alexandria
23 Sharia El Mina El Sharqia, Raml Station.
Open 8am–6pm daily (till 8pm in summer).
Tel (03) 485 1556.

Masr railway station.
Open 8am–8pm daily.
Tel (03) 392 5985.

Aswan
Aswan railway station.
Open 9am–3pm, 6–8pm daily; 9am–3pm, 7–9pm in summer.
Tel (097) 231 2811/2814.

Cairo
5 Sharia Adly.
Open 9am–6pm daily.
Tel (02) 2391 3454.

Terminal 1, Cairo airport.
Open 8am–9pm daily.
Tel (02) 2265 5000/1.

Ramses railway station.
Open 8:30am–8pm daily.
Tel (02) 2575 3555.

Giza Pyramids.
Open 8:30am–5pm daily.
Tel (02) 3570 2233.

Luxor
Opposite railway station (main office).
Open 8am–8pm daily.
Tel (095) 228 0902.

Inside railway station.
Open 8am–8pm daily.
Tel (095) 237 0259.

Luxor airport.
Open 24 hours daily.
Tel (095) 237 2306.

Disabled Travellers

Camel Dive Club
Sharm el-Sheikh, Sinai.
Tel (069) 360 0700.
🅦 **cameldive.com**

Misr Travel
7 Sharia Talaat Harb, Cairo.
Tel (02) 2393 0010, 19341.
🅦 **misrtraveleg.net**

Misr Travel UK
Old Inn House, Suite D, Carshalton Road, Sutton, SM1 4LE.
Tel (020) 8643 2429.

Egypt For All
🅦 **egyptforall.net**

Security

With the wave of unrest since the 2011 Revolution, it is advisable to check local Egyptian news sites such as english.ahram.org.eg for the current situation. Also, check your country's embassy website for security threat updates.

Egypt has far less crime than most other countries in the world and you will find Egyptians to be warm, welcoming and helpful. However, visitors should keep an eye out for possible scams and overcharging. Take the usual precautions of wearing a money belt and keeping a close watch on cameras and bags. In fact, tales abound of taxi drivers, hotel personnel and ordinary citizens returning lost property and keeping a look-out for the welfare of guests.

Police

Visitors to Egypt are often surprised by the numbers of police posted on street corners, at intersections and outside government buildings and historic sites. This is not a sign of imminent or recent trouble, but has simply been the status quo since the 1960s.

Different police forces deal with different aspects of law and order. The Municipal Police handle crime and are recognizable by their uniforms – khaki in winter and tan or white in summer. Traffic Police wear similar uniforms, with the addition of striped cuffs. Both forces deal with accidents and can help in emergencies, but few speak English.

The Tourist Police are the agency visitors should turn to in times of trouble. Ordinary ranks wear khaki uniforms, while officers wear black in winter, white in summer. Easily identified by "Tourist Police" armbands, they are stationed at ports, airports, stations, tourist sites and museums and usually speak some English.

The Central Security Police guard embassies, banks and highways. Dressed in black uniforms and armed with Kalashnikovs, they can appear very intimidating. In general they are no cause for concern, but if you do find yourself caught up in a demonstration, get right away immediately.

Unless drugs or espionage are suspected, foreigners are usually treated with politeness by the police.

Petty Crime

Egypt is proud of its low crime rate and in general visitors should have little trouble as long as they take sensible precautions and avoid travelling alone when away from tourist areas. As in any large city, crowded areas, such as the Khan al-Khalili, provide the ideal conditions for pickpockets and petty thieves. Keep your money and passport in a money belt or pouch and your camera and other valuables out of sight. Security on camp sites, hostels and cheap hotels is likely to be poor, so leave valuables at the reception desk, or take them with you.

Crowded street near Khan al-Khalili, where it is wise for visitors to mind their valuables

If travelling by car, do not leave anything of value visible or accessible.

Travel and Terrorism

Following demonstrations in 2011, it is sensible to be cautious when in large cities, listen to local advice and obey curfews. Generally most of the unrest has been in the outlying suburbs of Cairo and Northern Sinai. Get up-to-date advice from your ministry of foreign affairs before travelling. In the UK, call the Foreign and Commonwealth Office or visit their website. US citizens should check the US State Department's website for current advice for travellers. Middle Egypt – which includes the cities of Minya, Asyut and Sohag and the historic sites of the Tombs of Beni Hassan, Tell al-Amarna, Abydos, Dendara and several monasteries – is a potential hot spot for trouble (see p180). Because of this, the Egyptian authorities are vigilant over visitors to the area. There is heavy security and the movements of tourists are tightly controlled.

It is possible to arrange day trips as part of a group from Cairo and Luxor, but only under strict security. If you go alone by local bus or by service taxi, police at checkpoints may ask to see your passport and might even give you an escort into the sites, depending on the situation. Information about the causes and extent of the unrest is hard to come by and often conflicting. The threat is not always directed at tourists, but visitors do run the risk of being caught up in local violence.

Terrorist attacks on tourists in general have ceased since the massacre at the Temple of Hatshepsut in Luxor, on 17 November 1997. Since then, the government has tried to prevent such attacks and has increased security, particularly at the major historical sites.

In Case of Fire

Hostels, cheap hotels and even some of the more expensive establishments are unlikely to

Distinctive Egyptian fire engine, equipped for the rough terrain

have adequate fire exits or even fire extinguishers. Therefore, it is a good idea at least to familiarize yourself with the layout of the building and possible escape routes in case a fire does occur.

Women Travellers

Egypt has become more conservative in recent years, as witnessed by the increasing numbers of women wearing the *hijab* or headscarf. Women tourists are not expected to wear scarves, but may feel more at ease doing so in mosques or rural areas.

The social norms for women in Egypt are very different from those in the West and this, combined with images of women in Hollywood films, creates misconceptions. For example, women travellers unaccompanied by a man are often regarded as morally loose. While serious sexual assaults are rare, verbal harassment and groping do occur. The risk of harassment can be reduced by dressing modestly. Wear long, loose, opaque clothes that cover your chest, shoulders, upper arms and your legs below the knees. Many single women wear wedding rings, which signal respectability. Sit with other women on trains and buses and in the Cairo Metro, where there are cars reserved for women. Avoid eye contact and smiling at strange men as these can be misconstrued. If you are harassed, the best response is to ignore the offender. Using phrases such as *haram* (shame), or *sibnee le wahdi* (leave me alone) may bring help. Women in Islam are highly respected and help is frequently extended to female travellers in distress.

Embassies

If you find yourself in trouble, contact your embassy or consulate who will give legal advice and replace lost passports. They are unsympathetic to drug offenders and will not lend you money to get home, although, as a last resort, they will arrange repatriation. It is as well to remember that although you are a welcome visitor to the country, you are still subject to Egyptian laws.

DIRECTORY

Emergency Services

Fire Tel 180.
Tourist Police Tel 126.
Emergency Tel 123.

Travel Advice

W **fco.gov.uk** (in UK) or
Tel (020) 7008 1500.
W **travel.state.gov** (in US).

Embassies

Australia
World Trade Centre (11th floor),
Corniche el-Nil, Bulaq, Cairo.
Map 1 A3. **Tel** (02) 2770 6600.

Canada
26 Sharia Kamel el Shenawi,
Garden City, Cairo. **Map** 5 A5.
Tel (02) 2791 8700.

Ireland
22 Hassan Assem, Zamalek, Cairo.
Map 1 A3.
Tel (02) 2735 8264.

UK
7 Sharia Ahmed Ragheb, Garden
City, Cairo. **Map** 5 A4.
Tel (02) 2791 6000.

USA
5 Sharia Amerika al-Latineya,
Garden City, Cairo.
Map 5 B4.
Tel (02) 2797 3300.

A police escort accompanying tourists taking a camel ride at Aswan

Health and Insurance

Although travelling in Egypt might be thought to pose serious health risks, these can be minimized by careful pre-planning, taking sensible precautions while in the country and by taking out appropriate travel insurance before leaving home. The most common problems are mild gastric disturbances – simply caused by bacteria in food and drink to which the traveller has yet to acquire immunity – plus the range of ailments induced by a careless attitude to extreme heat and sunshine.

General Advice

For most visitors to Egypt, stomach upsets and over-exposure to the sun constitute the greatest health risks. It is a good idea, however, to pack a first-aid kit with plasters, bandages, antiseptic ointment and some painkillers. Insect repellent is vital, especially in the Western Desert oases, on the Sinai coast, in the Delta, and for felucca rides at sunset. Include some oral rehydration salts in your kit: these will help replace lost minerals if you do suffer a bad bout of diarrhoea.

Check the current requirements regarding prescription medicines with the Egyptian embassy before you travel; you may need to carry a letter from your GP. It's a good idea to bring your own supply of contact lens solution.

The sun is strong throughout Egypt, even in winter, and particularly in Upper Egypt, where there is very little shade. Wear a sunhat and sunglasses and use a sunscreen with a protection factor of at least 30.

Vaccinations

Visitors to Egypt do not require any vaccinations unless they are coming from an infected area. However you may like to ask your GP for the current World Health Organization (WHO) health bulletin on Egypt before travelling. As well as ensuring that your polio and tetanus cover is up to date, the most common recommendations include vaccinations against typhoid and Hepatitis A and B. A meningitis vaccination may

also be advised. Rabies is a problem throughout the country. Avoid touching any stray animals, including cats, dogs, bats and monkeys. If you think you have been exposed to the disease, seek help urgently.

Pharmacies

Egyptian pharmacists are a good source of help for minor health complaints. They generally speak English and can be trusted to advise on remedies for most common ailments. Pharmacies carry a wide range of drugs, which are cheap and can often be dispensed without a doctor's prescription. Pharmacists can also help you find a doctor.

Stomach Upsets

Mild diarrhoea is a common ailment for visitors to Egypt. However, a few simple precautions can reduce your chances of falling ill, or at least lessen the effects.

While tap water is generally safe, it is heavily chlorinated and rather unpleasant tasting. Bottled water is available everywhere – but make sure that the seal is unbroken when you buy it. Avoid raw vegetables and unpeeled fruit, or wash them thoroughly in

A Bedouin camel trek near Ain Hudra Oasis in South Sinai, with fierce sun and intense heat posing potential health hazards

purified water. Do not buy food from a street stall that has no running water, and beware of ice-cream that may have melted, then been refrozen. Choose budget restaurants with care and always check that meat has been cooked thoroughly.

If you do feel unwell, bottled water with a little added fresh lime juice can help settle an upset stomach.

Other Hazards

Dehydration, sunburn and heat exhaustion are of particular concern, especially in Upper Egypt. Lack of shade at archaeological sites, plus wind-blown sand and dust, can make for an uncomfortable experience. Sweat evaporates quickly in these dry conditions and you may become dehydrated without realizing it. Drink plenty of bottled water and add a little extra salt to your food to replace salts lost in sweat. Wear a sunhat and loose-fitting clothes made of natural fibres, and wear a T-shirt when swimming.

Heatstroke is a potentially fatal condition that occurs when the body temperature rises to dangerous levels. Symptoms include flushed skin, severe headaches and confusion. Immediate medical attention is essential.

Bilharzia, or schistosomiasis, is another hazard in Egypt. This disease is transmitted by water-borne flukes that infest the stagnant water found in canals or in slower-moving stretches of the Nile. Do not wade or bathe in such water or walk barefoot on the muddy banks. Never drink water from such a source.

Hospitals and Emergencies

Private hospitals provide the best medical care in Egypt, but they still fall short of standards found in the West. The most reliable private hospitals are

Local brand of Egyptian bottled water

in Cairo and Alexandria, and those attached to universities are generally competent and well equipped. Irrespective of whether the patient is insured, both private and state-run hospitals will probably ask for a cash payment before providing treatment of any kind. If you do not have sufficient funds to cover this, contact your embassy who may be able to arrange for relatives or your insurance company to cover the fees in advance of your claim. Be sure to obtain receipts for all the expenses you incur, since these will be required by your insurance company to support your claim for reimbursement.

With the exception of the private service run by As-Salaam Hospital in Cairo, ambulances do not carry paramedics or life-support equipment. Since telephone lines in Egypt are seriously overloaded, it is best, in a real emergency, to take a taxi to the nearest hospital rather than trying to call an ambulance.

Travel Insurance

Most travel policies cover you for lost belongings and cancellation as well as medical emergencies, and are strongly recommended. Be sure to inform the insurance company if you intend to take part in any dangerous sports, such as diving, otherwise your cover may be invalid. Keep the documents with you so that you can readily contact the company if necessary.

A typical red-and-white Egyptian ambulance

Communications and Media

Egyptian telephone and internet services have improved dramatically in recent years. Internet cafés are widely available in the more tourist-orientated areas and almost all hotels have a wireless connection. Unfortunately the same cannot be said of the postal service. Overseas letters sent from Egypt can still take weeks to arrive, if they do at all. Egypt has eight television channels and many satellite channels, as well as several English-language newspapers and magazines.

Useful Dialling Codes

- To dial locally: dial the 7- or 8-digit telephone number.
- To dial within Egypt: dial 0 + area code + telephone number.
- Area codes: Cairo and Giza: 2; Alexandria: 3; Aswan: 97; Fayoum: 84; Luxor: 95; Ismailia: 64; Hurghada: 65; Sharm el-Sheikh: 69.
- To dial internationally: dial 00 + country code + telephone number.
- Country codes: US and Canada: 1; France: 33; Germany: 49; Italy: 39; Netherlands: 31; Spain: 34; UK: 44; South Africa: 27; Australia: 61
- Mobile phone numbers are prefixed by 0100, 0102, 0106, 0109, 0110, 0111, 0122, 0127 or 0128.

Public Telephones

Menatel, identified by its green-and-yellow half-booths, is the most widespread of the public card phone services. Phonecards can be obtained from pharmacies, newspaper stands, tobacco shops and kiosks displaying the green-and-yellow Menatel sign. The LE 10 cards are for local calls and the LE 30 cards for international calls. Cheaper rates are available from 8pm–8am. All booths have instructions in Arabic and English.

Phone booths are gradually being phased out, however as the use of mobile phones is endemic in Egypt. The phone system as a whole remains overloaded and it can take numerous attempts to reach the person you are calling. Numbers change often and in such cases, a recorded message both in Arabic and English will provide you with the new number.

Mobile Phones

Not all networks provide roaming services in Egypt so if you are planning to use your mobile phone frequently, you can buy a SIM card from a local provider such as Mobinil, Vodafone or Etisalat. On some SIM cards incoming calls are free. All providers have shops in most towns and cities. SIM cards can be bought for about LE 50 and top-up cards for phone credit can be bought easily from kiosks and grocery shops.

A typical postbox in Egypt

Postal Services

Most post offices in Egypt are open from 9am to 3pm daily, except Friday and Saturday, although the central Cairo post office remains open 24 hours a day. Post offices are often overcrowded and difficult to use if you don't speak Arabic. It is probably simpler therefore to buy stamps and send mail from hotels. To send important letters or packages, it is strongly advised to use one of the international courier services, such as Federal Express or DHL. Both companies have several offices in Cairo. This is a more expensive option but the only way of guaranteeing that items will reach their intended recipient quickly.

Receiving letters *poste restante* at the post office is not always reliable and it is a better idea to have letters sent to your hotel. In addition, the main American Express office in Cairo at 15 Sharia Qasr el-Nil holds mail for people who have American Express cards or Amex travellers' cheques. Receiving packages or overstuffed envelopes from overseas is best avoided as all such parcels are inspected by customs and censors. Items such as compact discs, DVDs and computer games arrive very late or not at all. If they do arrive, expect to pay duty worth more than the package's contents.

Television and Radio

Television channels 1 and 2 are the national channels, with the latter broadcasting news in English and French. Channel 3 is the local Cairo channel. Channels 4 to 8 are broadcast from Ismailia, Alexandria, Tanta, Minya and Aswan respectively. All the channels broadcast

Man using a mobile phone while on a camel

Newspaper stand selling foreign papers in Mahattat Ramla, Alexandria

foreign-language programmes with Arabic subtitles, and the better hotels provide cable or satellite television. Increasing numbers of private television channels broadcast mainly entertainment programmes.

Foreign-language radio programmes are rare outside Cairo and Alexandria. In Cairo, FM 95 broadcasts programmes in English and French and a few other stations mix Western classical and pop music with Arabic music and news. Check the *Egyptian Gazette* for TV and radio schedules or *Egypt Today* magazine for satellite and cable TV highlights.

A selection of English-language newspapers and magazines

Newspapers and Magazines

The daily *Egyptian Gazette* and the weekly *Middle East Times* and *Al-Ahram Weekly* cover international and domestic news; the latter two provide good coverage of television, films and cultural events. The weekly *Cairo Times* is a mix of local and regional news, features and reviews. Outside Cairo, the *Egyptian Gazette* is the only local English-language paper.

There are a number of English-language magazines. The monthly *Egypt Today* contains comprehensive cultural and restaurant listings.

Other English- language magazines include *Egypt Today*'s sister publications *Business Today* and *Sports and Fitness*, which is useful for health clubs, sports and recreation listings. A broad range of Western newspapers is usually on sale the day after publication at street-side newspaper stands in affluent areas of large cities and at major hotels. *Time*, *Newsweek* and *The Economist* are also available.

Internet and Wi-Fi

Internet access is widespread in Egypt and internet cafés and Wi-Fi technology are fast-growing phenomena, especially in the tourist centres of Cairo, Alexandria and Luxor. Major hotels also offer internet access

and Wi-Fi. Some hotels charge for use; costs are usually LE 5–10 per hour, although five-star hotels can charge considerably more for access.

DIRECTORY
Main Post Offices

Cairo
Midan Ataba. **Map** 6 E2.

Luxor
Sharia al-Mahatta.

International Courier Services

Federal Express
1079 Corniche el-Nil, Garden City, Cairo. **Map** 5 A5. **Tel** 19985.

DHL
38 Sharia Abdel Khaleq Tharwat, Cairo. **Map** 5 C2. **Tel** 16345.

Internet Cafés

Internet Egypt
Ground floor, 2 Midan Simon Bolivar, Garden City, Cairo. **Map** 5 B4. **Tel** (02) 2796 2882.

Mohandiseen Cybercafé
Sharia Gamiat ad-Dowal al-Arabiyya, Cairo. **Tel** (02) 3305 0493.

Sun Café
Between Sharia Souq el-Tawfiqa and Sharia 26 July, Downtown, Cairo.

Zamalek Center
25a Sharia Ismail Mohammed, Zamalek. **Map** 5 B3. **Tel** (02) 2736 4004.

One of many internet cafés in Cairo

Banking and Currency

Egypt is still very much a cash economy. Both banks and exchange offices will change cash and travellers' cheques, but exchange offices usually offer better hours, shorter queues and more favourable rates. Credit cards, while accepted at most major hotels and some tourist shops, are not much use anywhere else. Automated Teller Machines (ATMs) are found outside many banks and can be used for cash withdrawals, although some credit card companies charge heavily for this service. Egypt prohibits the exportation of its currency, which, in any case, is useless outside the country.

Standard ATM with instructions in a range of languages

Banks and Bureaux de Change

The usual opening hours for banks in Egypt are Sunday to Thursday 8:30am to 2pm. Exchange offices are also open in the evenings from 6pm to 9pm. Most banks are closed on Friday and Saturday. As well as Egyptian banks, which include **Banque Misr**, there are a few well-known international names such as Barclays and Citibank. The best time to go is just as the bank opens – to avoid crowds.

Exchange offices can be found throughout major cities and tourist areas and are preferable to banks, shops and hotels for changing money. The black market for hard currency is now in decline and not worth the risk.

It is a good idea to change some money on arrival; both terminals at Cairo Airport have 24-hour exchange offices.

Thomas Cook exchange office on the Corniche, Luxor

Credit and Debit Cards

A large number of international bank ATMs have popped up around Cairo and other major tourist centres. The banks include HSBC, **Barclays** and **Citibank**. Local ATMs accept debit cards, but charge an international withdrawal fee.

Credit card usage is becoming more widespread in upmarket restaurants and shops. The most commonly accepted credit cards are **Visa** and **MasterCard**. In case you have to wire money from Egypt it must be in US dollars, not Egyptian pounds. It is advisable to make a photocopy or scan of your cards before you travel in case of loss or theft.

Travellers' cheques are still accepted at the leading exchange offices, though these may charge hefty commissions. A passport is required to change travellers' cheques.

Baksheesh and Tipping

People demanding *baksheesh* without rendering a service can be irritating, but calm and good-humoured refusals will eventually meet with success. Most Egyptians are paid such low salaries that *baksheesh,* in the form of a tip for service, is a vital part of their income. It is usual, in restaurants, to round up the bill or give an extra 10 per cent directly to the waiter. Small tips, in the 25 pt to LE 1 range, should be given to people who help you in some small way, such as lavatory attendants, and the

people who park cars, carry luggage or unlock tombs. Offers to bend the rules a bit, such as letting you into a site after hours or opening one

DIRECTORY

Banks

Banque Misr
151 Sharia Mohammed Farid, Cairo. **Map** 2 D5, 6 D4.
Tel 19888.

Barclays International
12 Midan al-Sheikh Yusuf, Garden City, Cairo. **Map** 3 B1, 5 A5.
Tel (02) 2366 2600 or 16222.

Citibank
4 Sharia Ahmed Pasha, Garden City, Cairo. **Map** 3 B1, 5 A5.
Tel 16644.

Bureaux de Change

American Express
15 Sharia Qasr el-Nil, Cairo.
Map 1 C5, 5 C3. **Tel** 16443.
Winter Palace Arcade, Luxor.
Tel (0122) 338 8717 or 16119.

Thomas Cook/Travel Choice
17 Sharia Mahmoud Bassiouni, Cairo. **Map** 5 B5. **Tel** 16119.
9 Sharia Abtal El-Tahrir, Corniche el-Nil, Aswan.
Tel (097) 230 6839.
Midan Saad Zaghloul, Alexandria. **Tel** (03) 484 7830.
Winter Palace Arcade, Luxor.
Tel (095) 237 2402.

Lost or Stolen Credit Cards

American Express
Tel 16443 (24 hours).

Visa/MasterCard
Tel (001) 410 581 9994 (reverse charge call), 19007.

supposedly closed, will cost a little more. However, don't assume money will buy you everything. Do not risk offence by refusing to pay small sums for even minor assistance, but also do not throw money at people to get your way.

Currency

The basic unit of currency in Egypt is the Egyptian pound or *ginee*, written as £E or LE. The Egyptian pound is divided into 100 piastres (pt) or *irsh*. The 50, 100 and 200 LE notes can sometimes be difficult to change, so always carry some smaller notes. It is also advisable to keep a separate supply of lower denomination notes for *baksheesh* and for taxis who invariably have no change. Do not accept ragged or mutilated notes because taxi drivers and vendors will also refuse them.

Banknotes

Banknotes are issued in 1, 5, 10, 20, 50, 100 and 200 pound denominations as well as 50 and 25 piastres. Smaller in size than pound notes, they are often refused by vendors and taxi drivers alike. Most smaller shops round prices up.

5 Egyptian pounds (LE 5)

10 Egyptian pounds (LE 10)

20 Egyptian pounds (LE 20)

50 Egyptian pounds (LE 50)

100 Egyptian pounds (LE 100)

200 Egyptian pounds (LE 200)

Coins

Coins come in denominations of 1 LE and 5, 10, 20, 25 and 50 piastres. Different versions of the same value can be found in circulation.

5 piastres (5 pt)

10 piastres (10 pt)

20 piastres (20 pt)

25 piastres (25 pt)

50 piastres (50 pt)

1 pound (LE 1)

TRAVEL INFORMATION

Most visitors to Egypt fly to Cairo, but flights are also available to Luxor, Alexandria, Hurghada and Sharm el-Sheikh. A holiday in Egypt can also be combined with a visit to another Middle Eastern or North African country, but flying within the region is comparatively more expensive than flying direct from the US or Europe. Another popular method of entry into Egypt is overland from Jordan, via Israel, although this entails some extra effort and time because of having to cross two borders on the way. An easier route from Jordan is on the regular ferry or catamaran service that runs between Aqaba and Nuweiba on the Gulf of Aqaba coast of Sinai.

Cairo International Airport, to the northeast of the city

Arriving by Air

Direct flights to Egypt are regularly available from most European capitals. Both **British Airways** and **EgyptAir** fly daily from Heathrow (with a flight time of approximately 5 hours) while **Air France** flies daily from Paris (4.5 hours). Other daily flights include KLM from Amsterdam, **Lufthansa** from Frankfurt, Malev from Budapest, Olympic from Athens, TAROM from Bucharest and **Turkish Airlines** from Istanbul. Charter flights are available to domestic and international destinations.

EgyptAir flies daily direct to Cairo from New York's JFK airport. The flight time is approximately 12 hours. **Delta** flies direct to and from New York four times a week. There are no direct flights to Egypt from Canada.

Travellers from Australia and New Zealand usually get to Egypt via London, or add on Cairo as part of a Round-the-World Ticket. However, EgyptAir offers daily flights to Bangkok (with a flight time of approximately 9 hours). Fares vary according to the time of year.

Transport from Cairo Airport

Cairo International Airport is 20 km (12 miles) to the northeast of the city and has three terminals. The latest addition, Terminal 3, serves all domestic and international EgyptAir flights, and all international flights from fellow Star Alliance airlines, such as Lufthansa. Terminal 2 (currently undergoing renovation) serves non-Star Alliance airlines, such as British Airways, and also Saudi and Gulf state airlines. All other international flights land at Terminal 1.

All terminals are connected to the city centre by bus, but the fastest and most comfortable transfer is by taxi. (For more general information regarding buses and taxis, see pp338–9.)

There is no difficulty in finding a taxi at the airport, as drivers descend on new arrivals the minute they have cleared Customs. The time of day, number, gender and appearance of the passengers, amount of luggage, volume of traffic and bargaining skills all factor into the fare. A trip from the airport to downtown Cairo typically costs between LE 60 and 80 per car load, not per person. New arrivals may also be offered a "limousine" service – the fixed rate for the trip in a decent saloon is around LE 80.

Transport from Other Airports

The airport in Alexandria is 5 km (3 miles) south of the city, however, flights into Alexandria are instead using Borg El-Arab airport, 40 km (24 miles) west of the city, while El-Nouzha airport is upgraded. Buses connect Borg El-Arab to the centre of town, but a taxi is easier, costing about LE 80–100. Most visitors arriving at Luxor are met at the airport by representatives from their hotels or cruise boats. If not,

Black-and-yellow taxi serving Alexandria airport

a taxi into town costs around LE 30. Similarly, most visitors to Sharm el-Sheikh are met by hotel transportation. Taxis from the airport, located north of Naama Bay, test the skills of the best bargainers. Expect to pay around LE 30 to 50 per trip. The situation at Hurghada airport is similar, but a taxi into town should cost only LE 40.

Arriving by Land from Israel and Jordan

Buses run twice a week, on Sundays and Thursdays at 8am, from Tel Aviv and Jerusalem to Egypt, crossing at Taba, the gateway to the Sinai coast. The journey between Jerusalem and Cairo takes 12–14 hours, depending on how long it takes to cross the border. The process has been streamlined slightly at the Taba crossing, which serves both the Israeli resort of Eilat and Egyptian resorts on the Gulf of Aqaba and the rest of the Sinai.

It is also possible to enter Egypt by land from Jordan through Israel. The journey involves a 5-km (3-mile) taxi or "service" taxi ride from Aqaba to the border, followed by a short walk to the Israeli side. From

Cruise ship passing through the Suez Canal

there, visitors can take a taxi into Eilat. Buses and taxis run from the centre of Eilat to the border with Egypt at Taba. Departure taxes must be paid when leaving Jordan and Israel, even if one is just passing through the latter.

Bear in mind that having Israeli stamps in your passport may preclude you from visiting other Arab countries.

Arriving by Sea

Although Egypt is served by several ports on both its Mediterranean and Red Sea coasts, the advent of cheap air fares and package holidays has inevitably seen the decline of passenger ferries bringing

travellers to the country. There is one exception to this – the crossing from Aqaba, in Jordan, to Nuweiba, in the Sinai. This route is served by both a ferry, which takes 3–5 hours, depending on the weather, and a high-speed catamaran service that does the trip in an hour.

There are no longer any direct ferries from Greece or Cyprus, but two cruise ships sail from Limassol to Port Said, taking passengers on a two-day group visa to Egypt.

Otherwise the only other arrivals by sea are passengers from the cruise ships in the surrounding waters, who come ashore on day trips to visit some of the sights.

DIRECTORY

Airports

Alexandria (Borg El-Arab)
Tel (03) 459 1486.

Aswan
Tel (097) 348 0333.

Cairo
Tel (02) 226 55000 (Terminal 1).
Tel 16707 (Terminal 3).
W cairo-airport.com

Hurghada
Tel (065) 346 2722.

Luxor
Tel (095) 232 4455.

Marsa Alam
Tel (065) 370 0029.

Sharm el-Sheikh
Tel (069) 362 3304.

Airline Offices in Cairo

Air France
Building B1, Sheraton Business District, Cairo.
Map 5 B4.
Tel (02) 2598 1010.
W airfrance.com

British Airways
InterContinental Residence Suites, Citystars Complex, Heliopolis, Cairo.
Tel (02) 2480 0380.
W britishairways.com

Delta
Jeddah Tower, 15 Sharia Ismail Mohammed Zamalek, Cairo.
Tel (02) 2736 2030.
W delta.com

EgyptAir
9 Sharia Talaat Harb.
Map 5 C3. Tel (02) 2393 0381. W egyptair.com
Cairo International Airport.
Tel (02) 2267 7010 (T1).
Tel (02) 2696 6798 (T3).

Lufthansa & Swiss
6 Sharia al-Sheikh al-Marsafi, Zamalek.
Map 1 A4. Tel 19380.
Cairo International Airport. Tel (02) 2269 5210 (Lufthansa).
W lufthansa.com
Tel (02) 2269 5201 (Swiss)
W swissair.com.

Singapore Airlines
8 Infinity Tower, 22 Fl., Sharia Gazirat El Arab, Mohandiseen, Cairo.
Tel (02) 2696 6805.
W singaporeair.com

Turkish Airlines
17 Sharia Sabri Abu Alam, Cairo.
Tel 19849.
W turkishairlines.com

Transport from Cairo Airport

Cairo Airport Shuttle Bus
Tel 19970.
W cairoshuttlebus.com

Buses to and from Israel

Mazada Tours
Cairo Sheraton,
11 Midan Gala, Cairo.
Tel (02) 3348 8600.

Travelling in Egypt

The overall standards of plane and train travel in Egypt are pretty good, but both services can be frustrating in terms of booking and scheduling. The rail network links the Nile Valley, the Delta and the Canal Zone, while EgyptAir and Air Sinai, the national carriers, serve the major cities. Costs for air travel, however, are substantially higher than trains and long-distance buses, so it is not an option for budget travellers. The bus service in Egypt is extensive and, for short trips, often preferable to trains, both in cost and transit time. For longer journeys, night buses are often available.

Train bound for Aswan departing from Ramses station in Cairo

Sign for the Abu Simbel airport in the Nile Valley

Domestic Flights

Flying within Egypt entails flying with EgyptAir as the company has a monopoly on air travel within the country. Air Sinai is part of the same company and was formed to serve Israel and the Sinai, thus protecting the mother carrier from losing its landing rights in other Arab countries. EgyptAir operates frequent daily flights between Cairo, Luxor, Hurghada and Aswan, and a slightly reduced service to Alexandria. All domestic flights leave from Terminal 1, the Old Airport, in Cairo. There are several flights a day between Aswan and Abu Simbel. Air Sinai offers daily flights between Cairo, Luxor, Hurghada and Sharm el-Sheikh.

Flight Reservations

Fares are average by inter-national standards and are calculated in US dollars. It is possible to pay in Egyptian pounds, backed up by an exchange receipt. Reservations should be made as far in advance as possible, especially during winter or if travelling at the time of important Muslim festivals such as Eid al-Adha

and Eid al-Fitr *(see p43)*. Overbooking is common on EgyptAir and Air Sinai: always confirm your flight reservation and make a note of the confirmation reference number. Delays are also common. It is a good idea to have something to read or to otherwise fill the time you may spend waiting. The baggage allowance for domestic flights is 20 kg (44 lb), but this rule is often flouted, especially with regard to hand luggage. It is important to arrive at the airport at least one hour before domestic flights and two hours before international flights.

Trains

Trains are the best option for long trips between major cities, offering a much more pleasant alternative to buses and taxis. For short journeys, however,

trains tend to be slower and less reliable. Trains in Egypt fall into two categories: air-conditioned (A/C), which includes the more luxurious sleeping trains, and non-A/C, or local stopping trains. A/C trains usually offer first- and second-class cars. First-class cars are less crowded and the seats are more comfortable. Second-class travel is not significantly worse and costs quite a bit less. Seats can be reserved up to a week in advance and it is best to book for the return journey at the same time. There are 10 A/C trains a day between Cairo and Alexandria and five daily between Cairo and Luxor and Aswan, but tourists are only

Façade of the Masr train station in central Alexandria

One of the buses used by the West Delta Bus Company

officially allowed on the night train, which departs from Ramses station at 10pm. It is impossible to buy advance tickets for the other trains.

Sleeping trains provide a fast, comfortable, but expensive overnight service between Cairo and Luxor and Aswan. Carpeted compartments have two bunks and a washbasin. There is a lounge car, and breakfast and dinner are served in the compartments. The meals are included in the price. The company that operates the sleeping trains has ticket offices at both Ramses and Giza railway stations. Tickets should be booked well in advance.

Non-A/C trains have only second- and third-class seats, the latter with open doors and windows for ventilation. Both classes are very dirty and crowded and cannot be used by foreign travellers.

Logo of the Superjet bus run by the Arab Union Transport Company

Long-Distance Buses

There are three main bus operators in Egypt. The **Upper Egypt Bus Company** operates services to the Nile Valley, Al-Fayoum, the Western Desert oases and towns along the Red Sea Coast down to Quesir. It also runs a luxury bus service every evening to Luxor and to Aswan. The **East Delta Bus Company** covers services to

the Sinai beach towns of Sharm el-Sheikh, Dahab, Nuweiba and Taba, as well as to St Catherine's Monastery and the Suez Canal towns of Port Said, Ismailia and Suez. Alexandria, Marsa Matruh, Siwa Oasis and the Delta towns are served by the **West and Middle Delta Bus Company**. Travellers have a choice between air-conditioned (A/C) buses, which are usually newer, and non-A/C vehicles which are generally in worse shape and can take much longer to arrive at their destination. Be aware that just because a bus is advertised as having air-conditioning does not mean that it will actually work; nor will passengers necessarily obey the "no smoking" signs.

The Arab Union Transport Company operates the super-comfortable **Superjet** buses along the main Cairo to Alexandria, Luxor, Hurghada, Sharm el-Sheikh and Aswan routes. Superjet buses also serve Port Said with around nine trips a day. The buses are air-conditioned, with toilets, videos and hostesses offering highly priced snacks.

All long-distance buses from Cairo now depart from the Cairo Gateway bus terminal near Ramses train station. Bus schedules, usually posted in Arabic, are erratic and change frequently so it is advisable to ask travel agencies, hotels and tourist offices to help check the departure times. Tickets are sold from small kiosks at city terminals, up to 24 hours in advance for A/C and long-haul services. In smaller towns, tickets may only be available an hour or so before departure.

Prices vary depending on the type of service and the time of travel. For popular trips, book as early as possible to be sure of a seat and to catch the bus at the main departure terminal.

DIRECTORY

Bus Companies

East Delta Bus Company
Tel (02) 2261 1883.
W bus.com.eg

Superjet
Tel (02) 2579 8181.

Upper Egypt Bus Company
Tel (02) 3572 5032.
W bus.com.eg

West and Middle Delta Bus Company
Tel (02) 2575 2157.
W bus.com.eg

Train Stations

Alexandria
Sidi Gaber Station.
Tel (03) 392 2882.

Cairo
Ramses Station,
Midan Ramses.
Map 2 D3.
Tel (02) 2575 3555.

Imposing entrance to Ramses train station, on Midan Ramses, Cairo

Road Travel in Egypt

Driving in Egypt is not for the faint-hearted. Traffic in Cairo is continually busy and horrendous and the main roads out of the metropolis are hazardous. In Alexandria, traffic is no more orderly than in Cairo, but it is less dense, except for summer when millions of Egyptians relocate to Alexandria and the Mediterranean coast. Service (pronounced *servees*) taxis go just about anywhere in the country, providing a fast, cheap form of transport. However their relative discomfort and lack of safety limit their usefulness on all but a few routes. For day trips, hiring a driver with car may be the best option.

Service Taxis

As in other Middle Eastern countries, service taxis form an important part of Egypt's internal transport system, providing a fast and cheap method of getting around the country. Drivers congregate at recognized locations – usually near bus and train stations – and tout for passengers by shouting out their destination. They leave when their vehicle is full. They will not leave before unless the passengers are prepared to pay the extra fares. There is no need to book a seat: just show up at the "terminal" and look for a vehicle that goes to your destination. Because the vehicles are always full to capacity, the ride can be hot and uncomfortable, especially over long distances. There is little room for luggage, though there is usually a roofrack where luggage can be stowed. More worryingly, the drivers are notorious for their reckless driving and their vehicles are often in poor condition.

Alternatively, you may like to hire a whole service taxi for your group if you wish to undertake a day trip to a destination that is not easily accessed by other means. This can be a cheaper option than hiring a car to drive yourself or using other forms of public transport. In Cairo, Giza and Alexandria, a taxi service called Yellow Cabs allows you to order a private car with a driver at any time of the day or night.

Parking sign for international car rental agencies in Egypt

Car Rental

International vehicle rental companies such as Hertz, Budget and Avis have offices at the airports and in major hotels in tourist areas. To rent a car, you must be between 25 and 70 years old and hold a valid International Driver's Licence. Cairo and the larger towns are well served by petrol stations but in rural and desert areas long distances can separate them, so always fill the tank to the limit. If driving off-road, always carry spare fuel, water and tools. Most petrol stations can perform minor repairs and Egyptian mechanics are quite good at solving problems, sometimes resorting to more creative or less orthodox measures.

Driving in Egypt

There are few fixed rules for driving in Egypt and in the cities anarchy prevails. Drivers ignore lane markings, drive the wrong way up one-way streets, back up in the face of oncoming traffic if they miss a turn and ignore red lights and non-signposted intersections. Drivers' intentions are often communicated by hand gestures rather than by conventional signals. A common gesture of drivers and pedestrians alike is raised fingers, tips pinched together. This means "Wait". A flip of the

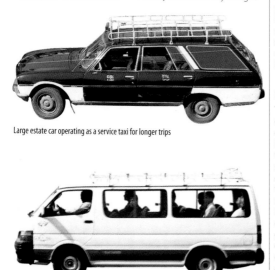

Large estate car operating as a service taxi for longer trips

Minibus holding up to 12 passengers, operating as a service taxi

hand forward means "Pass". Drivers will sometimes signal turns by pointing with their whole arm out of the window. However, it is compulsory to wear seatbelts and it is illegal to use a mobile phone while driving. Speed limits are 35 mph (60 kmph) on motorways, but these can vary, so look out for signs.

Other hazards in the cities include people jumping from moving buses, overloaded motorbikes, donkey carts and flocks of sheep, and pedestrians who also do not follow any rules of road etiquette.

Hazards on roads between cities are even more serious and numerous. Cars and trucks routinely overtake in the face of oncoming traffic or on the hard shoulder. Roads are in poor condition, with potholes, rough patches and drifting sand. Children often play alongside and in the road, and all manner of livestock, including camels, wander across. Motorists will stack rocks or construction debris in the road in lieu of hazard warning signs when they have pulled in because of a breakdown.

Typical heavy traffic near Midan Ramses in Cairo

Driving at night is best avoided. Egyptians tend not use their lights at night, except to flash them at oncoming vehicles. Off-road driving without a local guide in the Sinai, along the North Coast near El-Alamein and in the Canal Zone can be especially dangerous because of the presence of landmines, left over from World War II and the Arab-Israeli wars. Police checkpoints are a frequent occurrence. Foreign drivers are usually waved through, but be prepared to show your passport.

Hiring a private car with a driver can work out cheaper than renting a car. Check with travel agencies and hotels. Regular taxis can also be hired for the day at negotiable rates.

Maps

The best general map of Egypt is one published by Freytag & Berndt, which is available in most major tourist areas. Mobil's *Motoring Guide to Egypt* is a good choice if you are going to drive. It is sold in Mobil stations and tourist bookstores. Egyptians themselves seldom refer to maps and map coverage of cities other than Cairo is poor.

Stop sign   Uneven road   No car horns

DIRECTORY

Taxi Service

London Cabs
Tel 19670.

Nile Water Taxi
Tel (0128) 8011 8888.

Car Rental

Avis
Tel (02) 2794 7400 (24 hrs). Cairo International Airport. Tel (02) 2792 4400. Le Meridien Heliopolis Hotel, 51 El Orouba Street, Cairo. Tel (010) 0107 7400.
W avisegypt.com

Budget Rent-a-Car
Cairo International Airport, Terminals 1 and 3. Tel (011) 4443 9138. 22 Sharia el Mathaf el Zeraey, Agouza, Cairo. Tel (010) 2333 6723.

Hertz
Tel (0102) 224 2660 (24 hrs). Cairo International Airport. Danny Mall, Cairo–Alexandria Desert Road, Cairo. 195 Sharia 26 July, Agouza, Cairo.

Motoring Organizations

Automobile Association (AA)
Lambert House, Stockport Road, Cheadle SK8 2DY. Tel (0161) 495 8945.
W theaa.com

Automobile and Touring Club of Egypt
10 Sharia Qasr el-Nil, Cairo. Map 1 C5. Tel (02) 2574 3176.

Royal Automobile Club (RAC)
8 Surrey Street, Norwich, NR1 3NG. Tel (01922) 727 313. **W** rac.co.uk

Map Outlets

AUC Bookshop (Egypt)
AUC Hostel, 16 Sharia Mohammed Thakeb, Zamalek, Cairo.

Stanfords (UK)
12–14 Long Acre, London WC2E LP. Tel (020) 7836 1321.

Getting Around Cairo and Alexandria

The traffic in Cairo is notorious, both for its congestion and its chaos. Driving in the city is impractical for the visitor and many areas, such as the narrow streets and alleys of Islamic and Coptic Cairo, are best explored on foot. The city's public transport includes an extensive bus system, which is cheap but extremely overcrowded, and an efficient Metro, although it is of limited use to visitors. Taxis are the easiest way to get around and are plentiful, inexpensive and simple to use once the fare system is understood.

Alexandria's main form of transport is its tram system which covers most areas around the city centre. Downtown is compact enough to negotiate on foot, and minibuses run constantly east and west along the Corniche.

Tram in front of the basilica in Heliopolis (see pp140–41)

Walking

Walking in Cairo is the best way to experience the richness and diversity of this vibrant city. Tackling the streets for the first time, however, can be an intimidating prospect and care should be taken. Drivers do not obey lane markings, road signs or traffic lights. They will slow down to give you time to cross the street, but do not hesitate partway across as this confuses the dodge-and-dash flow of traffic and pedestrians and can increase the chances of an accident. Where possible, cross with groups of other people. Walking in the poorer quarters is remarkably safe, but be wary of petty thieves in crowded areas like the Khan al-Khalili. Women may also encounter verbal harassment and gropers downtown, on the bridges and in the Khan al-Khalili.

Taxis

To hail one of Cairo's taxis, stand on the side of the road and signal with your hand. State your destination by district or land-mark and be prepared for the driver to pick up other people travelling in the same direction.

Black-and-white taxis are becoming increasingly rare in Cairo. These do not have meters, so it is best to agree on a price beforehand. White cabs, which all have meters that start at LE 3, have made it much easier for locals and tourists alike. In general, most trips within the Downtown-Dokki-Mohandiseen-Zamalek area cost between LE 10–15. From Downtown to Heliopolis or Maadi charges are LE 35–40 and from Downtown to the airport, LE 55. Expect to pay a little more late at night. Taxis at five-star hotels charge higher fares but are good for

day hire as they are in better condition and the drivers speak some English. London Cabs (see p337) is also a useful service for tourists.

Taxis are generally cheaper in Alexandria than in Cairo, however, and journeys around the city centre cost no more than LE 5, while a ride to the bus station is LE 20.

Single women passengers are generally safe, but should ride in the back of cabs and not talk or make eye contact with the driver, as both of these actions can attract unwanted attention.

River Buses and Feluccas

An alternative means of getting around is by river bus. These are inexpensive, but a bit slow and run approximately every half-hour from near Coptic Cairo to the Arab Television Building north of the Egyptian Museum, stopping at Rhoda Island. There is also a fast water-taxi service available which can be booked online at niletaxi.com. The water taxis stop at numerous points on both banks of the Nile between downtown Cairo and Maadi. At weekends, the buses are full of revellers heading for the Nile Barrages (see p173) north of the city. River buses only run until 4pm.

Feluccas (sailing boats) are found along the river and can be hired out for short cruises (about LE 60 per hour). This is a

One of the yellow-and-black taxis in Alexandria

Felucca on the Nile in Central Cairo – a sedate mode of travel

great way to see Cairo from the Nile and cruises at sunset are particularly popular. One of the main departure points for felucca cruises is in Garden City by the Meridien Hotel.

Metro

The Cairo Metro is clean, safe and inexpensive but visitors will find it useful for only a few stops, the most prominent of which is the Mar Girgis station opposite Coptic Cairo. There are three lines, identified by direction. The al-Marg to Helwan line follows the east bank of the Nile for most of its length, the Shubra to Giza line runs north to southwest via Midan Tahrir, and the third line runs from Attaba downtown to Al Ahram, in the heart of the Korba in Heliopolis. The last stop on the line is displayed on the front of each train and maps of the network can be found at each station.

Tickets are available at all stations and are valid for one trip, including transfers. A trip costs a flat rate of LE 1 to any destination. Ticket-operated turnstiles control access to all platforms, so you will need to keep your ticket in order to exit at your destination. The Metro is extremely crowded during the morning and evening rush hours.

The middle one or two carriages on each train is reserved for women only, but women can and do choose to ride on any car.

Buses

City buses are usually green, blue or red, with route numbers displayed in Arabic on the front. The buses are often overcrowded and are not really recommended. However, they do cover almost all destinations and are very cheap. The city-run minibuses (usually white or green) are a slightly more pleasant experience and are still very inexpensive. These have fixed routes and charge a flat fare, which is paid as you board. Buses leave from Midan Abdel Moneim Riad, next to Midan Tahir, or from where you see metal shelters, signs mounted on lampposts, or more commonly, crowds of people waiting along the road.

Air-conditioned buses (No. 158 and No. 381, which has Wi-Fi) travel to and from the airport and Tahrir Bus Station and Ramses respectively. The city also has microbuses and service taxis that operate on fixed routes and stop on request. Like the local buses, they are overcrowded and used mainly by workers and residents. Check cairobusroutes.com for more details.

Getting Around Alexandria

Alexandria has an aged tram system. The cars are worn and the pace is slow, but fares are cheap. The service runs from 5:30am to midnight, and to 1am during the summer months. Ramla is the main downtown terminal, located east of the bus depot on Midan Saad Zaghloul. Trams headed east from Ramla are blue, while those travelling west are yellow. Note that on trams that are made up of three cars the middle car is normally reserved for women.

Useful tram routes for visitors include No. 15 and No. 36 (yellow) for the Mosque of Abu al-Abbas Mursi (see pp248–9) and Fort Qaitbey (see p249). Heading east, route No. 2 (blue) travels two thirds of the way to Montazah Palace (see p251). All tram and route numbers are in Arabic script only.

As in Cairo, buses are old and overcrowded. Minibuses are a better option, following most of the same routes and operating hours as the tram. City minibuses are white while private ones are blue or grey and cost under LE 1.

The minibuses that travel along the Corniche day and night are convenient. Look out for red double-decker buses along the Corniche – they stop on demand and charge LE 5.

City taxis are black and orange, or yellow, and follow the same rules as taxis in Cairo (see p338).

Horse-drawn carriages ply the Corniche and Masr Station and can be a relaxing way of getting around the city, providing traffic is light. The price is negotiable. An hourly rate of LE 30 is reasonably equitable to all.

A westbound tram on a busy thoroughfare in Alexandria

General Index

Acknowledgments

Dorling Kindersley would like to thank the following people whose contributions and assistance have made the preparation of this book possible.

Publishing Manager
Jane Ewart.

Managing Editor
Anna Streiffert.

Director of Publishing, Travel Guides
Gillian Allan.

Publisher
Douglas Amrine.

Production
Joanna Bull, Sarah Dodd.

Main Contributors
Jane Dunford, Dr Joann Fletcher, Carole French, Robin Gauldie, Andrew Humphreys, Kyle Pakka, Richard Williams.

Additional Contributors and Consultants
Vanessa Betts, Carole French, Mohammed Saad El-Essawy, David Stone, Hugh Taylor, Wendy Wrangham.

Additional Illustrations
Rebecca Milner.

Additional Photography
Max Alexander, Vanessa Betts, Jo Doran, Alistair Duncan, Eddie Gerald, Minesh Modha, Ian O'Leary, Rough Guides/Eddie Gerald, Jon Spaull, Clive Streeter, Stuart West, Wendy Wrangham.

Revisions Team
Ashwin Adimari, Claire Baranowski, Vanessa Betts, Imogen Corke, Surya Deogun, Hossam Elsawwaf, Helen Foulkes, Rachel Fox, Dale Harris, Victoria Heyworth-Dunne, Cincy Jose, Juliet Kenny, Shikha Kulkarni, Claire Jones, Jude Ledger, Carly Madden, Samira Mahmoud, Nicola Malone, Alison McGill, Michael Mitchell, Sonal Modha, Marisa Renzullo, Rada Radojicic, Lucy Richards, Ellen Root, Collette Sadler, Sands Publishing Solutions, Kareen Sharawy, Beverly Smart, Meredith Smith, Stuti Tiwari, Conrad Van Dyk, Deepika Verma.

Proof Readers
Samantha Cook, Stewart J Wild.

Indexer
Zoe Ross.

Special Assistance
Ben Faulks, Gamal, Peter Sheehan, Shehad, Hisham Youssif.

Additional Picture Research
Nicole Kaczynski.

Photography Permissions
The publisher would like to thank all the churches, museums, hotels, restaurants, shops, galleries and sights too numerous to thank individually, for their co-operation and contribution to this publication.

Picture Credits
a=above; b=below/bottom; c =centre; f=far; l=left; r=right; t=top.

The publisher would like to thank the following individuals, companies and picture libraries for permission to reproduce their photographs:

123RF.com: Pius Lee 281tr; Takepicsforfun 194cr.

1886 Restaurant: 289bc.

4corners Images: Günter Grafenhain 184–5; Paul Panayiotou 68–9.

AFP, London: Amr Mammoud-STR 301cr; Manoocher Deghati-STF 43clb; Marwan Naamani-STF 42cr; Mohammed al-Sihiti-STR 44bl, 45t, 305tr; Narwan Naamani-STR 44b; Patrick Hertzog-STF 46b; STR 43tr; STR-STR 45b.

AKG London: 59tc; 187t, 249ca; François Guenet 178b; Erich Lessing 87cl, 179tr, 187t, 201bl, 242tr; Gilles Mermet 114bc.

Al Tarfa Desert Sanctuary: 271tc, 277tr.

Alamy Images: Anna Stowe Travel 210–11; Peter Bowater 310bl; Adam Butler 313cb; Peter Chadwick 310c; Charles Stirling (Travel) 326b; Ian Dagnall 230tl; Danita Delimont 198cr; dbimages/Amanda Ahn 332cla; Dacorum Gold 315c; F1online digitale Bildagentur Gmbh 256; Nick Hanna 313ca; 313cr; Peter Horree 144cla, 162; imagebroker/Manfred Bail 313br; Paul Ives 308br; Korivo 158–9; Stan Kujawa 310tr, 336b; Celia Mannings 316bc; Barry Mason 314bc; Michele Molinari 283c; B.O'Kane 2–3; Wolfgang Pölzer 312tr; Profimedia International s.r.o./Jaroslav Hejzlar 312cl; PSI 338br; Robert Harding Picture Library Ltd 232–3; SAS 283tl; Mike P Shepherd 262–3; Gordon Sinclair 309cl; Stock Connection Blue 10bl; travelpixs 180bl, 248tl; WaterFrame 312crb; Andrew Woodley 315bl; WoodyStock/McPhoto 316tl.

Ancient Art & Archiitecture Collection: 26tr, 28cl, 30–31, 30br, 32tr, 33cl, 35tl, 52br, 53b, 54crb,

55b, 56clb, 56bc, 60bc, 74cb, 81tl, 109tl, 136br, 172cr, 178tr, 179cl, 194br, 197cr, 197bl, 199br; Dr. S Coyne 215tr, 215cl, 215br; Muhammed al-Agsarai 60crb; R Sheridan 24tl, 26br, 38br, 250b.

The Ancient Egypt Picture Library: 34bl, 78cl, 178cr, 179br, 181tr, 198tr, 198bl, 243cl.

Jon Arnold: 1c.

The Art Archive: Mander & Mitcheson Theatre Col/ Eileen Tweedy 65ca; Museo Civico Revoltella Trieste/ Dagli Orti 64–5c; Museum Correr, Venice/Dagli Orti 62cb, 219cra; Dagli Orti 62t; Museum of Islamic Art Cairo/Dagli Orti 83c; The Egyptian Museum, Cairo/ Dagli Orti 31tr, 78clb, 80br, 81bc.

AWL Images: Travel Pix Collection 134–5.

Axiom: Heidi Grassley 219bl, James Morris 35crb, 168br, 181cb, 181bl, 219tc, 243br, 264cb.

Baladina: 287tr.

Basma Hotel Aswan: 269tr.

Bawiti Oasis Resort: 268bl, 293br.

Bildarchiv Preussischer Kulturbwwesitz: Johannes Laurentius 58cl.

Bordiehn's B's at Marina: 279br.

Bridgeman Art Library, London/New York: 34tr, 34cr, 36ca, 59tr, 61br, 63bc, *The Flight into Egypt* by Jean-Leon Gerome 127t, 132tr; Bargello, Florence 61bc; Magdelen College, Oxford 61br; Musée des Beaux-Arts, Beziers 58–9c; Musée du Louvre 26cl, 26–7, 30bl, 182br; Stapleton Collection 28b, 136clb, 218tr, 301bl; The British Library, London 62bc; The British Museum, London 50bl; Whitford & Hughes 127t.

Rob Den Braasem: photographersdirect.com 146cla.

Cairo Marriott: 272bl.

Jean-loup Charmet: 57bl.

Citystars: 295br.

Thomas Cooke Archive: 195cr.

Corbis: 64tr; Yann Arthus-Bertrand 19b; Bettman 59ca; Bettmann 22c; Design Pics/Peter Langer 252–3; Hulton Deutsch Collection 24br; William Manning 104–5; Masterfile/Mark Downey 15bl; Jose Fuste Raga 315tr; Carmen Redondo 203cl; Reuters New Media Inc, 58c, 261cl; Galen Rowell 265crb; Stephane Compoint/Sygma 23t; STR/epa 67cl; Sygma 24/25c; Vanni Archive/Gian Berto Vanni 202cra; KM Westermann 64–5, 306cl; Sander de Wilde 67tr.

G. Dagli Orti: 114cl; Graeco-Roman Museum, Alexandria 59tl, 246clb, 247cra; Graeco-Roman Museum, Alexandria.

Crust: 286bl.

DK Picture Library: 64b, 298tr, 298br; Alan Hills 298bl; Alistair Duncan 25t, 29b, 29cra; British Museum 27cb, 35br; British Museum/ Peter Hayman 126t, 126tr; Dave King 299br; Frank Greenaway 59cb;

Geoff Brightling 25br, 35clb; Peter Hayman 34cbl; Philip Dowell 299br; Philip Enticknap 195cl.

DK Picture Library/british Museum, London: 32cla, 32cl, 32cr, 32crb, 32br, 32bcl, 33tl, 33tr, 33cla, 33ca, 33crb, 33bl, 52t, 59bl.

Jo Doran: 119br, 205t.

Dreamstime.com: Alex7370 235br; Richard Carey 308br; Jakub Gojda 231br; Jacek Golonka 309tr; Amr Hassanein 170–71; Icon72 14tr; Stanislav Moroz 13tl; Mohamed Osama 72; Jose I. Soto 12bc; Vlad1949 41bl; Zanozaru 28tr; Viktor Zhugin 122–3.

Edimedia France: 38c.

Egyptair: 340c.

El Gezira Hotel: 288tr.

Mary Evans Picture Library: 60tc, 61tl, 63tr, 63cr, 63clb, 63br, 64cl, 195crb, 195br, 301cb.

Werner Forman Archive: 55ca, 138cr, 167tc, 168cl, 196tr, 199cb; British Museum London 34ca; Dr. E Strouhal 35bl, 35c, 203bc, 207tl; Graeco-Roman Museum, Alexandria 57tc, 246cl, 246bl, 247bl; J Paul Getty Museum, Malibu 173bc; Metropolitan Museum of Art, New York 81c, Musée du Louvre 35cla; Schimmel Collection New York 27tl, 126cl; The Egyptian Museum, Cairo 24clb, 54ca, 55cb, 78bc, 79tr, 79cra, 79cr, 79cb, 80cr, 80cla.

Keneth Garrett: 198b.

Getty Images: AFP/Cris Bouroncle 46bl; Dean Conger 238; Cultura Travel/Seb Oliver 18; DEA/C. Sappa 11cr; DEA/G. Dagli Orti 142–3; Franz Marc Frei 113tr; Richard l'Anson 266–7; Jean-Pierre Lescourret 318–19; Dominik Pabis 130; Stringer 100cr; Ulana Switucha 291tr; The Image Bank/Stuart Westmorland 282cl; Stuart Westmorland 84–5.

Patrick Godeau, Egypt: 118bc.

Ronald Grant Archive: 59b.

Hilton Alexandria Green Plaza: 269bl.

© **Michael Holford**: 27tr, 29crb, 121tc, 201br.

Angelo Hornak Library: 39ca, 97cr.

Hulton Getty: Hulton Getty 58tr.

Katameya Heights Golf & Tennis Resort: 309br.

Leonardo Media Ltd: 278bl.

Jurgen Liepe: 49bl, 50tl, 51tc, 51crb, 51bl, 53cb, 126bl, 136tr, 301cla.

Magnum: Bruno Barbey 67bc.

Maritim Jolie Ville Kings Island: 268cr.

Mena House: 270bc, 273tl.

Miramar Resort Taba Heights: 275bl.

Movenpick Resort Elephantine Island: 274tr.

Nile City Investments: 22b.

Richard T Nowitz: 114tr, 118cla, 120bl, 129c, 188b, 189b, 191cr, 191br, 308c.

Oronoz Archivo Fotografico: British Museum 26bl.

Lesley Orsen: 241cla.

Christine Osborne: 29tl, 35cra, 39cb, 96bl, 107br, 110tr, 110cl, 111t, 115bl, 118clb, 124br, 125bc, 127b, 180tl, 180c.

Oxford Scientific Films: Mark Webster 220.

Pa Photos: 65br.

Photolibrary: JTB Photo 314cl.

Popperfoto: 24tr, 24cla, 24cl, 25cr, 65bl, 66tl, 66cb, 67bl, 126br, 129br, 139bc; Donald McLeish 77tr.

Porto Marina Resort & Spa: 276br.

Rana El Nemr Photography: photographersdirect.com 146br.

Retrograph Archive Ltd: 195bl.

Roastery: 292tr.

Robert Harding Picture Library: Michael DeFreitas 90; Tony Waltham 174.

Scala Group S.P.A.: 120cr; Archaeological Museum, Palestine 48; Coptic Museum, Cairo 118tr, 120t; The Egyptian Museum, Cairo 49bc, 70crb.

Sofra: 279tl.

STA Travel Group: 322crb.

Superstock: Caroline Von Tuempling 328bl.

Terrace Cafe: 284bl.

Thomas Cook Egypt: 330bl.

Topham Picturepoint: 24bl.

Wawson Wood: 231cra, 231clb, 231bl.

Front End Paper

Left: **Alamy Images**: F1online digitale Bildagentur Gmbh clb; **Getty Images**: Dean Conger cl; **Robert Harding Picture Library**: Tony Waltham bc.

Right: **Alamy Images**: Peter Horree tc; **DK Images**: Eddie Gerald cb; **Dreamstime.com**: Mohamed Osama c; **Getty Images**: Dominik Pabis crb; **Oxford Scientific Films**: Mark Webster tr; **Robert Harding Picture Library**: Michael DeFreitas cr.

Jacket

Front: **4Corners**: Günter Grafenhain main; **DK Images**: Eddie Gerarld bl.

Spine: **4Corners**: Günter Grafenhain.

All other images © Dorling Kindersley.
For further information see: www.dkimages.com

Special Editions of DK Travel Guides

DK Travel Guides can be purchased in bulk quantities at discounted prices for use in promotions or as premiums. We are also able to offer special editions and personalized jackets, corporate imprints, and excerpts from all of our books, tailored specifically to meet your own needs.

To find out more, please contact:
in the United States **specialsales@dk.com**
in the UK **travelguides@dk.com**
in Canada DK Special Sales at **specialmarkets@dk.com**
in Australia **penguincorporatesales@penguinrandomhouse.com.au**

Phrase Book

The official language of Egypt is Arabic. While it is not an easy language for newcomers to learn, it is well worth taking the time to practise and memorize a few key words and phrases. Most urban Egyptians speak a little English but they will greet any attempt to speak Arabic with delight and encouragement.

The Arabic given here is the Modern Standard Arabic. This is the Arabic written in newspapers, spoken on the radio and recited in prayers in the mosque. This varies somewhat from the language spoken on the street (Egyptian Colloquial Arabic), which is in fact a dialect of the standard language. Nevertheless if you speak slowly and clearly, you should have no difficulty being understood.

Transliteration from Arabic script to the Roman alphabet is a difficult task. Although many attempts have been made, there is no satisfactory system and you will repeatedly come across contradictory spellings in Egypt.

In this phrase book we have given a simple phonetic transcription only. The underlined letter indicates the stressed syllable.

Pronunciation

a, ah	as in "mad"
aa	as in "far"
aw	as in "law"
ay	as in "day"
e	as in "bed"
ee	as in "keen"
i	as in "bit"
o	as in "rob"
oo	as in "food"
u	as in "book"
A	pronounced as an emphasized "a" as in "both of us – you And me!"
D	a heavily pronounced "d"
gh	like a French "r" – from the back of the throat
H	a heavily pronounced "h"
kh	as in the Scottish pronunciation of "loch"
q	a "k" sound from the back of the mouth as in "caramel"
S, T	heavily pronounced "s", "t"
th	as in "thin"
Z	heavily pronounced "z"
'	this sounds like a small catch in the breath

When two different vowels occur together, for example Ae- and aA- each is pronounced separately.

In Emergency

Help!	an-najdah!
Stop!	qeff!
I want to go to a doctor	oreed al zehab lel tabeeb
I want to go to a pharmacist	oreed al zehab lel saydaliya
Where is the nearest telephone?	ayn yoogad aqrab telifoon?
Where is the hospital?	ayn toogad al mostahfa?
I'm allergic to… …penicillin/aspirin	Andee Hasaaseeyah men… penicillin/aspirin

Communication Essentials

Yes/No	naAm/laa
Thank you	shokran
No, thank you	laa shokran
Please *(asking for something)*	min faDlak
Please *(offering)*	tafaDal
Good morning	sabaaH al-khayr
Good afternoon	as-salaam Alaykum
Good evening	masa' al-khayr
Good night *(when going to bed)*	teSbaH Ala khayr
Good night *(leaving group early)*	maA as-salaamah *or* as-salaam Alaykum
Goodbye	maA as-salaamah
Excuse me, please	min faDlak, law samaHt
today	al-yawm
yesterday	al-ams
tomorrow	ghadan
this morning	haza aS-sabaaH
this afternoon	al-yawm baAd aZ-Zohr
this evening	haza al-masa'
here	hona
there	honaak
what?	maza?
which?	ay?
when?	mata?
who?	man?
where?	ayn?

Useful Phrases

I don't understand	la afham
Do you speak English/French?	hal tatakalam engleezee/faransee?
I can't speak Arabic	la ataklam al Arabeya
I don't know	la aAref
Please speak more slowly	men faDlak tahadath bebote'
Please write it down for me	men faDlak ektob ala hazeehee al-waraqah
My name is…	esmee…
How do you do, pleased to meet you	kayf Haalak, tasharafna be-meArefatak
How are you?	kayf Haalak?
Sorry!	aasef
I'm really sorry	aasef jeddan
Can you help me, please?	min faDlak, momken tosaAednee?
Can you tell me…?	men faDlak qol lee…?
I would like…	oreed…
Is there…here?	yugad…hona?
Where can I get…?	ayn ajed…?
How much is it?	kam thaman haza (m) hazeehee (f)?
What time is it?	as-saAh kam?
I must go now	labod an ajhab al-a'n
Do you take credit cards?	hal taqbal Visa, Access?
Where is the toilet?	ayn ajed al-hamam?
Go away! *(for children only)*	emshee!
Excellent!	momtaaz!
left	yasaar
right	yameen
up	fawq
down	asfal

Travel

I want to go to…	oreed al zehab le…
How do you get to…?	kayef tazhab le…?
I'd like to rent a car	oreed asta'jer sayaarah
driver's licence	rokhSat qiyaadah
I've lost my way	ana Dalayt aT-Tareeq
Where is the nearest garage?	ayn yoogad aqrab warshet sayarat?
garage (for repairs)	garaaj meekaaneekee
petrol/gas	banzeen
petrol/gas station	maHaTTat banzeen
When is there a flight to…?	mata toogad reHalat tayaran ela…?
What is the fare to…?	kam thaman al tazkarah le…?
A ticket to…please	law samaHt, tazkarat zehaab le…
airport	maTaar
ticket	tazkarah
passport	jawaaz safar
visa	veeza
airport shuttle	baaS al-maTaar

When do we arrive in…?	mata nasel ela…?	How much is this?	be-kam haza?
When is the next train to…?	mata yaqoom al-qeTaar alzaheb le…?	I'll give you…	ha aAteek…
		Two for…	ethnayn be…
What station is this?	hazehe ay maHaTTah?	Where do I pay?	ayn adfaA?
train	qeTaar	to buy	yashtaree
first-class *(train)*	darajah oolah	to go shopping	yatasawwaq
second-class	darajah thaaneeyah		
sleeping car	Arabat nawm		
bus	otobees		

Sightseeing

bus station	mahatet el-otobees	mosque	jaamea
boat	markeb	street, road	shaareA
cruise	jawlah baHareeyah	house	bayt
ferry	Abaarah	square	midan
taxi	taaksee	beach	shaaTee'
		museum	matHaf
		church	kaneesah

Making a Telephone Call

may I use your telephone?	momken astaAmel teleefoonak?	castle, palace	qasr

Eating Out *(see also pp282–3)*

How much is a call to…?	be-kam al-mokaalamah le…?	A table for…one/two, please	ma'eda le-shakhS waHed/ le- shakhSayn, law samaHt
Can I call abroad from here?	momken ataSel bel- khaarej men hona?		
Hello, this is…speaking	alloo, …yatakalam	I'd like…	oreed…
I would like to speak to…	oreed atakalam maA…	May we have the bill, please?	momken al-Hesaab, law samaHt?
Could you leave him a message?	momken tatrok laho resaalah?	May we have some more…?	momken al-mazeed mendfadlak…?
My number is…	raqamee…		
telephone call	mokaalamah	My compliments to the chef!	taheyaty le-Tahy!
emergency	Tawaare'	beer	beerah
operator	sentraal	bottle	zojaajah
		cake	kayk

Post Offices and Banks

How much is a letter to…?	kam taklefat ersal kheTab ela…?	coffee	qahwah
This is to go airmail	erselha bel-bareed al-jawee	– no sugar	– saadah
		– medium	– maZbooT
I'd like to change this into…	oreed oghayyer haza ela	– sweet	– sukkar zeyaadah
bank	bank	– with milk	– bel-Haleeb
dollar (US)	dollar	cup	fenjaan
exchange rate	seAr at-taghyeer	glass	koob
letter	kheTaab	plate	Tabaq
postbox	sondooq bareed	sandwich	sandwetsh
package	tard	snack	wajbah khafeefah
post	boosTah	sugar	sukkar
postcard	beTaaqah bareedeeyah	table	ma'eda
post office	maktab al-bareed	tea	shaay
stamp	TaabeA bareed	mint	neAnaA
travellers' cheque	sheek siyaaHee	(mineral) water	miyaah (maAdaneeyah)
		wine	nabeez

Staying in a Hotel

Food and Drink

Have you got any vacancies?	hal yoogad ghoraf khaaleeyah?	soup	shorbah
		fish	samak
I have a reservation	Andee Hajz	aubergine salad	salaaTat baazenjaan
I'd like a room with a bathroom	oreed ghorfah be-Hammam	melon	shammaam
		pickles	mekhallalaat
May I have the bill please?	momken al-hesaab law samaHat?	hummus	Hommos
		falafel - fried balls of ground fava beans or chickpeas	falaafel
I'll pay by credit card	sa-asfaA al-fatoorah law Visa, Access		
		fried balls of ground fava beans with herbs	taAmeeyah
I'll pay by cash	sa-adfaA naqdan		
hotel	fondoq	olives	zaytoon
air-conditioning	takyeef	stuffed vine leaves	waraq Aenab maHsee
double room	ghorfa mozdawajah	aubergine and tahina paté	baaba ghanooj
single room	ghorfa be-sareer waaHed	cheese	jebnah
shower	dosh	curd cheese	labnah
toilet	towaaleet	egg	bayDah
toilet paper	waraq towaleet	macaroni	makaroonah
key	meftaaH	noodles	sheAreeyah
lift/elevator	mesAd		

Fish

breakfast	foToor	grilled fish	samak mashwee
restaurant	maTAm	fried fish	samak maqlee
bill	faatoorah	fish with rice	samak sayaadeeyah
		smoked fish	samak medakhan

Shopping

I'd like…	oreed…	shrimp	jambaree
Do you have…?	hal Andak…?	squid	Habaar
		tuna	toonah

Meat and Poultry

beef	laHm baqaree
chicken	firaakh
chicken pieces	koftat dajaaj
duck	baTT
grilled lamb kebab	kebaab
lamb	laHm Daanee
meat	laHm
meatballs	koftah
mixed grilled meats	luHoom mashweeyah
pigeon	Hamaam
roast beef	roosbeef
sliced spit-roast lamb	shaawerma
steak	boftayk

Vegetables

aubergine	baazenjaan
avocado	abookaado
cabbage	koronb
celery	karafs
chillies	felfel Haamee
cucumber	khiyaar
lentils	Adas
lettuce	khass
okra	baamyah
onions	baSal
potatoes	baTaaTes
rice	rozz
tomatoes	TamaaTem
vegetables	khoDaar

Fruit and Nuts

almonds	looz
apricots	meshmesh
bananas	mooz
dried fruits	fawaakeh mojaffafah
figs	teen
fruits	fawaakeh
lemon	laymoon HaameD
pistachio nuts	fostoq
watermelon	baTeekh

Desserts

cake	kayk
baclava	baqlaawah
biscuits	baskooweet
dessert	Halawiyaat
fritters in syrup	zalaabeeyah
fruit salad	salaatet fawaakeh
ice cream	aays kreem
"Mother of Ali"	omm Alee
– milk pudding with raisins	
pastry with nuts and syrup	konaafah
yogurt	zabaadee

Methods of Cooking

baked	feel-forn
barbecued	mashwee Ala al-faHm
boiled	maslooq
fried	maqlee

grilled	mashwee
pickled	mekhaalil
spiced	metabbel
stewed	mesabbek
stuffed	maHshee

Numbers

0	sefr	30		thalaatheen
1	waaHed	31		waaHed wa thalaatheen
2	ethnayn	32		ethnayn wa thalaatheen
3	thalaathah	40		arbaAeen
4	arbaAh	50		khamseen
5	khamsah	60		setteen
6	settah	70		sabAeen
7	sabAh	80		thamaaneen
8	thamaaneeyah	90		tesAeen
9	tesAh	100		me'ah
10	Asharah	110		me'ah wa Asharah
11	Hedaash	200		me'tayn
12	etnaash	300		thalaathme'ah
13	thalaathaash	400		arbaAme'ah
14	arbaAtaash	500		khamsme'ah
15	khamastaash	600		setme'ah
16	settaash	700		sabAme'ah
17	sabaAtaash	800		thamaanme'ah
18	thamaantaash	900		tesAme'ah
19	tesAtaash	1,000		alf
20	Aeshreen	2,000		alfayn
21	waaHed wa Aeshreen	10,000		Asharat aalaaf
22	ethnayn wa Aeshreen	1,000,000		malyoon

Days, Months and Seasons

Sunday	yawm al-aHad
Monday	yawm al-ethnayn
Tuesday	yawm ath-tholatha'
Wednesday	yawm al-arbeAa'
Thursday	yawm al-khamees
Friday	yawm al-jomAh
Saturday	yawm as-sabt
January	yanaayer
February	febraayer
March	Maars
April	ebreel
May	maayo
June	yoonyo
July	yoolyo
August	aghosTos
September	sebtember
October	oktoober
November	noofember
December	deesember
spring	al-ar-rabeeA
summer	aS-Sayf
autumn	al-khareef
winter	ash-sheta'

Things You'll Hear

enshaallah	God (Allah) willing
tasharafna	you're welcome
esmak eh?	What is your name?
bel-hanaa' wash-shefaa'	Enjoy your meal